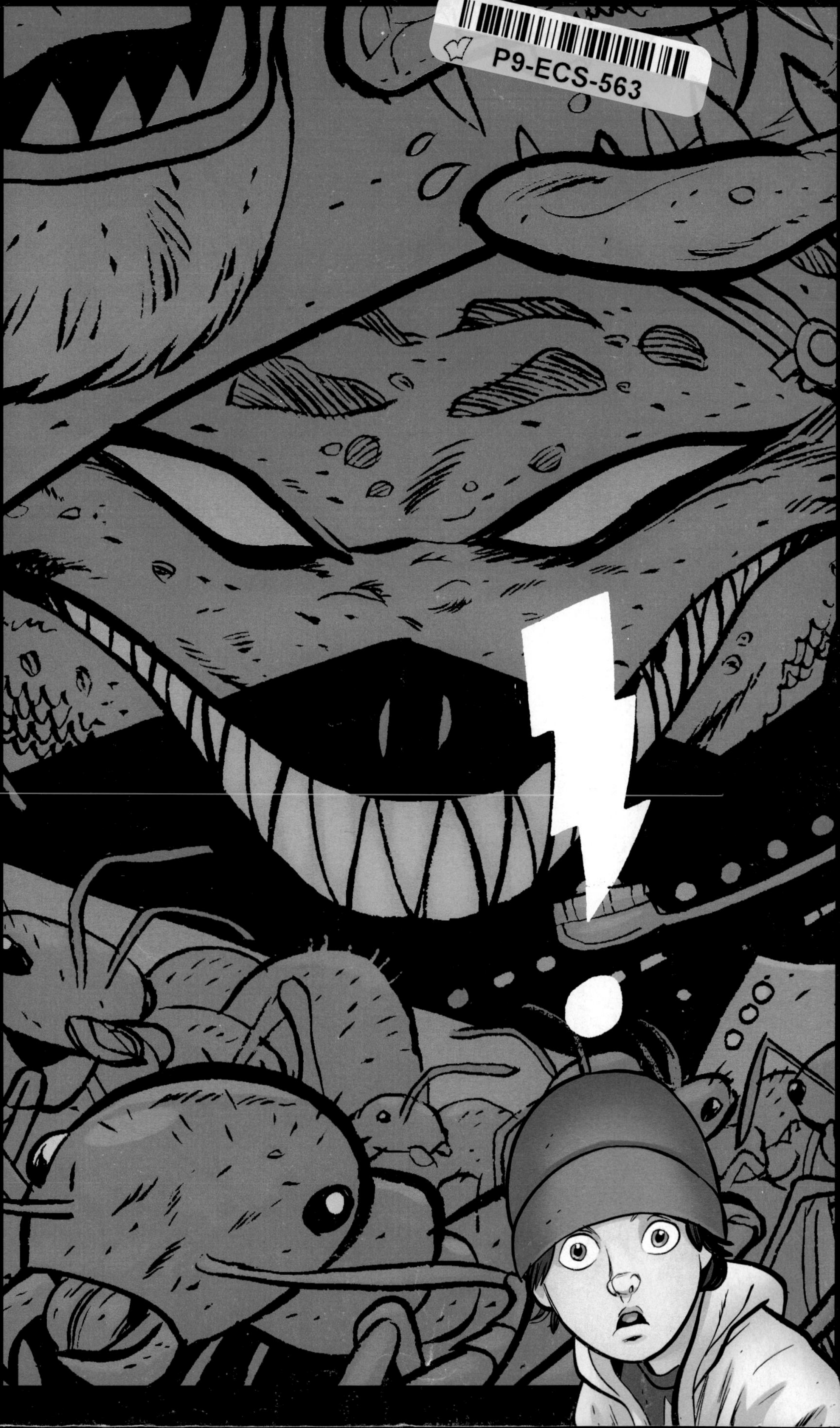

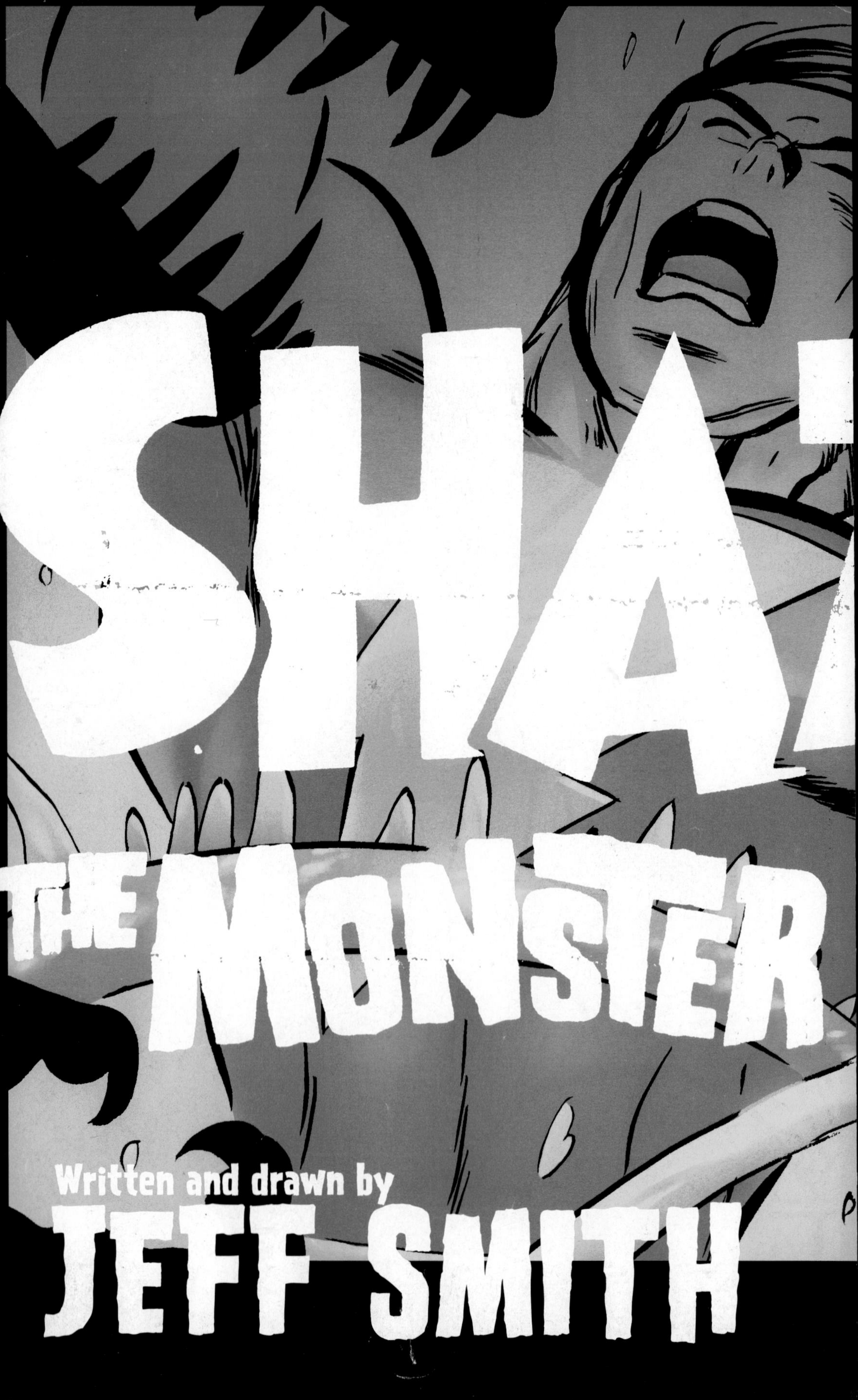
SHA
THE MONSTER
Written and drawn by
JEFF SMITH

# AM!

# SOCIETY OF EVIL



Colored by STEVE HAMAKER

Introduction by ALEX ROSS

MIKE CARLIN Editor - Original Series
TOM PALMER JR. Associate Editor- Original Series
JEB WOODARD Group Editor - Collected Editions
BOB HARRAS Editor - Collected Edition
STEVE COOK Design Director - Books
LOUIS PRANDI Publication Design

BOB HARRAS Senior VP - Editor-in-Chief, DC Comics
PAT McCALLUM Executive Editor, DC Comics

DAN DiDIO Publisher
JIM LEE Publisher & Chief Creative Officer
AMIT DESAI Executive VP - Business & Marketing Strategy,
Direct to Consumer & Global Franchise Management
BOBBIE CHASE VP & Executive Editor, Young Reader & Talent Development
MARK CHIARELLO Senior VP - Art, Design & Collected Editions
JOHN CUNNINGHAM Senior VP - Sales & Trade Marketing
BRIAR DARDEN VP - Business Affairs
ANNE DePIES Senior VP - Business Strategy, Finance & Administration
DON FALLETTI VP - Manufacturing Operations
LAWRENCE GANEM VP - Editorial Administration & Talent Relations
ALISON GILL Senior VP - Manufacturing & Operations
JASON GREENBERG VP - Business Strategy & Finance
HANK KANALZ Senior VP - Editorial Strategy & Administration
JAY KOGAN Senior VP - Legal Affairs
NICK J. NAPOLITANO VP - Manufacturing Administration
LISETTE OSTERLOH VP - Digital Marketing & Events
EDDIE SCANNELL VP - Consumer Marketing
COURTNEY SIMMONS Senior VP - Publicity & Communications
JIM (SKI) SOKOLOWSKI VP - Comic Book Specialty Sales & Trade Marketing
NANCY SPEARS VP - Mass, Book, Digital Sales & Trade Marketing
MICHELE R. WELLS VP - Content Strategy

Cover art by JEFF SMITH with STEVE HAMAKER

# Introduction by Alex Ross

**Charm.**

That's a quality that few comics deliver these days. Even though the root of comic books comes mostly from entertaining youth, the medium has evolved to the point of not wanting to recognize its origins. Despite the adult tenor of the modern superhero comics, it still is, at its base, stories about colorfully clad, magical human beings who do impossible feats. For the mostly adult audience that reads them, we still want these playful representations of the ideals of youth but we rarely come to terms with why. Yes, we desire dramatic, colorful entertainment done in a more sophisticated fashion for our adult tastes, but why do we still need the guys in tights? Charm. The subliminal quality of being charming is something that we all respond to, no matter what the age. Superheroes embody that quality like no other. The titans of myth found a new home in our rainbow-clad friends, and the world still needs their creative stimulation.

It's not often that we see the approach taken to superheroes stripped down to its original skin. The "comic" part of comic books had its origins with humorous cartooning. Combined with traditional illustration, the medium of comics made a hybrid of all influences and archetypes. The invention of the superhero was the ultimate grab bag of all genres; science fiction, adventure, fantasy, myth, mystery, and horror all found their aesthetic worth blended together. Those that were first spawned in the golden era of the superhero were the trailblazers who innovated the form. Few characters have contributed more than the great Captain Marvel. In one of the first creative twists on the dual-identity framework of super-people, Captain Marvel shared his existence with a young boy he transforms from and back into. Young readers got the ultimate wish fulfillment from the hero's being just like them. With just one magic word—Shazam!—an instantaneous switch is made from one personality and physical being to another. This magical change would be replicated for many years to come, in a host of many characters.

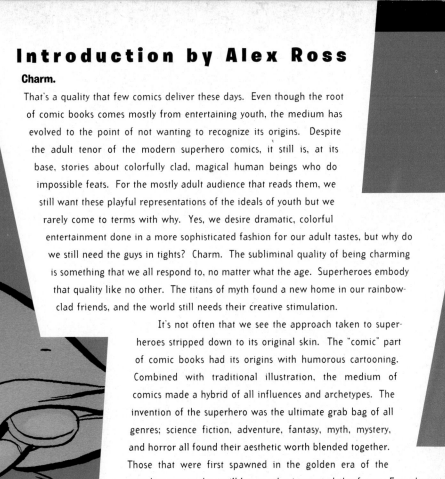

The Captain's sister, Mary Marvel, was also something of an innovation in the realm of young girls empowered like the boys. The bald scientist villain, Sivana, and the numerous other villains the Marvel family would face, had more creative juices flowing into the bloodstream of comics. Behind all of this was the talented team of artist C.C. Beck and writer Otto Binder. The greatest asset of their talents was the childlike whimsy their comics captured, perfectly crafted for the audience they knew well.

Beck's art style kept a strong link to comics' humorous cartooning roots, existing in somewhat of its own hybrid landscape of realism and fable. Binder kept that same bridge between the unfettered imagination of youth and the maturity of the modern world. Captain Marvel's prime period of impact was during the Second World War, where he provided entertainment of juvenile distraction and simultaneously directed attention to the war effort. His effect was felt far beyond the shores of America, as he served to inspire readers in a growing international comics market.

Today in comics the divide between the whimsy of cartoon entertainment and realistic illustrated fare has never been more separate. Most often it doesn't attempt to bridge the two, keeping the medium a ghettoized environment. Jeff Smith is one of the only people to challenge that separation and successfully hurdle its boundaries. The amazing accomplishment of his *Bone* saga, done over the last several years, truly recaptured a seemingly lost quality in comics. The mixing of animation-style rendering with whimsical characters wandering into an epic fantasy created one of the most charming comics in decades. Jeff also self-published from the start, making his mark in the comic book field on his own terms. As well, the character of Bone and his accompanying mythos is one that Jeff brought up through his childhood into the published reality of adulthood. His story is truly one to be an inspiration to us all.

Jeff's first project since *Bone* is this new use of Captain Marvel and his cast of characters, delighting Shazam fans like myself that an approach like Jeff's might find something lost in the character's presentation. He didn't disappoint, as Jeff returned to the roots of this superhero's magic, finding that balance between the child and man. Retelling the Marvel family's story from the beginning with an eye for detail often forgotten from his origins, both in tone and art, the story innovates further by melding that with a modern sensibility. Jeff's interpretation of Billy Batson as a tiny boy adds so much to the magic wish fulfillment of the story. Truly spending time with an all-too-young homeless orphan regained an important perspective on this character. The gentle care Jeff takes to tell his story is a welcome shock from comics' more standard storytelling approach.

I had the privilege of seeing the book's progress at a point when Jeff came through Chicago, where I saw the lengths he took to realize Captain Marvel's feline friend Tawky Tawny as a true tiger. Knowing that Jeff was revitalizing this character to his original state with a slight spin was purely inspiring. And, frankly, nothing is cuter than seeing Mary Marvel represented as a little tiny girl, impishly accompanying her "big" brother.

I must also say I'm grateful for the creative contribution to Captain Marvel's personal definition Jeff gave. For many years, the standard approach to his character has been that he was simply a boy inside a man's body. Jeff knew the original concept to his characterization was much more than that. Bringing back the quality of how Captain Marvel was much like a genie inside Billy Batson's bottle, with some distinction of minds and maturity, was a welcome change.

Jeff approached this story with great passion and purpose, not just to provide his perspective on a legend but to make a metaphor for our times. It's no accident the book has a post-9-11 haunting feel to it.

Jeff's creativity and contribution to comics is worthy of great attention and celebration. Inspiring like his work, he's also one of the nicest people you could ever meet. I'm proud to know him. Thanks for the great Shazam book, Jeff!

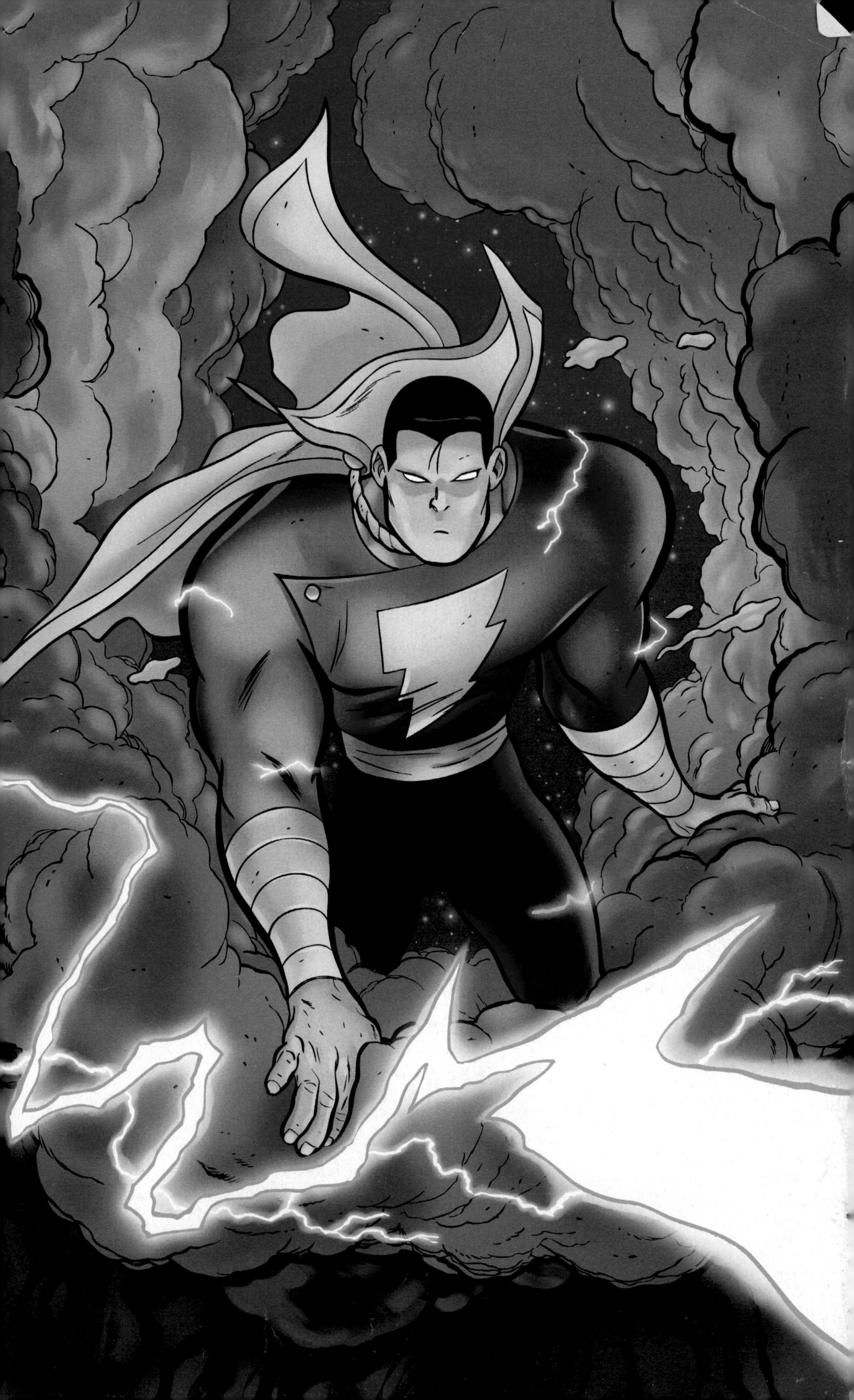

# THE MONSTER SOCIETY OF EVIL

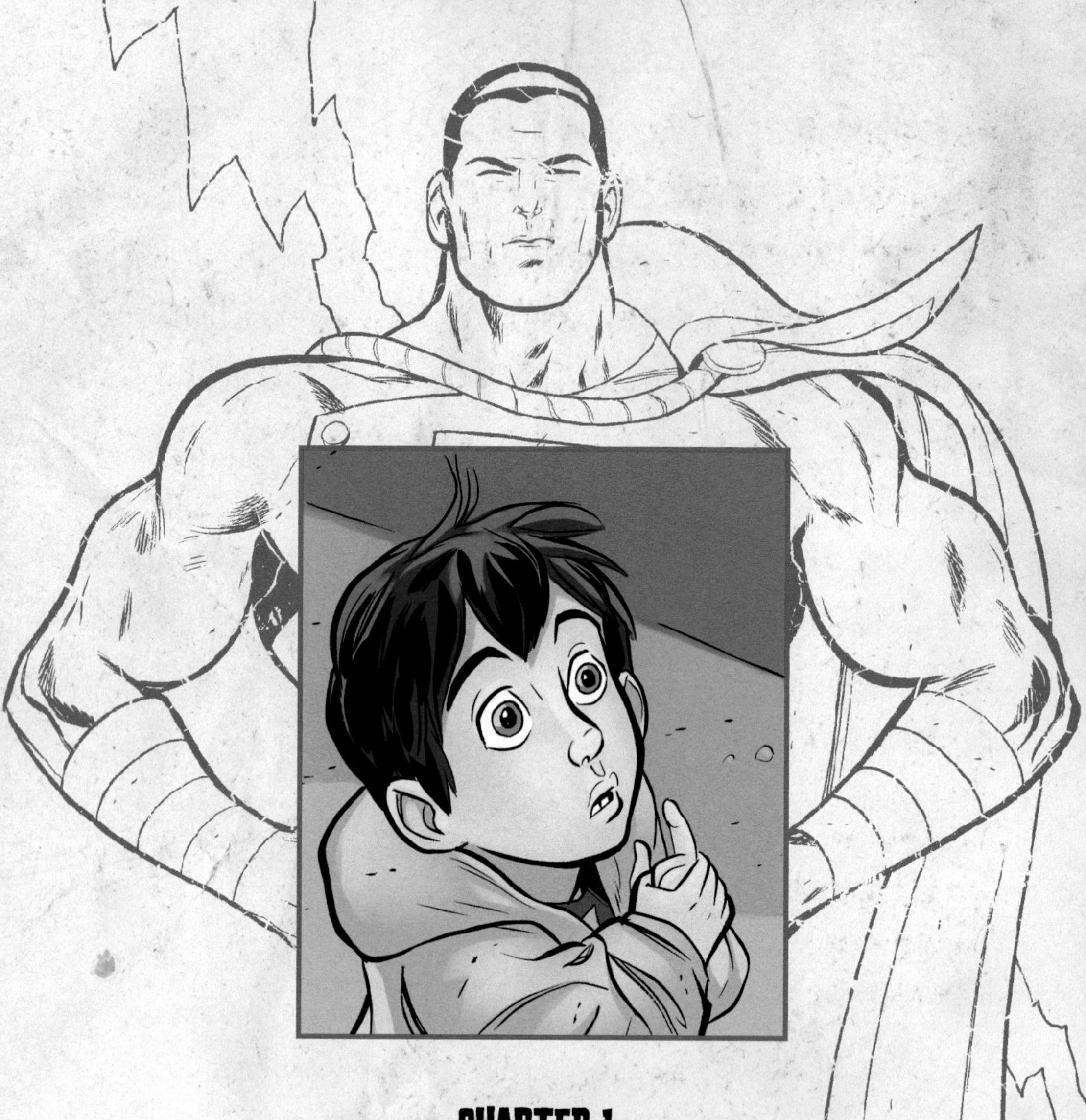

## CHAPTER 1:

## YROOB SZH Z HVXIVG!*

*THE MONSTER SOCIETY CODE

| A | B | C | D | E | F | G | H | I | J | K | L | M | N | O | P | Q | R | S | T | U | V | W | X | Y | Z |
|---|---|---|---|---|---|---|---|---|---|---|---|---|---|---|---|---|---|---|---|---|---|---|---|---|---|
| Z | Y | X | W | V | U | T | S | R | Q | P | O | N | M | L | K | J | I | H | G | F | E | D | C | B | A |

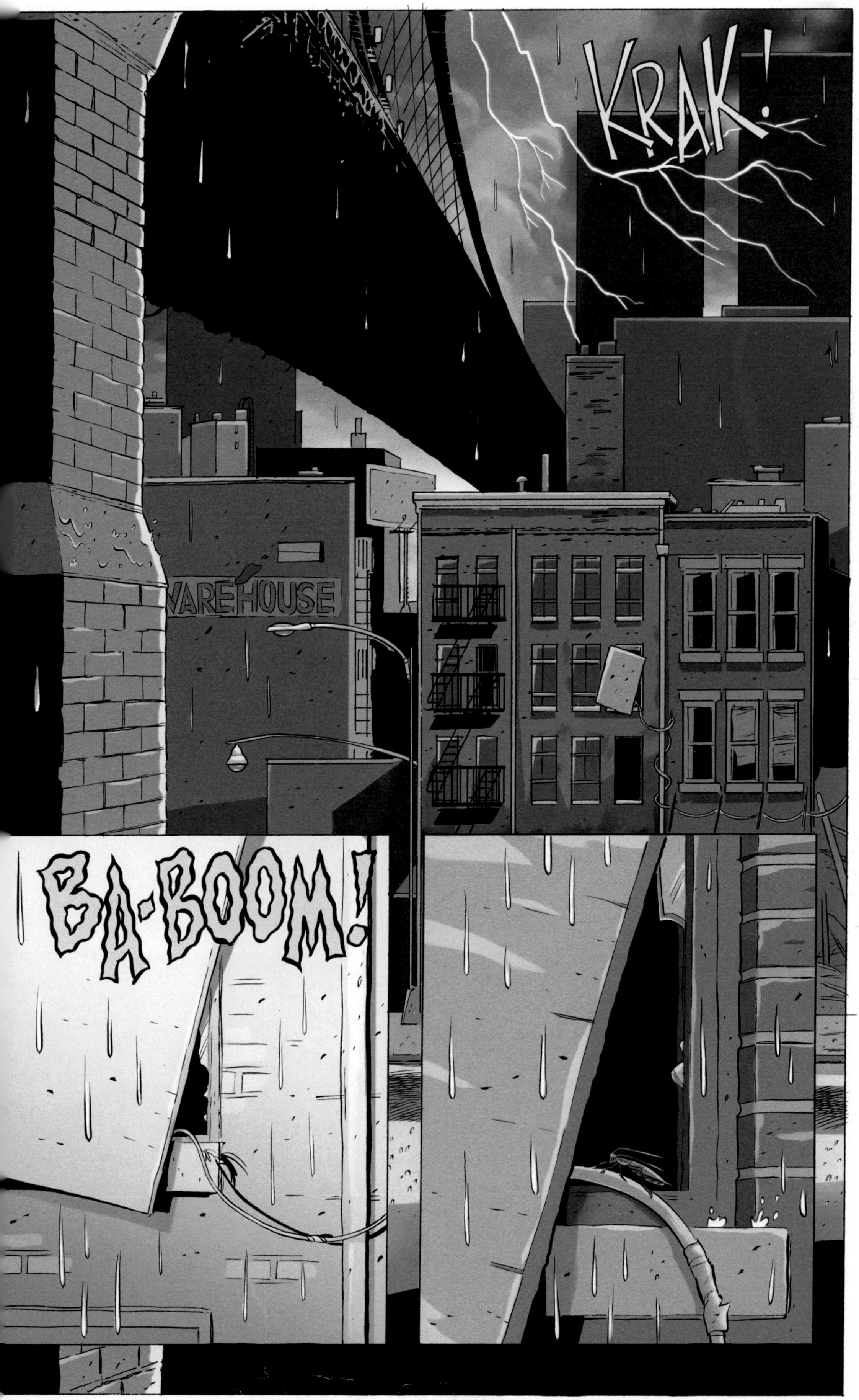
KRAK!
WAREHOUSE
BA-BOOM!

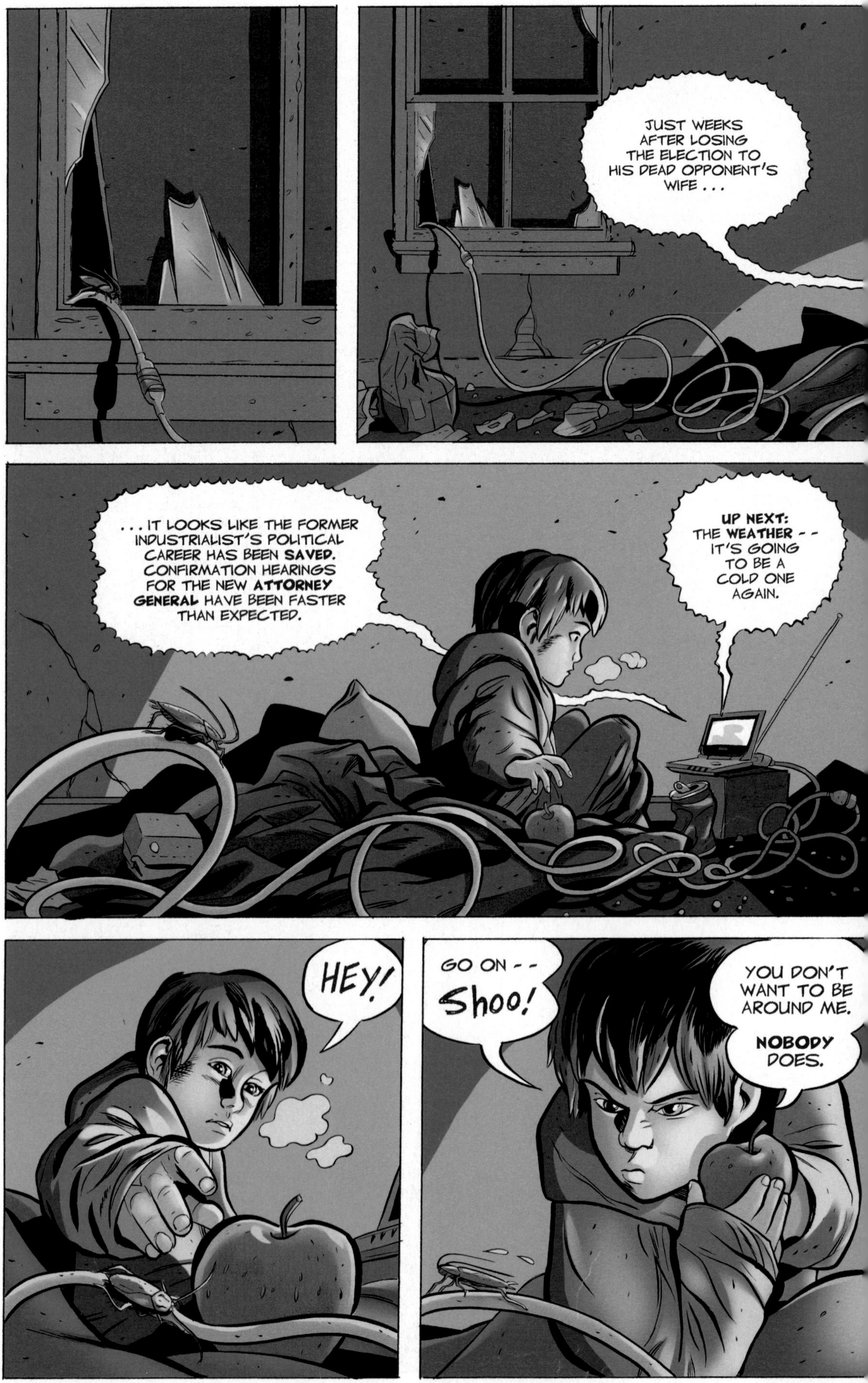
JUST WEEKS AFTER LOSING THE ELECTION TO HIS DEAD OPPONENT'S WIFE . . .
. . . IT LOOKS LIKE THE FORMER INDUSTRIALIST'S POLITICAL CAREER HAS BEEN SAVED. CONFIRMATION HEARINGS FOR THE NEW ATTORNEY GENERAL HAVE BEEN FASTER THAN EXPECTED.
UP NEXT: THE WEATHER - - IT'S GOING TO BE A COLD ONE AGAIN.
HEY!
GO ON - - Shoo!
YOU DON'T WANT TO BE AROUND ME.
NOBODY DOES.

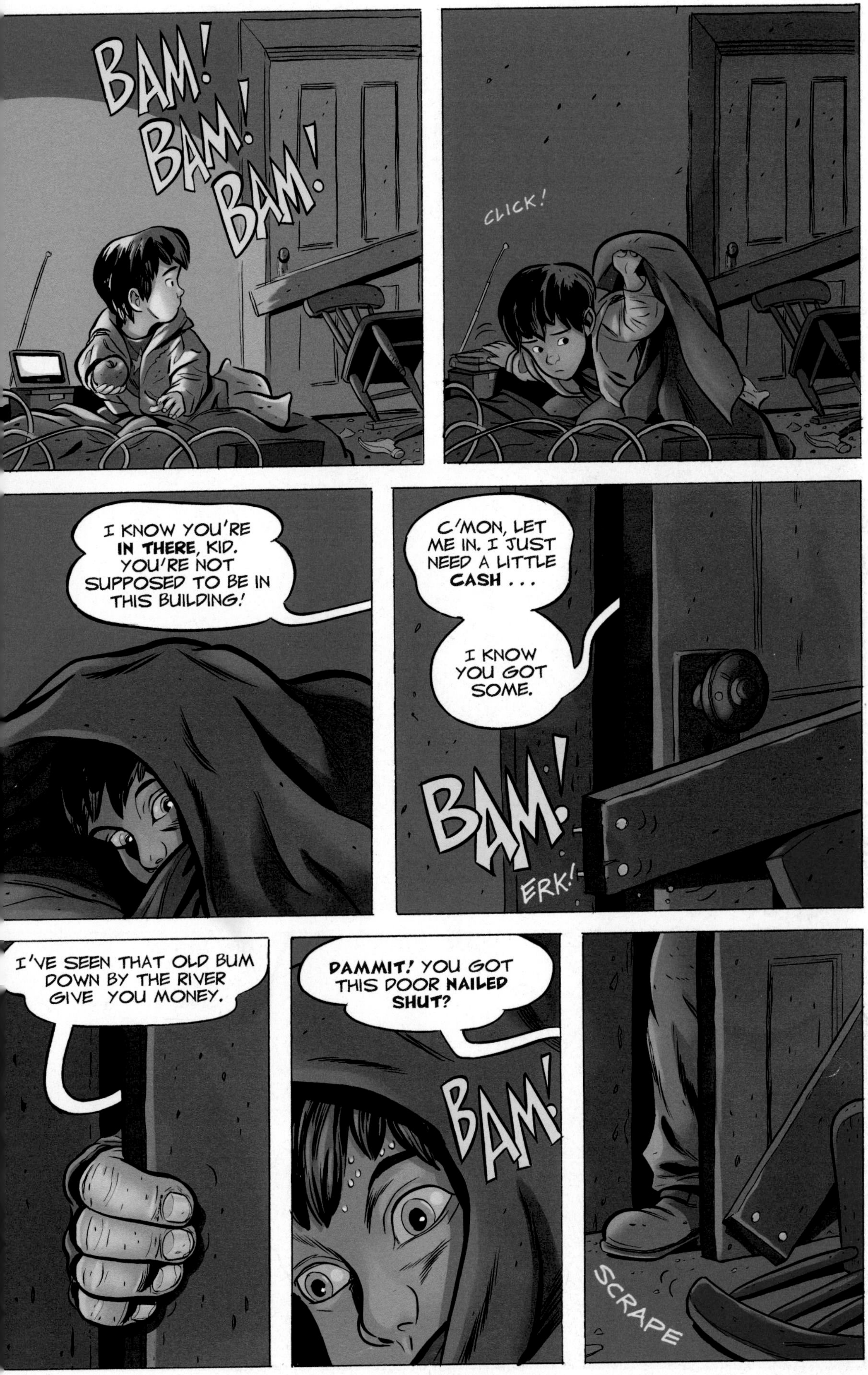
BAM! BAM! BAM!
CLICK!
I KNOW YOU'RE IN THERE, KID. YOU'RE NOT SUPPOSED TO BE IN THIS BUILDING!
C'MON, LET ME IN. I JUST NEED A LITTLE CASH . . .
I KNOW YOU GOT SOME.
BAM!
ERK!
I'VE SEEN THAT OLD BUM DOWN BY THE RIVER GIVE YOU MONEY.
DAMMIT! YOU GOT THIS DOOR NAILED SHUT?
BAM!
SCRAPE

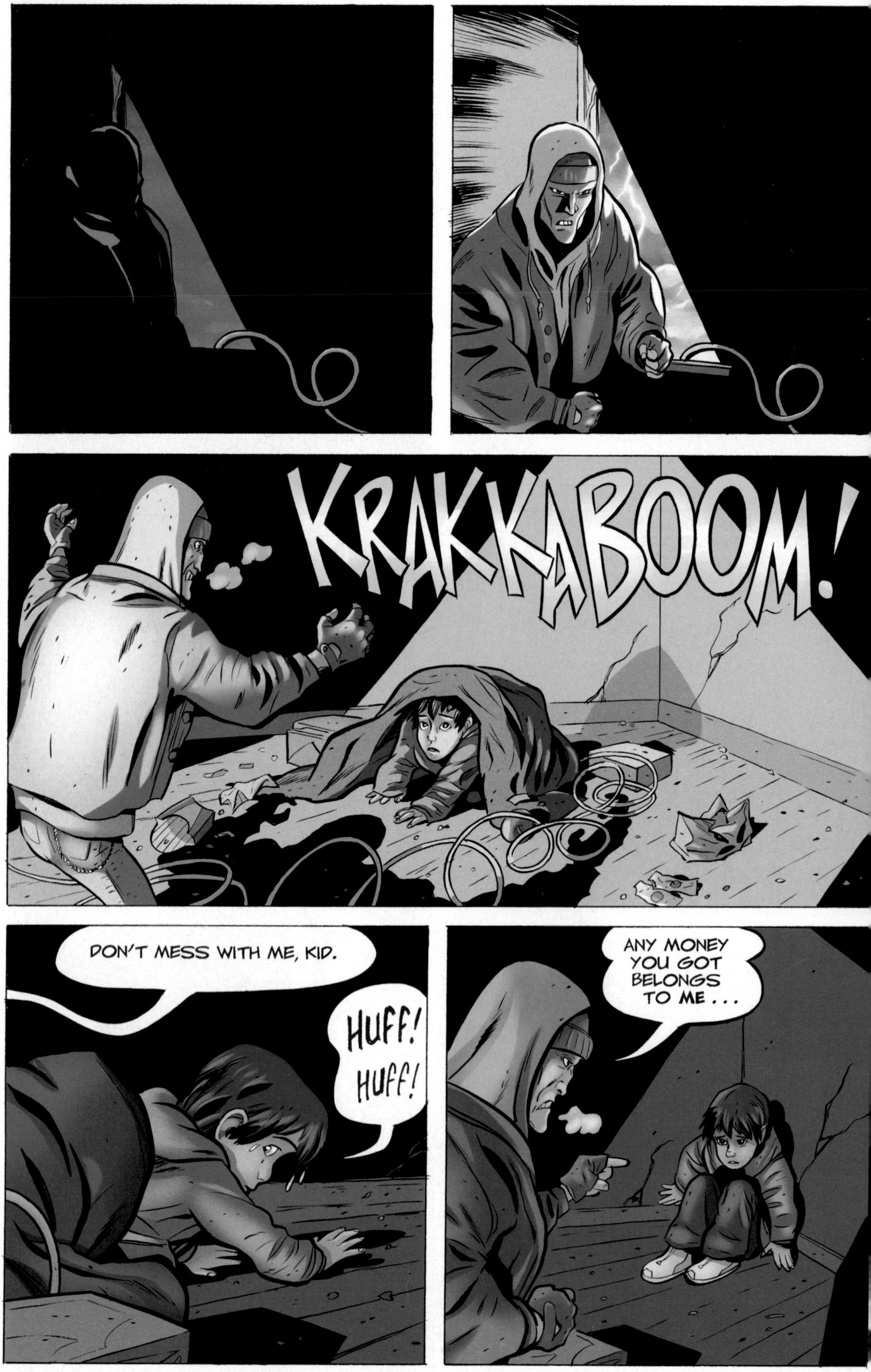
KRAKKABOOM!
DON'T MESS WITH ME, KID.
HUFF! HUFF!
ANY MONEY YOU GOT BELONGS TO ME . . .

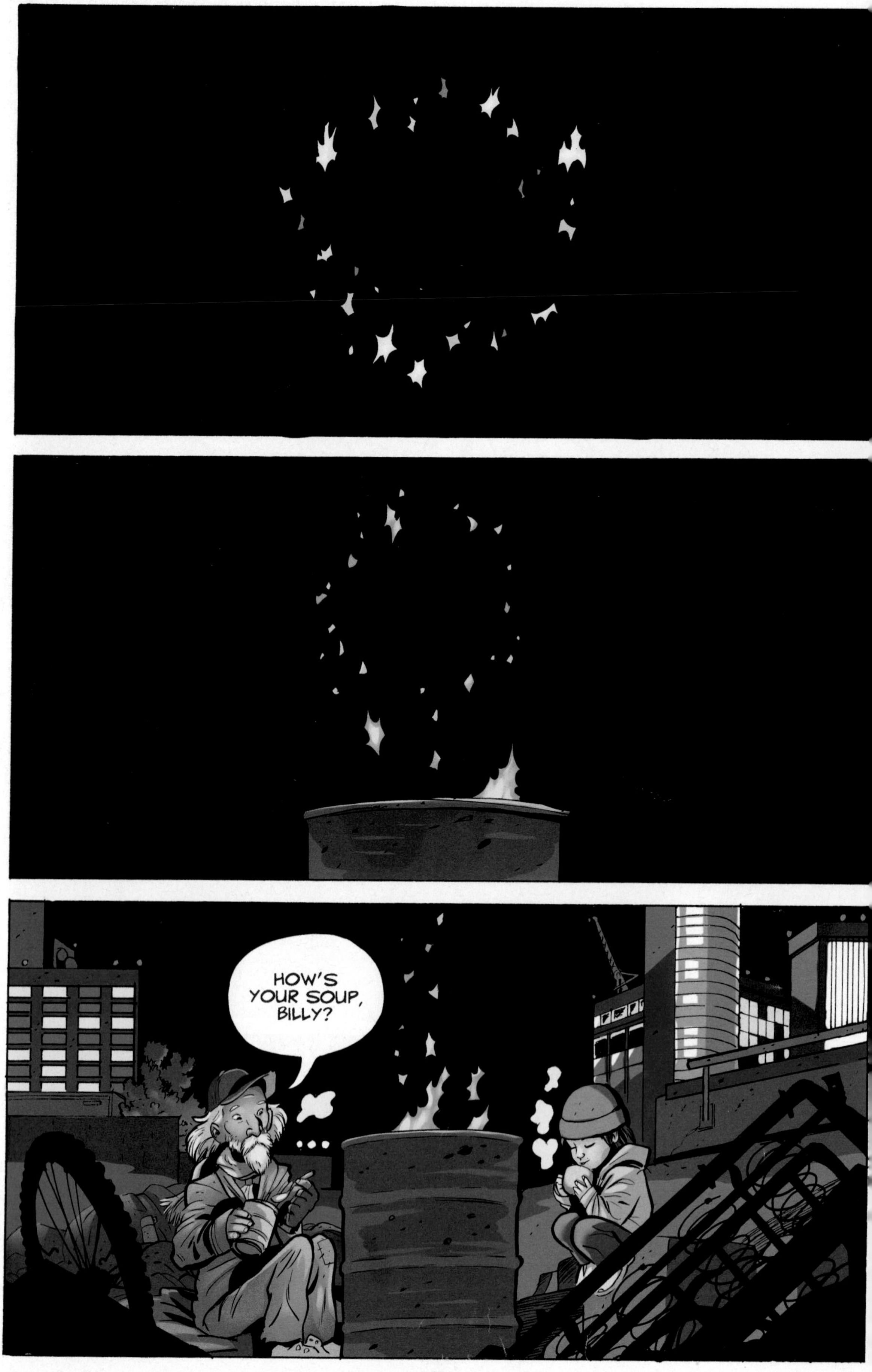
HOW'S YOUR SOUP, BILLY?

IT'S GOOD AND IT'S **REAL HOT!**

I BROUGHT YOUR CHANGE. YOU WANT TO COUNT IT?

NO, NO, YOU KEEP IT! IT IS YOUR **TIP** FOR RUNNING ERRANDS FOR ME.

BUT ALL I DID WAS PICK UP A FEW GROCERIES. ARE YOU **SURE?**

YOU KNOW HOW HARD IT IS FOR ME TO GO INTO THE CITY, BILLY. IT HELPS WHEN YOU DO IT.

WOW! THANKS, TALKY! I WOULDN'T KNOW WHAT TO DO WITHOUT YOU.

RAIN'S COMIN'... I CAN FEEL IT IN MY HIP. COLD, **WINTER** RAIN.

THAT'S NOT GOOD FOR PEOPLE LIKE US.

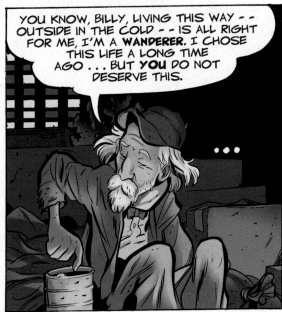

YOU KNOW, BILLY, LIVING THIS WAY -- OUTSIDE IN THE COLD -- IS ALL RIGHT FOR ME, I'M A **WANDERER.** I CHOSE THIS LIFE A LONG TIME AGO ... BUT **YOU** DO NOT DESERVE THIS.

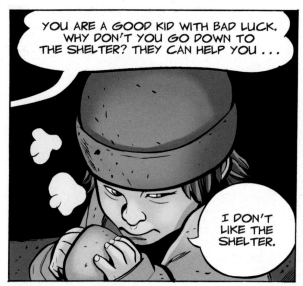

16

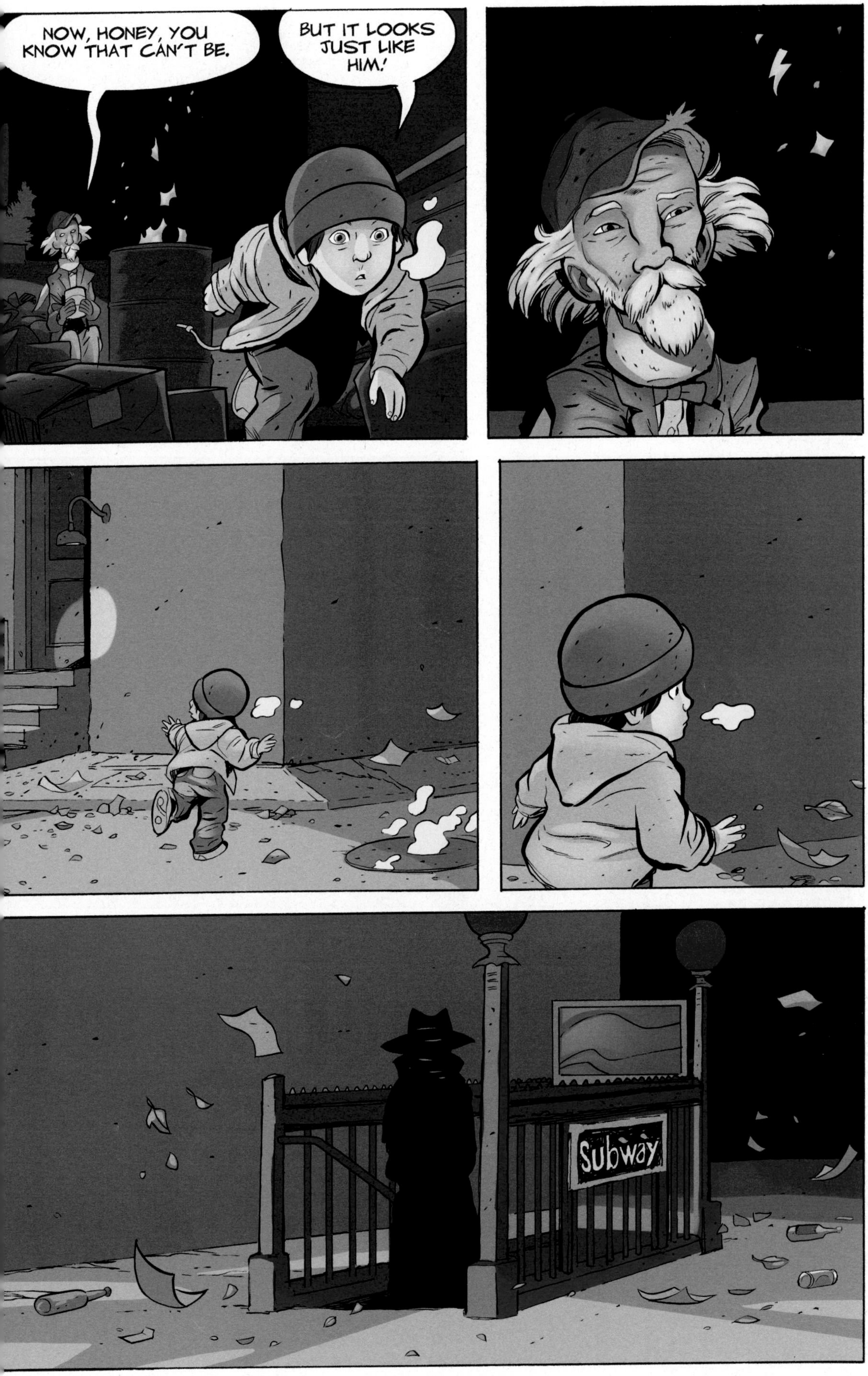
NOW, HONEY, YOU KNOW THAT CAN'T BE.
BUT IT LOOKS JUST LIKE HIM!
Subway

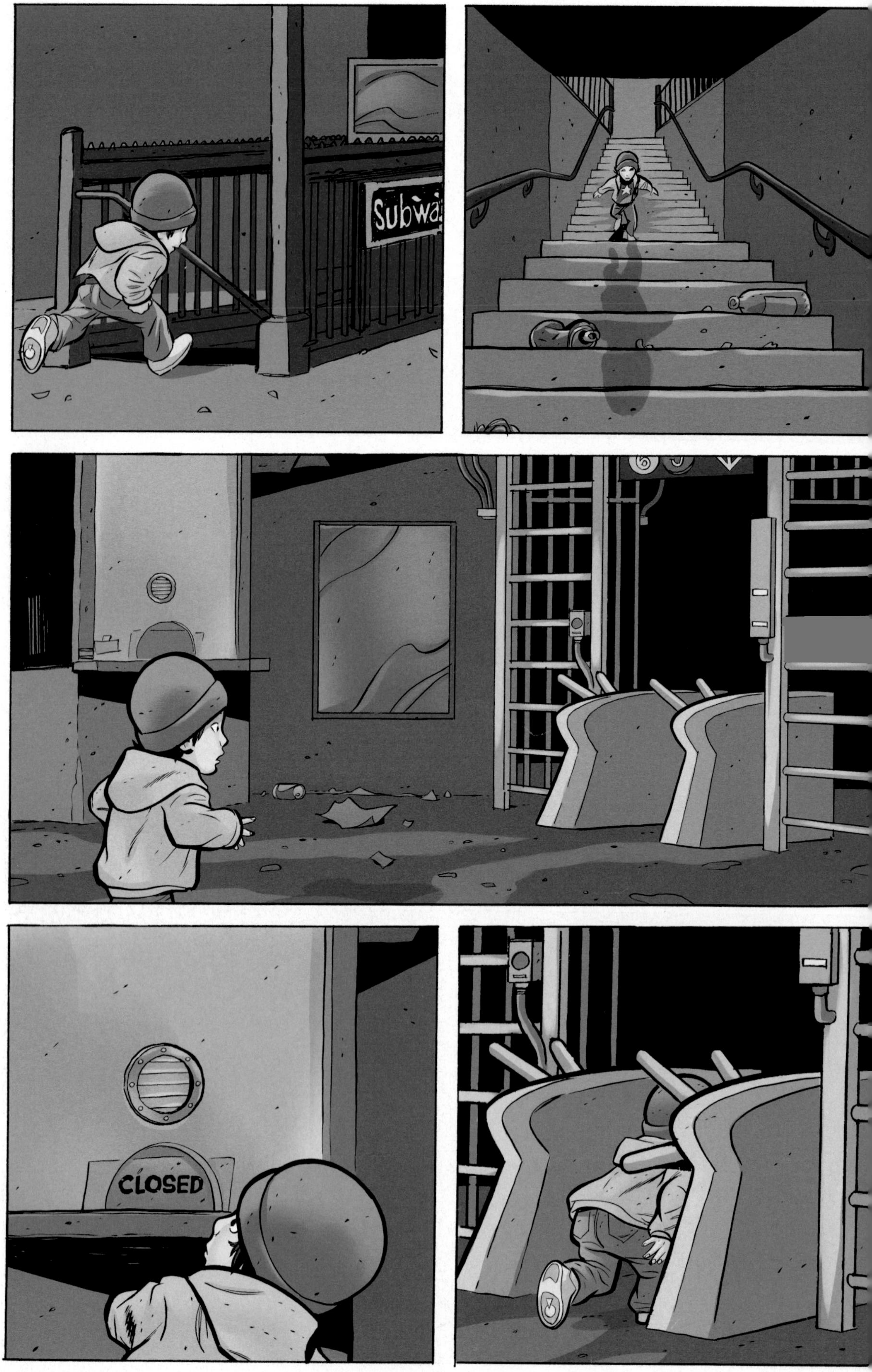
CLOSED

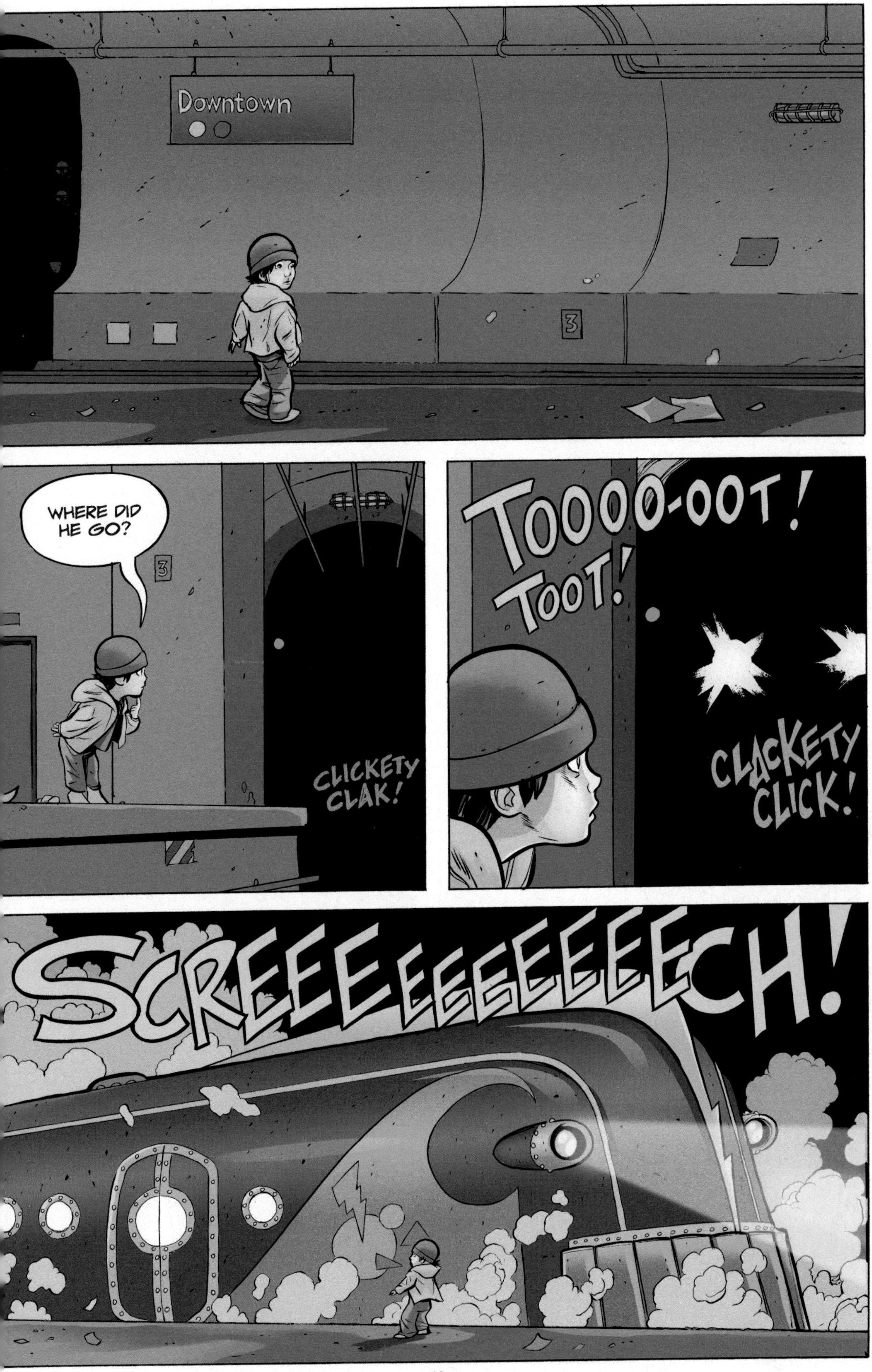
Downtown
3
WHERE DID HE GO?
3
CLICKETY CLAK!
TOOOO-OOT! TOOT!
CLACKETY CLICK!
SCREEEEEEEEEEECH!

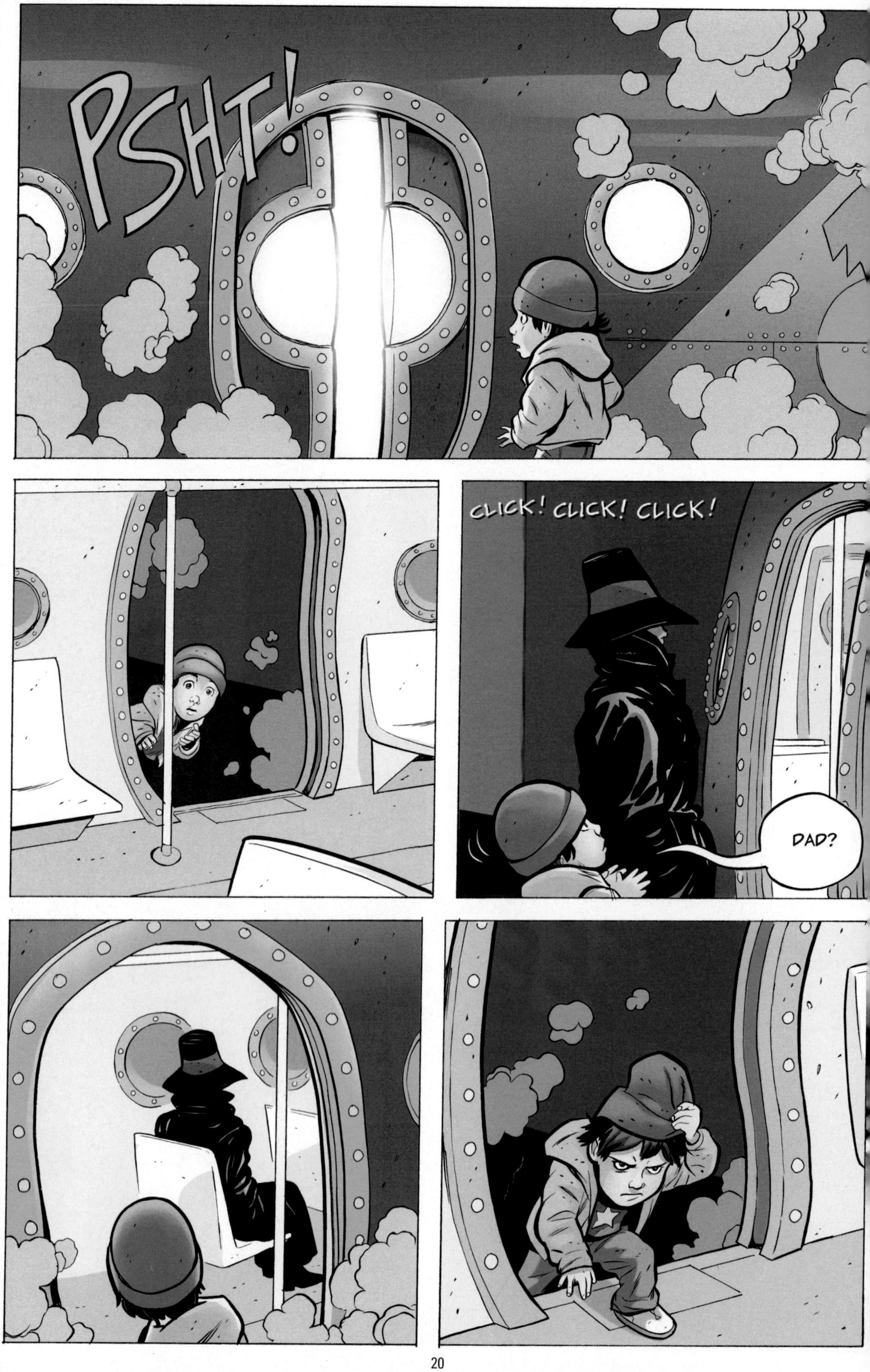
PSHT!
CLICK! CLICK! CLICK!
DAD?

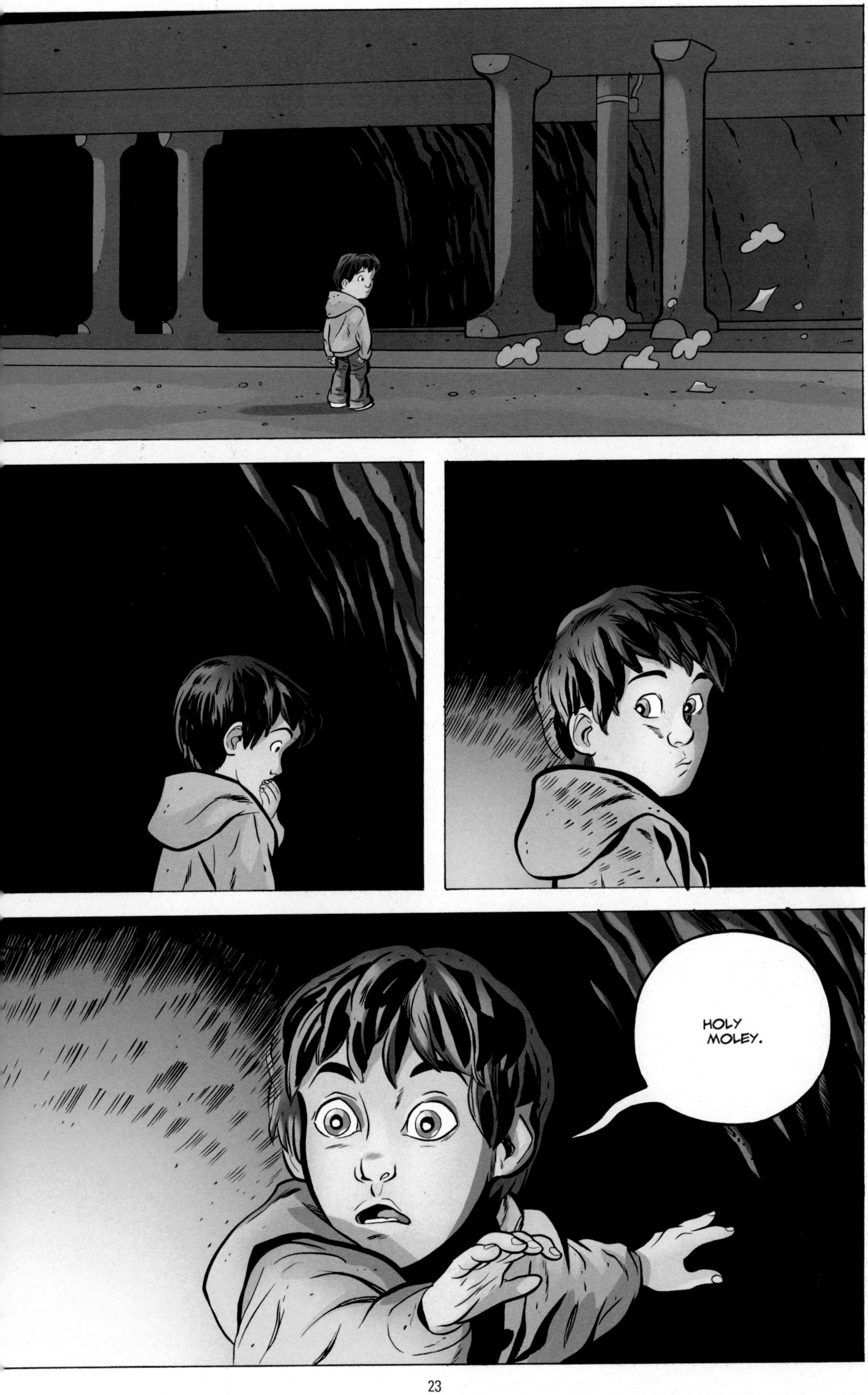
HOLY MOLEY.

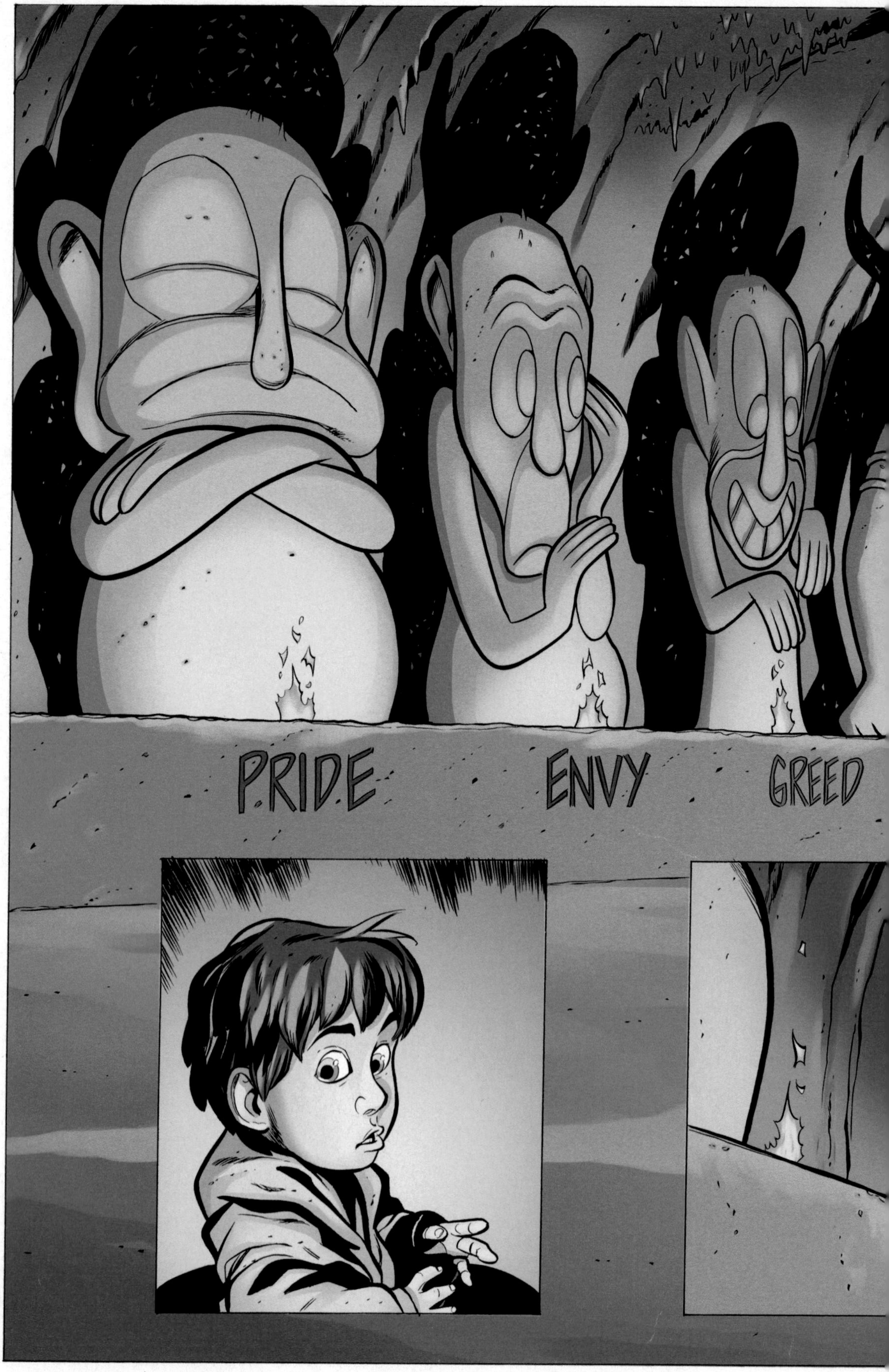
PRIDE
ENVY
GREED

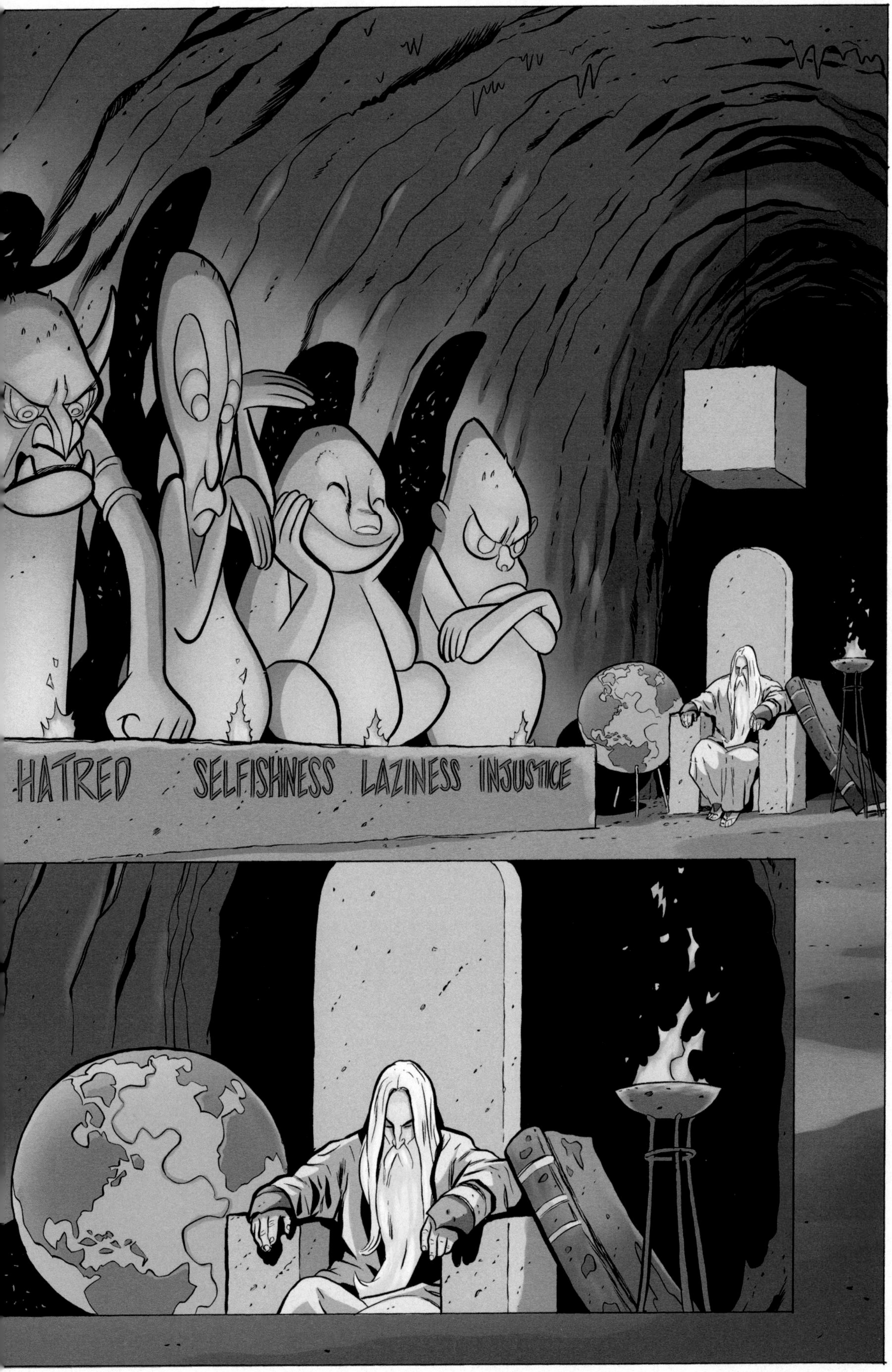
HATRED
SELFISHNESS
LAZINESS
INJUSTICE

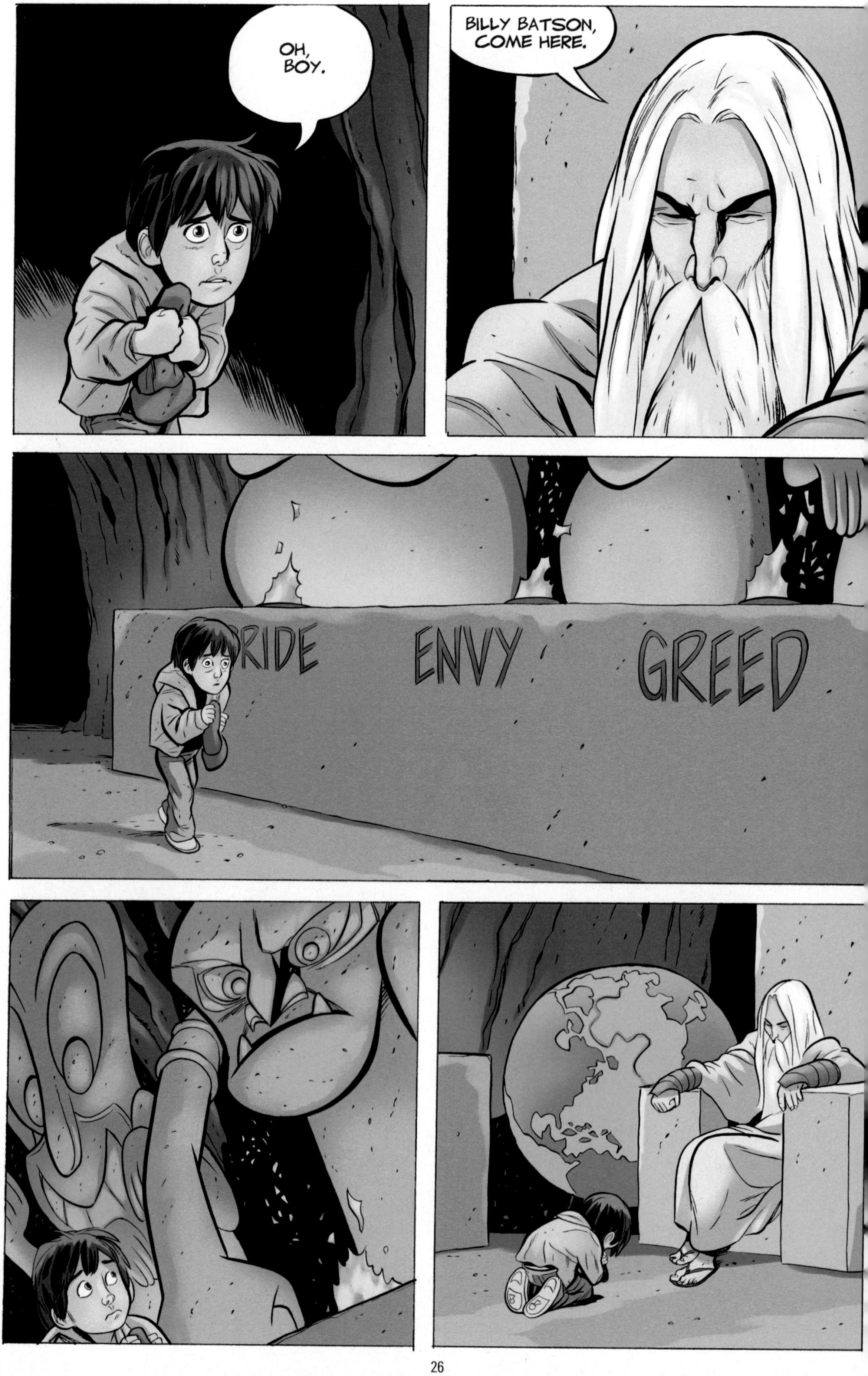
OH, BOY.
BILLY BATSON, COME HERE.
PRIDE
ENVY
GREED

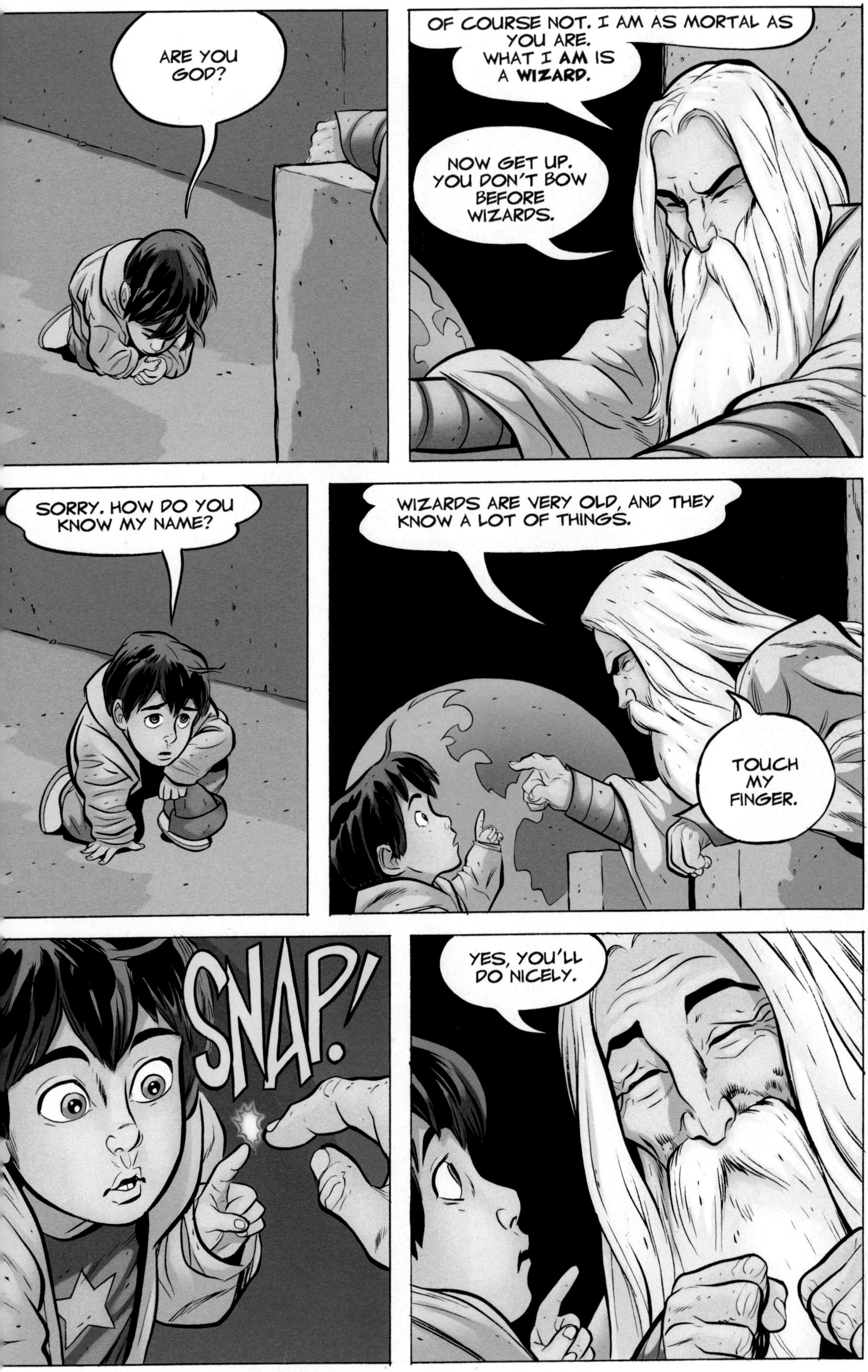
ARE YOU GOD?
OF COURSE NOT. I AM AS MORTAL AS YOU ARE. WHAT I AM IS A WIZARD.
NOW GET UP. YOU DON'T BOW BEFORE WIZARDS.
SORRY. HOW DO YOU KNOW MY NAME?
WIZARDS ARE VERY OLD, AND THEY KNOW A LOT OF THINGS.
TOUCH MY FINGER.
SNAP!
YES, YOU'LL DO NICELY.

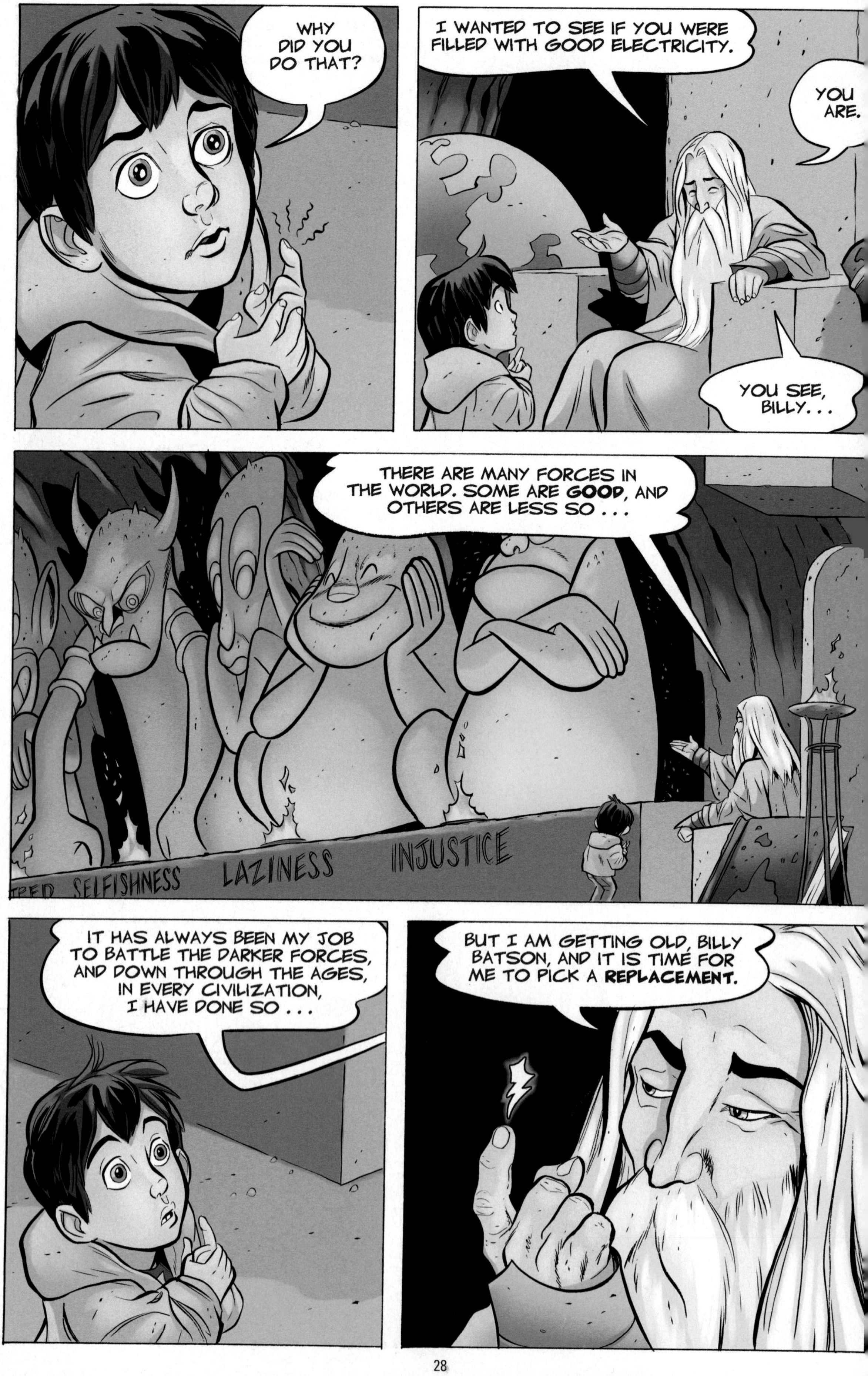
WHY DID YOU DO THAT?
I WANTED TO SEE IF YOU WERE FILLED WITH GOOD ELECTRICITY.
YOU ARE.
YOU SEE, BILLY. . .
THERE ARE MANY FORCES IN THE WORLD. SOME ARE GOOD, AND OTHERS ARE LESS SO . . .
SELFISHNESS
LAZINESS
INJUSTICE
IT HAS ALWAYS BEEN MY JOB TO BATTLE THE DARKER FORCES, AND DOWN THROUGH THE AGES, IN EVERY CIVILIZATION, I HAVE DONE SO . . .
BUT I AM GETTING OLD, BILLY BATSON, AND IT IS TIME FOR ME TO PICK A REPLACEMENT.

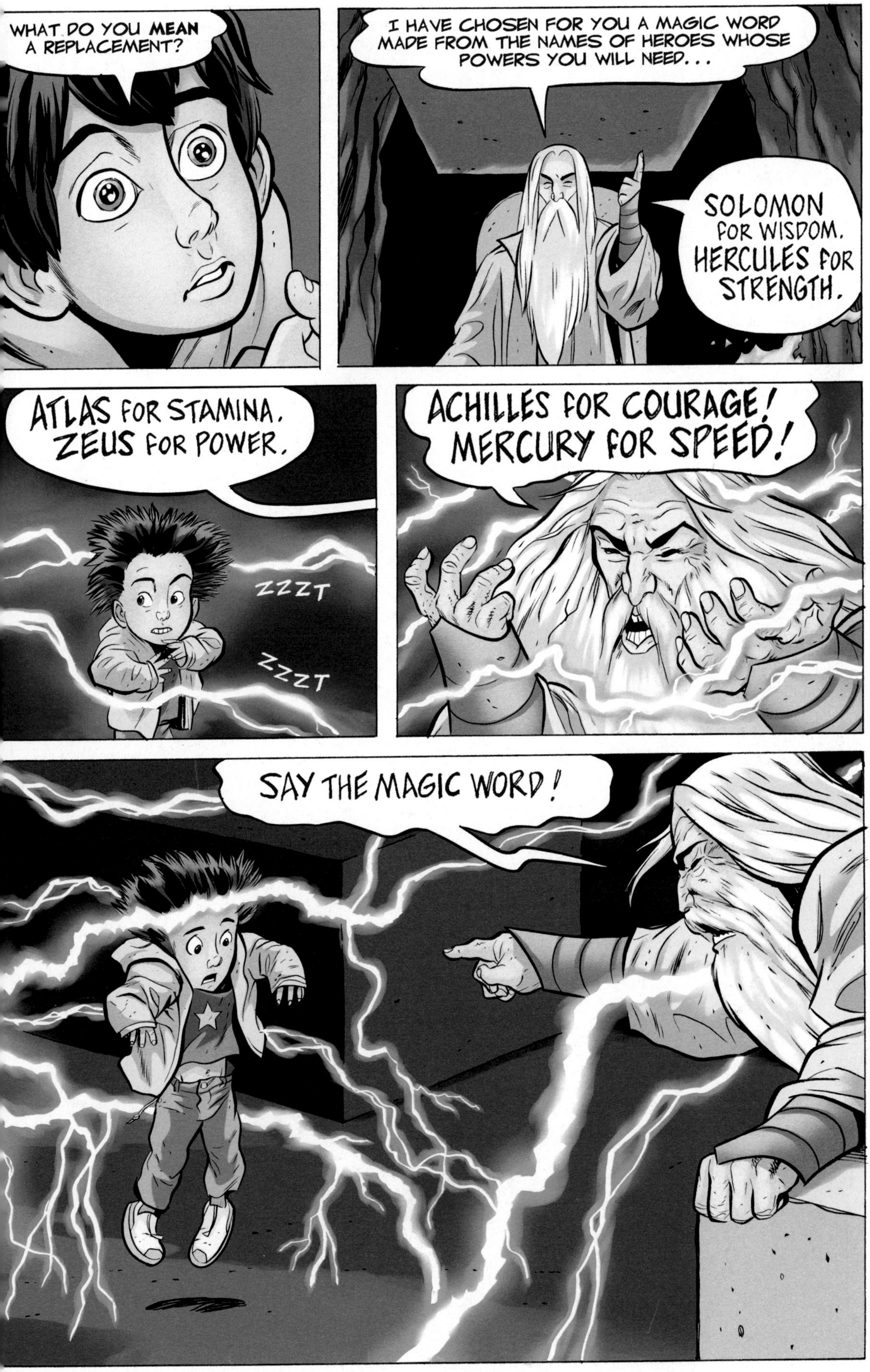
WHAT DO YOU MEAN A REPLACEMENT?
I HAVE CHOSEN FOR YOU A MAGIC WORD MADE FROM THE NAMES OF HEROES WHOSE POWERS YOU WILL NEED...
SOLOMON FOR WISDOM. HERCULES FOR STRENGTH.
ATLAS FOR STAMINA. ZEUS FOR POWER.
ZZZT
ZZZT
ACHILLES FOR COURAGE! MERCURY FOR SPEED!
SAY THE MAGIC WORD!

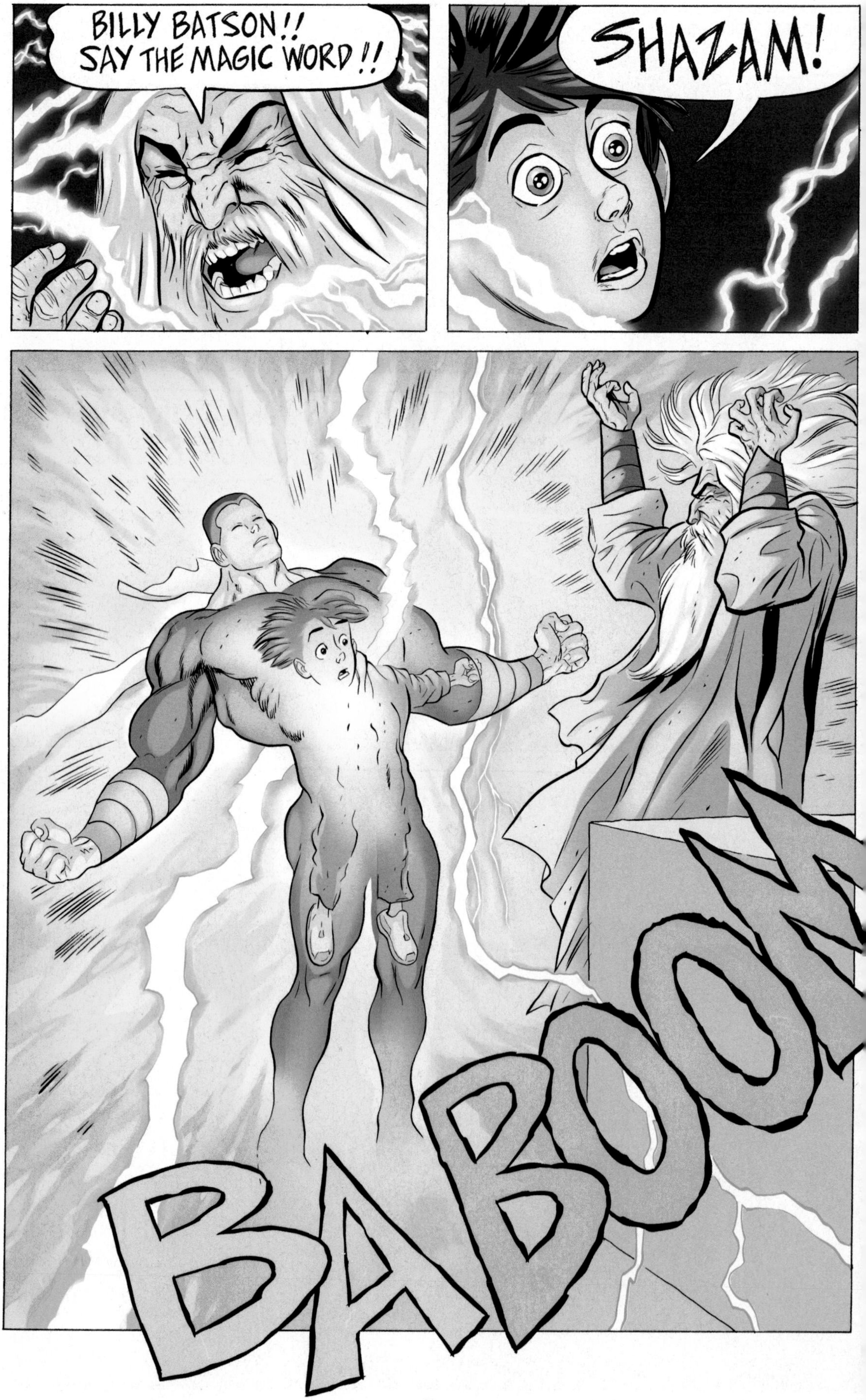
BILLY BATSON!! SAY THE MAGIC WORD!!
SHAZAM!
BABOOM

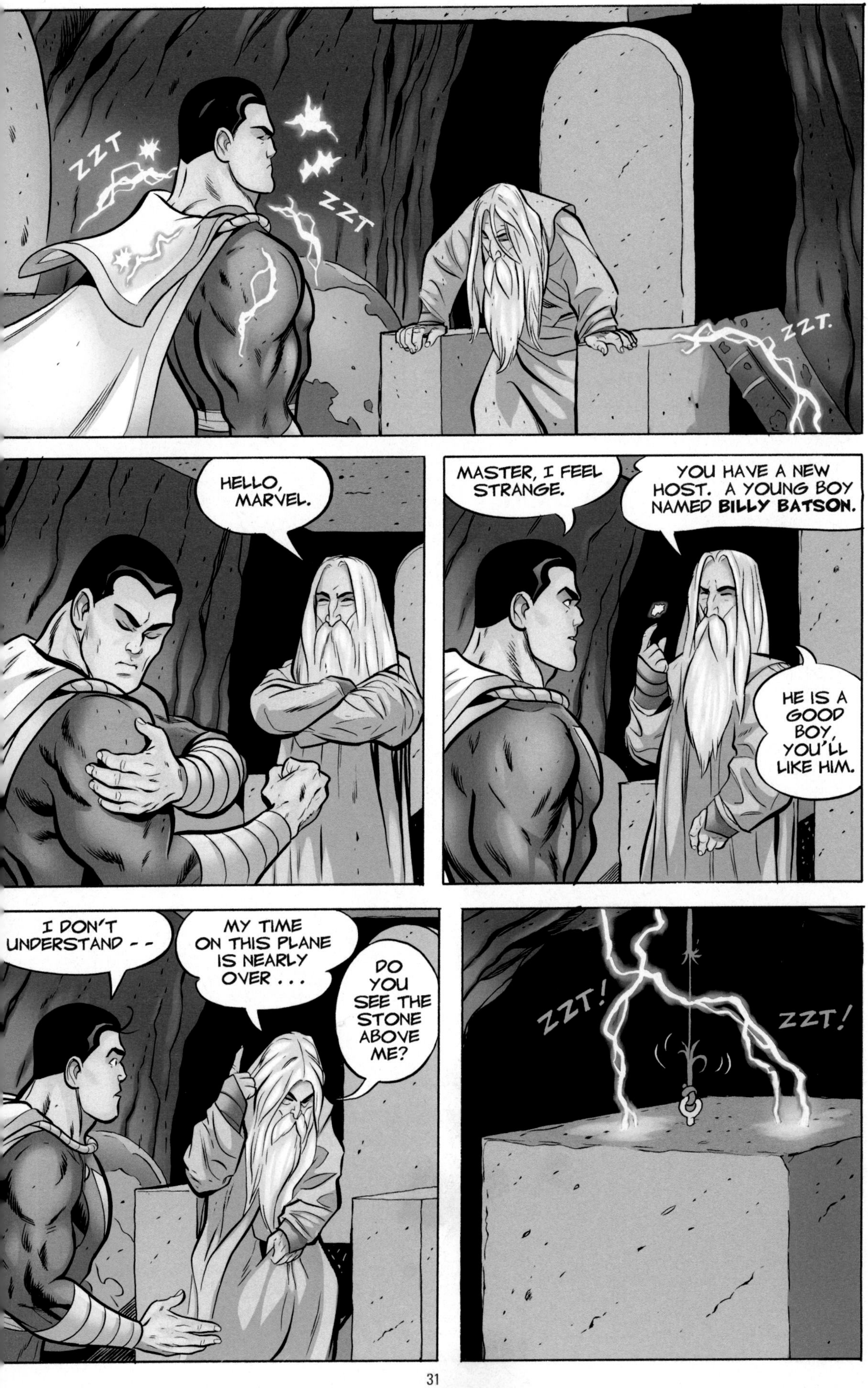
ZZT
ZZT
ZZT.
HELLO, MARVEL.
MASTER, I FEEL STRANGE.
YOU HAVE A NEW HOST. A YOUNG BOY NAMED **BILLY BATSON.**
HE IS A GOOD BOY, YOU'LL LIKE HIM.
I DON'T UNDERSTAND - -
MY TIME ON THIS PLANE IS NEARLY OVER . . .
DO YOU SEE THE STONE ABOVE ME?
ZZT!
ZZT!

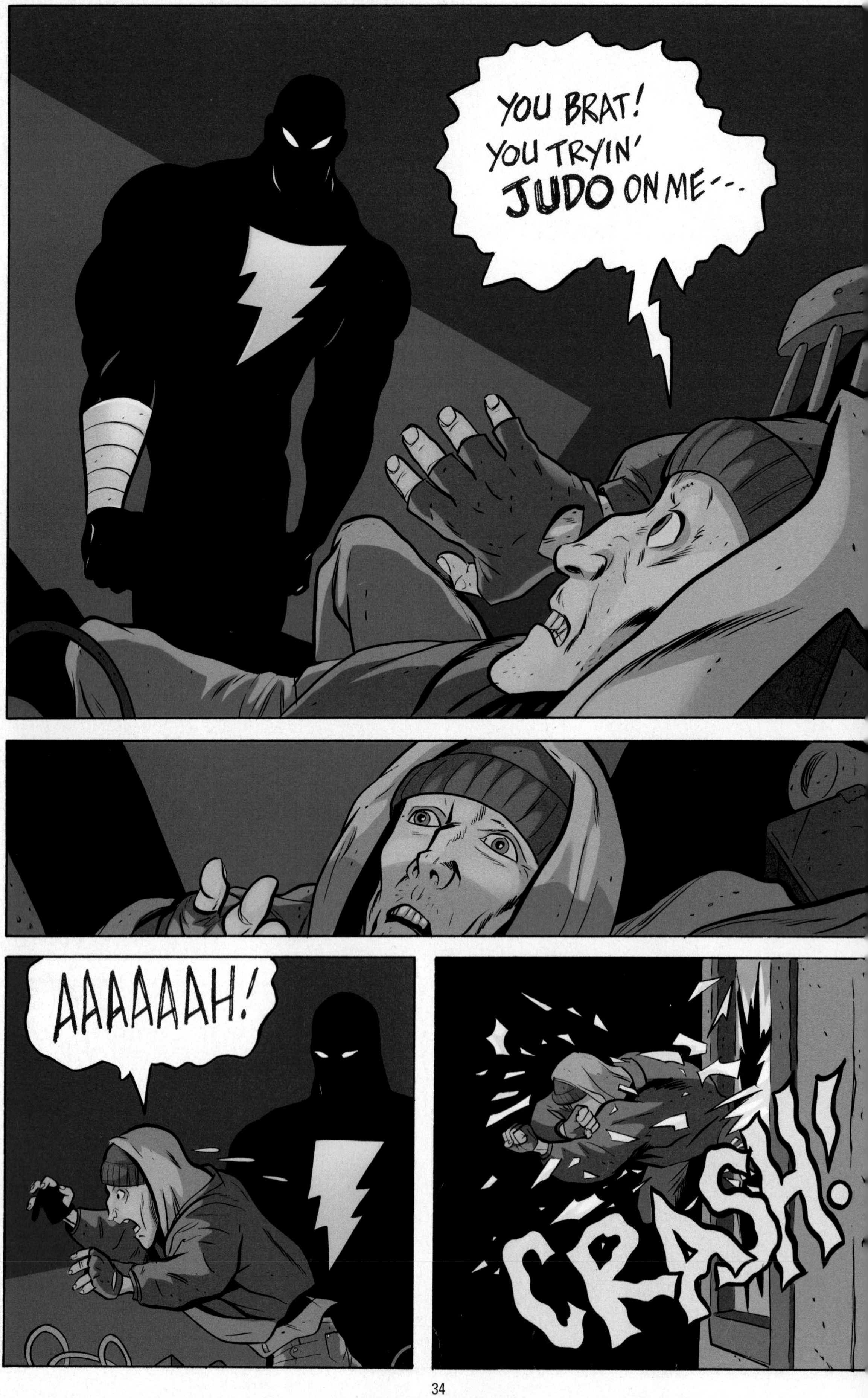
YOU BRAT!
YOU TRYIN'
JUDO ON ME--.
AAAAAH!
CRASH!

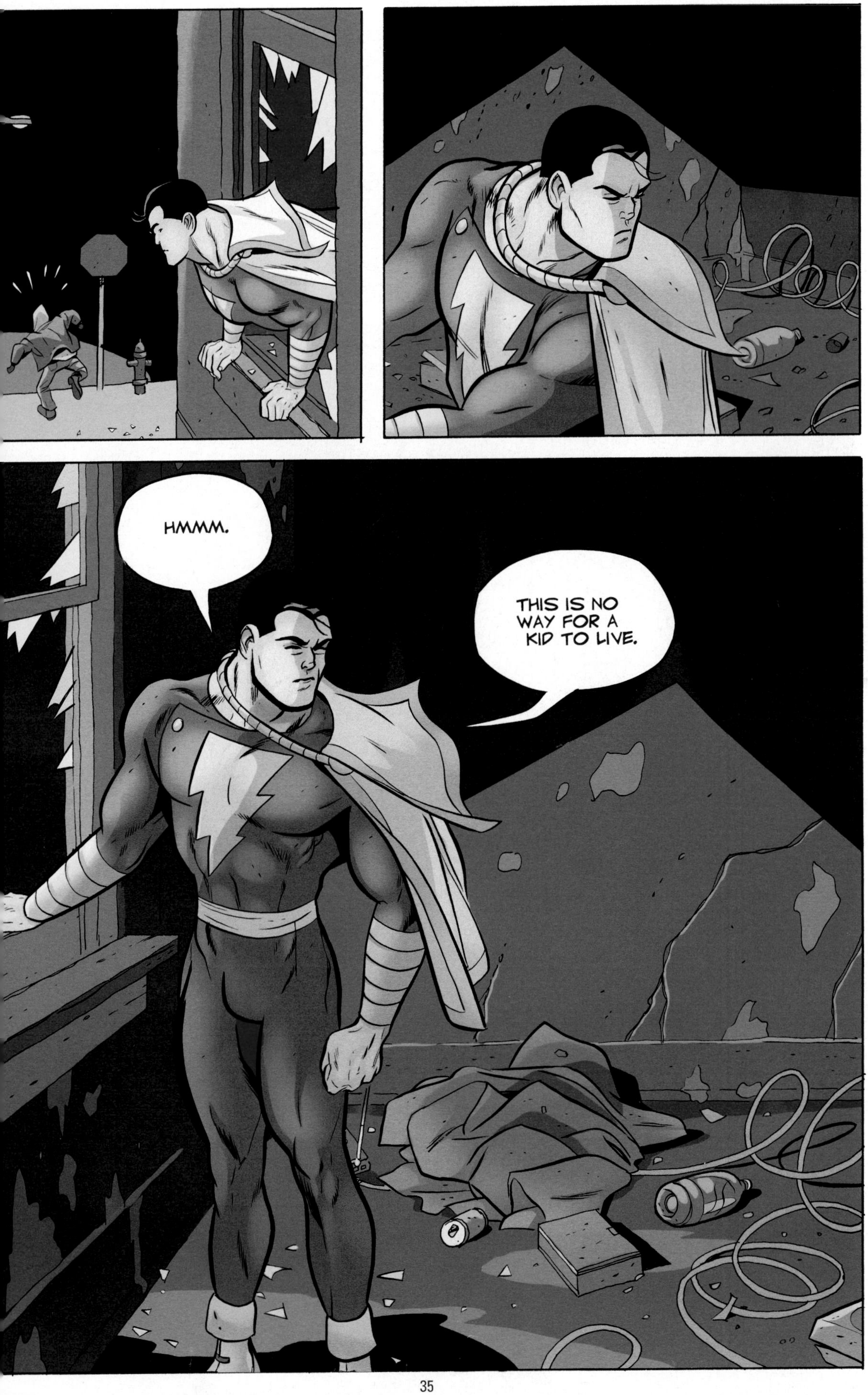
HMMM.
THIS IS NO WAY FOR A KID TO LIVE.

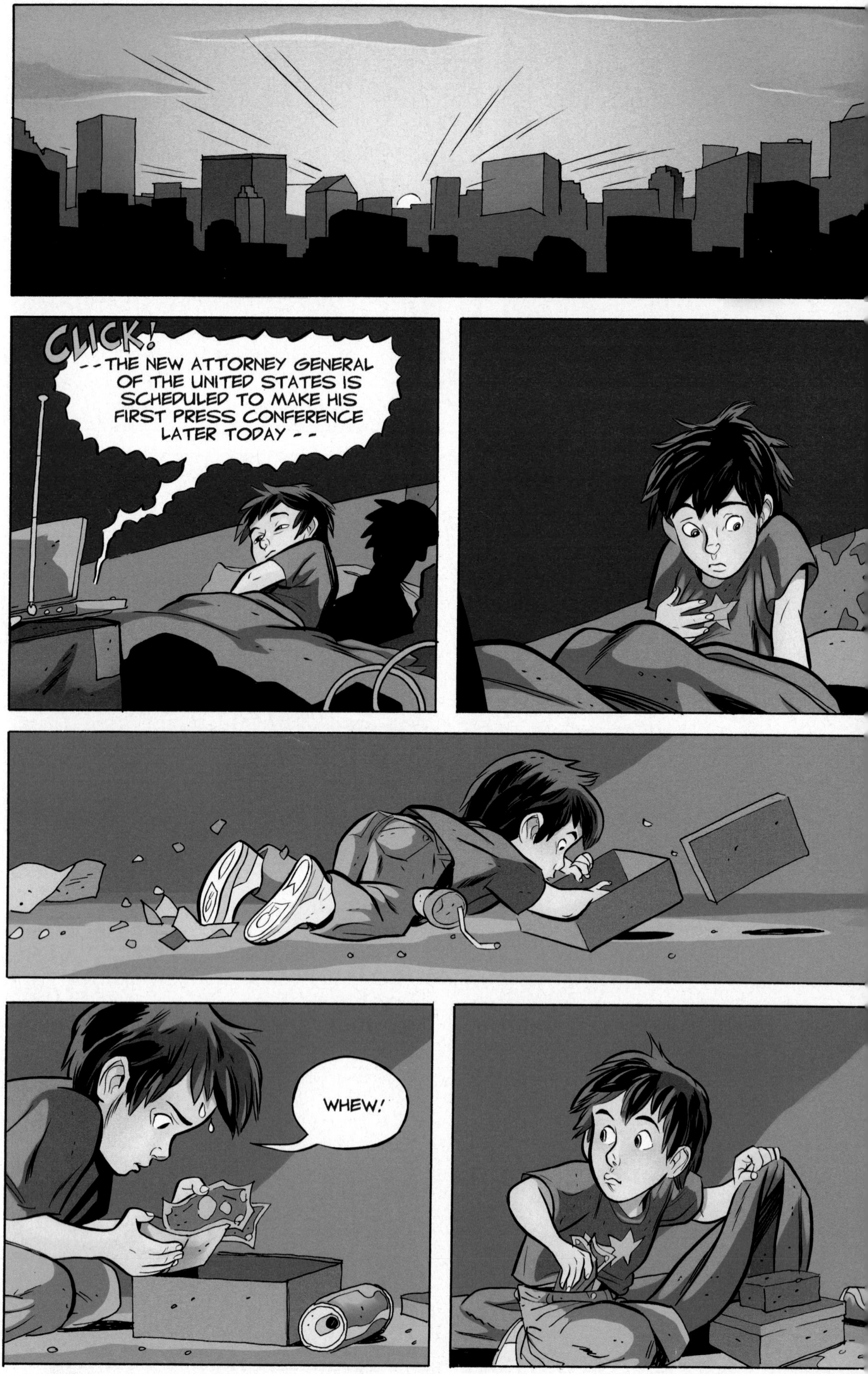
CLICK!
--THE NEW ATTORNEY GENERAL OF THE UNITED STATES IS SCHEDULED TO MAKE HIS FIRST PRESS CONFERENCE LATER TODAY --
WHEW!

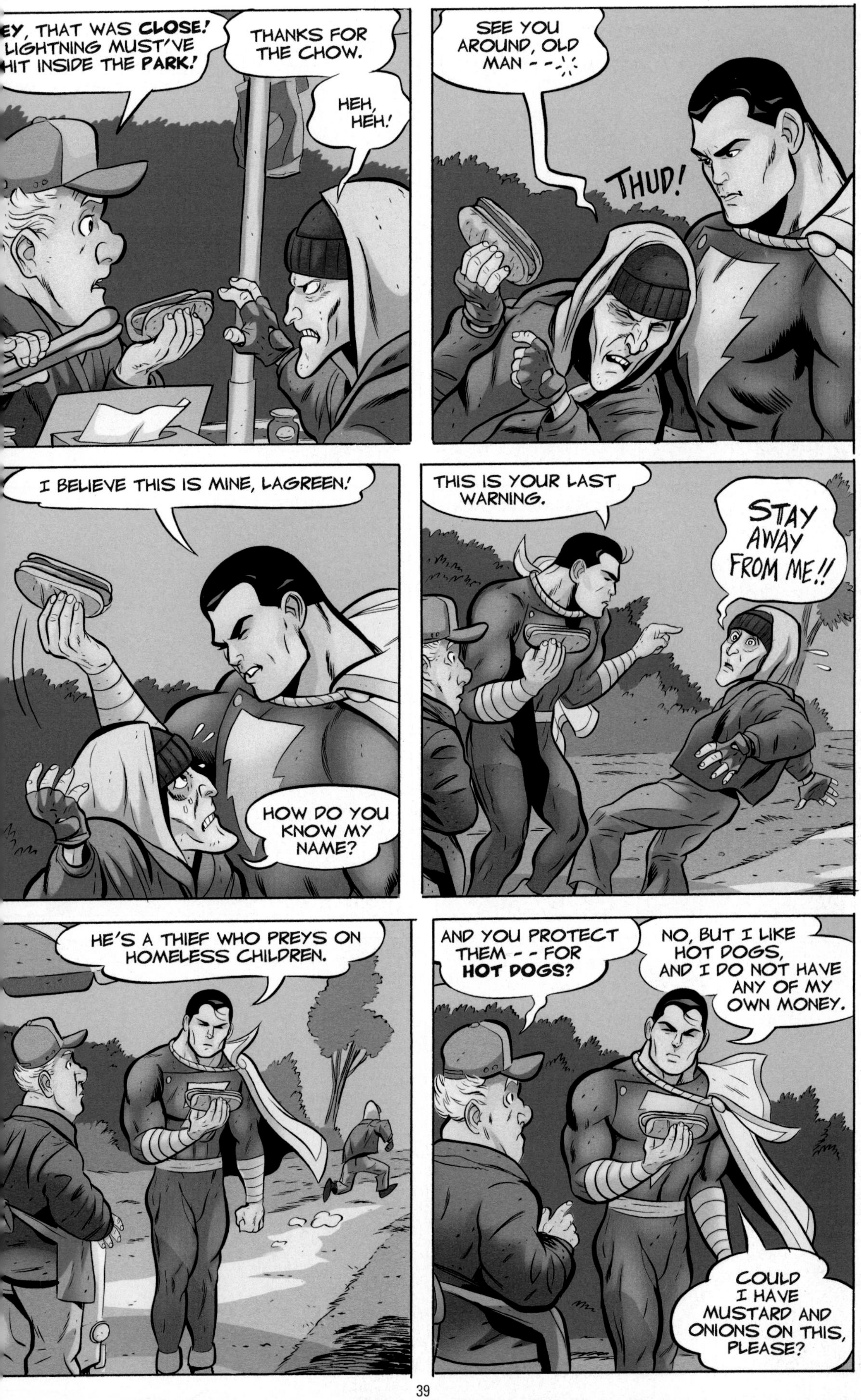
EY, THAT WAS CLOSE! LIGHTNING MUST'VE HIT INSIDE THE PARK!
THANKS FOR THE CHOW.
HEH, HEH!
SEE YOU AROUND, OLD MAN - -
THUD!
I BELIEVE THIS IS MINE, LAGREEN!
HOW DO YOU KNOW MY NAME?
THIS IS YOUR LAST WARNING.
STAY AWAY FROM ME!!
HE'S A THIEF WHO PREYS ON HOMELESS CHILDREN.
AND YOU PROTECT THEM - - FOR HOT DOGS?
NO, BUT I LIKE HOT DOGS, AND I DO NOT HAVE ANY OF MY OWN MONEY.
COULD I HAVE MUSTARD AND ONIONS ON THIS, PLEASE?

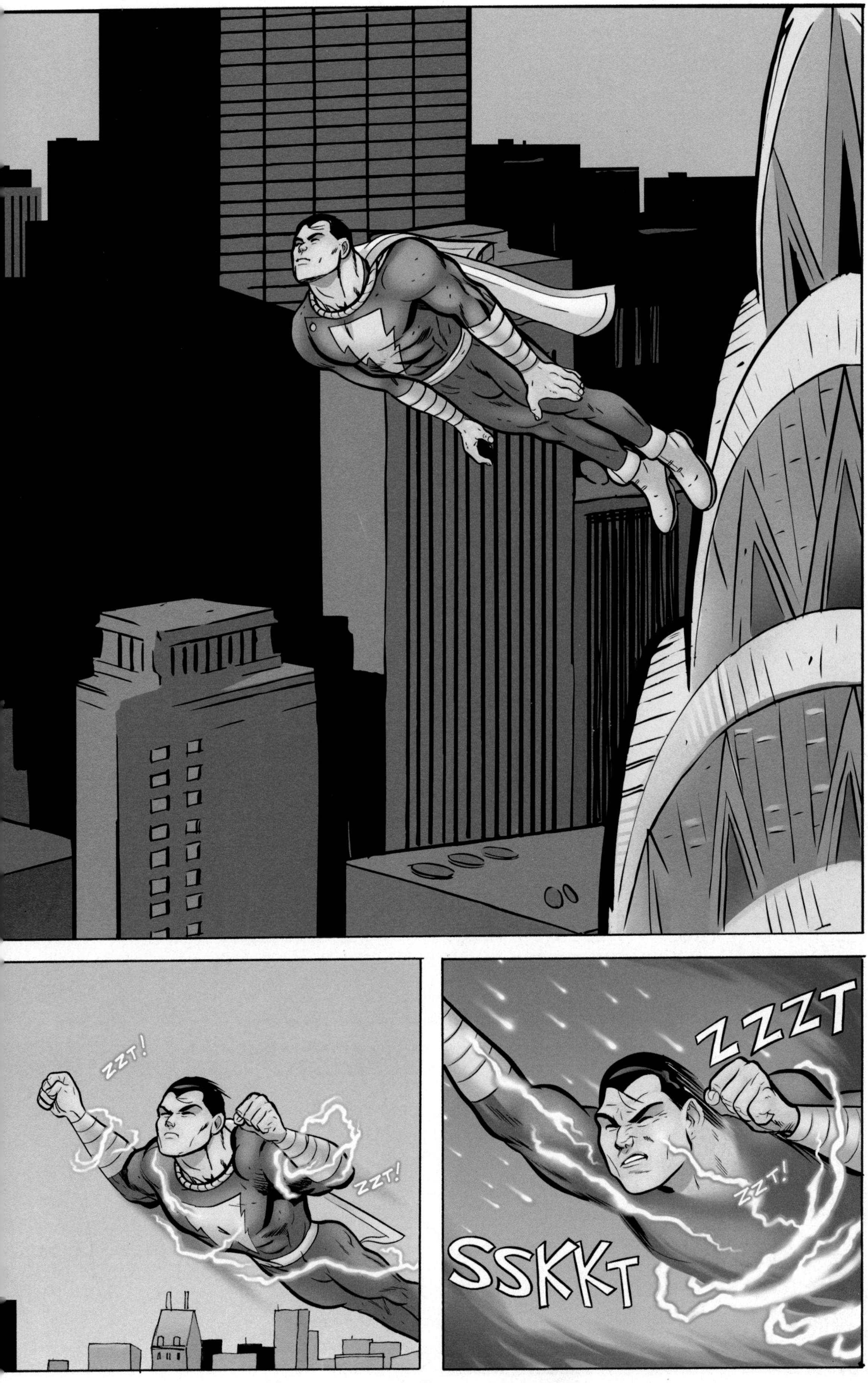
ZZT!
ZZT!
ZZZT
ZZT!
SSKKT

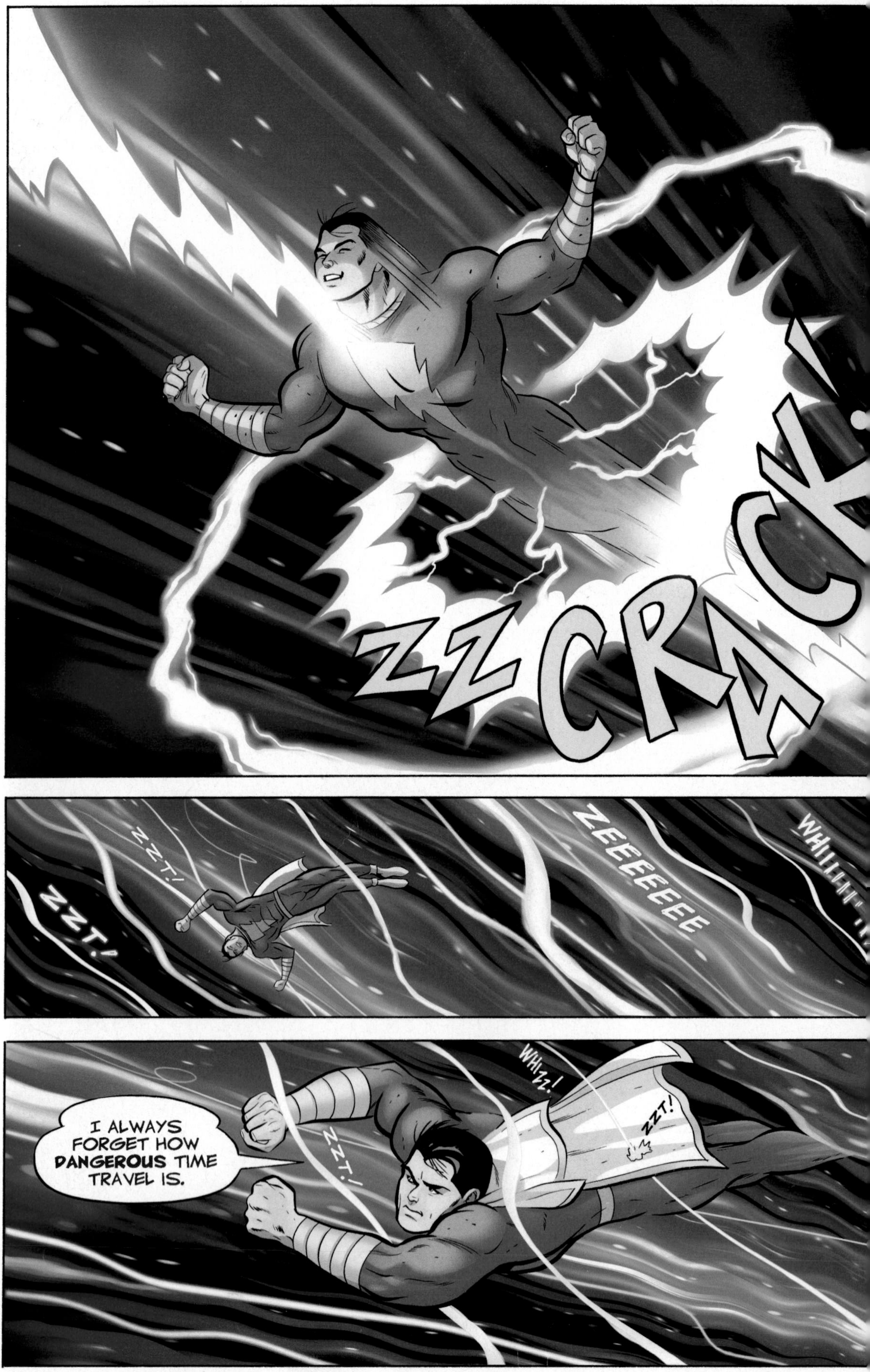
ZZCRACK!
ZZT!
ZZT!
ZEEEEEEE
WHIIIIII
WHIZZ!
ZZT!
ZZT!
I ALWAYS FORGET HOW **DANGEROUS** TIME TRAVEL IS.

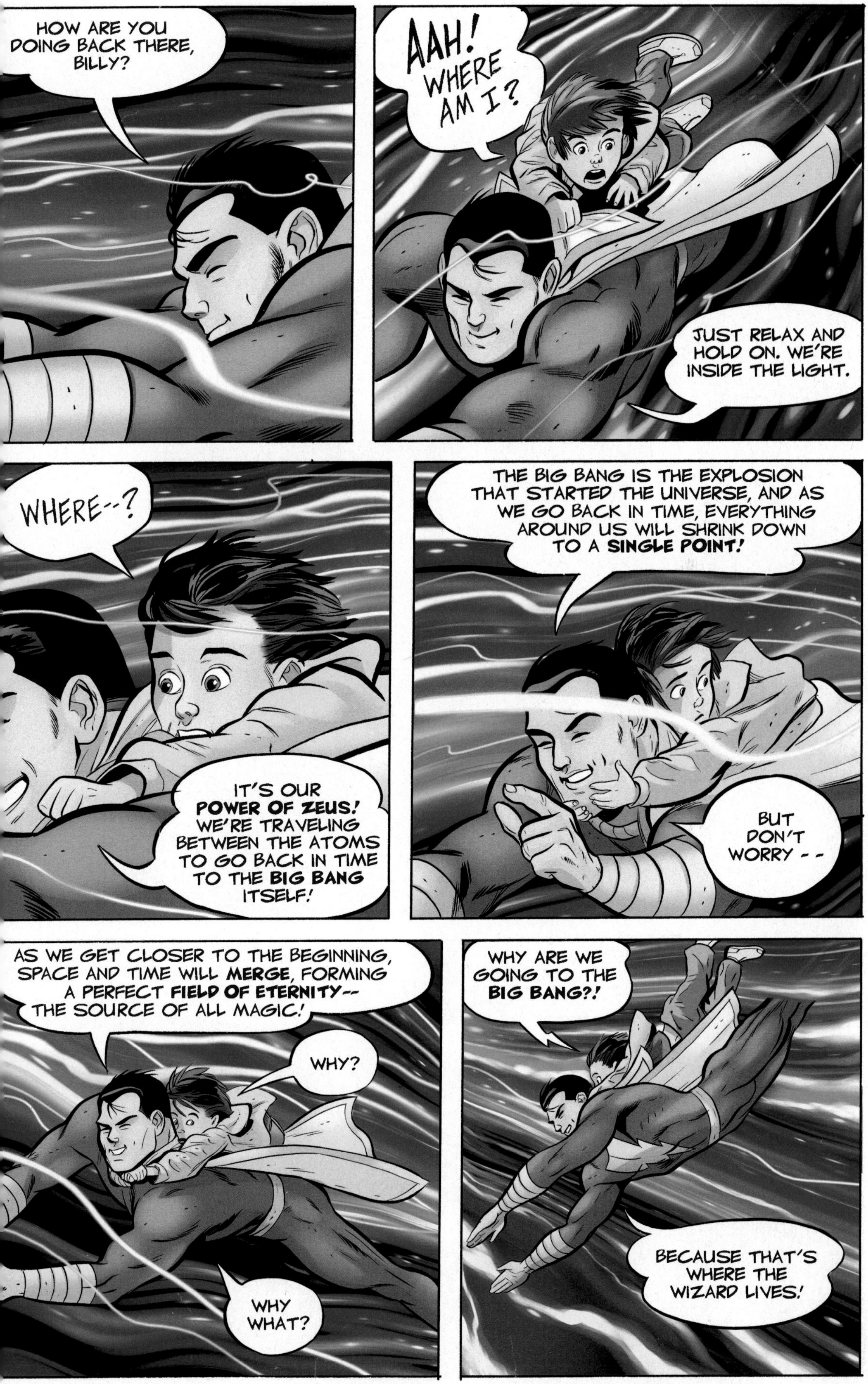
HOW ARE YOU DOING BACK THERE, BILLY?
AAH! WHERE AM I?
JUST RELAX AND HOLD ON. WE'RE INSIDE THE LIGHT.
WHERE--?
IT'S OUR POWER OF ZEUS! WE'RE TRAVELING BETWEEN THE ATOMS TO GO BACK IN TIME TO THE BIG BANG ITSELF!
THE BIG BANG IS THE EXPLOSION THAT STARTED THE UNIVERSE, AND AS WE GO BACK IN TIME, EVERYTHING AROUND US WILL SHRINK DOWN TO A SINGLE POINT!
BUT DON'T WORRY - -
AS WE GET CLOSER TO THE BEGINNING, SPACE AND TIME WILL MERGE, FORMING A PERFECT FIELD OF ETERNITY-- THE SOURCE OF ALL MAGIC!
WHY?
WHY WHAT?
WHY ARE WE GOING TO THE BIG BANG?!
BECAUSE THAT'S WHERE THE WIZARD LIVES!

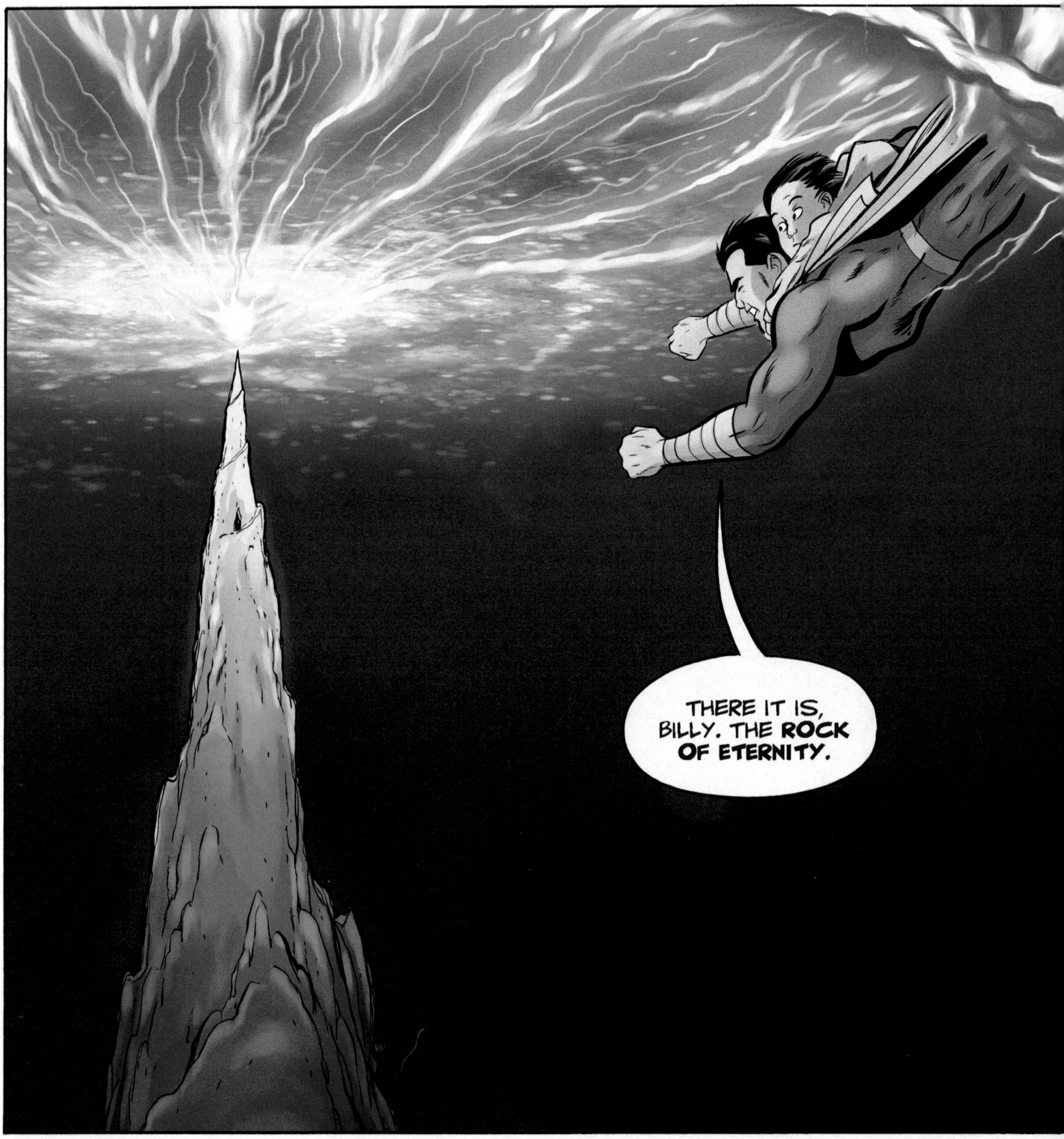
THERE IT IS, BILLY. THE ROCK OF ETERNITY.

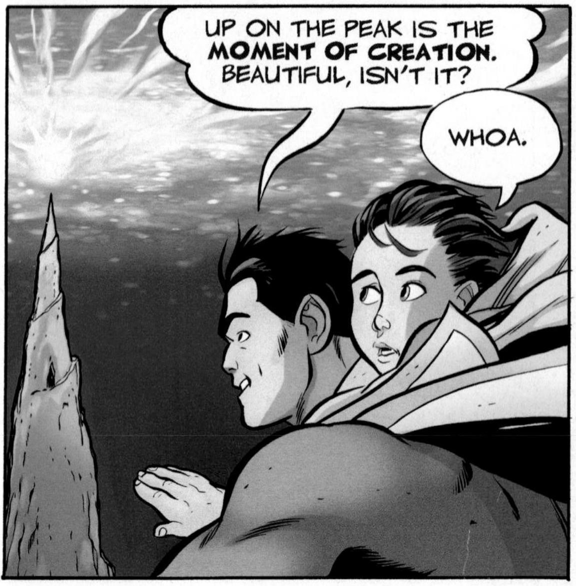
UP ON THE PEAK IS THE MOMENT OF CREATION. BEAUTIFUL, ISN'T IT?
WHOA.

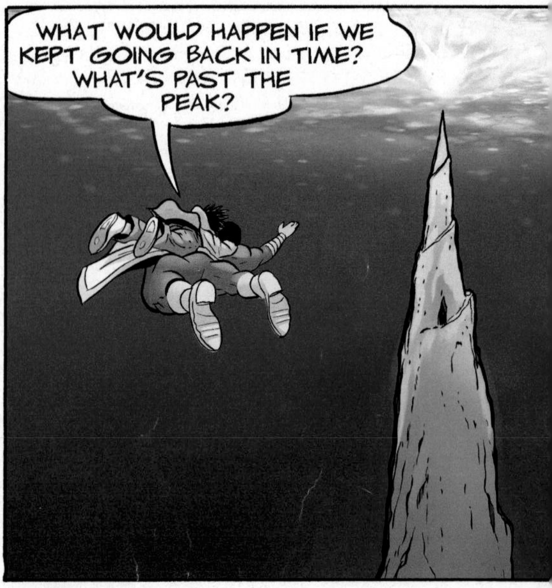
WHAT WOULD HAPPEN IF WE KEPT GOING BACK IN TIME? WHAT'S PAST THE PEAK?

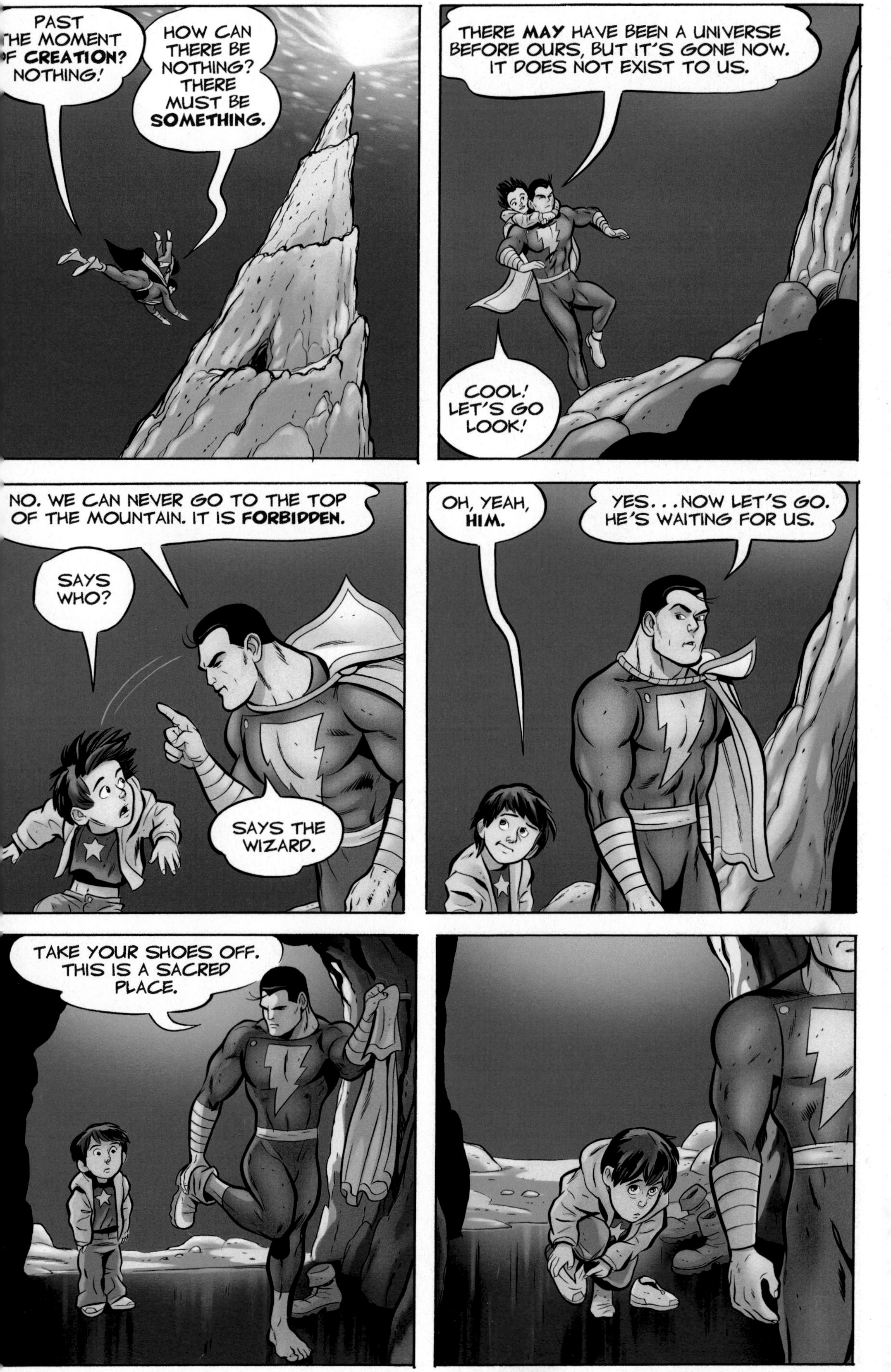
PAST THE MOMENT F CREATION? NOTHING!
HOW CAN THERE BE NOTHING? THERE MUST BE SOMETHING.
THERE MAY HAVE BEEN A UNIVERSE BEFORE OURS, BUT IT'S GONE NOW. IT DOES NOT EXIST TO US.
COOL! LET'S GO LOOK!
NO. WE CAN NEVER GO TO THE TOP OF THE MOUNTAIN. IT IS FORBIDDEN.
SAYS WHO?
SAYS THE WIZARD.
OH, YEAH, HIM.
YES. . .NOW LET'S GO. HE'S WAITING FOR US.
TAKE YOUR SHOES OFF. THIS IS A SACRED PLACE.

46

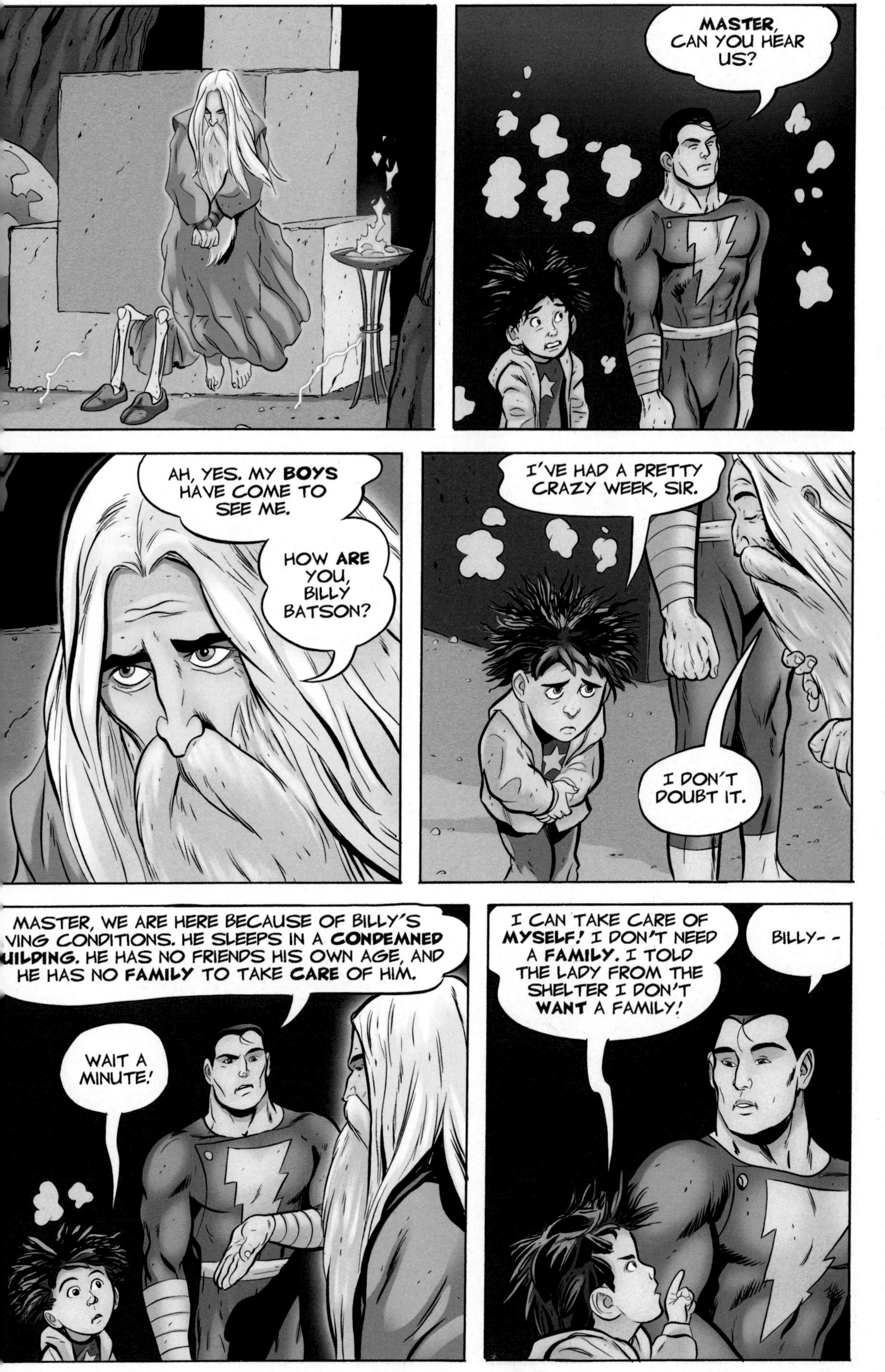
MASTER, CAN YOU HEAR US?
AH, YES. MY BOYS HAVE COME TO SEE ME.
HOW ARE YOU, BILLY BATSON?
I'VE HAD A PRETTY CRAZY WEEK, SIR.
I DON'T DOUBT IT.
MASTER, WE ARE HERE BECAUSE OF BILLY'S VING CONDITIONS. HE SLEEPS IN A CONDEMNED UILDING. HE HAS NO FRIENDS HIS OWN AGE, AND E HAS NO FAMILY TO TAKE CARE OF HIM.
WAIT A MINUTE!
I CAN TAKE CARE OF MYSELF! I DON'T NEED A FAMILY. I TOLD THE LADY FROM THE SHELTER I DON'T WANT A FAMILY!
BILLY--

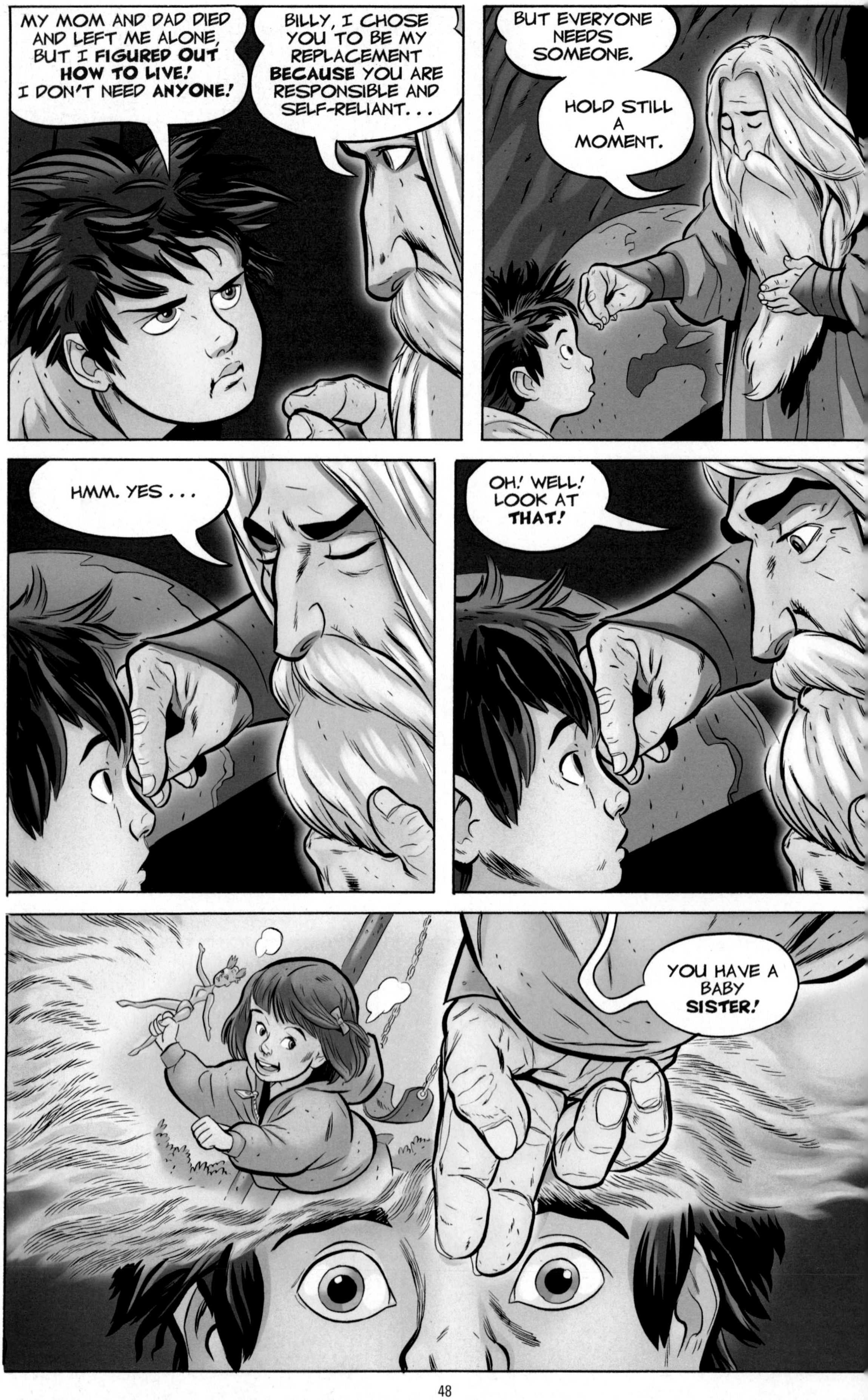
MY MOM AND DAD DIED AND LEFT ME ALONE, BUT I FIGURED OUT HOW TO LIVE! I DON'T NEED ANYONE!
BILLY, I CHOSE YOU TO BE MY REPLACEMENT BECAUSE YOU ARE RESPONSIBLE AND SELF-RELIANT...
BUT EVERYONE NEEDS SOMEONE.
HOLD STILL A MOMENT.
HMM. YES...
OH! WELL! LOOK AT THAT!
YOU HAVE A BABY SISTER!

HE LOOKS SURPRISED.

HE **IS** SURPRISED. **I'M** SURPRISED.

I WONDER WHERE SHE IS?

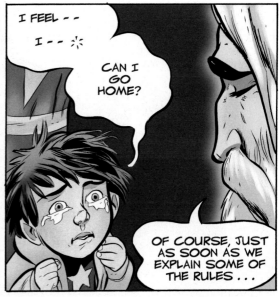

I FEEL -- I -- ✳

CAN I GO HOME?

OF COURSE, JUST AS SOON AS WE EXPLAIN SOME OF THE RULES . . .

WHAT RULES? I JUST HAVE TO SAY **SHAZ** --

**NO!!** DON'T SAY IT, BILLY! MAGIC IS **UN-PREDICTABLE** HERE!

THIS IS **VERY IMPORTANT!** THE RULES OF THE **ORDINARY** WORLD DO NOT APPLY IN ETERNITY.

WHY?

BECAUSE **TIME** AND **SPACE** ARE SMASHED TOGETHER HERE -- LIKE IN A **BLACK HOLE!** I'M YOUR **FUTURE SELF!**

CALLING UPON THE MAGIC **HERE** COULD CAUSE A **TERRIBLE PARADOX!**

PRIDE EN

PERHAPS YOU'D LIKE TO WAIT OUTSIDE FOR CAPTAIN MARVEL.

PRIDE

HE'S VERY YOUNG.

AND YET YOU AND HE ARE ONE. **TOGETHER** YOU WILL SOLVE YOUR PROBLEMS.

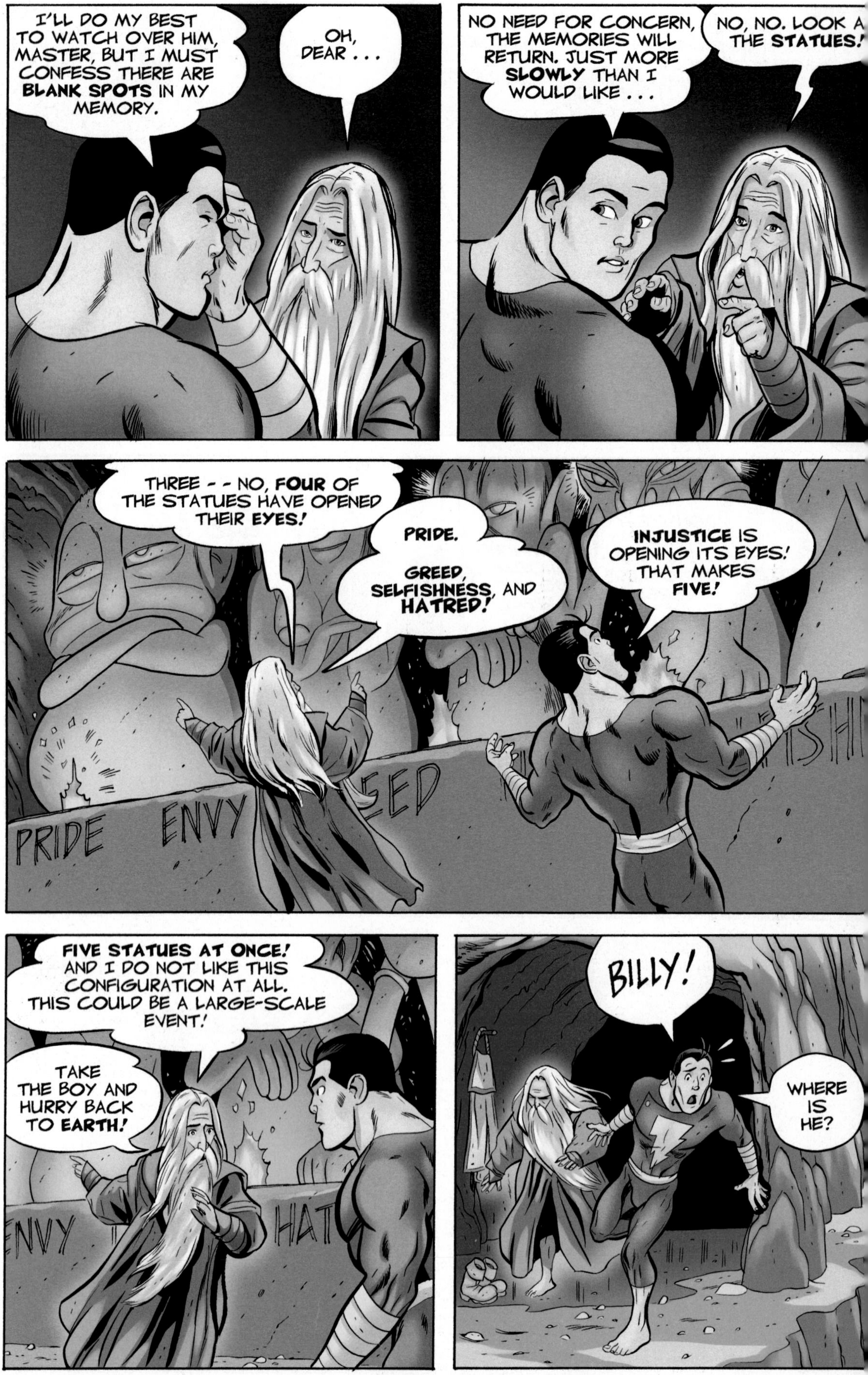

I'LL DO MY BEST TO WATCH OVER HIM, MASTER, BUT I MUST CONFESS THERE ARE BLANK SPOTS IN MY MEMORY.
OH, DEAR . . .
NO NEED FOR CONCERN, THE MEMORIES WILL RETURN. JUST MORE SLOWLY THAN I WOULD LIKE . . .
NO, NO. LOOK A THE STATUES!
THREE - - NO, FOUR OF THE STATUES HAVE OPENED THEIR EYES!
PRIDE.
GREED, SELFISHNESS, AND HATRED!
INJUSTICE IS OPENING ITS EYES! THAT MAKES FIVE!
PRIDE
ENVY
FIVE STATUES AT ONCE! AND I DO NOT LIKE THIS CONFIGURATION AT ALL. THIS COULD BE A LARGE-SCALE EVENT!
TAKE THE BOY AND HURRY BACK TO EARTH!
BILLY!
WHERE IS HE?

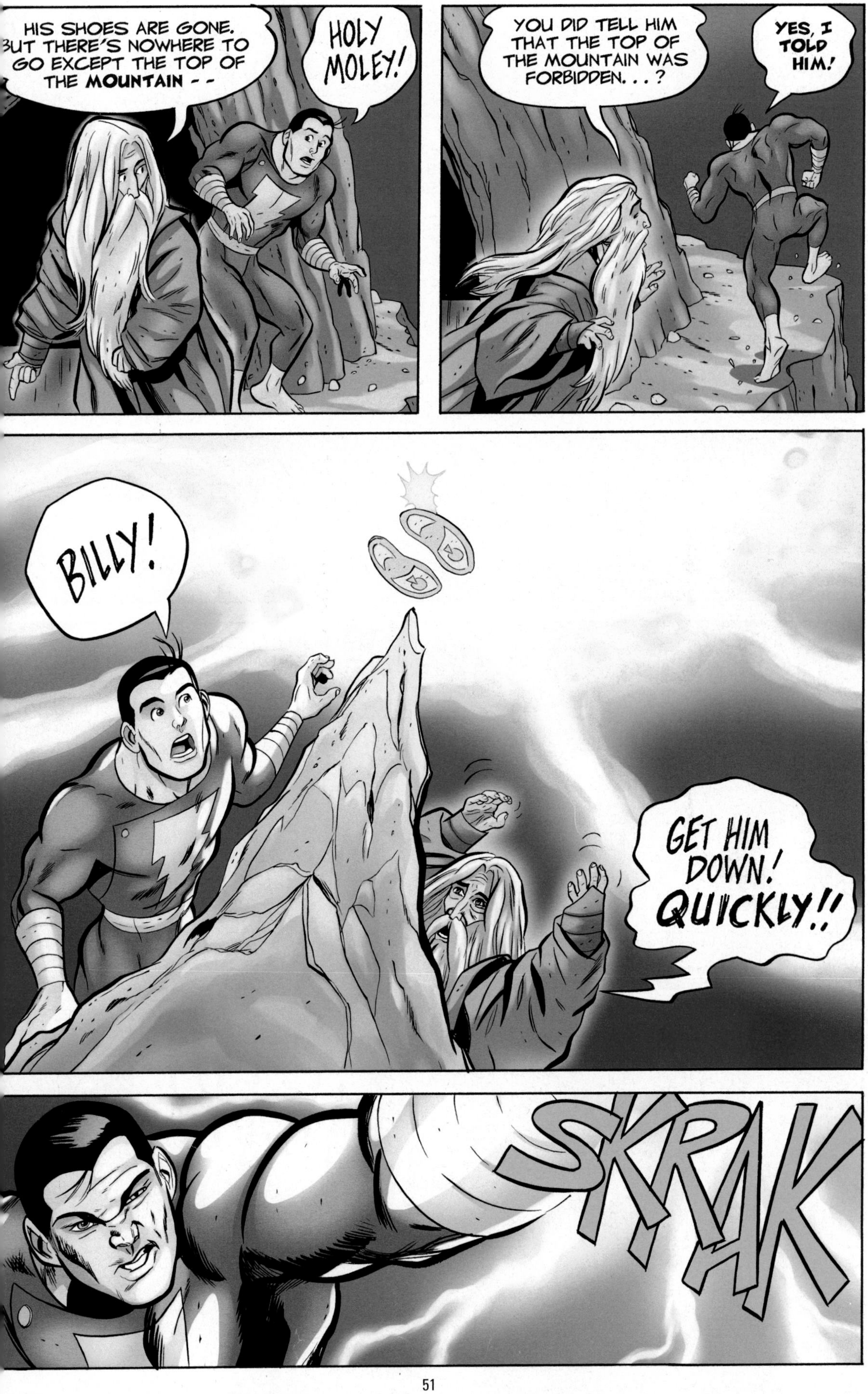
HIS SHOES ARE GONE. BUT THERE'S NOWHERE TO GO EXCEPT THE TOP OF THE **MOUNTAIN** - -
HOLY MOLEY!
YOU DID TELL HIM THAT THE TOP OF THE MOUNTAIN WAS FORBIDDEN. . . ?
YES, I **TOLD** HIM!
BILLY!
GET HIM DOWN! **QUICKLY!!**
SKRAK

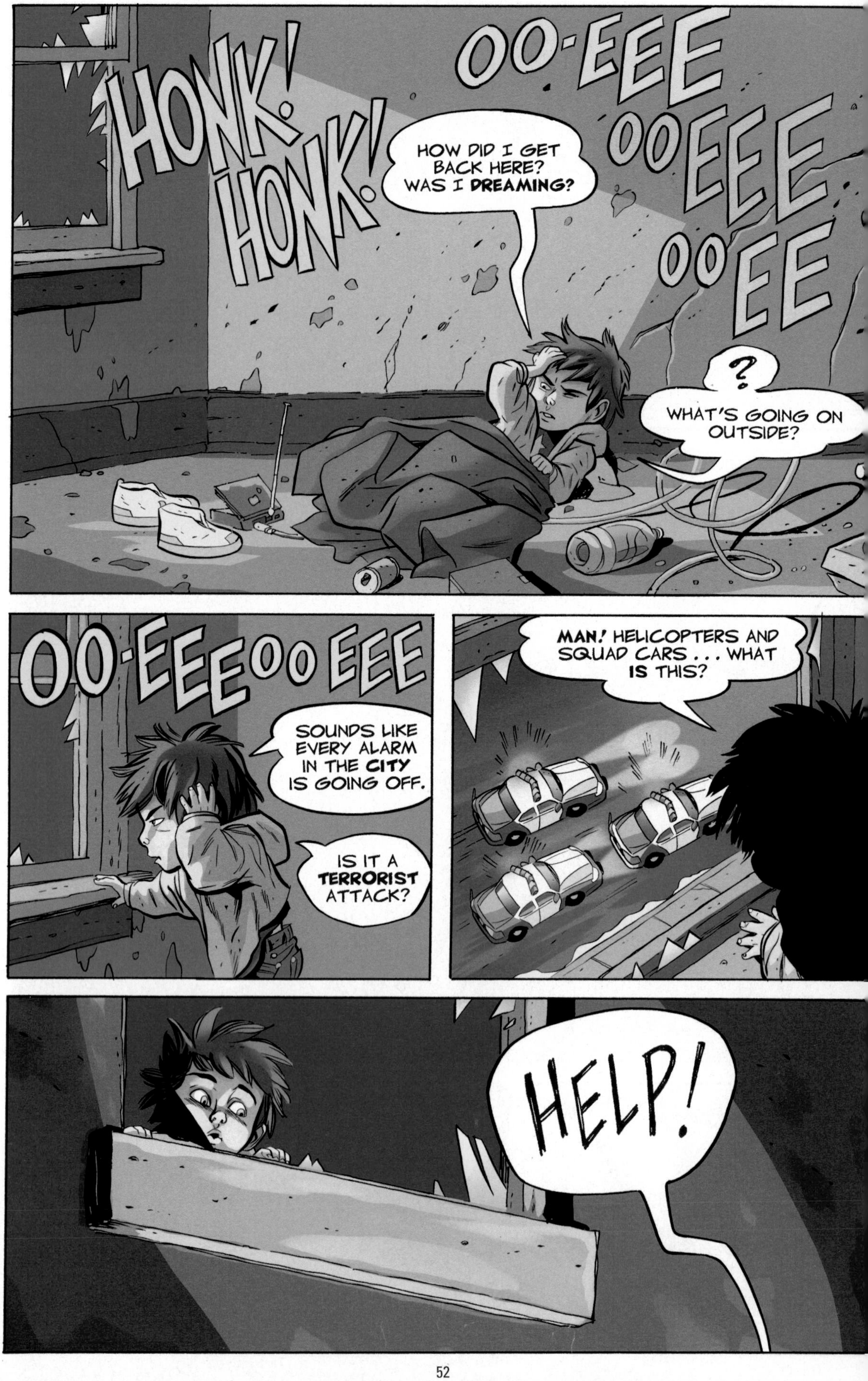
HONK! HONK!
OO-EEE OOEEE OOEE
HOW DID I GET BACK HERE? WAS I **DREAMING?**
?
WHAT'S GOING ON OUTSIDE?
OO-EEEOO EEE
SOUNDS LIKE EVERY ALARM IN THE **CITY** IS GOING OFF.
IS IT A **TERRORIST** ATTACK?
**MAN!** HELICOPTERS AND SQUAD CARS . . . WHAT **IS** THIS?
HELP!

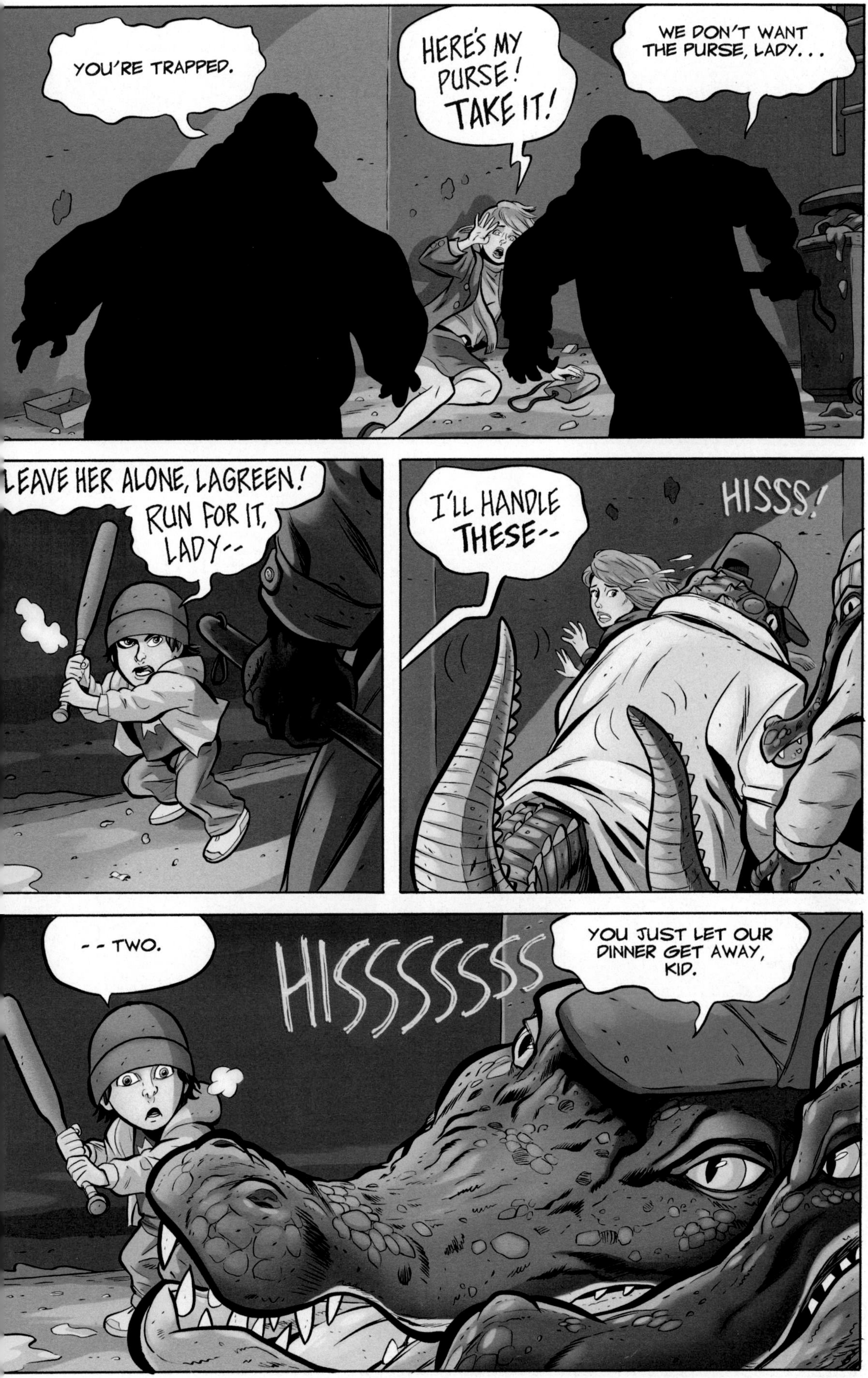
YOU'RE TRAPPED.
HERE'S MY PURSE! TAKE IT!
WE DON'T WANT THE PURSE, LADY...
LEAVE HER ALONE, LAGREEN! RUN FOR IT, LADY--
I'LL HANDLE THESE--
HISSS!
--TWO.
HISSSSSSS
YOU JUST LET OUR DINNER GET AWAY, KID.

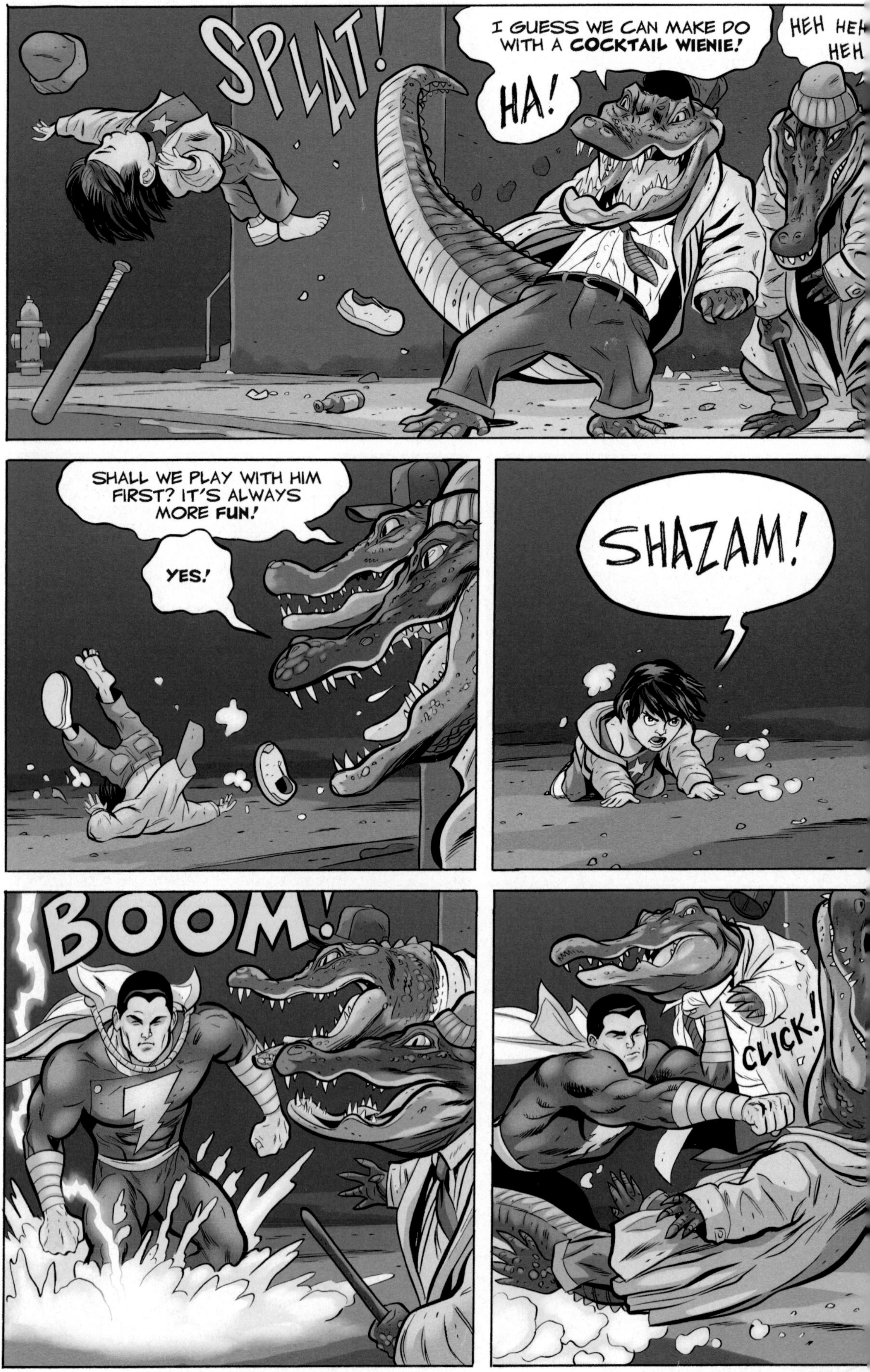
SPLAT!
I GUESS WE CAN MAKE DO WITH A COCKTAIL WIENIE!
HA!
HEH HEH HEH
SHALL WE PLAY WITH HIM FIRST? IT'S ALWAYS MORE FUN!
YES!
SHAZAM!
BOOM!
CLICK!

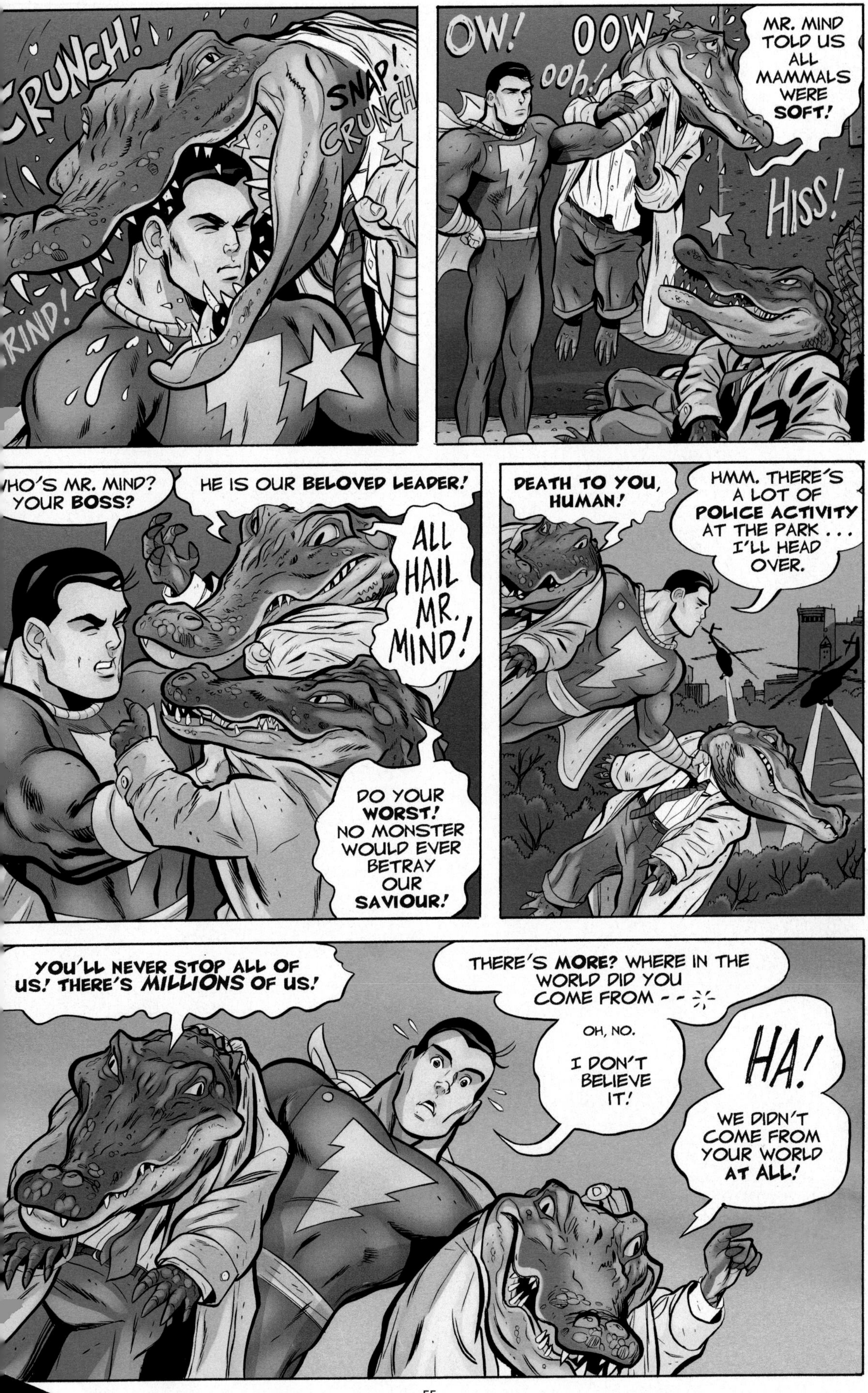
CRUNCH!
SNAP!
CRUNCH
RIND!
OW!
OOW
ooh!
MR. MIND TOLD US ALL MAMMALS WERE SOFT!
HISS!
WHO'S MR. MIND? YOUR BOSS?
HE IS OUR BELOVED LEADER!
ALL HAIL MR. MIND!
DO YOUR WORST! NO MONSTER WOULD EVER BETRAY OUR SAVIOUR!
DEATH TO YOU, HUMAN!
HMM. THERE'S A LOT OF POLICE ACTIVITY AT THE PARK . . . I'LL HEAD OVER.
YOU'LL NEVER STOP ALL OF US! THERE'S MILLIONS OF US!
THERE'S MORE? WHERE IN THE WORLD DID YOU COME FROM - -
OH, NO.
I DON'T BELIEVE IT!
HA!
WE DIDN'T COME FROM YOUR WORLD AT ALL!

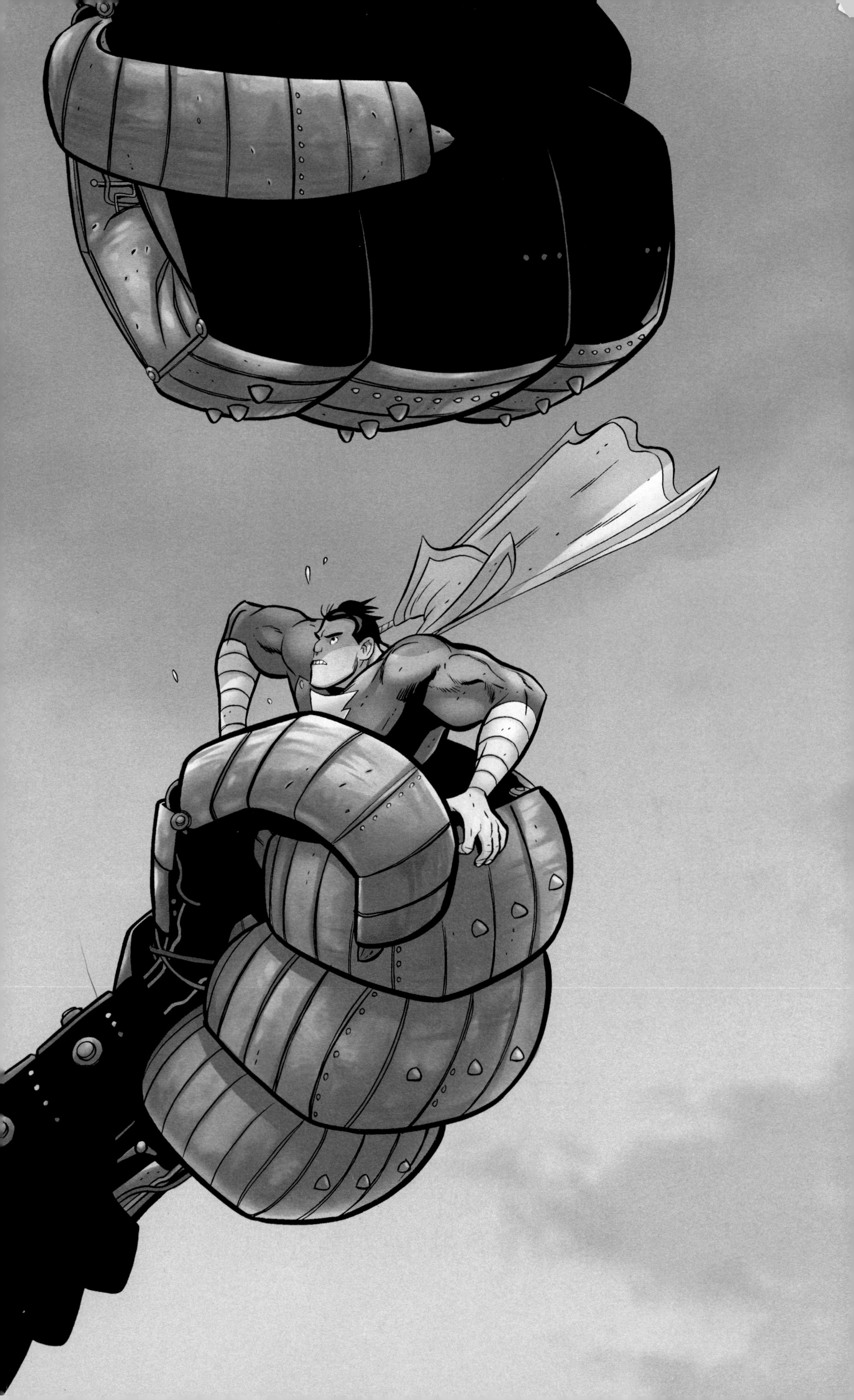

# THE MONSTER SOCIETY OF EVIL

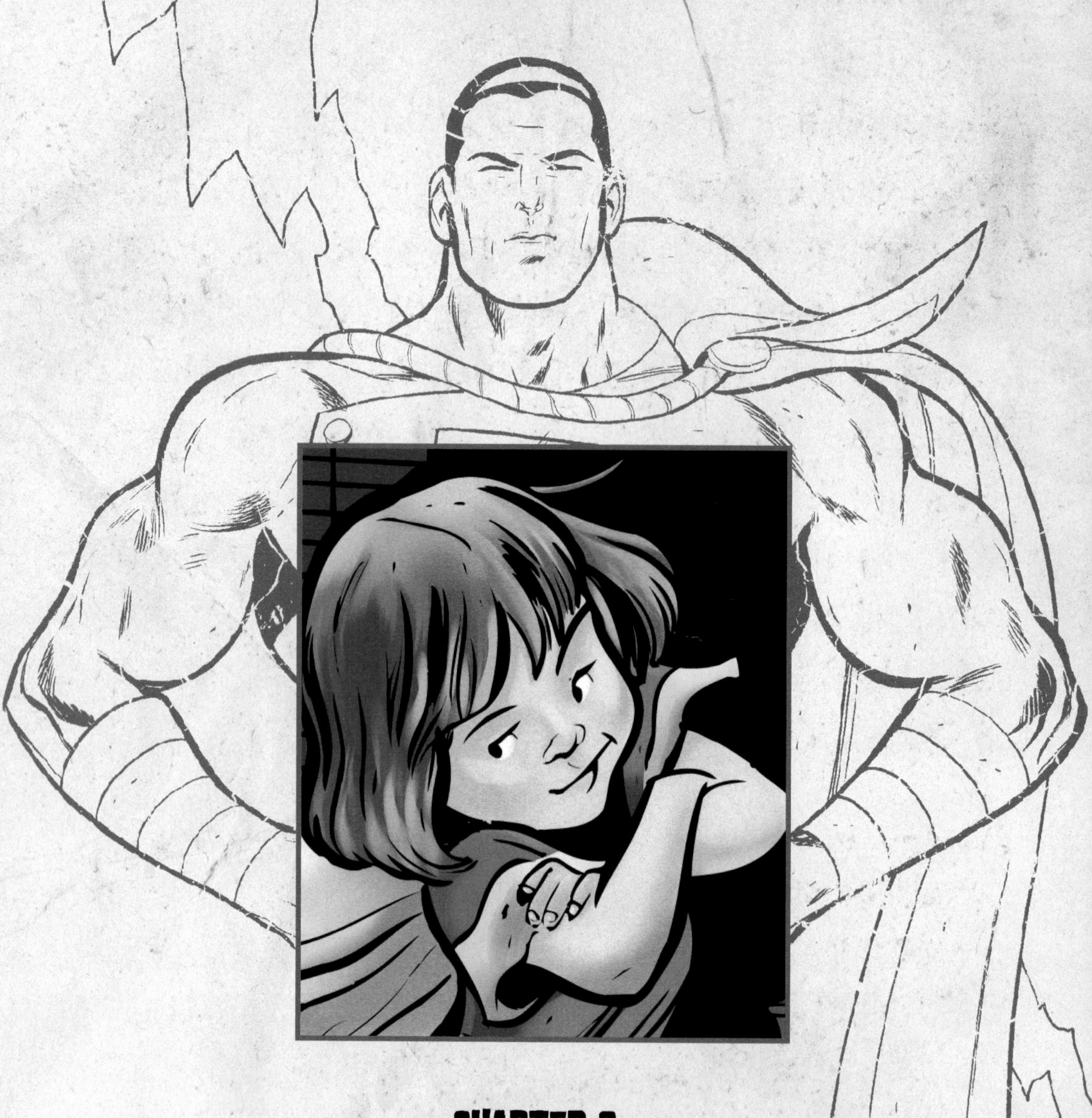

## CHAPTER 2:
## NZIB GZPVH GSV XZPV!*

*THE MONSTER SOCIETY CODE

| | | | | | | | | | | | | | | | | | | | | | | | | | |
|---|---|---|---|---|---|---|---|---|---|---|---|---|---|---|---|---|---|---|---|---|---|---|---|---|---|
| A | B | C | D | E | F | G | H | I | J | K | L | M | N | O | P | Q | R | S | T | U | V | W | X | Y | Z |
| Z | Y | X | W | V | U | T | S | R | Q | P | O | N | M | L | K | J | I | H | G | F | E | D | C | B | A |

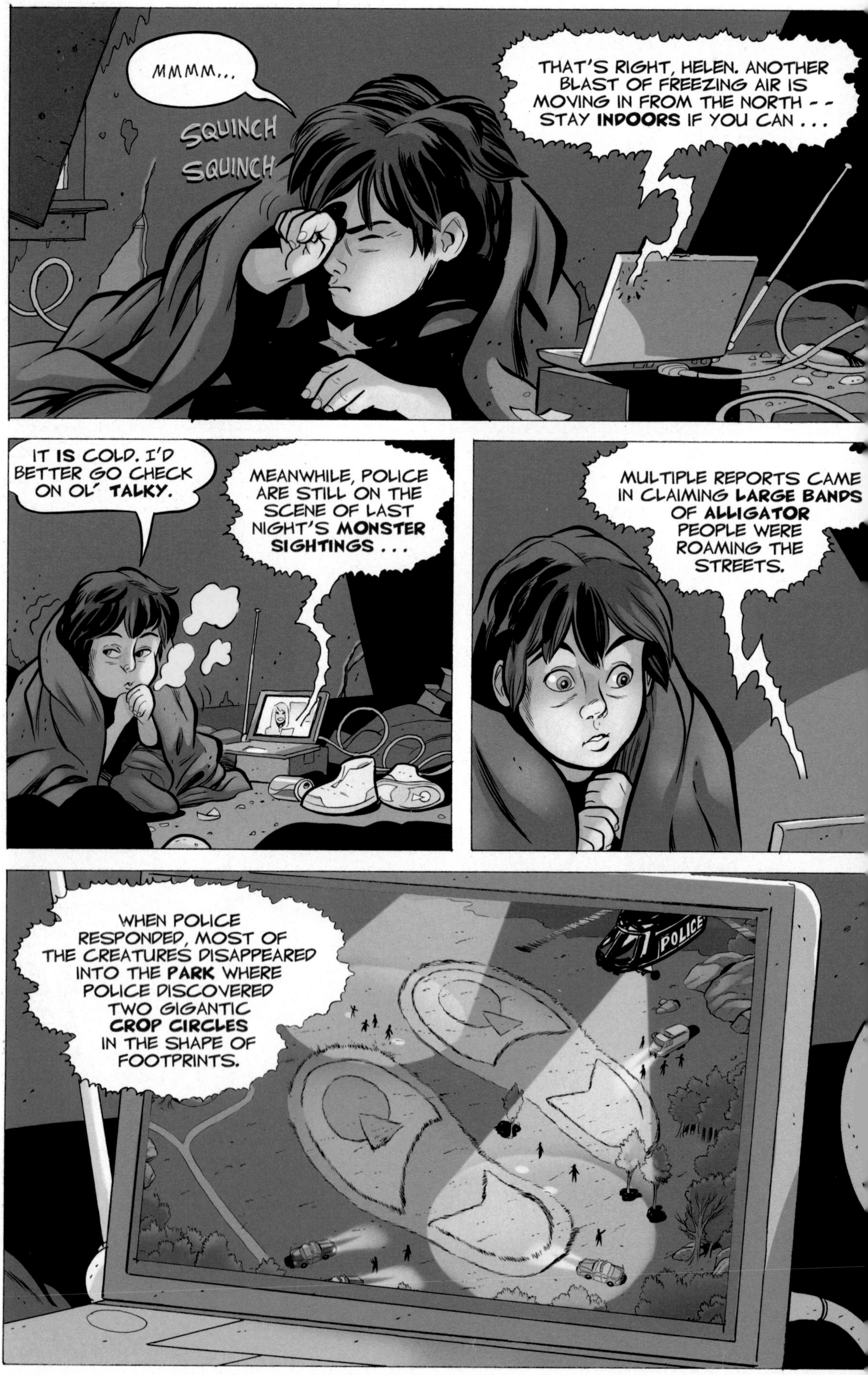
MMMM...
THAT'S RIGHT, HELEN. ANOTHER BLAST OF FREEZING AIR IS MOVING IN FROM THE NORTH -- STAY INDOORS IF YOU CAN . . .
SQUINCH SQUINCH
IT IS COLD. I'D BETTER GO CHECK ON OL' TALKY.
MEANWHILE, POLICE ARE STILL ON THE SCENE OF LAST NIGHT'S MONSTER SIGHTINGS . . .
MULTIPLE REPORTS CAME IN CLAIMING LARGE BANDS OF ALLIGATOR PEOPLE WERE ROAMING THE STREETS.
WHEN POLICE RESPONDED, MOST OF THE CREATURES DISAPPEARED INTO THE PARK WHERE POLICE DISCOVERED TWO GIGANTIC CROP CIRCLES IN THE SHAPE OF FOOTPRINTS.
POLICE

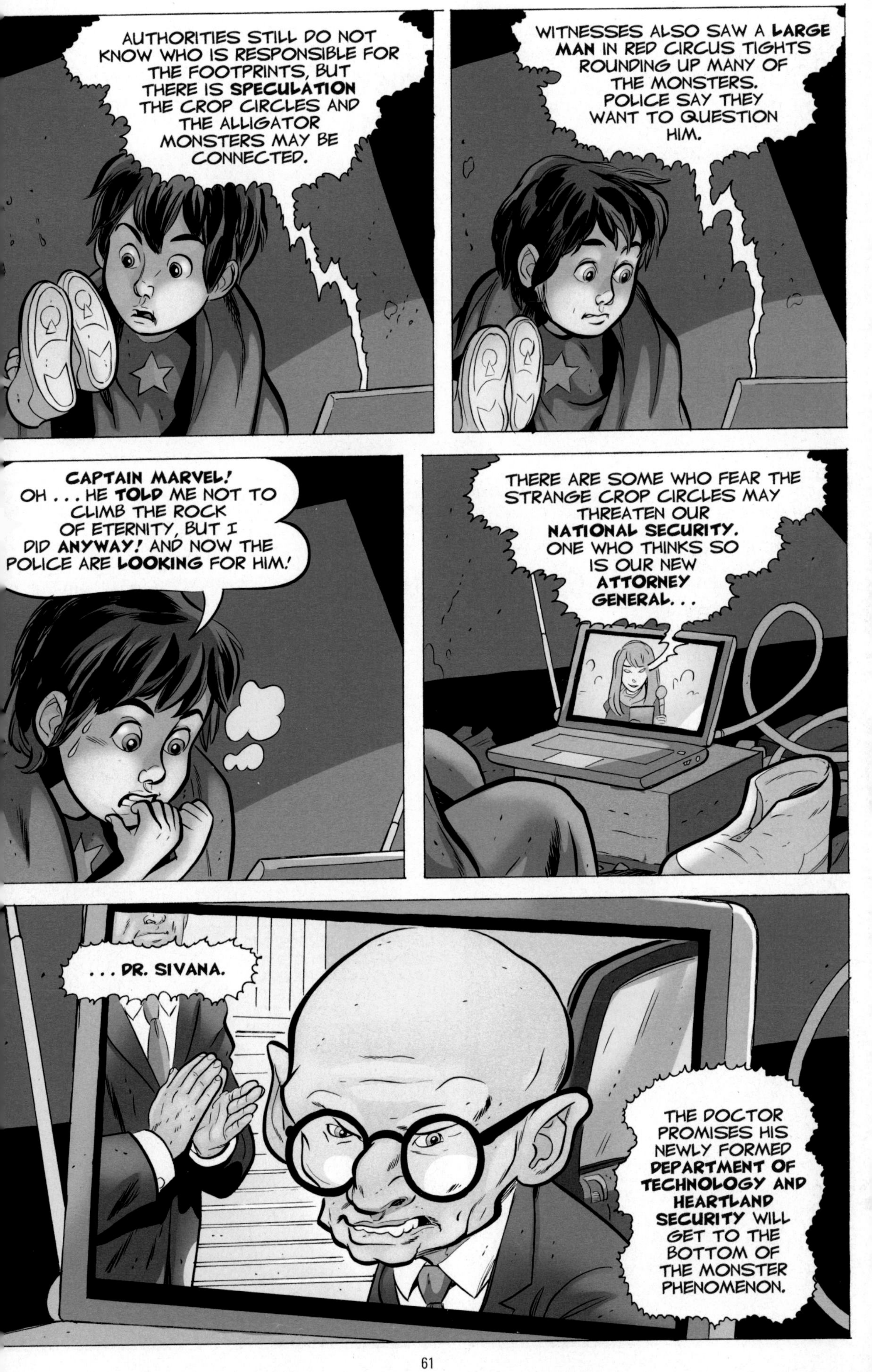
AUTHORITIES STILL DO NOT KNOW WHO IS RESPONSIBLE FOR THE FOOTPRINTS, BUT THERE IS SPECULATION THE CROP CIRCLES AND THE ALLIGATOR MONSTERS MAY BE CONNECTED.
WITNESSES ALSO SAW A LARGE MAN IN RED CIRCUS TIGHTS ROUNDING UP MANY OF THE MONSTERS. POLICE SAY THEY WANT TO QUESTION HIM.
CAPTAIN MARVEL! OH . . . HE TOLD ME NOT TO CLIMB THE ROCK OF ETERNITY, BUT I DID ANYWAY! AND NOW THE POLICE ARE LOOKING FOR HIM!
THERE ARE SOME WHO FEAR THE STRANGE CROP CIRCLES MAY THREATEN OUR NATIONAL SECURITY. ONE WHO THINKS SO IS OUR NEW ATTORNEY GENERAL. . .
. . . DR. SIVANA.
THE DOCTOR PROMISES HIS NEWLY FORMED DEPARTMENT OF TECHNOLOGY AND HEARTLAND SECURITY WILL GET TO THE BOTTOM OF THE MONSTER PHENOMENON.

ATTORNEY GENERAL SIVANA IS SCHEDULED TO MAKE A STATEMENT ON THE COURTHOUSE STEPS IN JUST A FEW MINUTES. WE'LL BRING YOU THE DOCTOR'S SPEECH **LIVE** -- AFTER THIS BREAK!

COME ONE, COME ALL! THE CIRCUS IS IN TOWN!! LA-TA-TOTTY-TOTTY-TOT-TAH **TAH-DAH!**

HMM . . . **THAT'S** WHAT I SHOULD DO. **JOIN THE CIRCUS!** SAY THE MAGIC WORD AND WATCH THE FREAK PICK UP AN **ELEPHANT.**

AND DON'T MISS THE WORLD'S **GREATEST** COLLECTION OF **CLAWS, JAWS AND MAN-EATING TEETH!**

IN A SPECIAL MATINEE TODAY YOU CAN SEE THE WORLD'S MOST FAMOUS **DEATH-DEFYING ACT** -- **THE MONSTER SOCIETY OF EVIL!!**

GROWL! ROAR!

MONSTER SOCIETY OF **EVIL,** HM?

MAYBE I **WILL** GO DOWN THERE . . .

CLICK

EVEN IF THERE'S NO CONNECTION TO THE **ALLIGATOR PEOPLE,** I CAN AT LEAST TRY TO GET A JOB CLEANING UP AFTER THE ANIMALS.

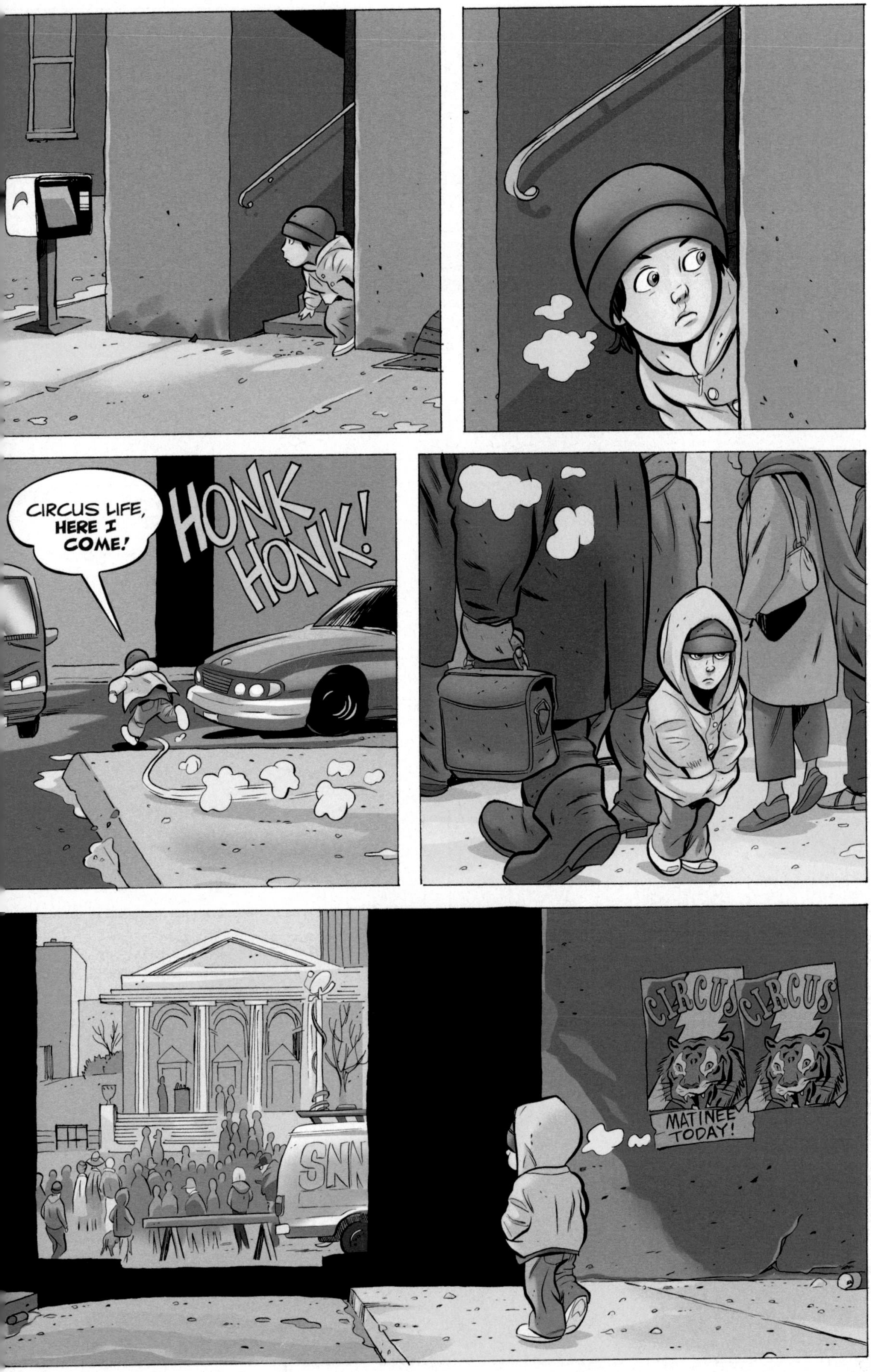
CIRCUS LIFE, HERE I COME!
HONK HONK!
SNN
CIRCUS
CIRCUS
MATINEE TODAY!

. . . ATTORNEY GENERAL SIVANA WILL NOW MAKE A BRIEF STATEMENT. DR. SIVANA.

OH, I'M SORRY, SIR. DO YOU NEED HELP?

GET ME A **BOX** TO STAND ON, YOU FOOL!

HERE, LET ME ADJUST THE MICRO-PHONES - -

RR-SQUEENK!

I CAN DO IT MYSELF!

WHEEE*

SQUEEEE~

IS THIS THING ON?

GOOD.

HELLO.

LAST NIGHT AT APPROXIMATELY **NINE P.M.** A SET OF FOOTPRINTS AN **ACRE WIDE** APPEARED IN OUR PARK. YOUR GOVERNMENT IS WORKING AROUND THE CLOCK TO **FIND THOSE RESPONSIBLE**. . .

. . .THE FOOTPRINTS MAY BE WARNING US OF A **TERRORIST PLOT**, OR THEY MAY BE A **HOAX**, BUT WE HAVE THE TECHNOLOGY TO FIND **WHOEVER CAUSED THIS!**

YOU HAVE MY **PERSONAL ASSURANCE** THAT THE **DEPARTMENT OF TECHNOLOGY AND HEARTLAND SECURITY** WILL GO THROUGH THE CREDIT ACCOUNTS OF EVERY CITIZEN UNTIL WE FIND SOMETHING **SUSPICIOUS!**

AND WHEN WE **DO**, WE'LL LOCK THE EVILDOERS UP, AND **THROW AWAY THE KEY!!**

REMEMBER, THE TERRORISTS WIN IF WE CHANGE OUR **LIFESTYLES**, SO GO IMMEDIATELY TO YOUR LOCAL **MALL** AND SPEND, SPEND, SPEND!

**KEEP OUR ECONOMY STRONG!!**

YAY! CLAP! CLAP

I'LL NEVER UNDER-STAND GROWN-UPS.

HEY, WHAT'S THIS?

ANTS?

WHOA. **NO WAY!** THIS MUST BE THE BIGGEST **ANT WAR** EVER!

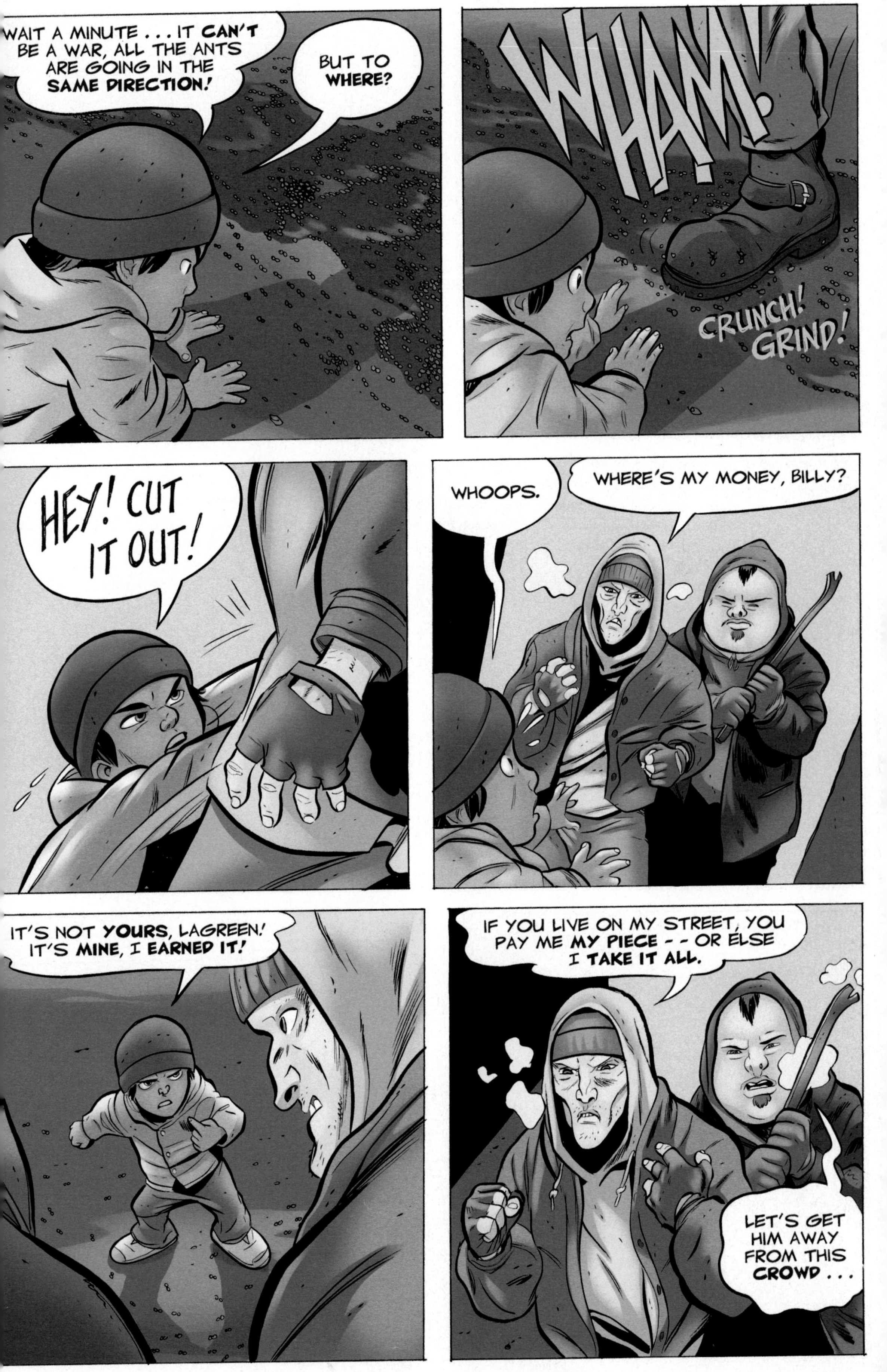
WAIT A MINUTE . . . IT CAN'T BE A WAR, ALL THE ANTS ARE GOING IN THE SAME DIRECTION!
BUT TO WHERE?
WHAM!
CRUNCH! GRIND!
HEY! CUT IT OUT!
WHOOPS.
WHERE'S MY MONEY, BILLY?
IT'S NOT YOURS, LAGREEN! IT'S MINE, I EARNED IT!
IF YOU LIVE ON MY STREET, YOU PAY ME MY PIECE - - OR ELSE I TAKE IT ALL.
LET'S GET HIM AWAY FROM THIS CROWD . . .

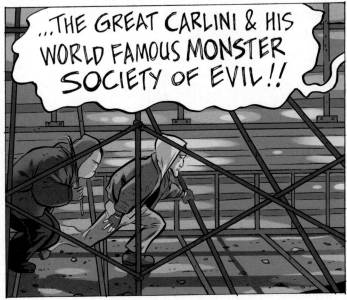

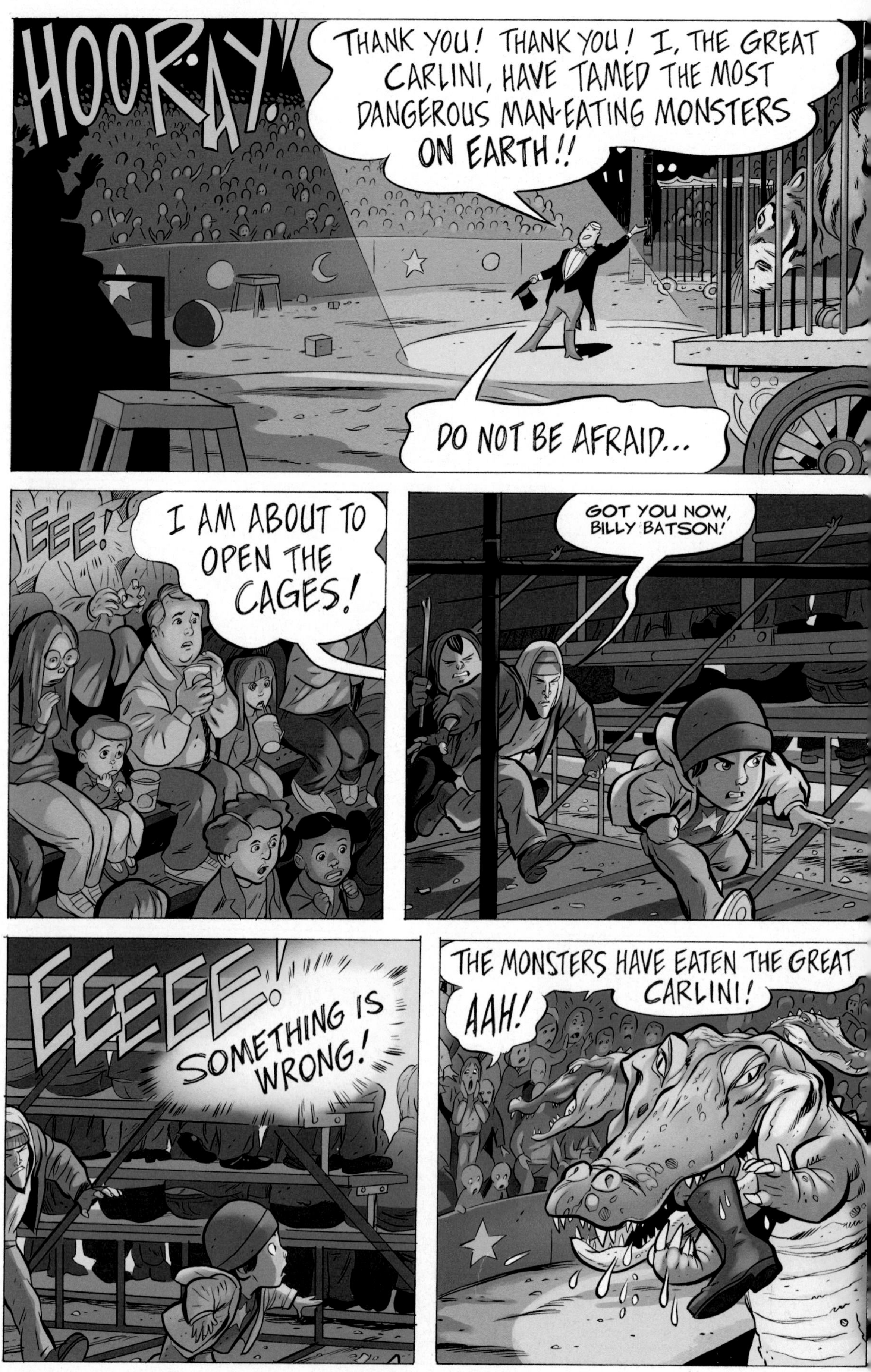
HOORAY!
THANK YOU! THANK YOU! I, THE GREAT CARLINI, HAVE TAMED THE MOST DANGEROUS MAN-EATING MONSTERS ON EARTH!!
DO NOT BE AFRAID...
EEE!
I AM ABOUT TO OPEN THE CAGES!
GOT YOU NOW, BILLY BATSON!
EEEEE!
SOMETHING IS WRONG!
THE MONSTERS HAVE EATEN THE GREAT CARLINI!
AAH!

71

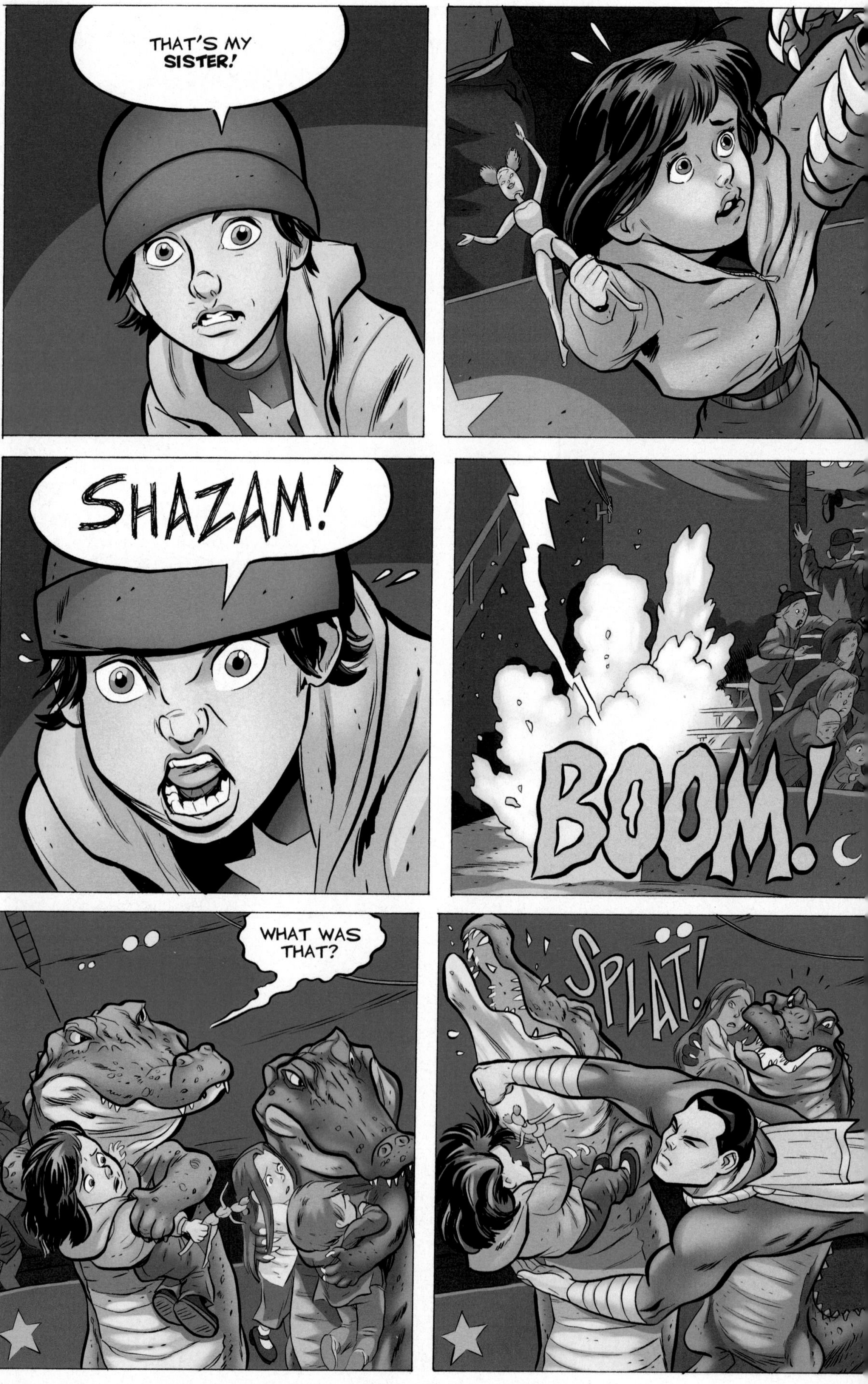
THAT'S MY SISTER!
SHAZAM!
BOOM!
WHAT WAS THAT?
SPLAT!

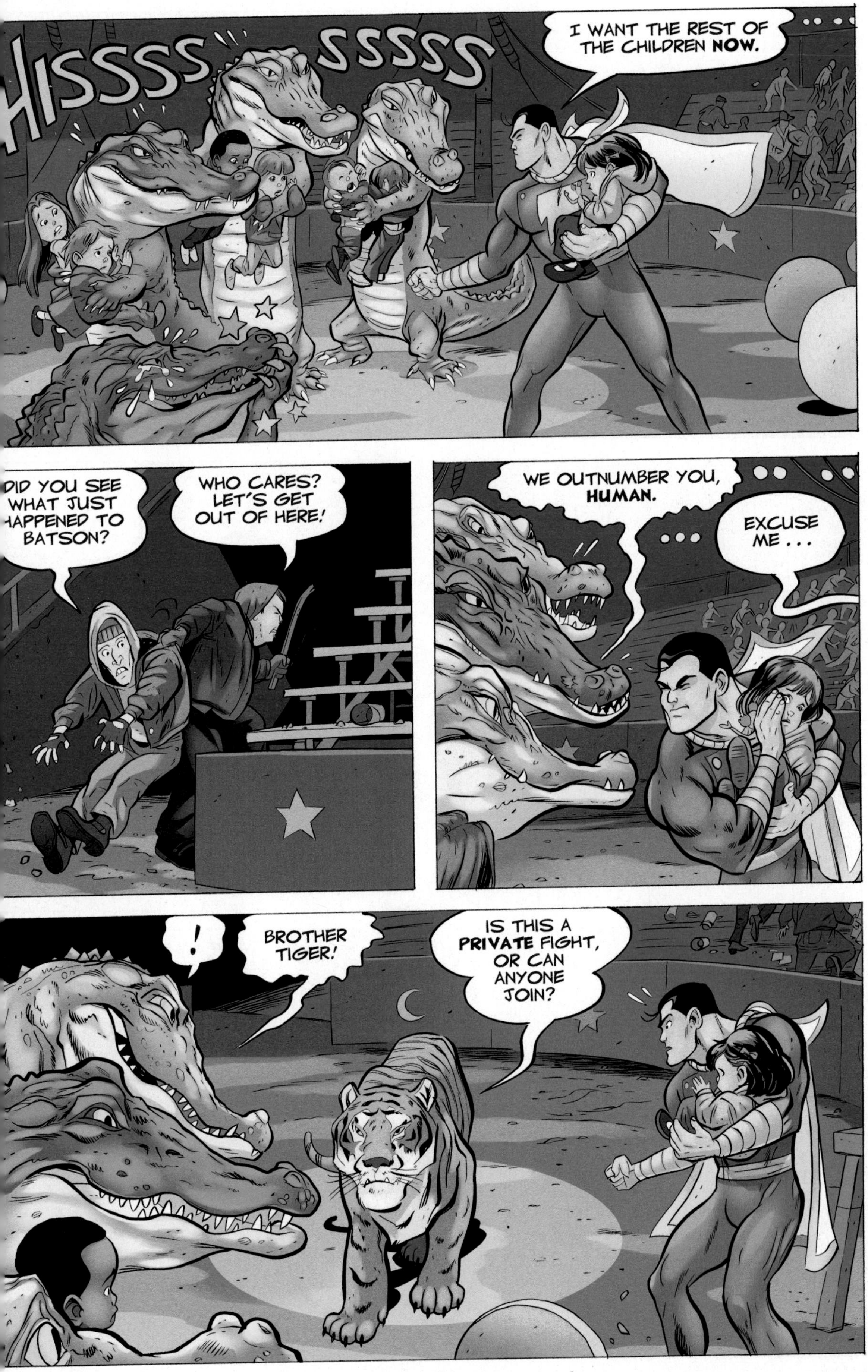
HISSSS
SSSSS
I WANT THE REST OF THE CHILDREN NOW.
DID YOU SEE WHAT JUST HAPPENED TO BATSON?
WHO CARES? LET'S GET OUT OF HERE!
WE OUTNUMBER YOU, HUMAN.
...
EXCUSE ME ...
!
BROTHER TIGER!
IS THIS A PRIVATE FIGHT, OR CAN ANYONE JOIN?

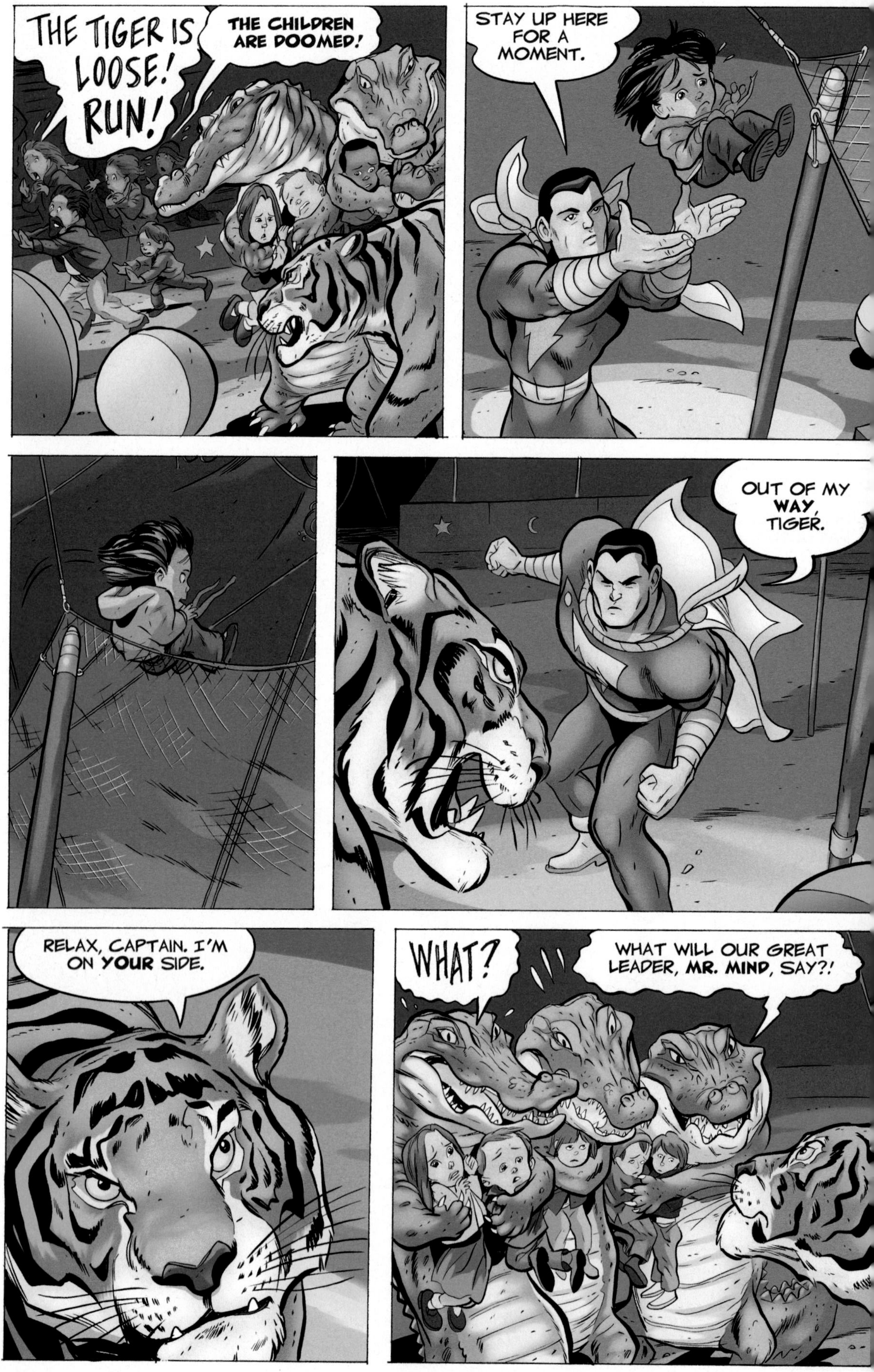
THE TIGER IS LOOSE! RUN!
THE CHILDREN ARE DOOMED!
STAY UP HERE FOR A MOMENT.
OUT OF MY WAY, TIGER.
RELAX, CAPTAIN. I'M ON YOUR SIDE.
WHAT?
WHAT WILL OUR GREAT LEADER, MR. MIND, SAY?!

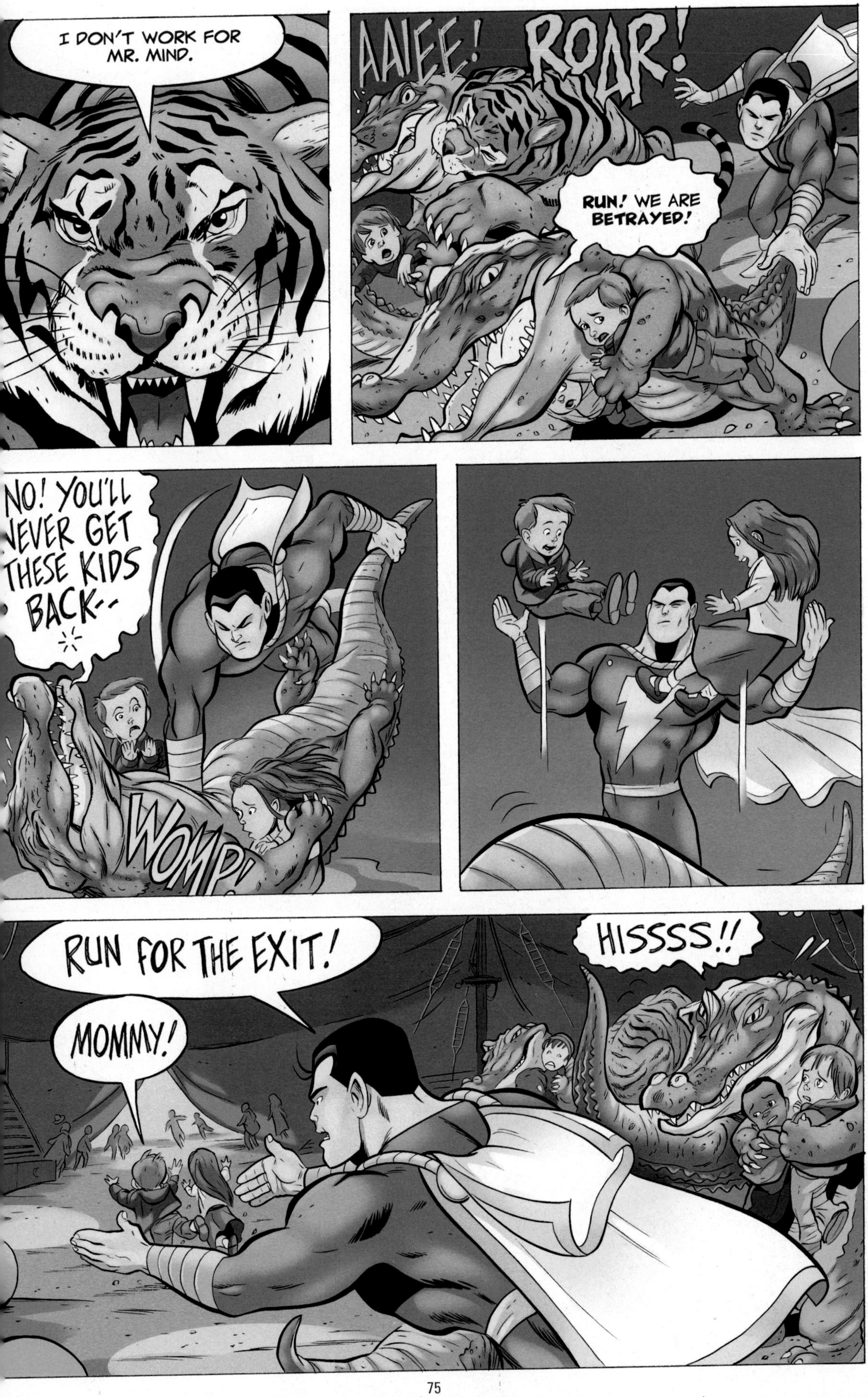
I DON'T WORK FOR MR. MIND.
AAIEE!
ROAR!
RUN! WE ARE BETRAYED!
NO! YOU'LL NEVER GET THESE KIDS BACK--
WOMP!
RUN FOR THE EXIT!
MOMMY!
HISSSS!!

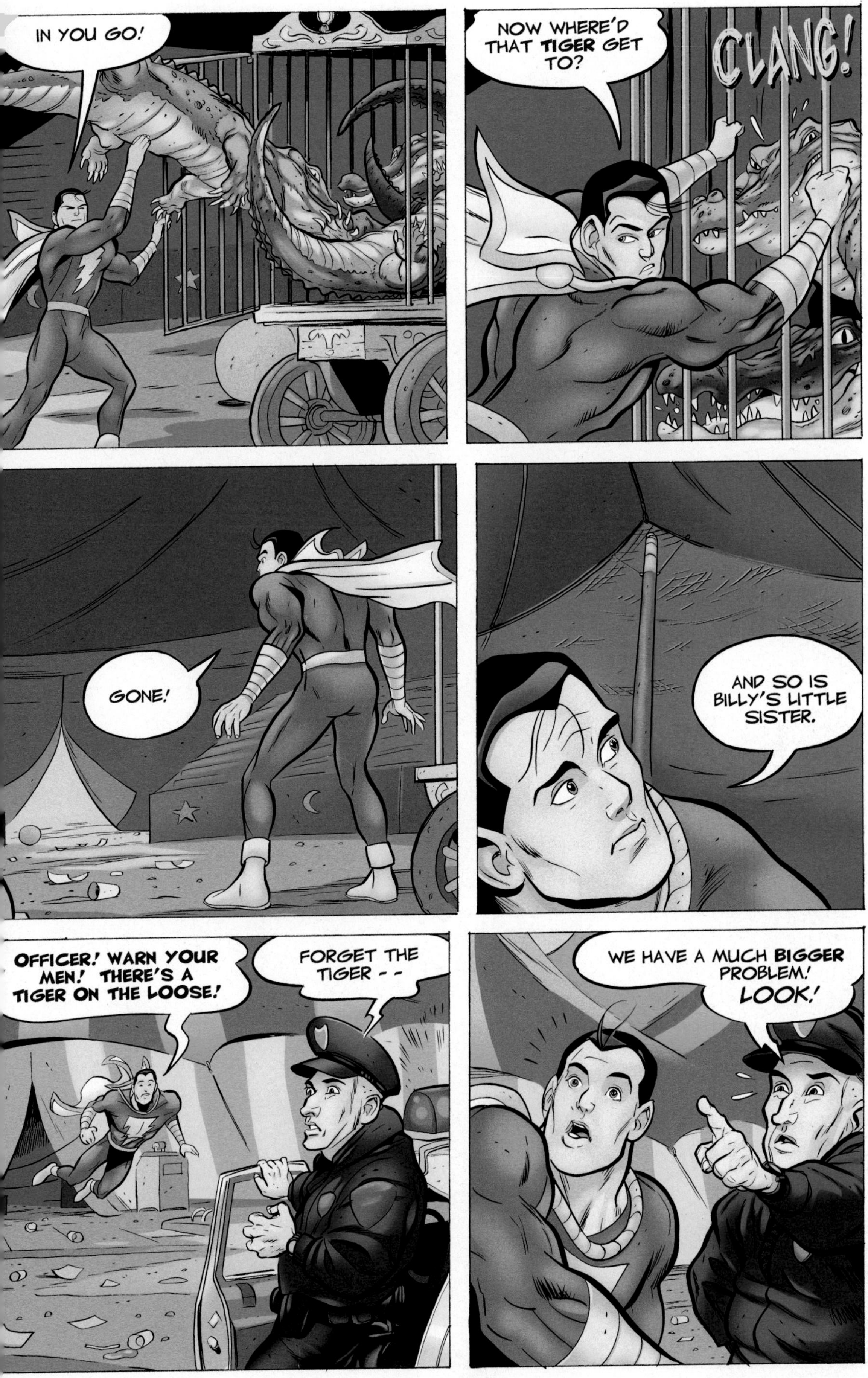

IN YOU GO!
NOW WHERE'D THAT TIGER GET TO?
CLANG!
GONE!
AND SO IS BILLY'S LITTLE SISTER.
OFFICER! WARN YOUR MEN! THERE'S A TIGER ON THE LOOSE!
FORGET THE TIGER - -
WE HAVE A MUCH BIGGER PROBLEM! LOOK!

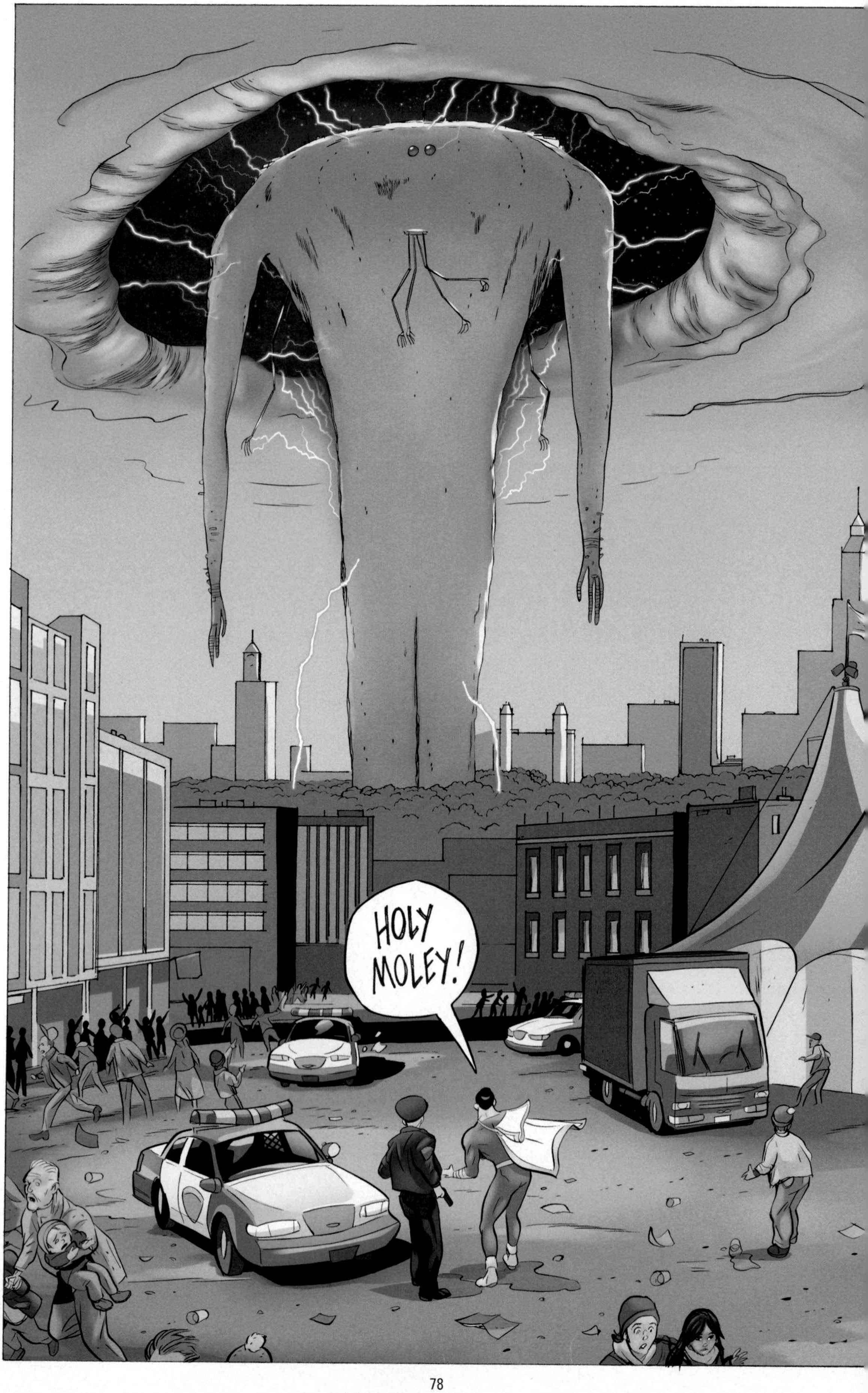
HOLY MOLEY!

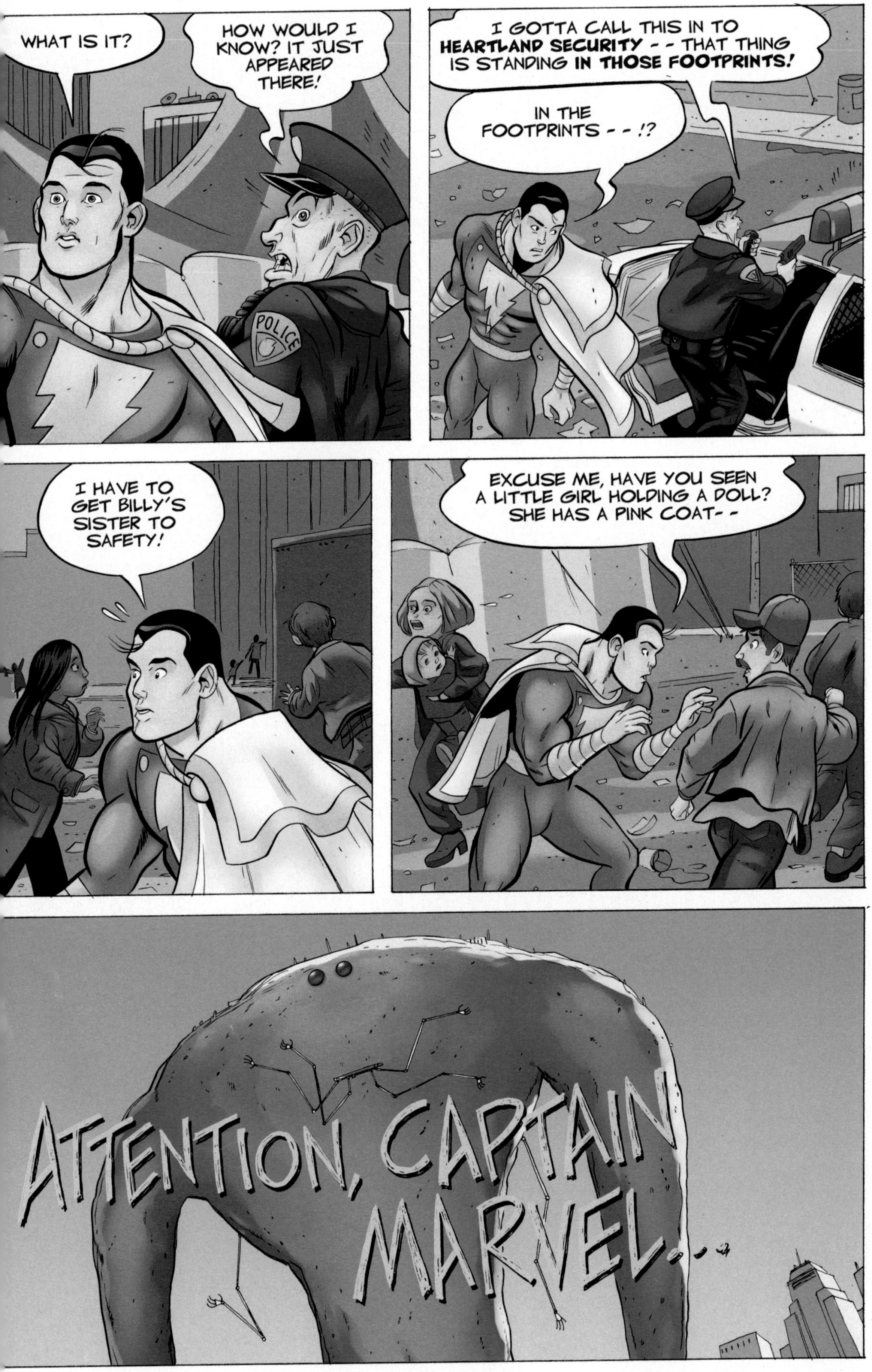
WHAT IS IT?
HOW WOULD I KNOW? IT JUST APPEARED THERE!
POLICE
I GOTTA CALL THIS IN TO HEARTLAND SECURITY - - THAT THING IS STANDING IN THOSE FOOTPRINTS!
IN THE FOOTPRINTS - - !?
I HAVE TO GET BILLY'S SISTER TO SAFETY!
EXCUSE ME, HAVE YOU SEEN A LITTLE GIRL HOLDING A DOLL? SHE HAS A PINK COAT- -
ATTENTION, CAPTAIN MARVEL...

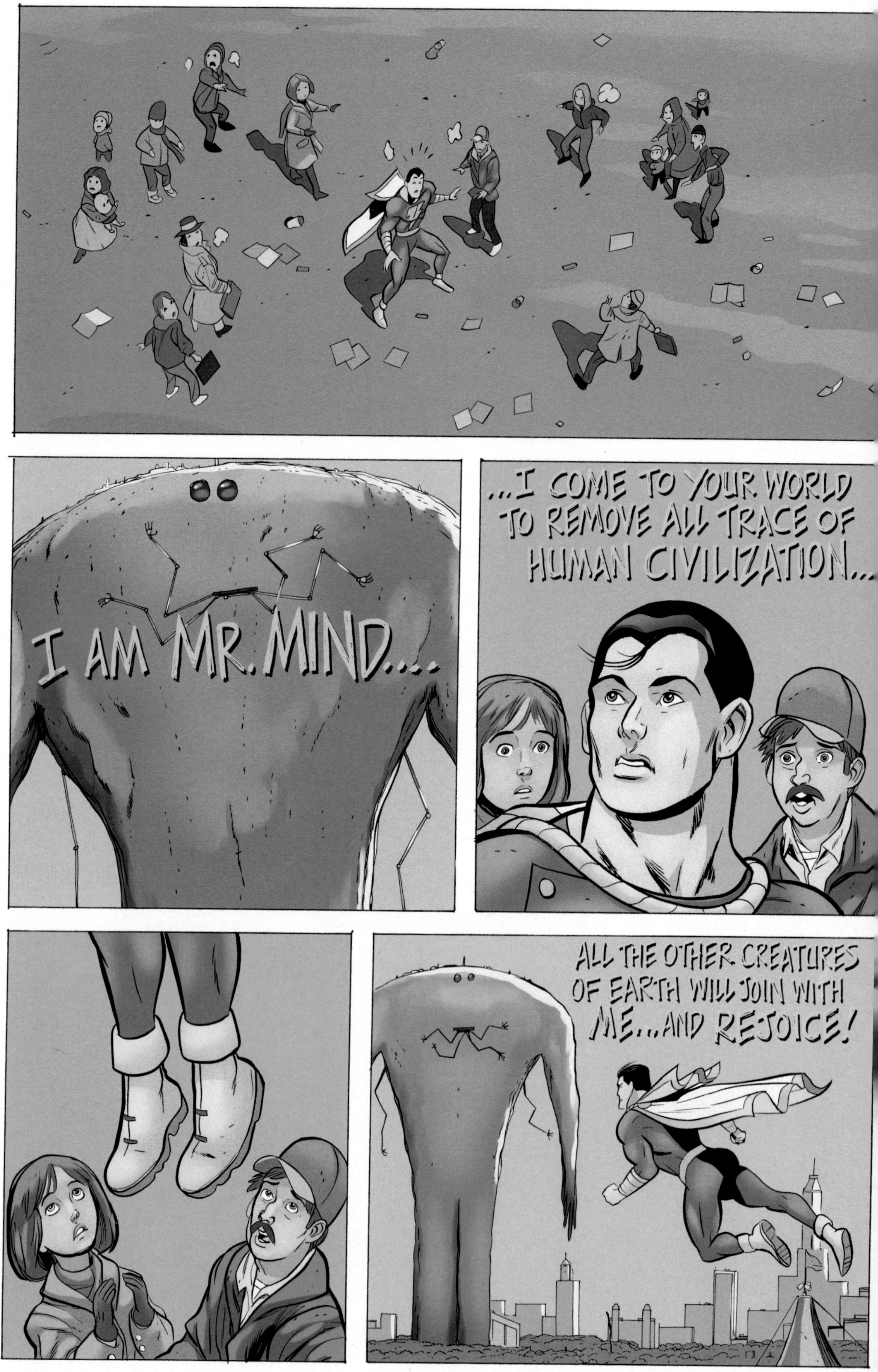
I AM MR. MIND....
...I COME TO YOUR WORLD TO REMOVE ALL TRACE OF HUMAN CIVILIZATION...
ALL THE OTHER CREATURES OF EARTH WILL JOIN WITH ME...AND REJOICE!

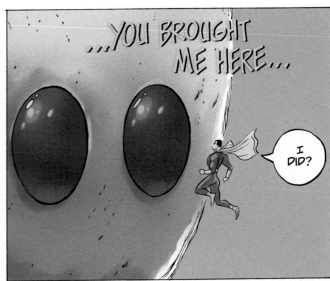

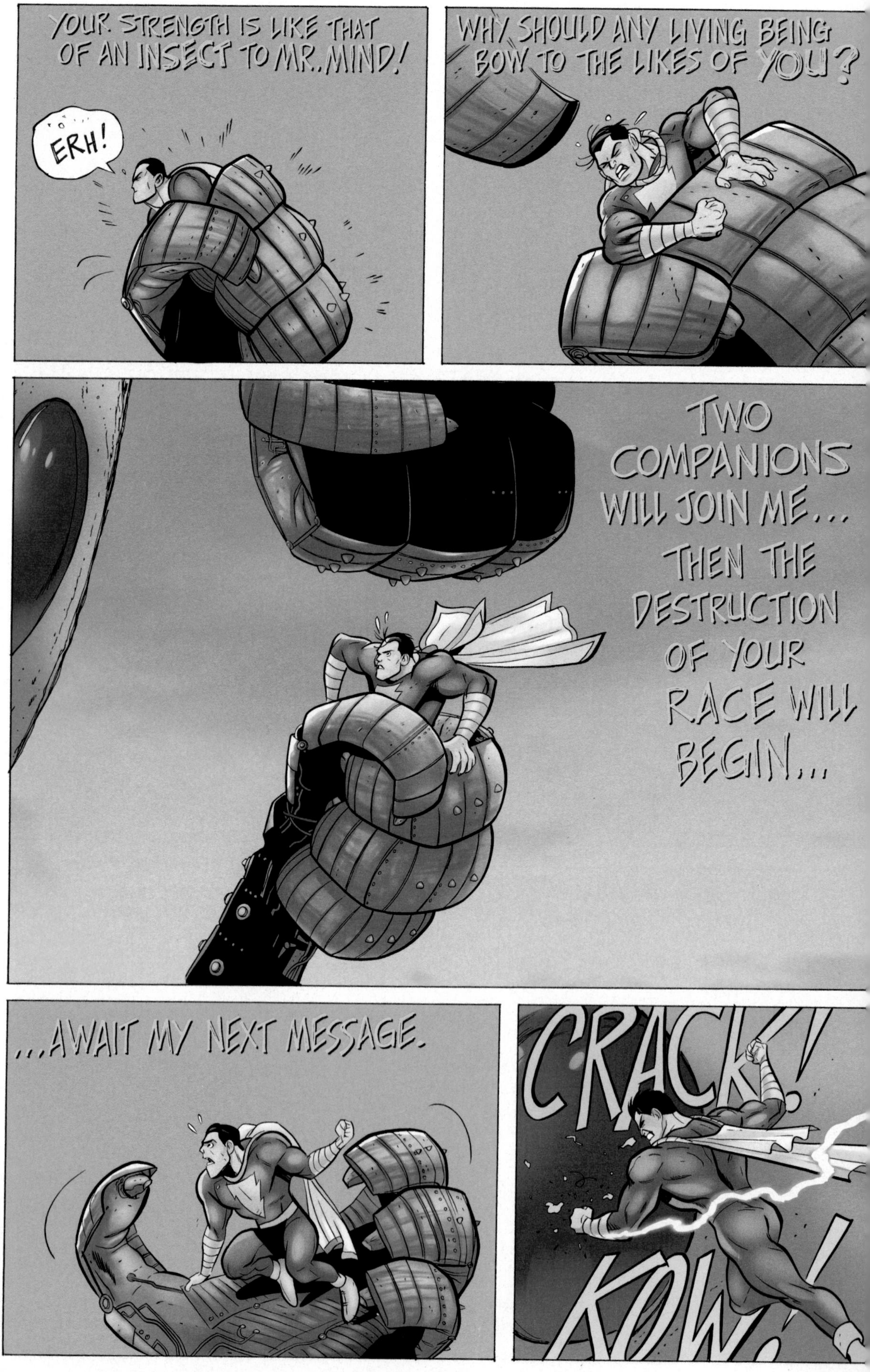
YOUR STRENGTH IS LIKE THAT OF AN INSECT TO MR. MIND!
ERH!
WHY SHOULD ANY LIVING BEING BOW TO THE LIKES OF YOU?
TWO COMPANIONS WILL JOIN ME... THEN THE DESTRUCTION OF YOUR RACE WILL BEGIN...
...AWAIT MY NEXT MESSAGE.
CRACK!
KOW!

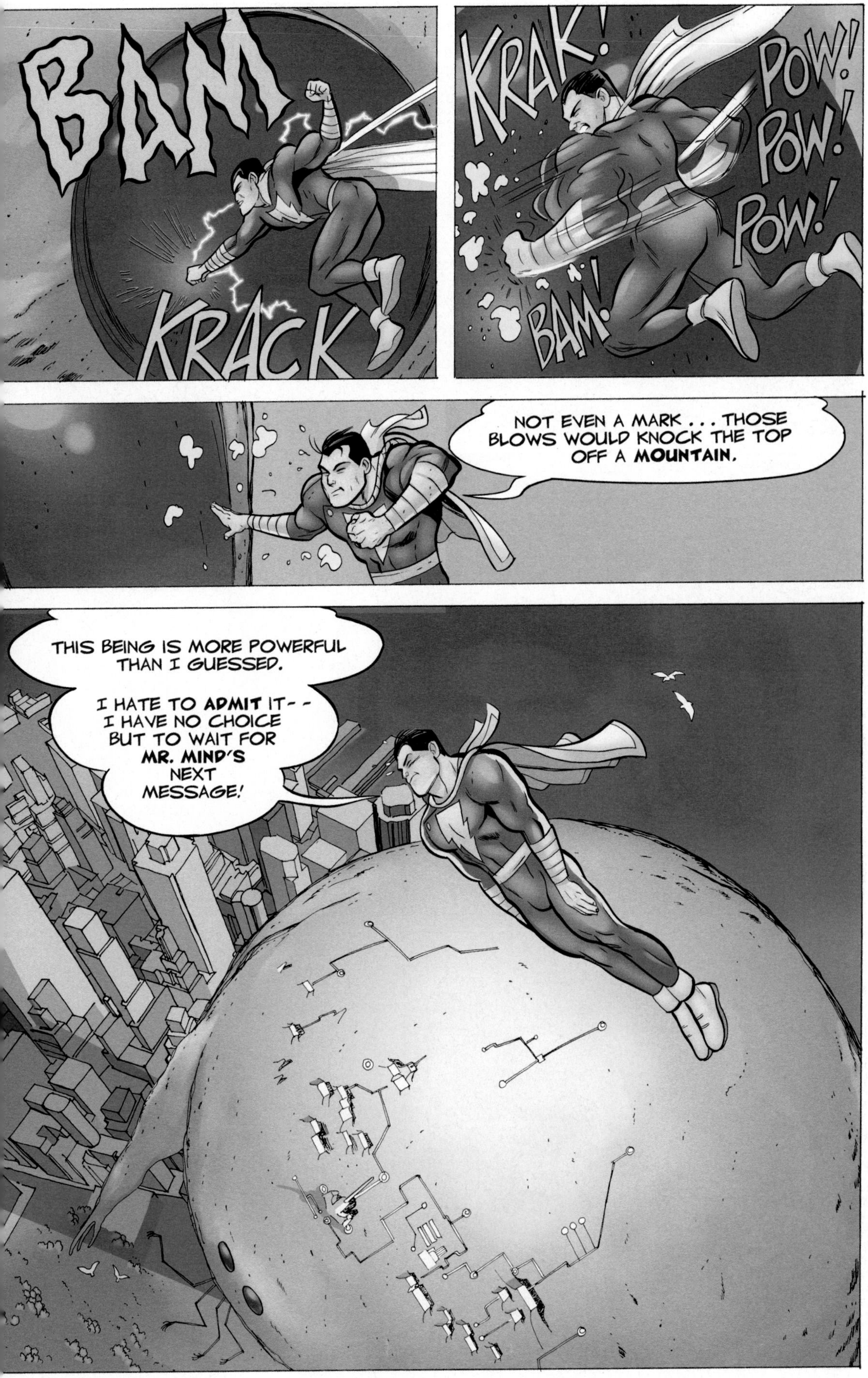
BAM
KRACK
KRAK!
POW!
POW!
POW!
BAM!
NOT EVEN A MARK . . . THOSE BLOWS WOULD KNOCK THE TOP OFF A MOUNTAIN.
THIS BEING IS MORE POWERFUL THAN I GUESSED.
I HATE TO ADMIT IT- - I HAVE NO CHOICE BUT TO WAIT FOR MR. MIND'S NEXT MESSAGE!

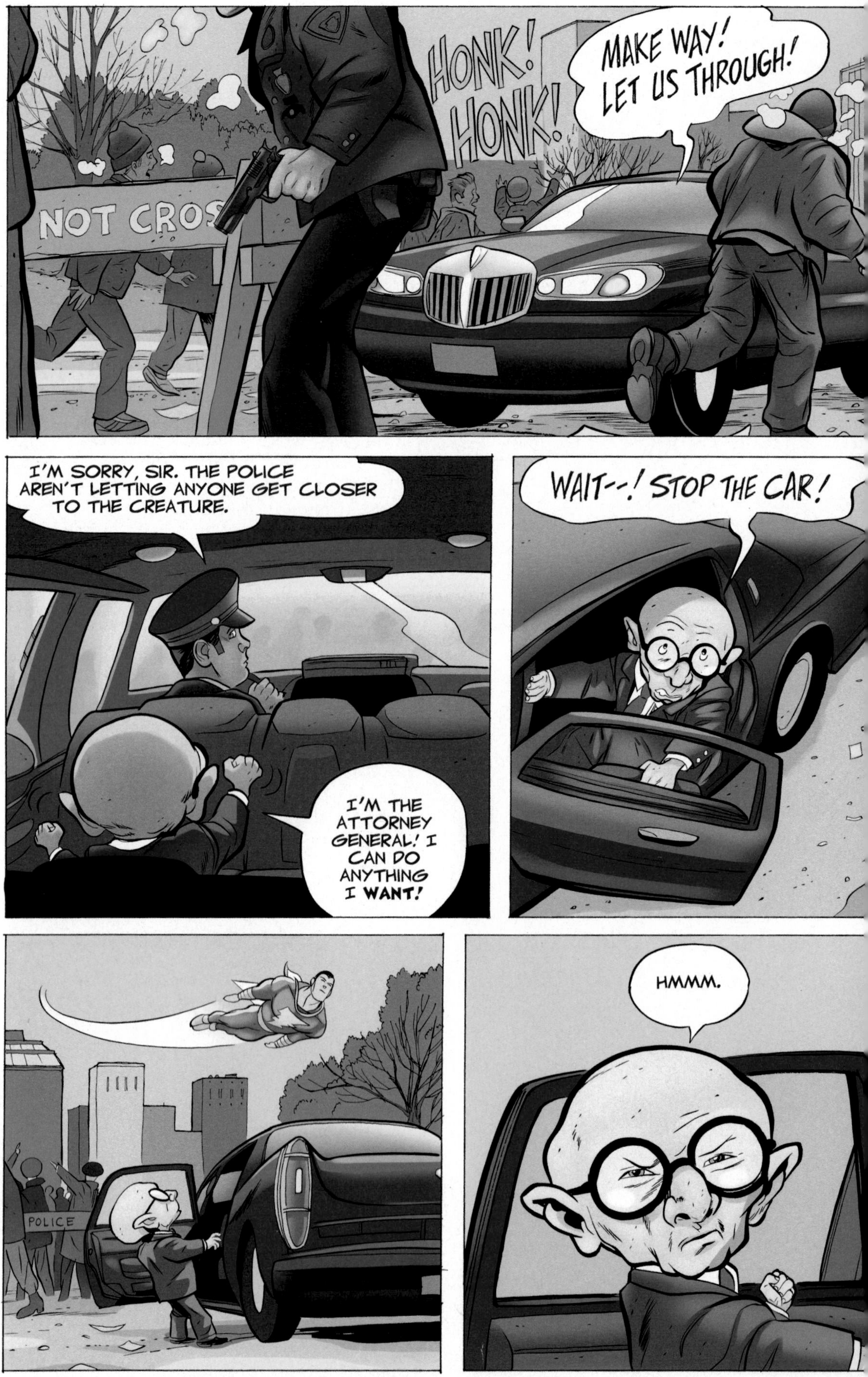
NOT CROS
HONK! HONK!
MAKE WAY! LET US THROUGH!
I'M SORRY, SIR. THE POLICE AREN'T LETTING ANYONE GET CLOSER TO THE CREATURE.
I'M THE ATTORNEY GENERAL! I CAN DO ANYTHING I WANT!
WAIT--! STOP THE CAR!
POLICE
HMMM.

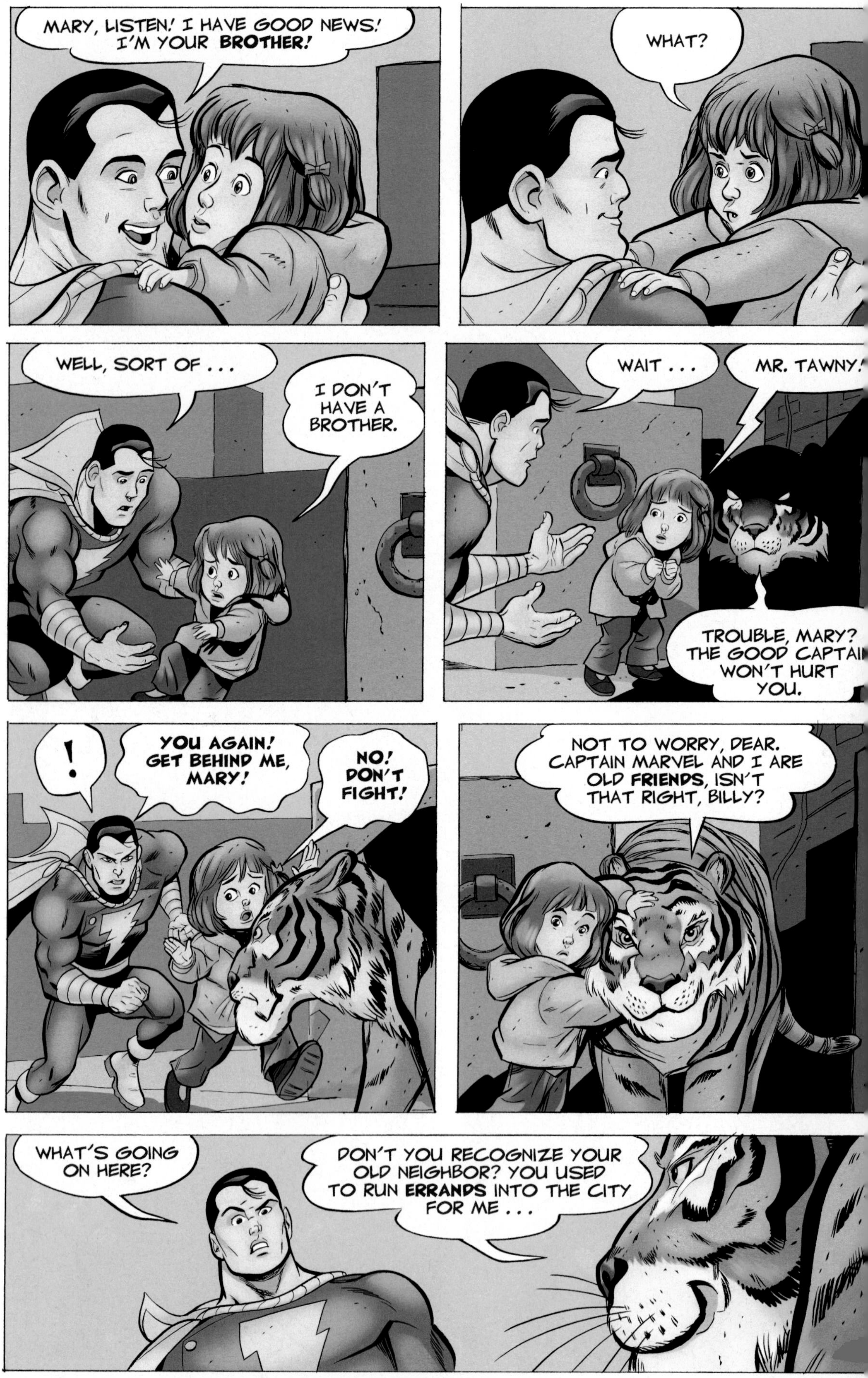

MARY, LISTEN! I HAVE GOOD NEWS! I'M YOUR **BROTHER!**
WHAT?
WELL, SORT OF . . .
I DON'T HAVE A BROTHER.
WAIT . . .
MR. TAWNY!
TROUBLE, MARY? THE GOOD CAPTAI WON'T HURT YOU.
!
YOU AGAIN! GET BEHIND ME, MARY!
NO! DON'T FIGHT!
NOT TO WORRY, DEAR. CAPTAIN MARVEL AND I ARE OLD **FRIENDS**, ISN'T THAT RIGHT, BILLY?
WHAT'S GOING ON HERE?
DON'T YOU RECOGNIZE YOUR OLD NEIGHBOR? YOU USED TO RUN **ERRANDS** INTO THE CITY FOR ME . . .

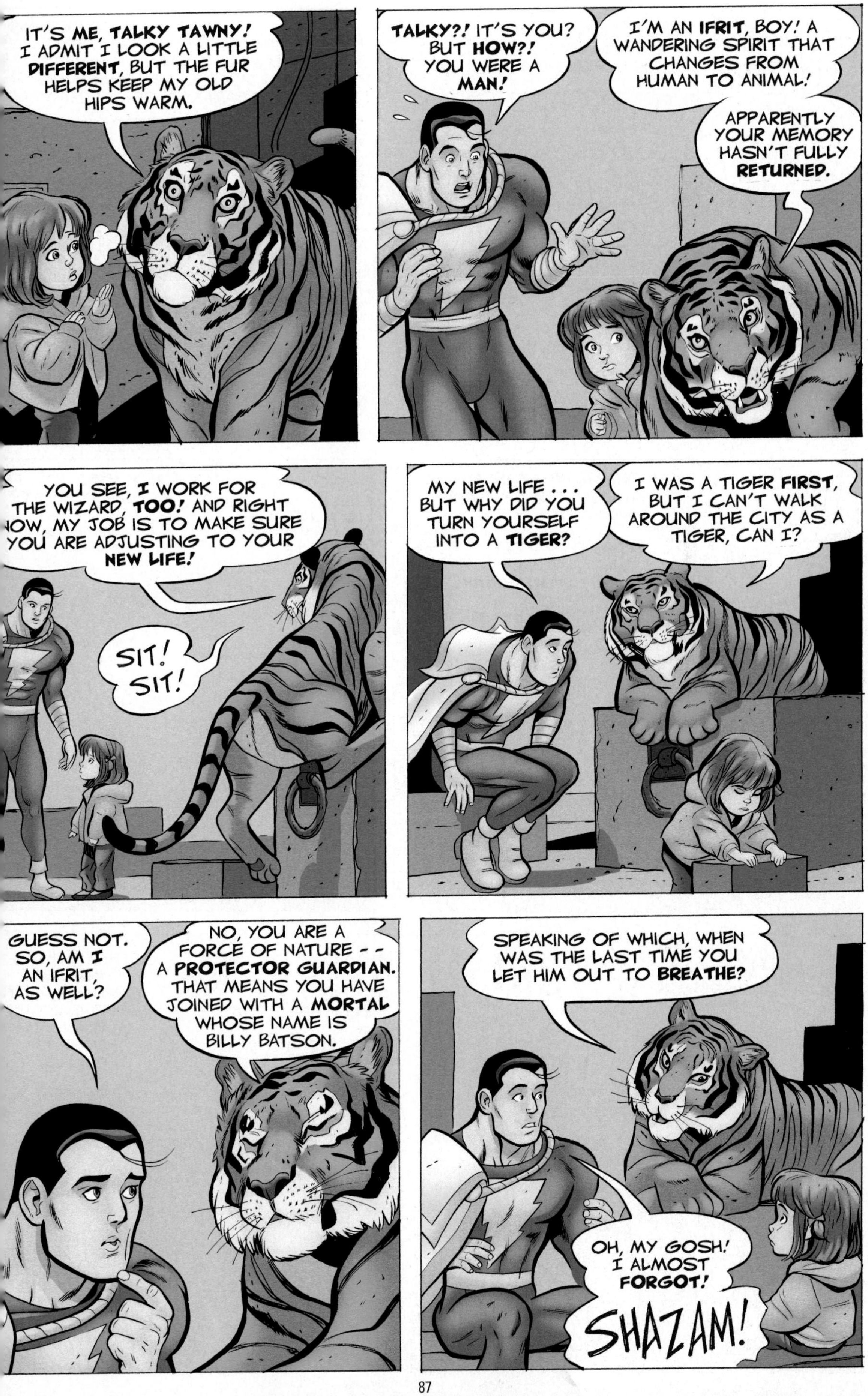
IT'S ME, TALKY TAWNY! I ADMIT I LOOK A LITTLE DIFFERENT, BUT THE FUR HELPS KEEP MY OLD HIPS WARM.
TALKY?! IT'S YOU? BUT HOW?! YOU WERE A MAN!
I'M AN IFRIT, BOY! A WANDERING SPIRIT THAT CHANGES FROM HUMAN TO ANIMAL!
APPARENTLY YOUR MEMORY HASN'T FULLY RETURNED.
YOU SEE, I WORK FOR THE WIZARD, TOO! AND RIGHT NOW, MY JOB IS TO MAKE SURE YOU ARE ADJUSTING TO YOUR NEW LIFE!
SIT! SIT!
MY NEW LIFE . . . BUT WHY DID YOU TURN YOURSELF INTO A TIGER?
I WAS A TIGER FIRST, BUT I CAN'T WALK AROUND THE CITY AS A TIGER, CAN I?
GUESS NOT. SO, AM I AN IFRIT, AS WELL?
NO, YOU ARE A FORCE OF NATURE - - A PROTECTOR GUARDIAN. THAT MEANS YOU HAVE JOINED WITH A MORTAL WHOSE NAME IS BILLY BATSON.
SPEAKING OF WHICH, WHEN WAS THE LAST TIME YOU LET HIM OUT TO BREATHE?
OH, MY GOSH! I ALMOST FORGOT!
SHAZAM!

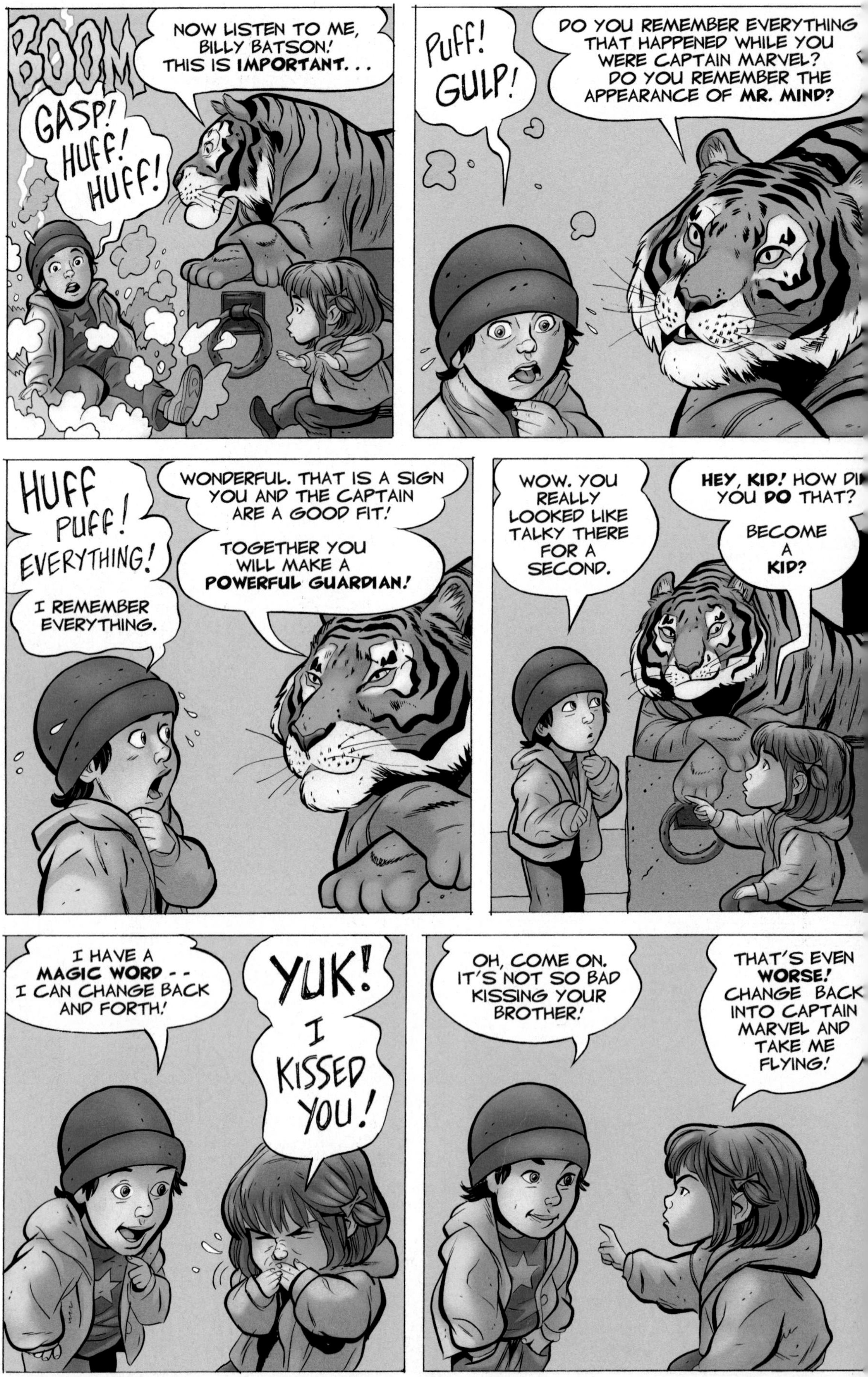

BOOM
NOW LISTEN TO ME, BILLY BATSON! THIS IS IMPORTANT. . .
GASP! HUFF! HUFF!
PUFF! GULP!
DO YOU REMEMBER EVERYTHING THAT HAPPENED WHILE YOU WERE CAPTAIN MARVEL? DO YOU REMEMBER THE APPEARANCE OF MR. MIND?
HUFF PUFF! EVERYTHING!
I REMEMBER EVERYTHING.
WONDERFUL. THAT IS A SIGN YOU AND THE CAPTAIN ARE A GOOD FIT!
TOGETHER YOU WILL MAKE A POWERFUL GUARDIAN!
WOW. YOU REALLY LOOKED LIKE TALKY THERE FOR A SECOND.
HEY, KID! HOW DI YOU DO THAT?
BECOME A KID?
I HAVE A MAGIC WORD - - I CAN CHANGE BACK AND FORTH!
YUK! I KISSED YOU!
OH, COME ON. IT'S NOT SO BAD KISSING YOUR BROTHER!
THAT'S EVEN WORSE! CHANGE BACK INTO CAPTAIN MARVEL AND TAKE ME FLYING!

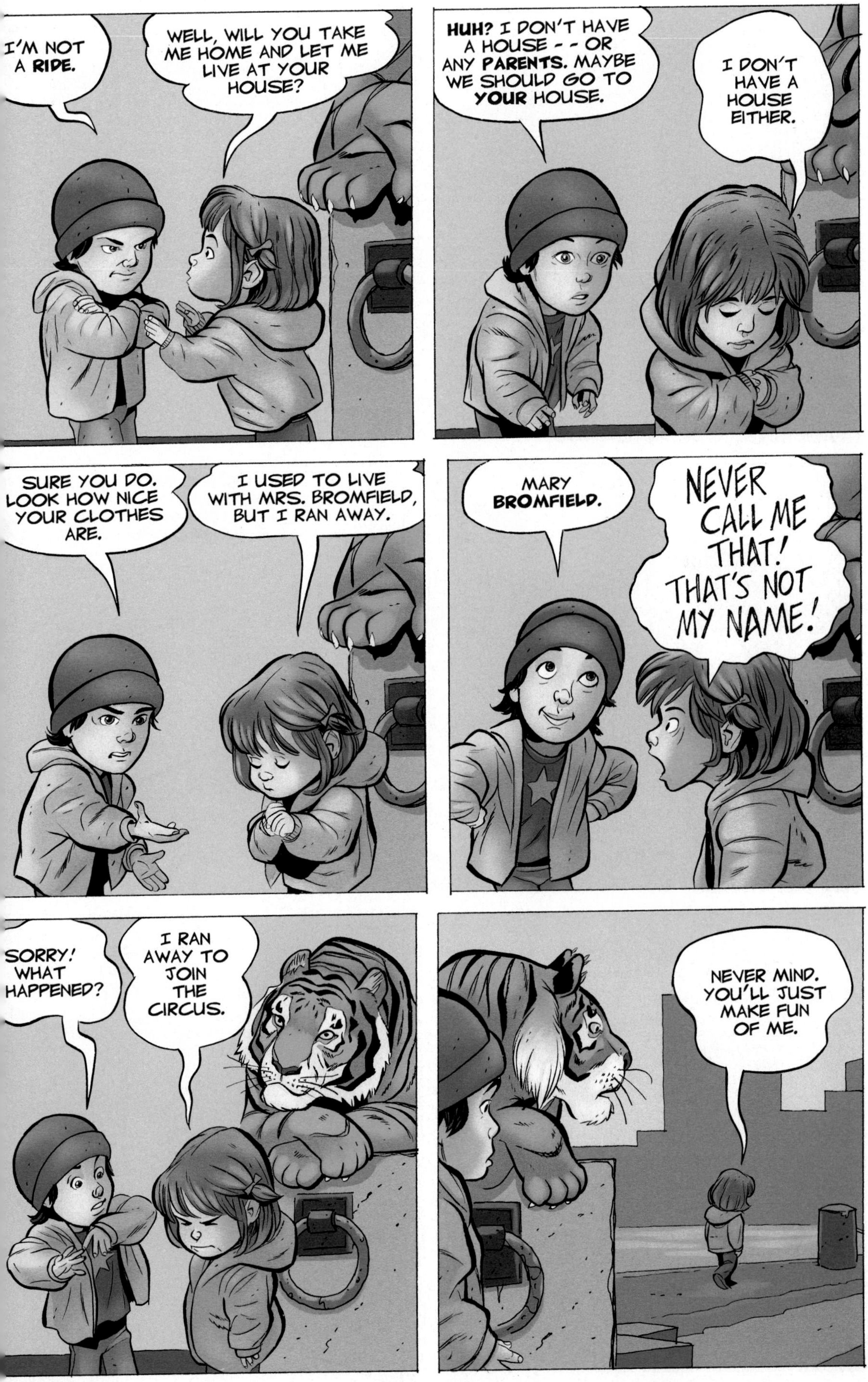
I'M NOT A RIDE.
WELL, WILL YOU TAKE ME HOME AND LET ME LIVE AT YOUR HOUSE?
HUH? I DON'T HAVE A HOUSE - - OR ANY PARENTS. MAYBE WE SHOULD GO TO YOUR HOUSE.
I DON'T HAVE A HOUSE EITHER.
SURE YOU DO. LOOK HOW NICE YOUR CLOTHES ARE.
I USED TO LIVE WITH MRS. BROMFIELD, BUT I RAN AWAY.
MARY BROMFIELD.
NEVER CALL ME THAT! THAT'S NOT MY NAME!
SORRY! WHAT HAPPENED?
I RAN AWAY TO JOIN THE CIRCUS.
NEVER MIND. YOU'LL JUST MAKE FUN OF ME.

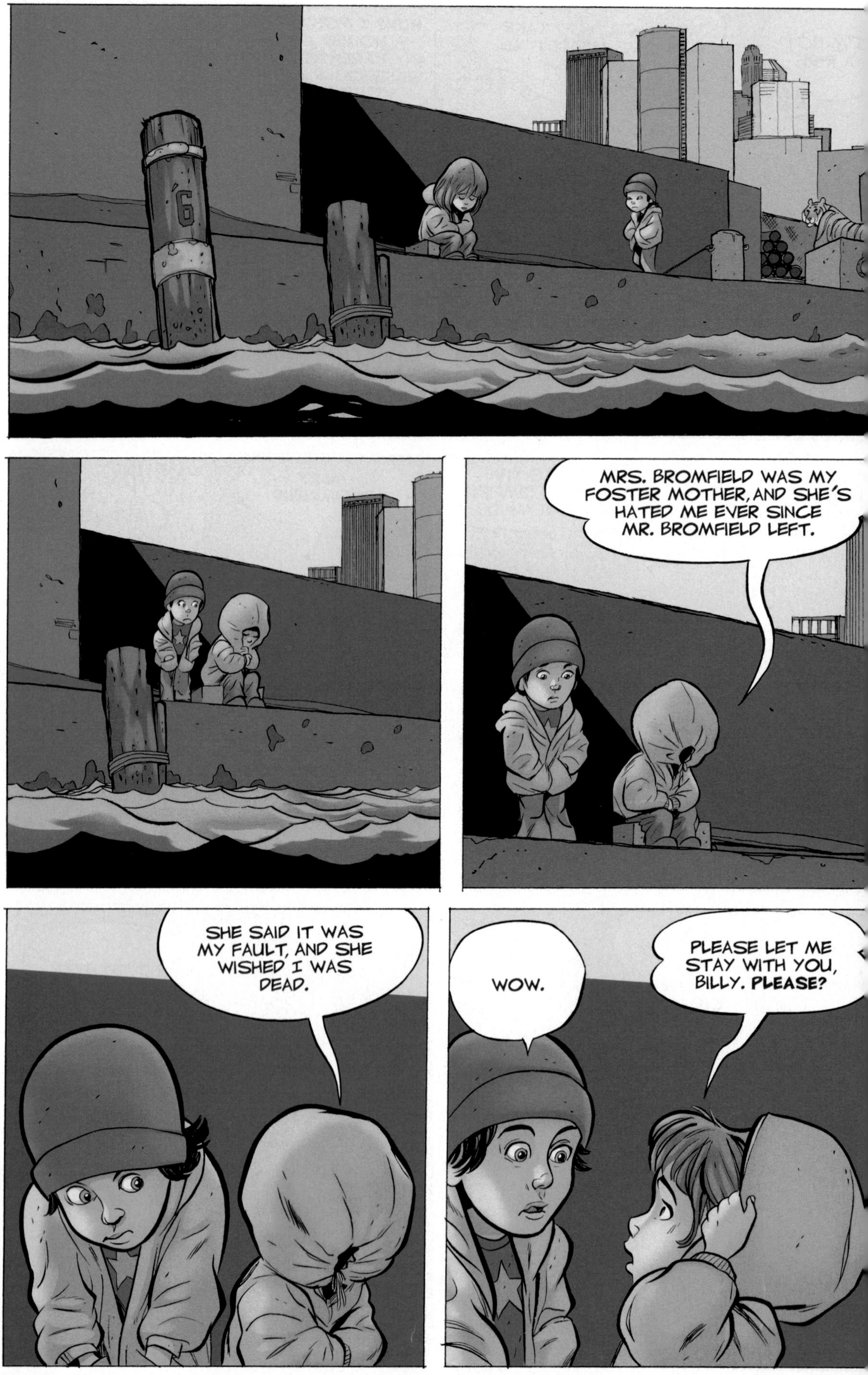
MRS. BROMFIELD WAS MY FOSTER MOTHER, AND SHE'S HATED ME EVER SINCE MR. BROMFIELD LEFT.
SHE SAID IT WAS MY FAULT, AND SHE WISHED I WAS DEAD.
WOW.
PLEASE LET ME STAY WITH YOU, BILLY. **PLEASE?**

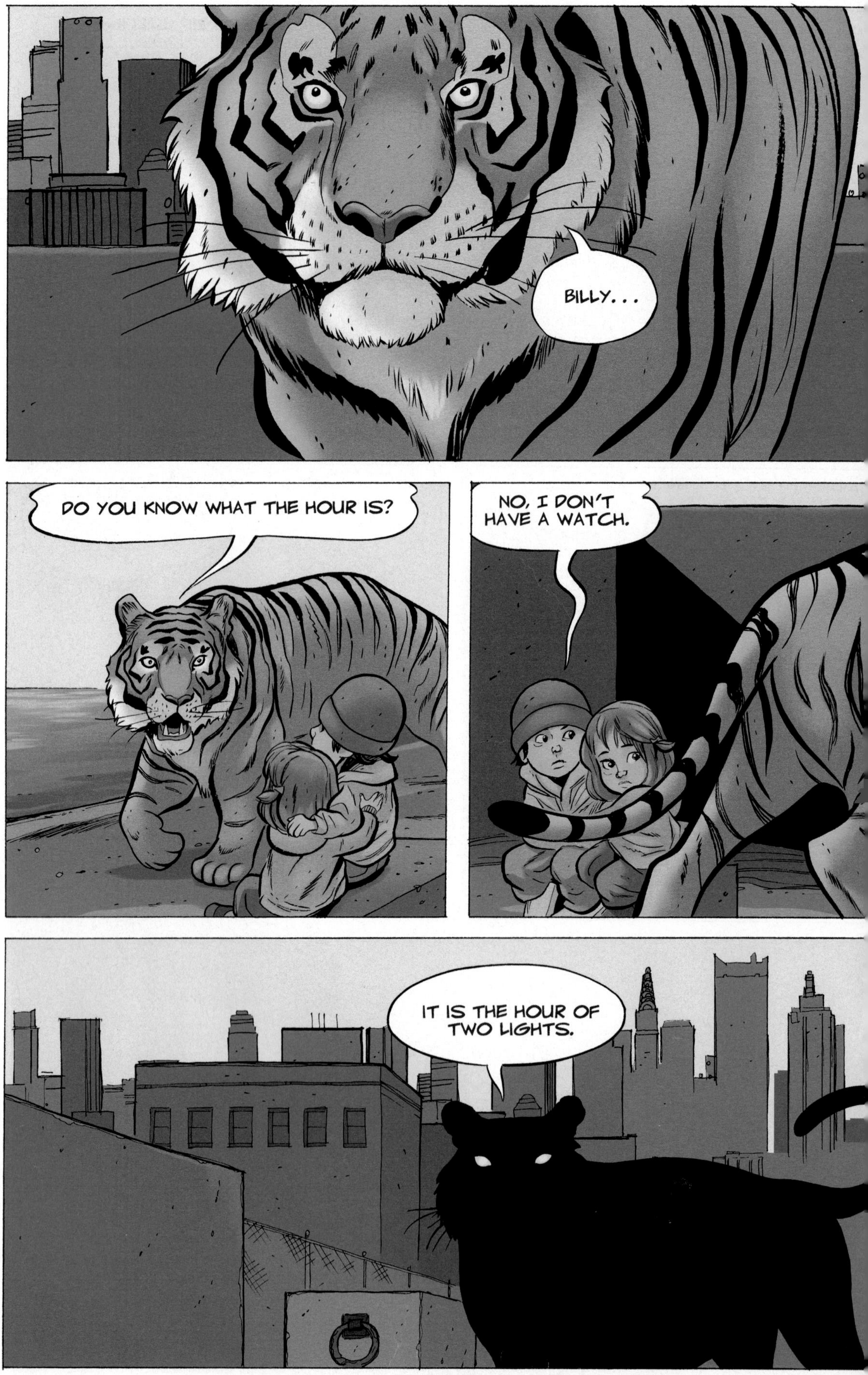
BILLY...
DO YOU KNOW WHAT THE HOUR IS?
NO, I DON'T HAVE A WATCH.
IT IS THE HOUR OF TWO LIGHTS.

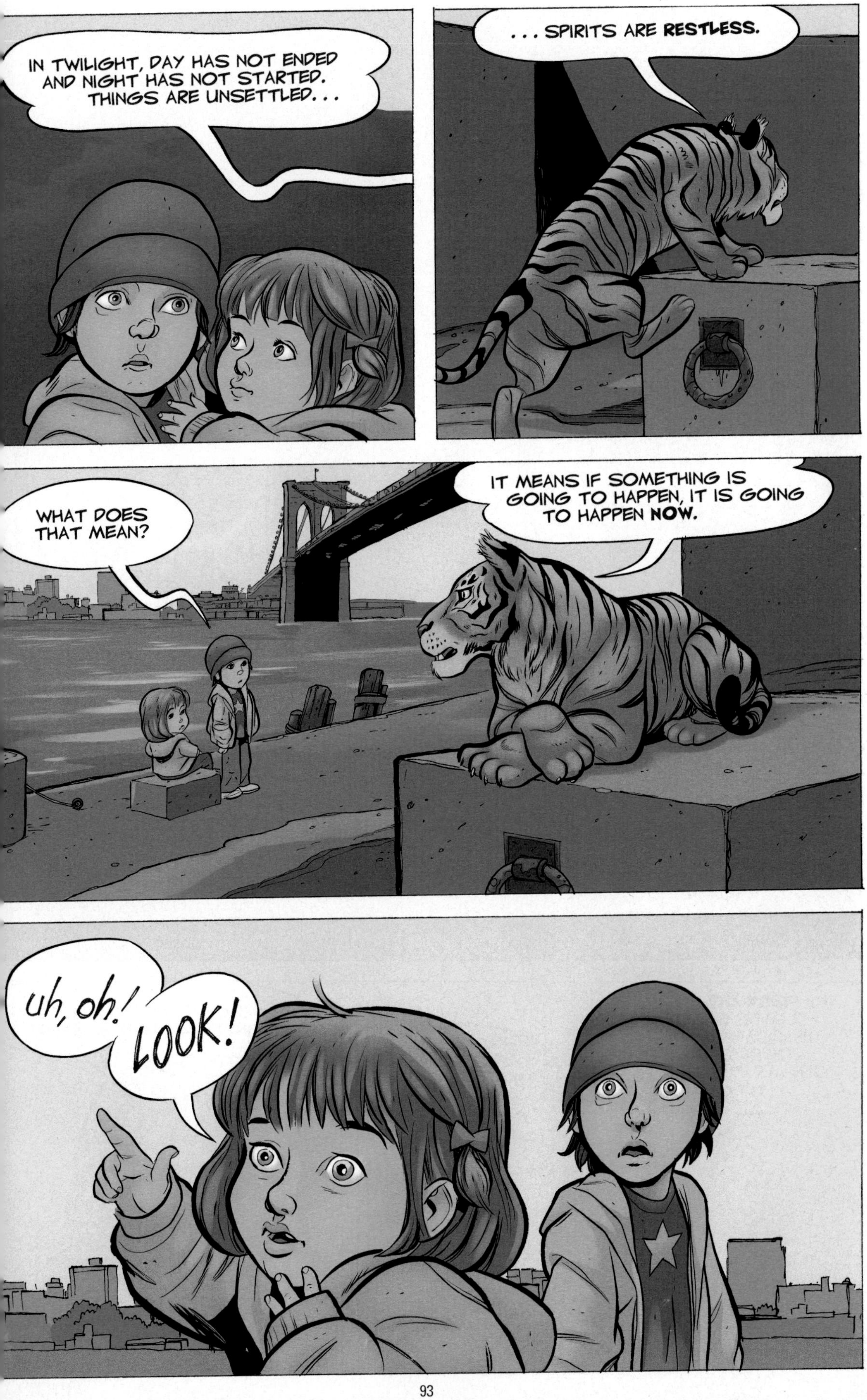
IN TWILIGHT, DAY HAS NOT ENDED AND NIGHT HAS NOT STARTED. THINGS ARE UNSETTLED...
... SPIRITS ARE **RESTLESS.**
WHAT DOES THAT MEAN?
IT MEANS IF SOMETHING IS GOING TO HAPPEN, IT IS GOING TO HAPPEN **NOW.**
uh, oh!
LOOK!

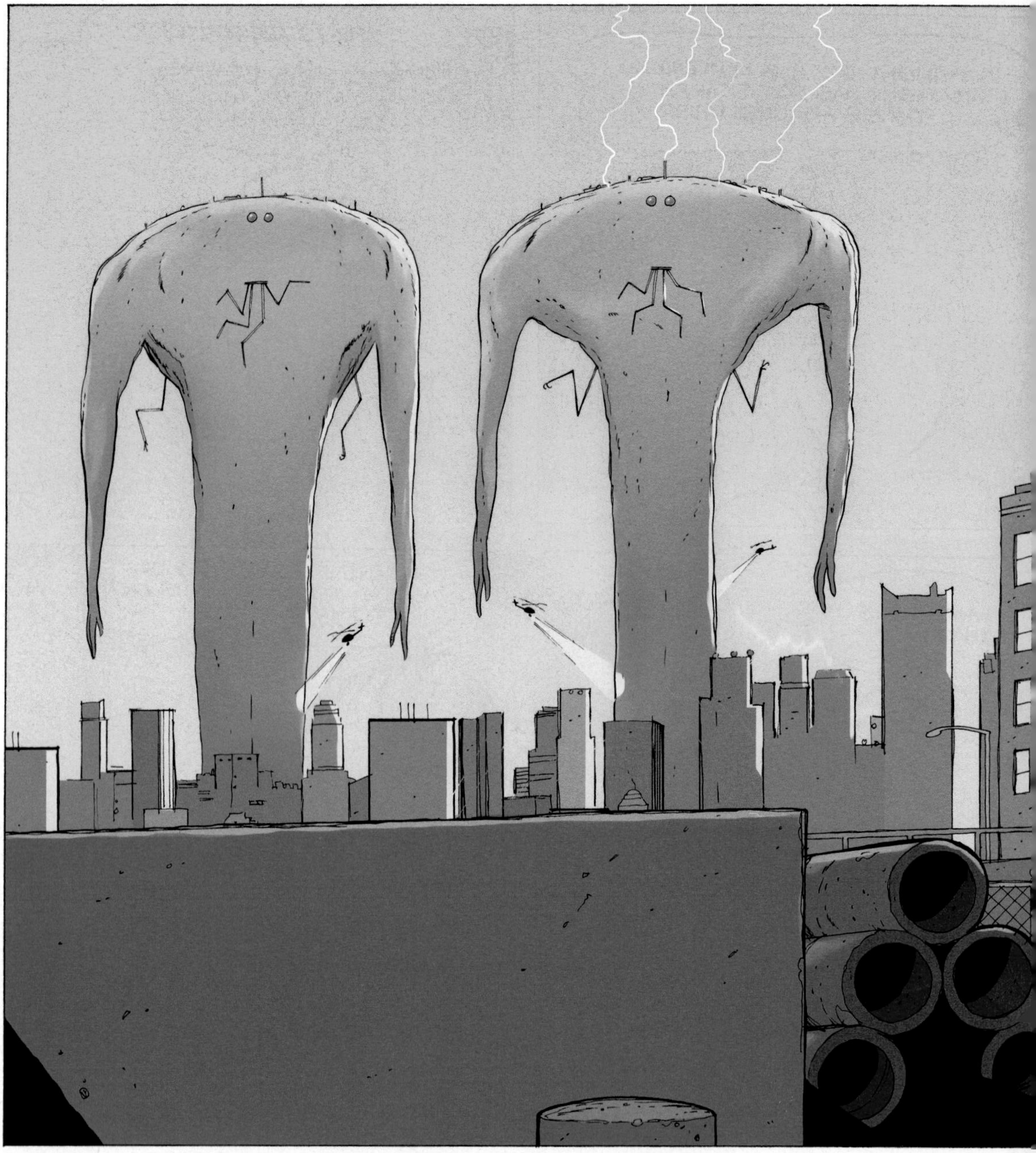

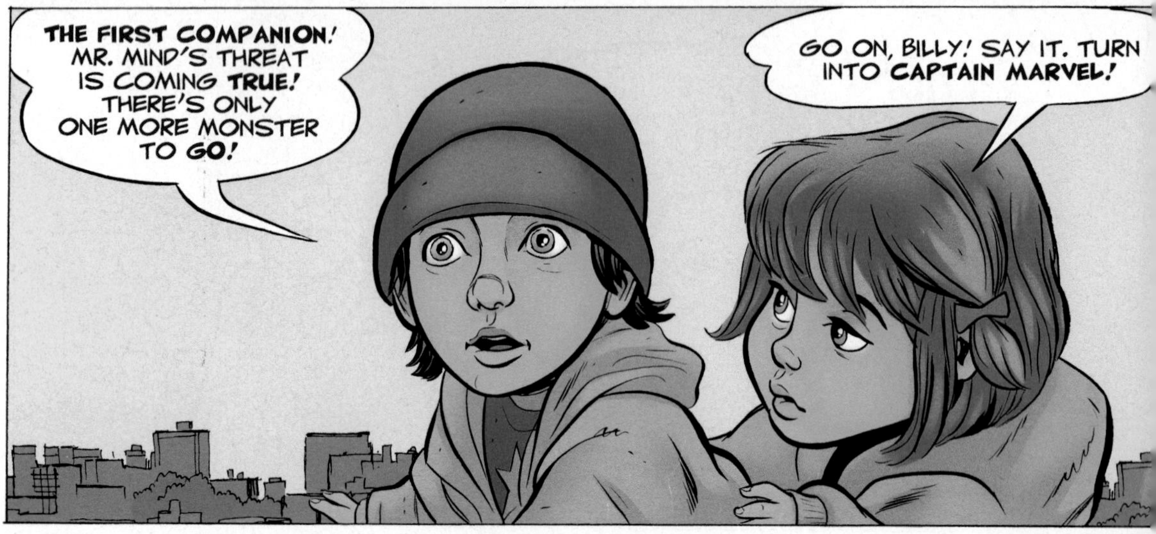
THE FIRST COMPANION! MR. MIND'S THREAT IS COMING TRUE! THERE'S ONLY ONE MORE MONSTER TO GO!
GO ON, BILLY! SAY IT. TURN INTO CAPTAIN MARVEL!

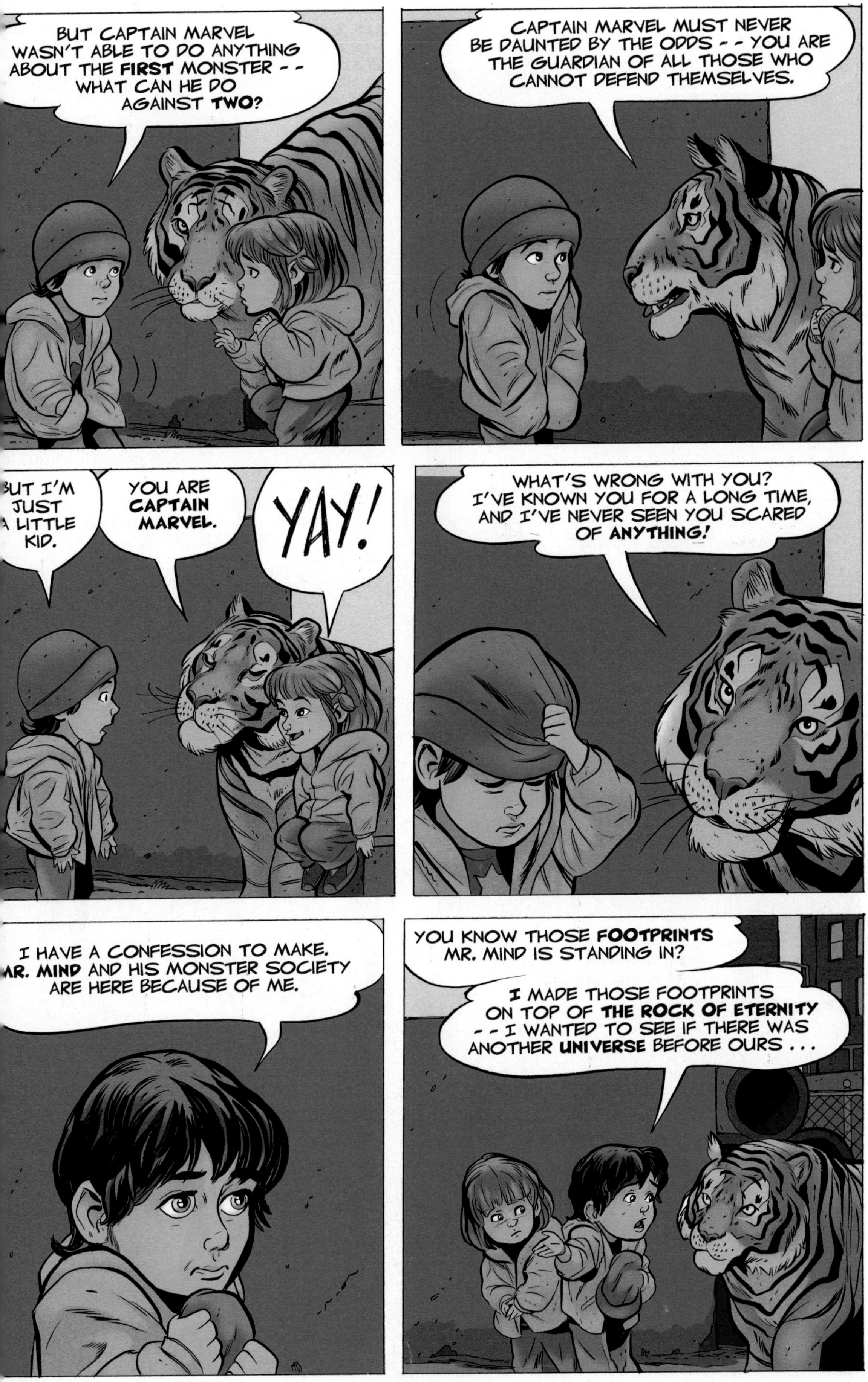
BUT CAPTAIN MARVEL WASN'T ABLE TO DO ANYTHING ABOUT THE **FIRST** MONSTER - - WHAT CAN HE DO AGAINST **TWO**?
CAPTAIN MARVEL MUST NEVER BE DAUNTED BY THE ODDS - - YOU ARE THE GUARDIAN OF ALL THOSE WHO CANNOT DEFEND THEMSELVES.
BUT I'M JUST A LITTLE KID.
YOU ARE **CAPTAIN MARVEL**.
YAY!
WHAT'S WRONG WITH YOU? I'VE KNOWN YOU FOR A LONG TIME, AND I'VE NEVER SEEN YOU SCARED OF **ANYTHING**!
I HAVE A CONFESSION TO MAKE. **MR. MIND** AND HIS MONSTER SOCIETY ARE HERE BECAUSE OF ME.
YOU KNOW THOSE **FOOTPRINTS** MR. MIND IS STANDING IN?
**I** MADE THOSE FOOTPRINTS ON TOP OF **THE ROCK OF ETERNITY** - - I WANTED TO SEE IF THERE WAS ANOTHER **UNIVERSE** BEFORE OURS . . .

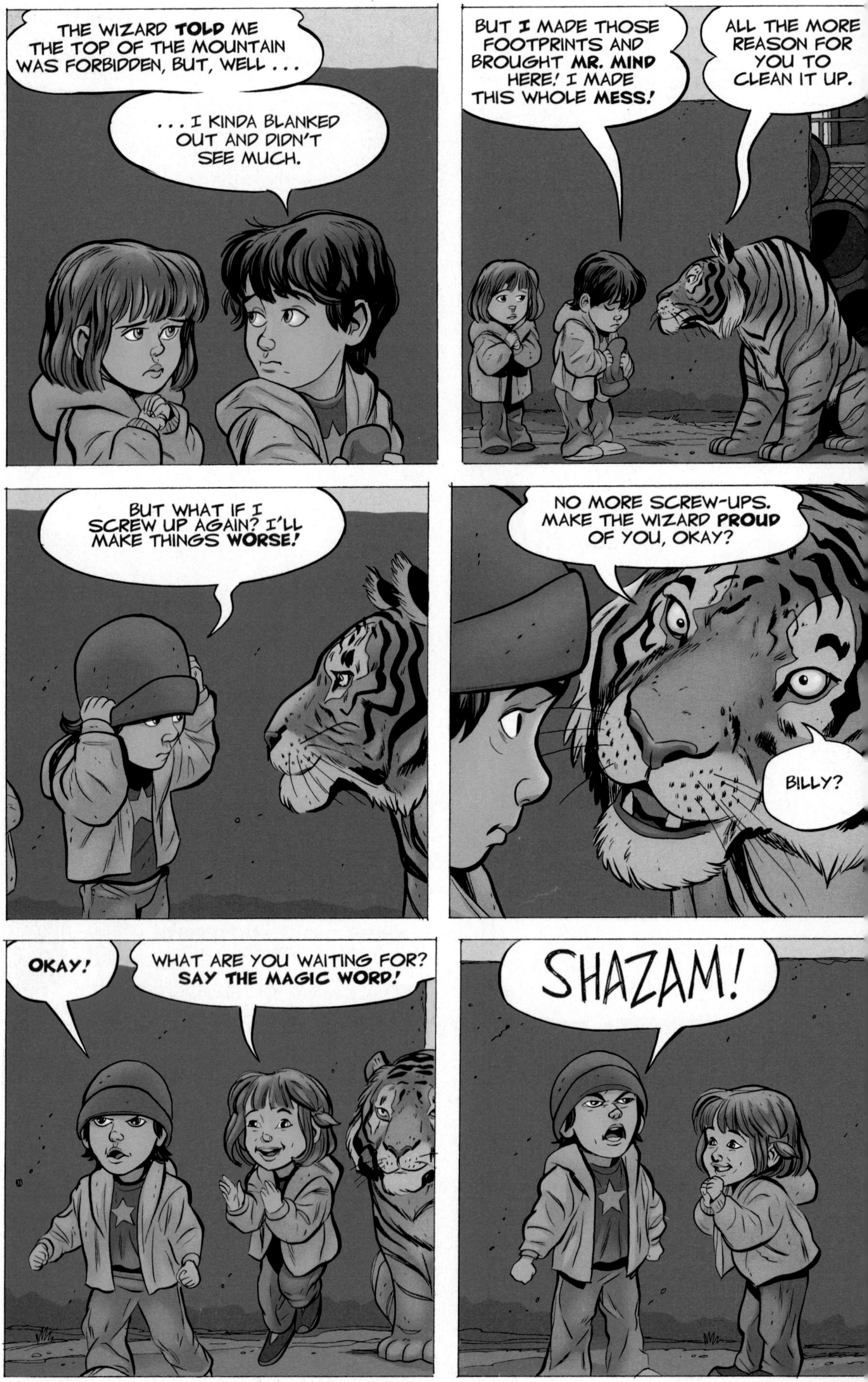
THE WIZARD TOLD ME THE TOP OF THE MOUNTAIN WAS FORBIDDEN, BUT, WELL . . .
. . . I KINDA BLANKED OUT AND DIDN'T SEE MUCH.
BUT I MADE THOSE FOOTPRINTS AND BROUGHT MR. MIND HERE! I MADE THIS WHOLE MESS!
ALL THE MORE REASON FOR YOU TO CLEAN IT UP.
BUT WHAT IF I SCREW UP AGAIN? I'LL MAKE THINGS WORSE!
NO MORE SCREW-UPS. MAKE THE WIZARD PROUD OF YOU, OKAY?
BILLY?
OKAY!
WHAT ARE YOU WAITING FOR? SAY THE MAGIC WORD!
SHAZAM!

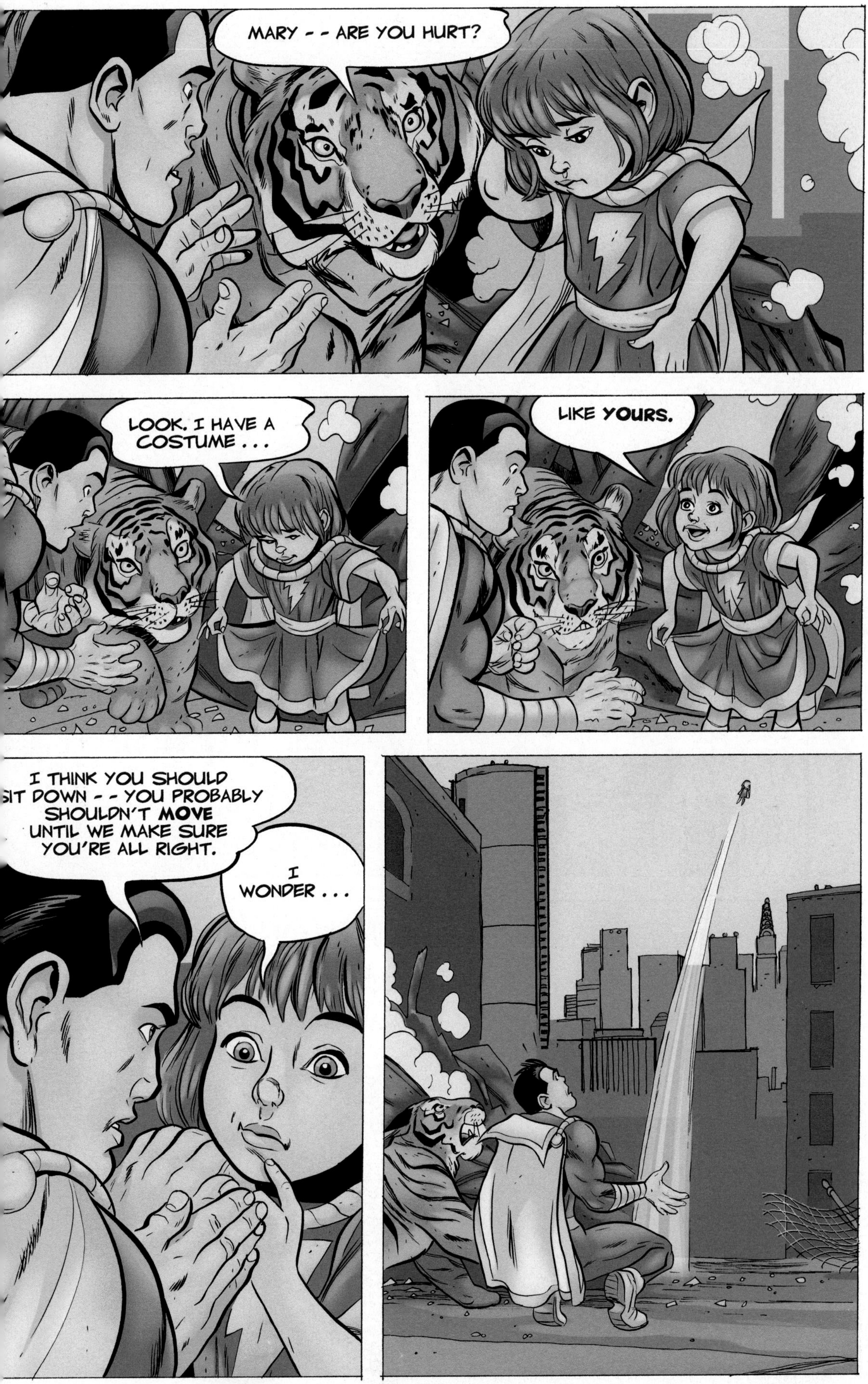
MARY - - ARE YOU HURT?
LOOK. I HAVE A COSTUME . . .
LIKE YOURS.
I THINK YOU SHOULD SIT DOWN - - YOU PROBABLY SHOULDN'T MOVE UNTIL WE MAKE SURE YOU'RE ALL RIGHT.
I WONDER . . .

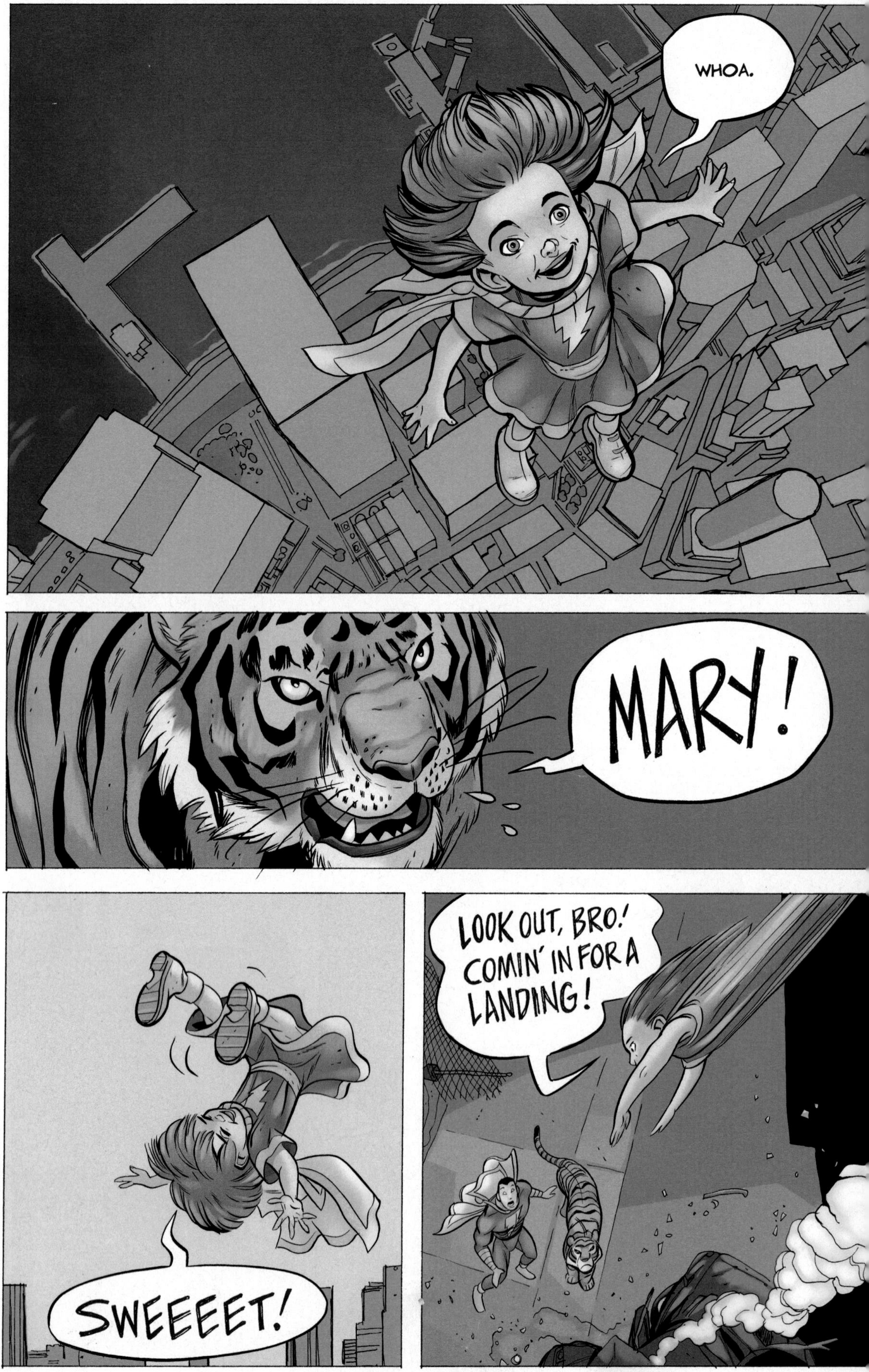
WHOA.
MARY!
SWEEEEET!
LOOK OUT, BRO! COMIN' IN FOR A LANDING!

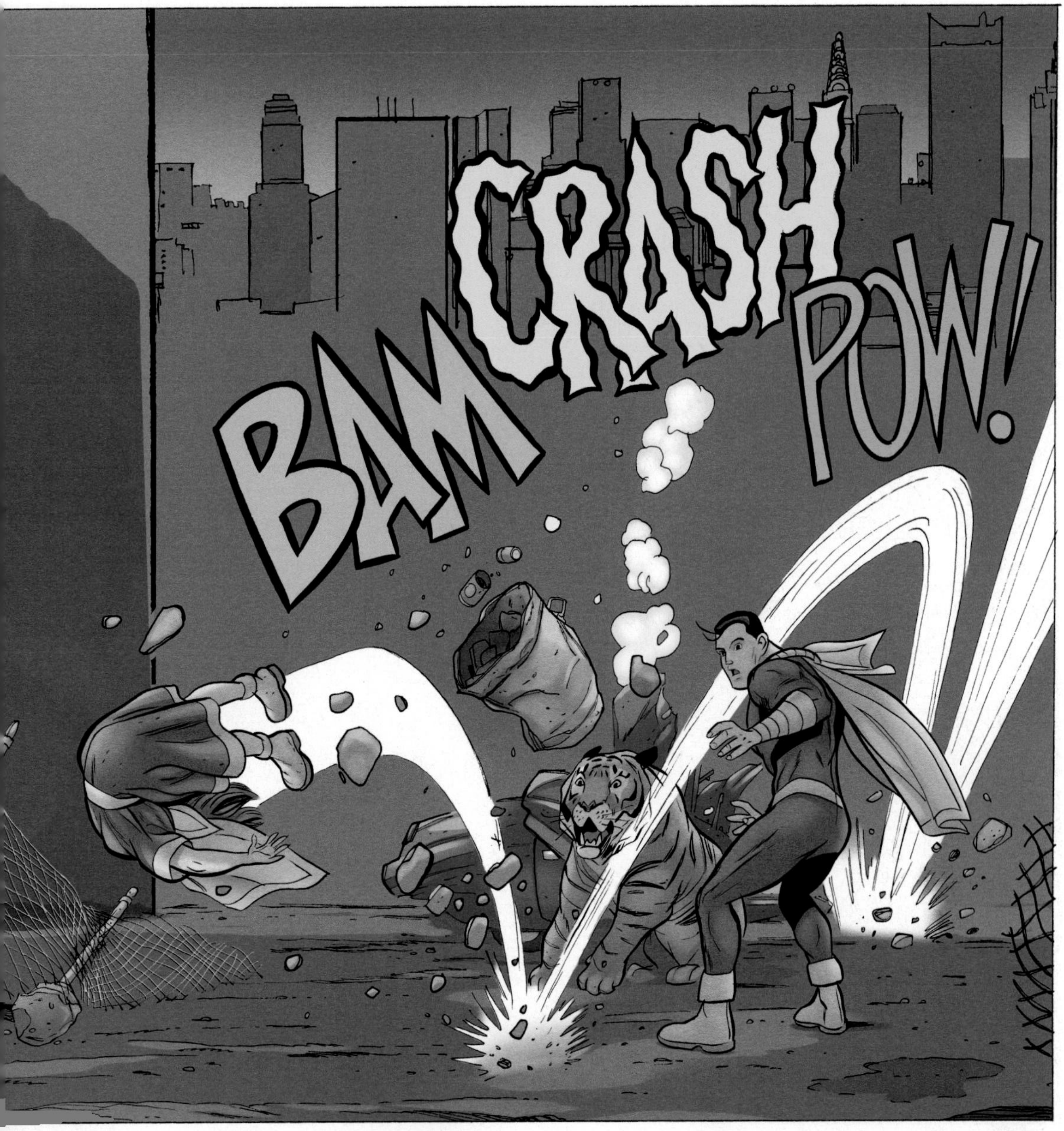
BAM
CRASH
POW!

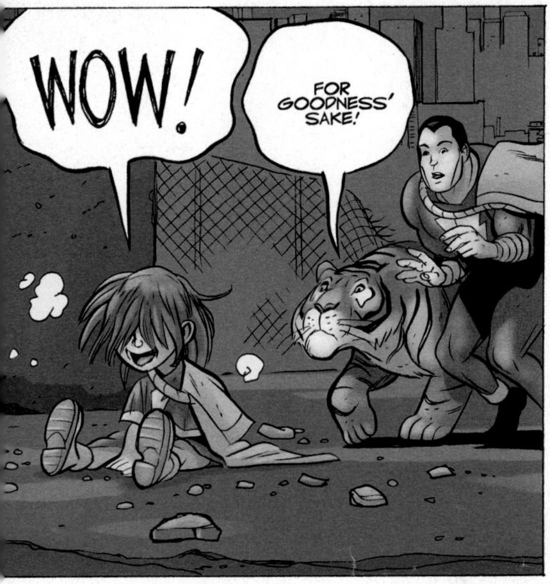
WOW!
FOR GOODNESS' SAKE!

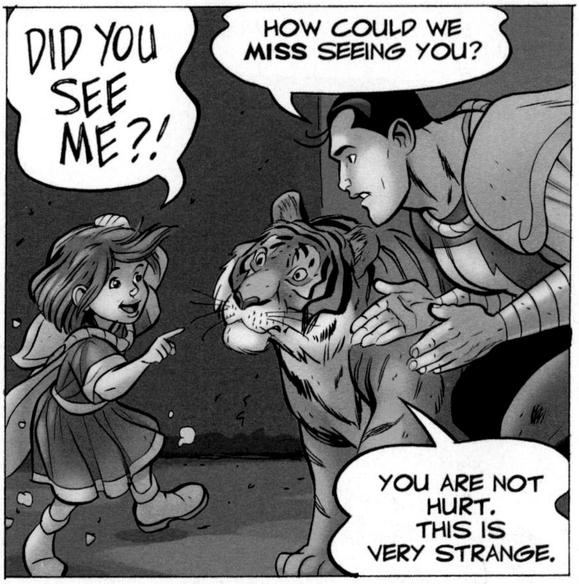
DID YOU SEE ME?!
HOW COULD WE MISS SEEING YOU?
YOU ARE NOT HURT. THIS IS VERY STRANGE.

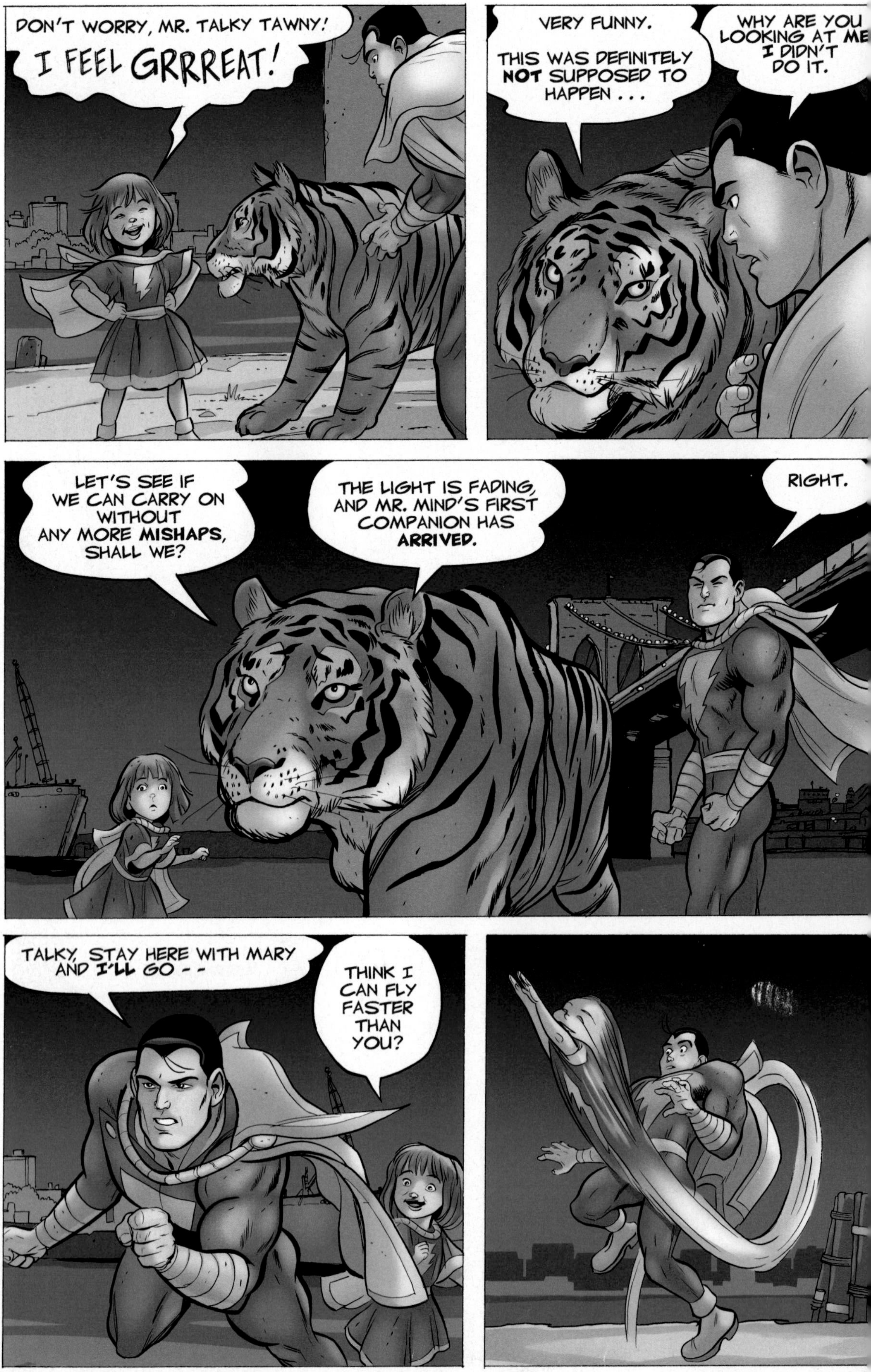
DON'T WORRY, MR. TALKY TAWNY!
I FEEL GRRREAT!
VERY FUNNY.
THIS WAS DEFINITELY NOT SUPPOSED TO HAPPEN . . .
WHY ARE YOU LOOKING AT ME? I DIDN'T DO IT.
LET'S SEE IF WE CAN CARRY ON WITHOUT ANY MORE MISHAPS, SHALL WE?
THE LIGHT IS FADING, AND MR. MIND'S FIRST COMPANION HAS ARRIVED.
RIGHT.
TALKY, STAY HERE WITH MARY AND I'LL GO --
THINK I CAN FLY FASTER THAN YOU?

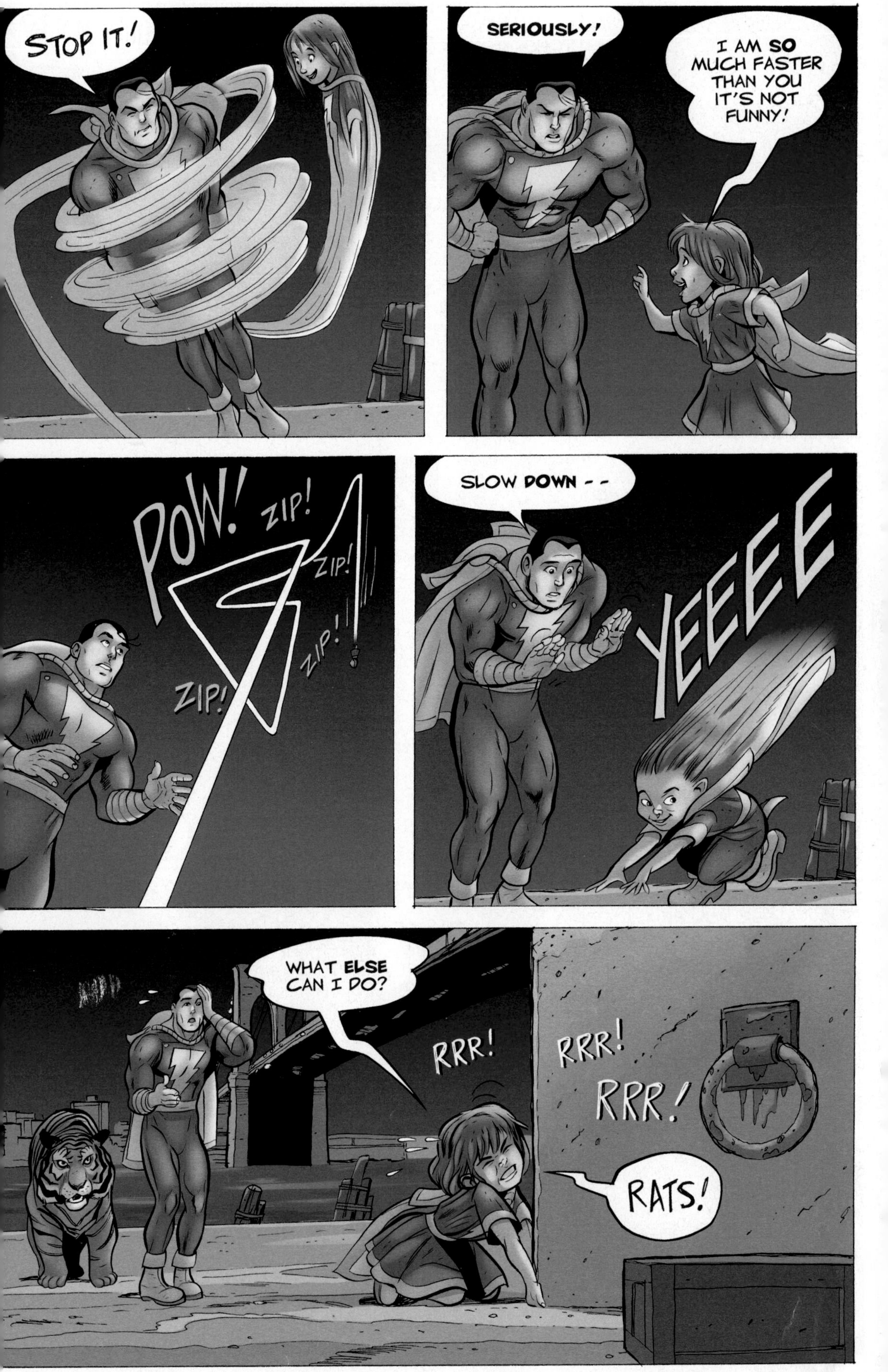
STOP IT!
SERIOUSLY!
I AM SO MUCH FASTER THAN YOU IT'S NOT FUNNY!
POW!
ZIP!
ZIP!
ZIP!
ZIP!
SLOW DOWN - -
YEEEE
WHAT ELSE CAN I DO?
RRR!
RRR!
RRR!
RATS!

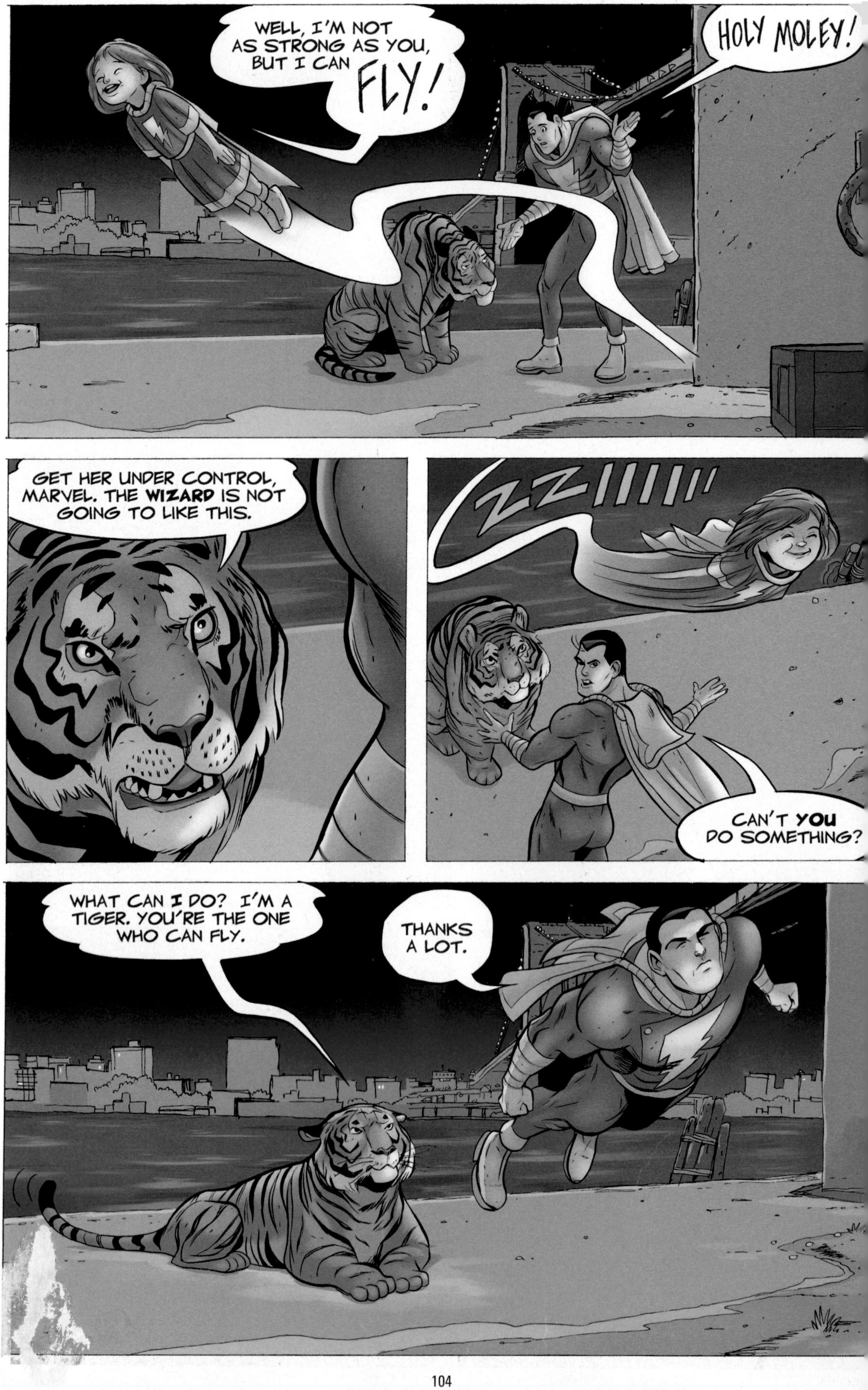
WELL, I'M NOT AS STRONG AS YOU, BUT I CAN FLY!
HOLY MOLEY!
GET HER UNDER CONTROL, MARVEL. THE WIZARD IS NOT GOING TO LIKE THIS.
ZZIIIIII
CAN'T YOU DO SOMETHING?
WHAT CAN I DO? I'M A TIGER. YOU'RE THE ONE WHO CAN FLY.
THANKS A LOT.

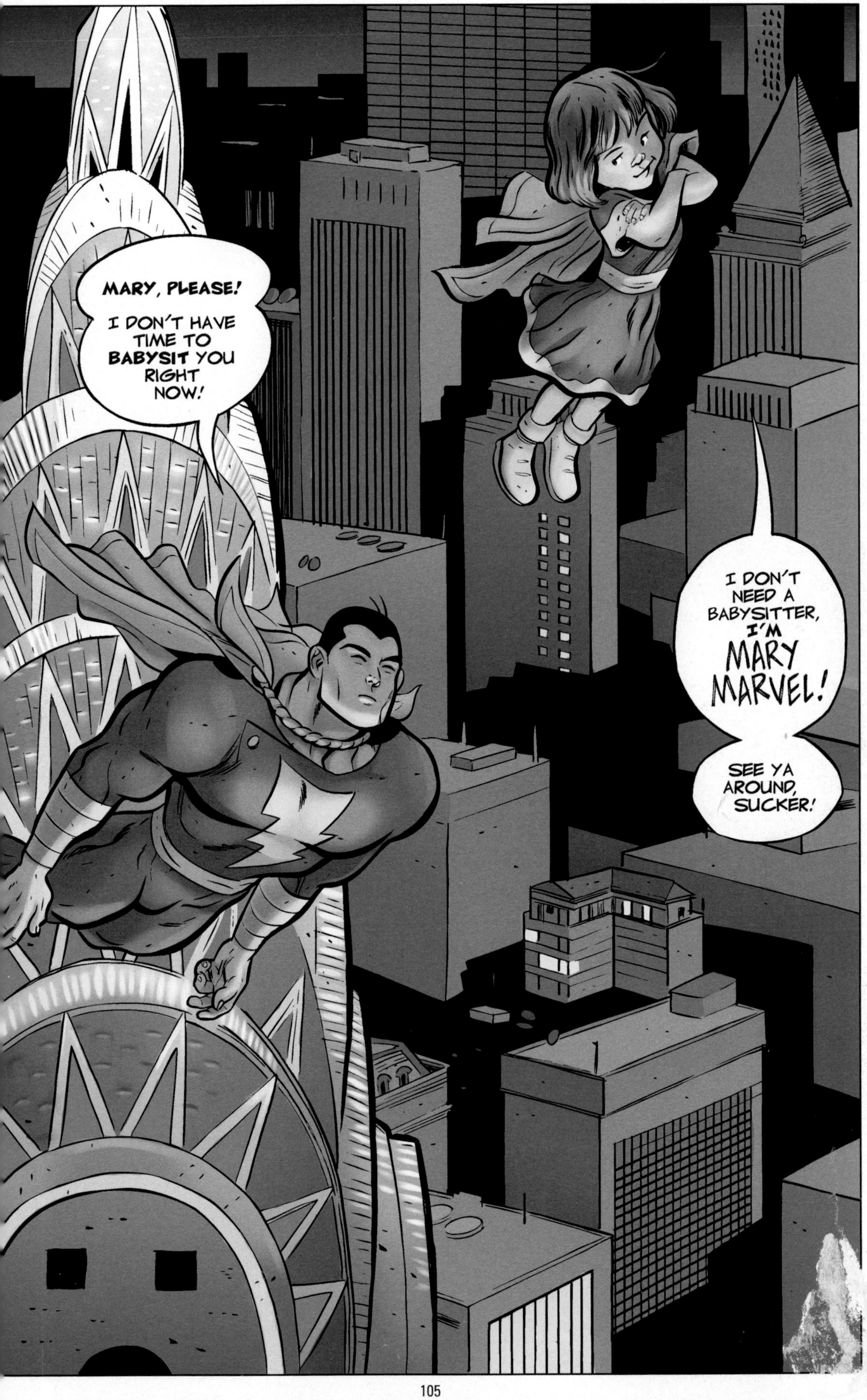
MARY, PLEASE!
I DON'T HAVE TIME TO BABYSIT YOU RIGHT NOW!
I DON'T NEED A BABYSITTER, I'M MARY MARVEL!
SEE YA AROUND, SUCKER!

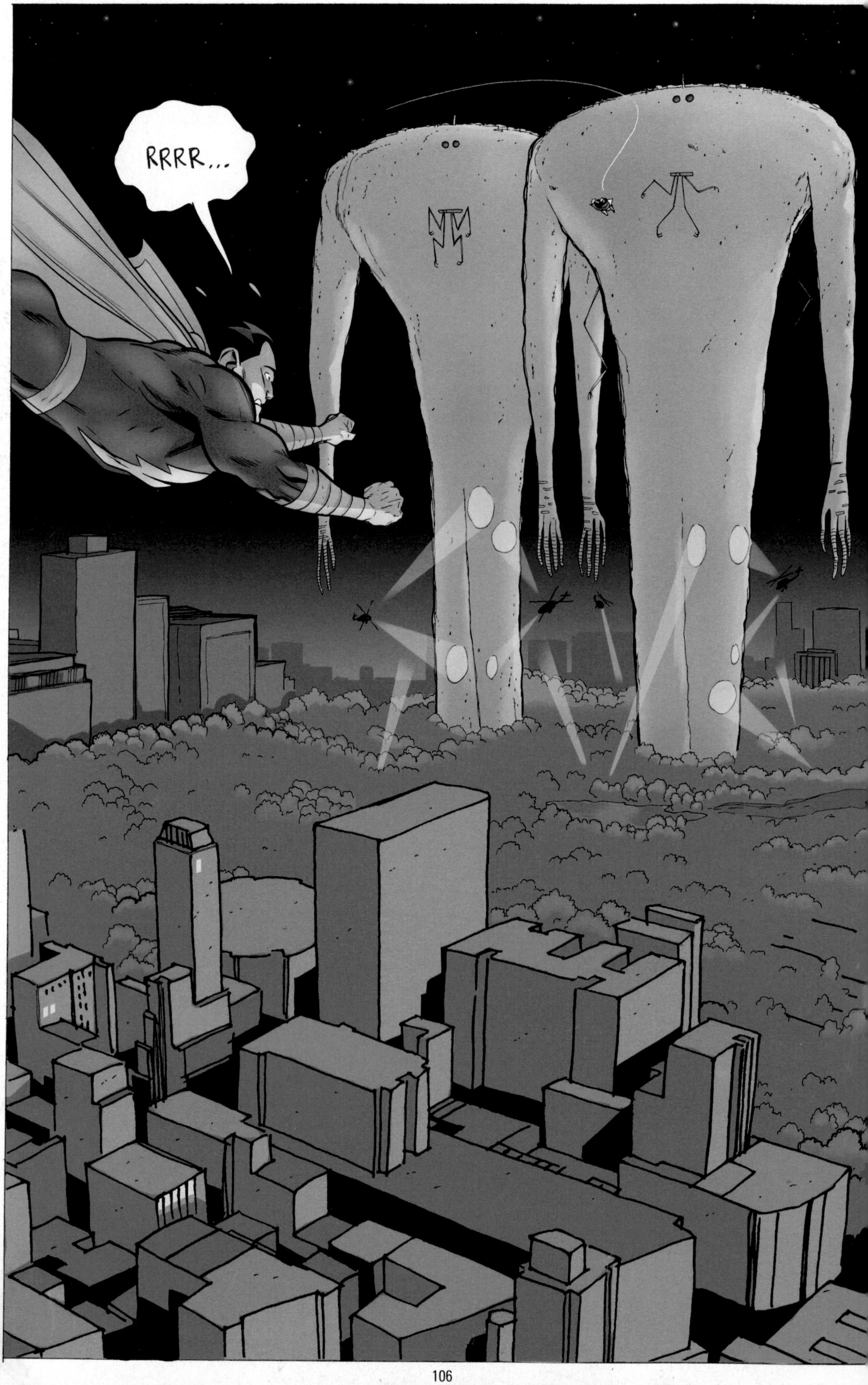
RRRR...

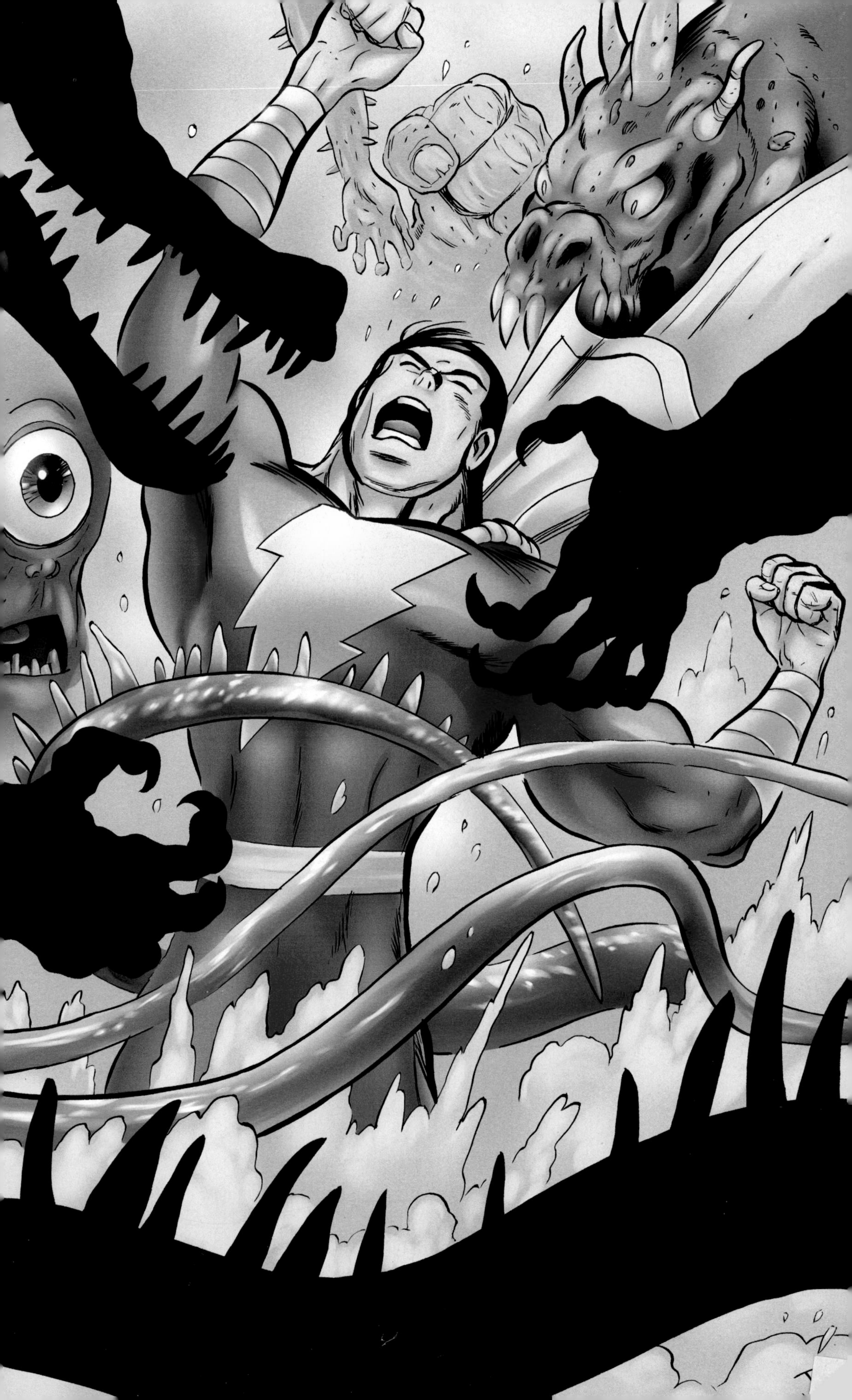

# THE MONSTER SOCIETY OF EVIL

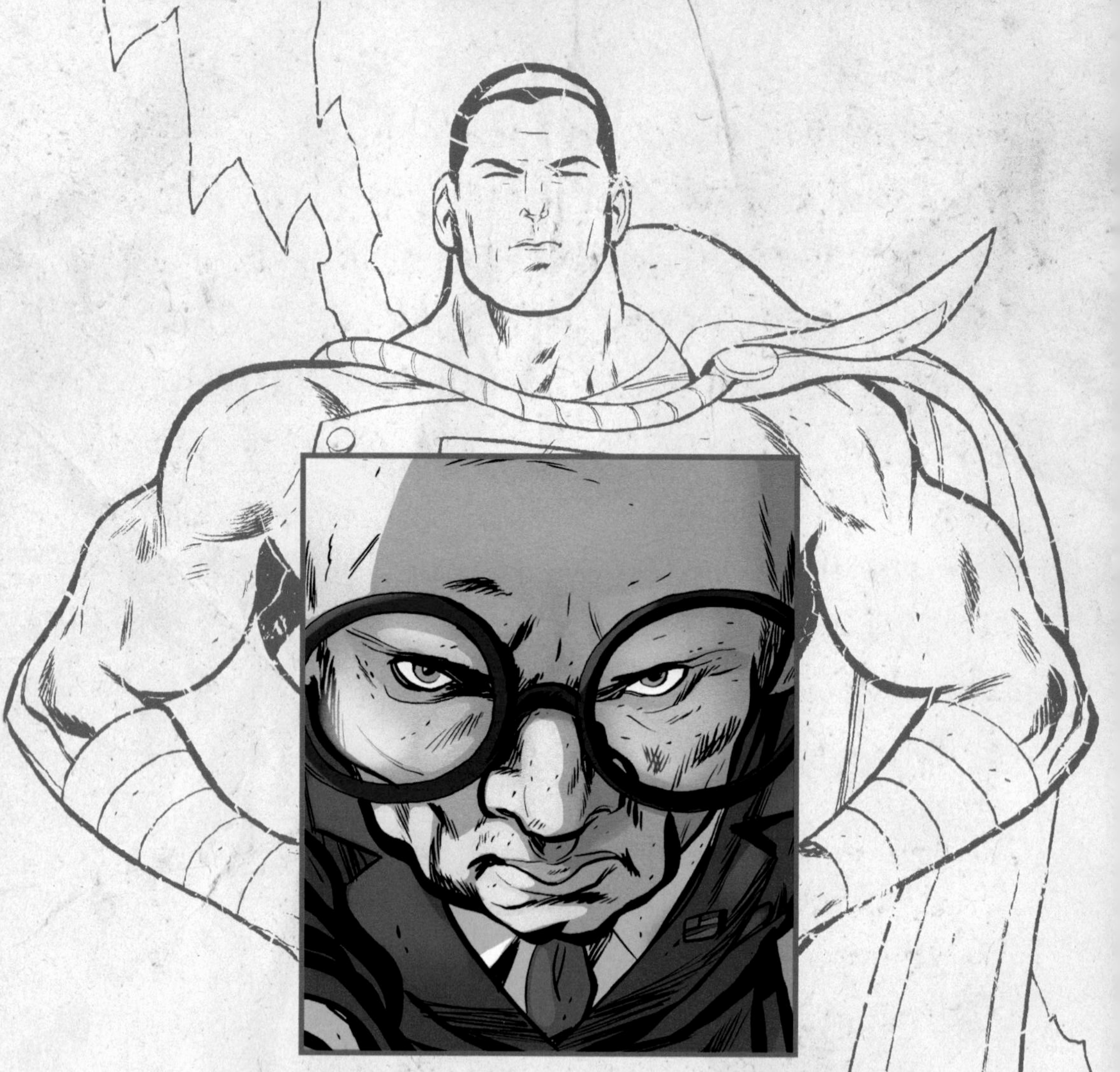

## CHAPTER 3:

# HREZMZ XLNVH LM HGILMT!*

*THE MONSTER SOCIETY CODE

| A | B | C | D | E | F | G | H | I | J | K | L | M | N | O | P | Q | R | S | T | U | V | W | X | Y | Z |
|---|---|---|---|---|---|---|---|---|---|---|---|---|---|---|---|---|---|---|---|---|---|---|---|---|---|
| Z | Y | X | W | V | U | T | S | R | Q | P | O | N | M | L | K | J | I | H | G | F | E | D | C | B | A |

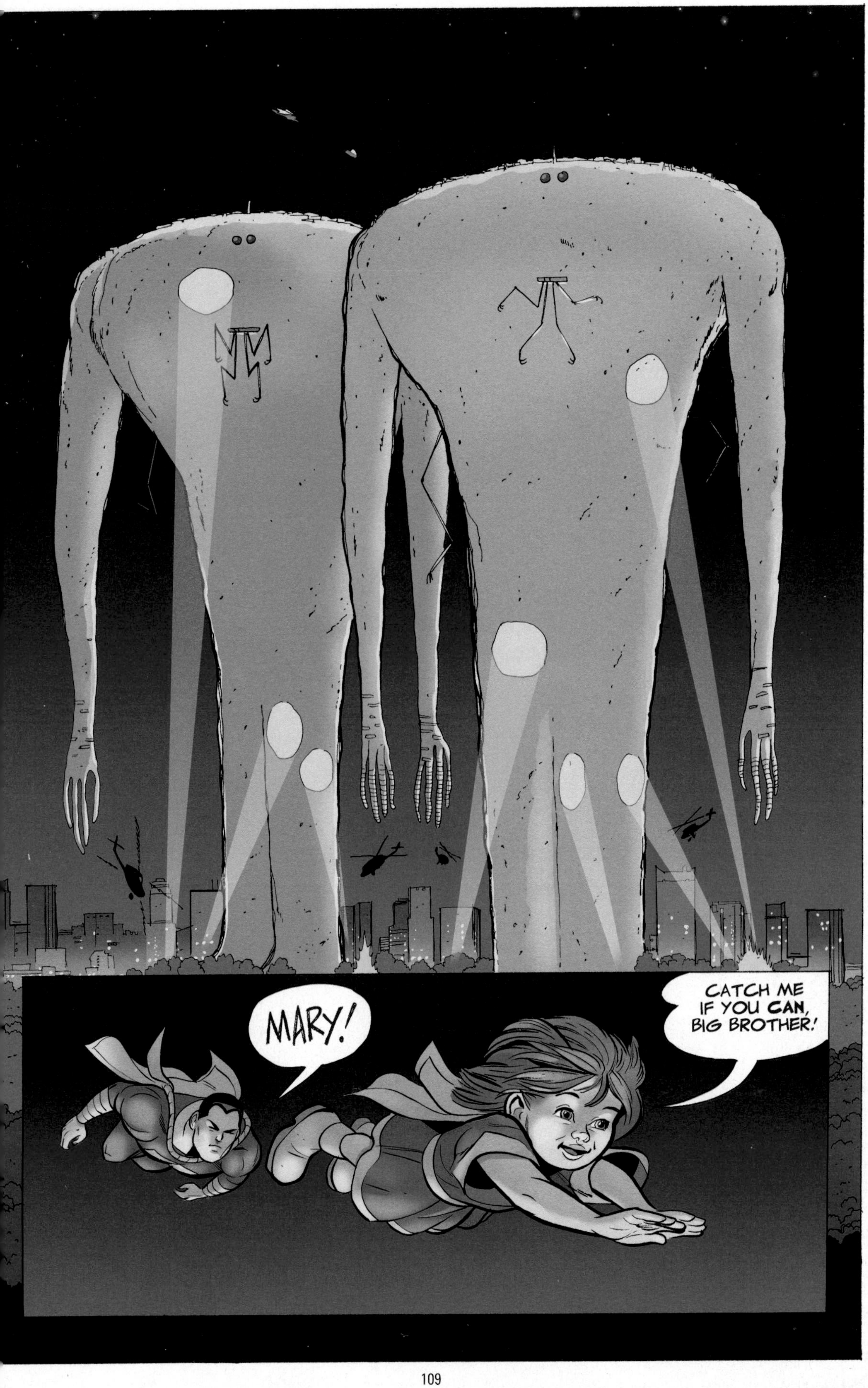
MARY!
CATCH ME IF YOU CAN, BIG BROTHER!

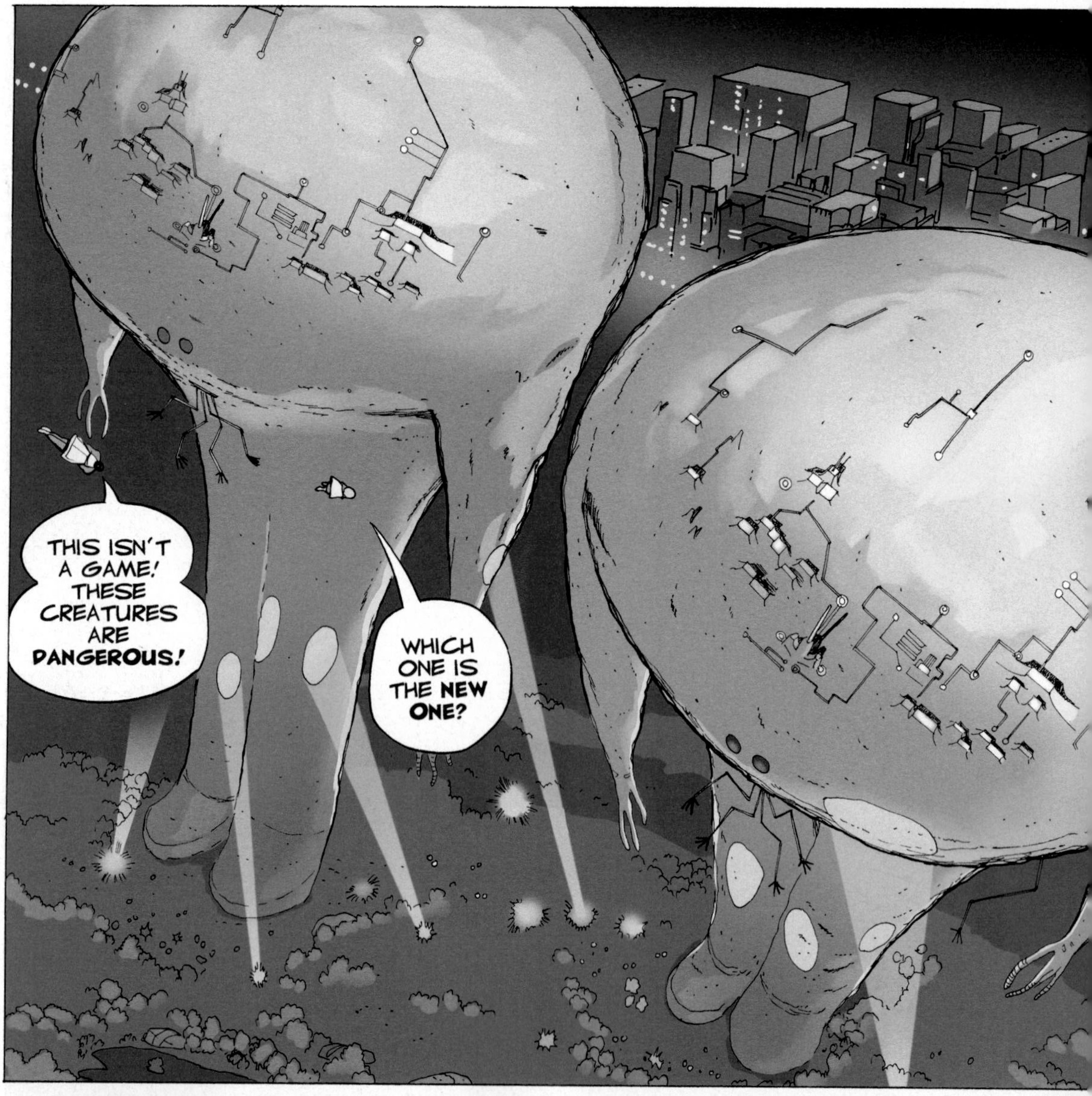
THIS ISN'T A GAME! THESE CREATURES ARE DANGEROUS!
WHICH ONE IS THE NEW ONE?

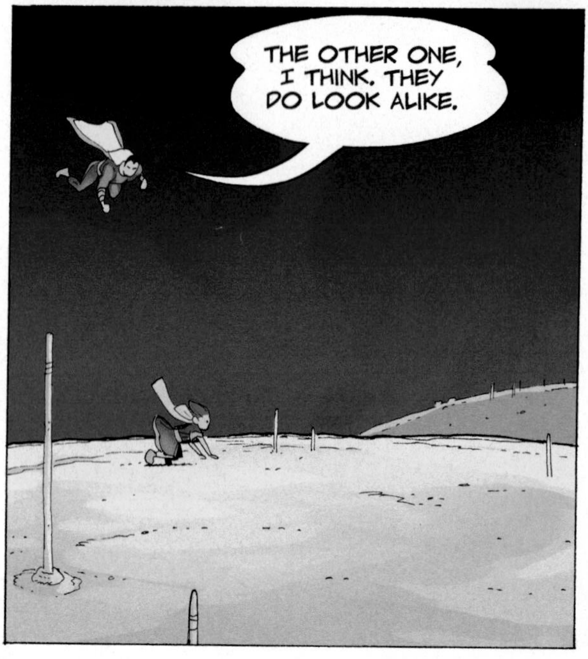
THE OTHER ONE, I THINK. THEY DO LOOK ALIKE.

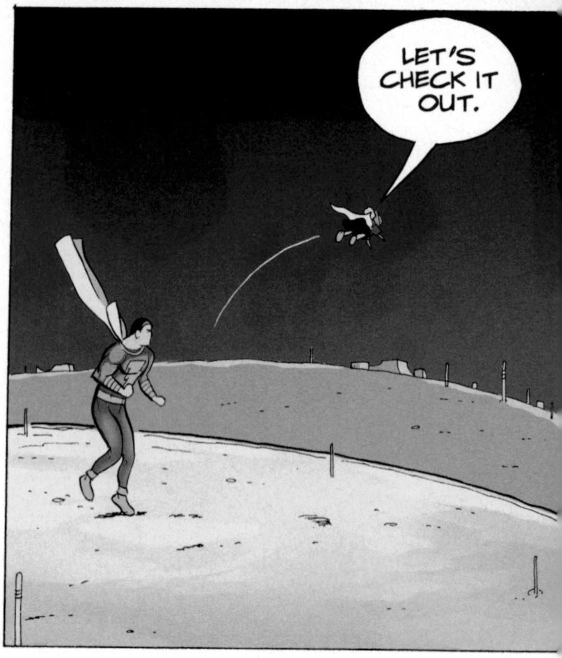
LET'S CHECK IT OUT.

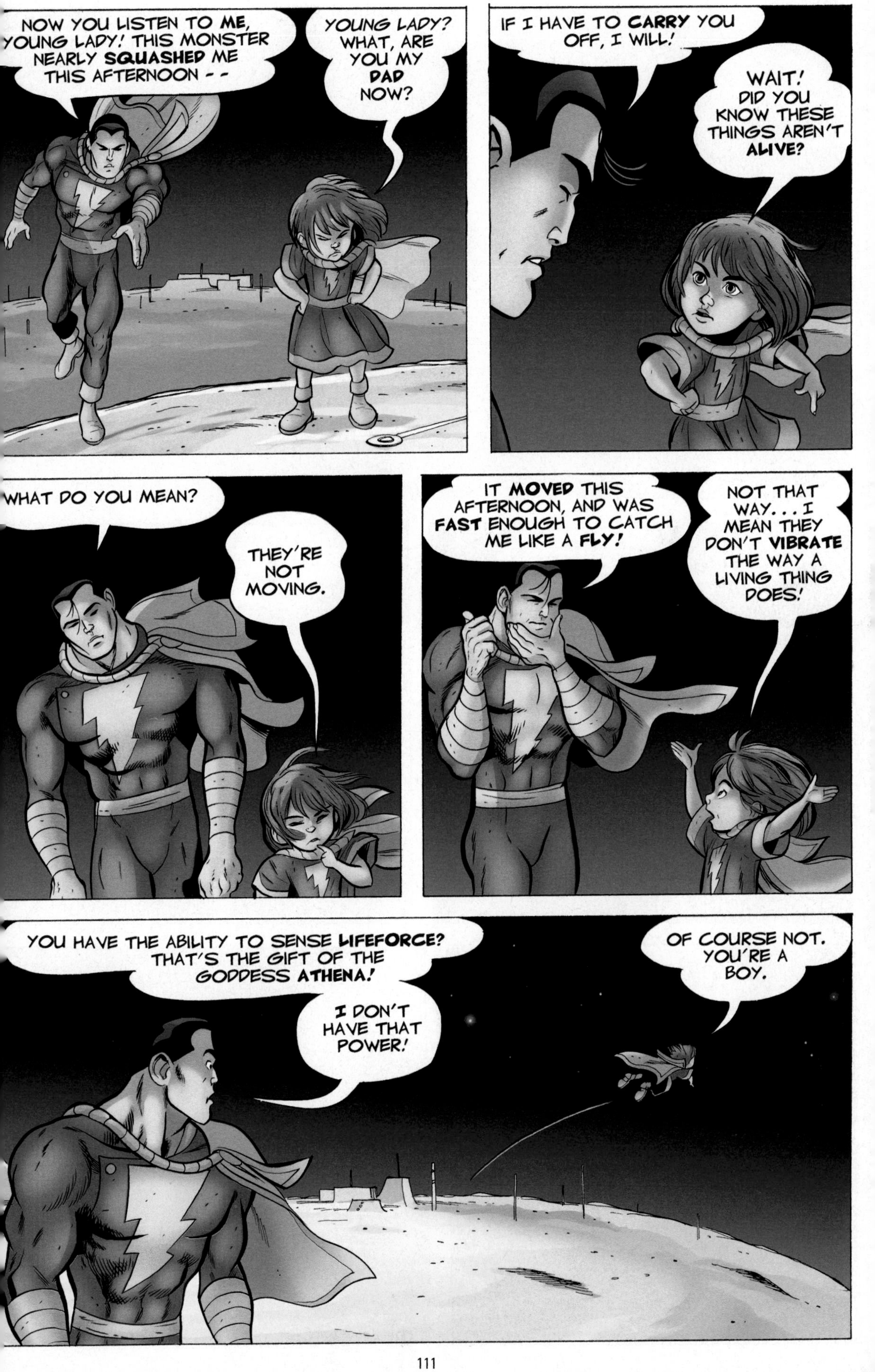
NOW YOU LISTEN TO ME, YOUNG LADY! THIS MONSTER NEARLY SQUASHED ME THIS AFTERNOON - -
YOUNG LADY? WHAT, ARE YOU MY DAD NOW?
IF I HAVE TO CARRY YOU OFF, I WILL!
WAIT! DID YOU KNOW THESE THINGS AREN'T ALIVE?
WHAT DO YOU MEAN?
THEY'RE NOT MOVING.
IT MOVED THIS AFTERNOON, AND WAS FAST ENOUGH TO CATCH ME LIKE A FLY!
NOT THAT WAY. . . I MEAN THEY DON'T VIBRATE THE WAY A LIVING THING DOES!
YOU HAVE THE ABILITY TO SENSE LIFEFORCE? THAT'S THE GIFT OF THE GODDESS ATHENA!
I DON'T HAVE THAT POWER!
OF COURSE NOT. YOU'RE A BOY.

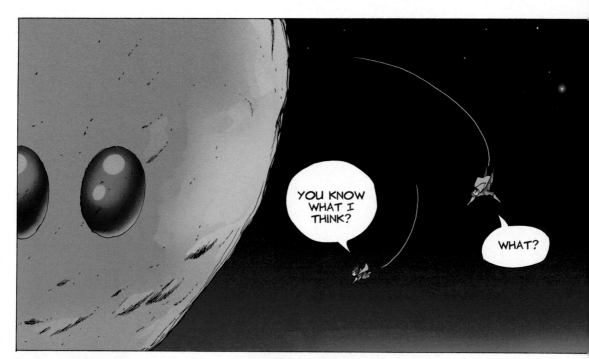

112

TAKE IT EASY--

WE'RE ON YOUR SIDE!

TATTA! TA-TTA! TATTA

WATCH OUT, MARY!

SPOW!
SPIING!

TAT!
TAT

TAT!
TATTA
TATTA TATTA

POW! POW!

WHY ARE THEY SHOOTING AT US?

THEY MUST THINK WE'RE IN LEAGUE WITH THE MONSTERS -- BUT THEY DIDN'T EVEN TRY TO FIND OUT.

HALT!

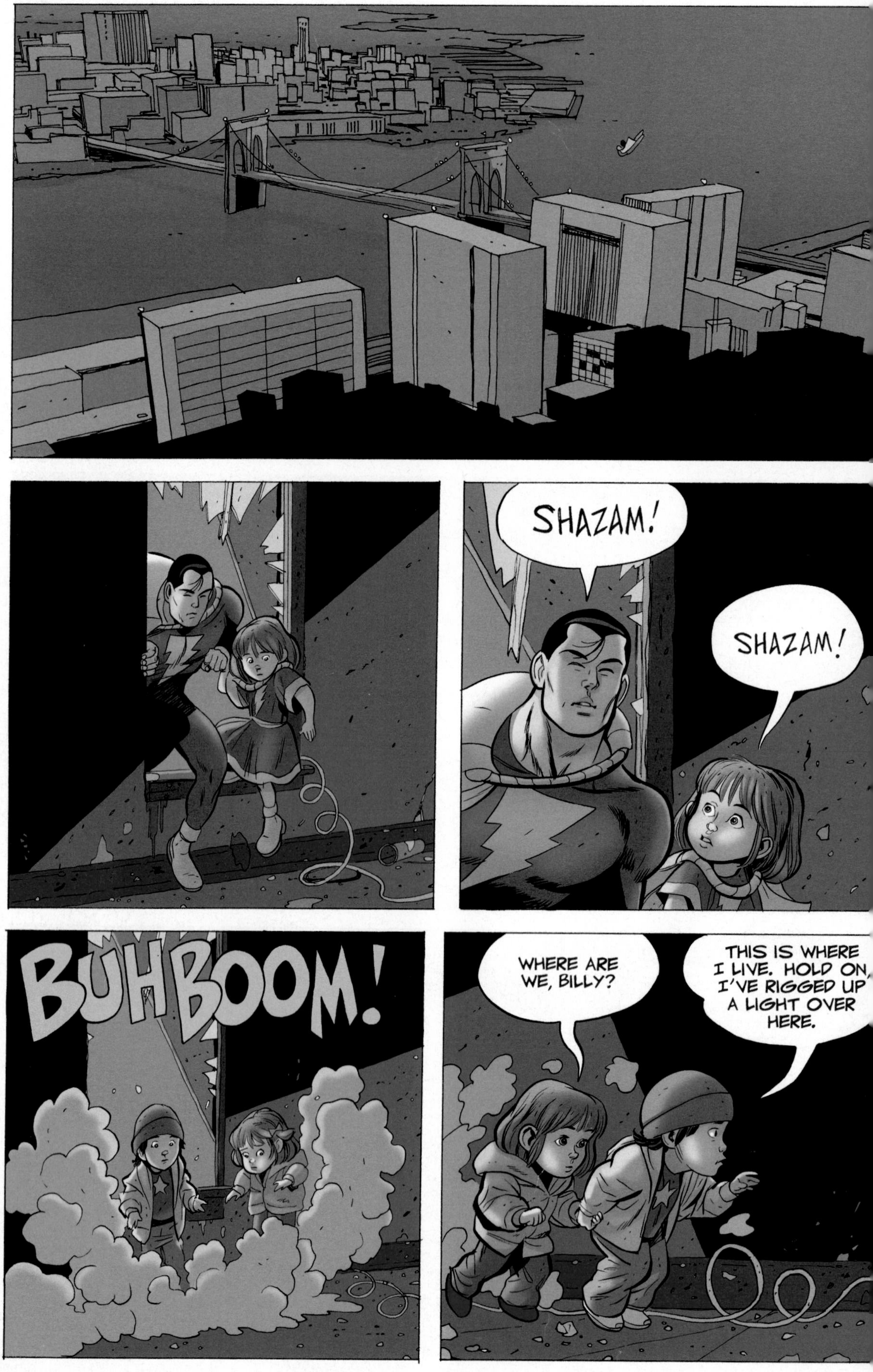
SHAZAM!
SHAZAM!
BUHBOOM!
WHERE ARE WE, BILLY?
THIS IS WHERE I LIVE. HOLD ON, I'VE RIGGED UP A LIGHT OVER HERE.

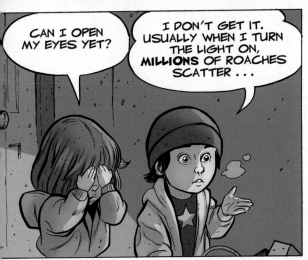

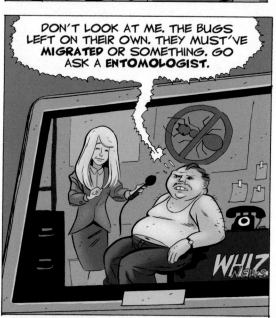

121

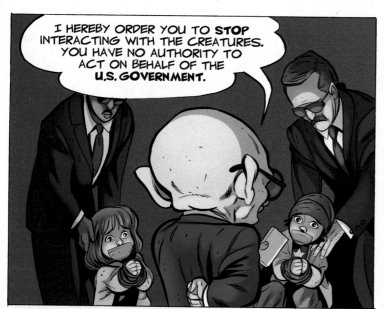

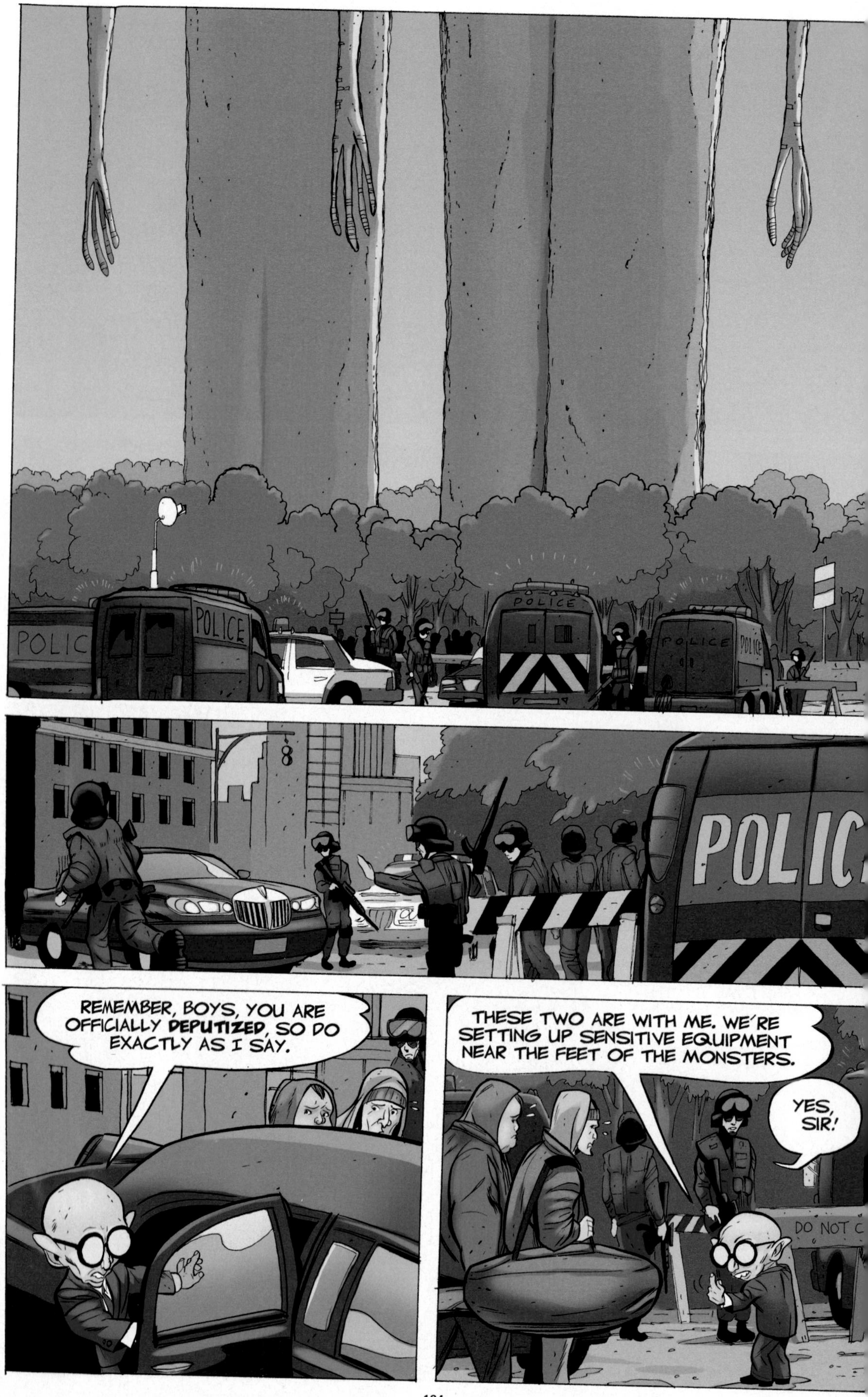
POLICE
POLIC
POLICE
POLICE
POLICE
POLIC
REMEMBER, BOYS, YOU ARE OFFICIALLY **DEPUTIZED**, SO DO EXACTLY AS I SAY.
THESE TWO ARE WITH ME. WE'RE SETTING UP SENSITIVE EQUIPMENT NEAR THE FEET OF THE MONSTERS.
YES, SIR!
DO NOT C

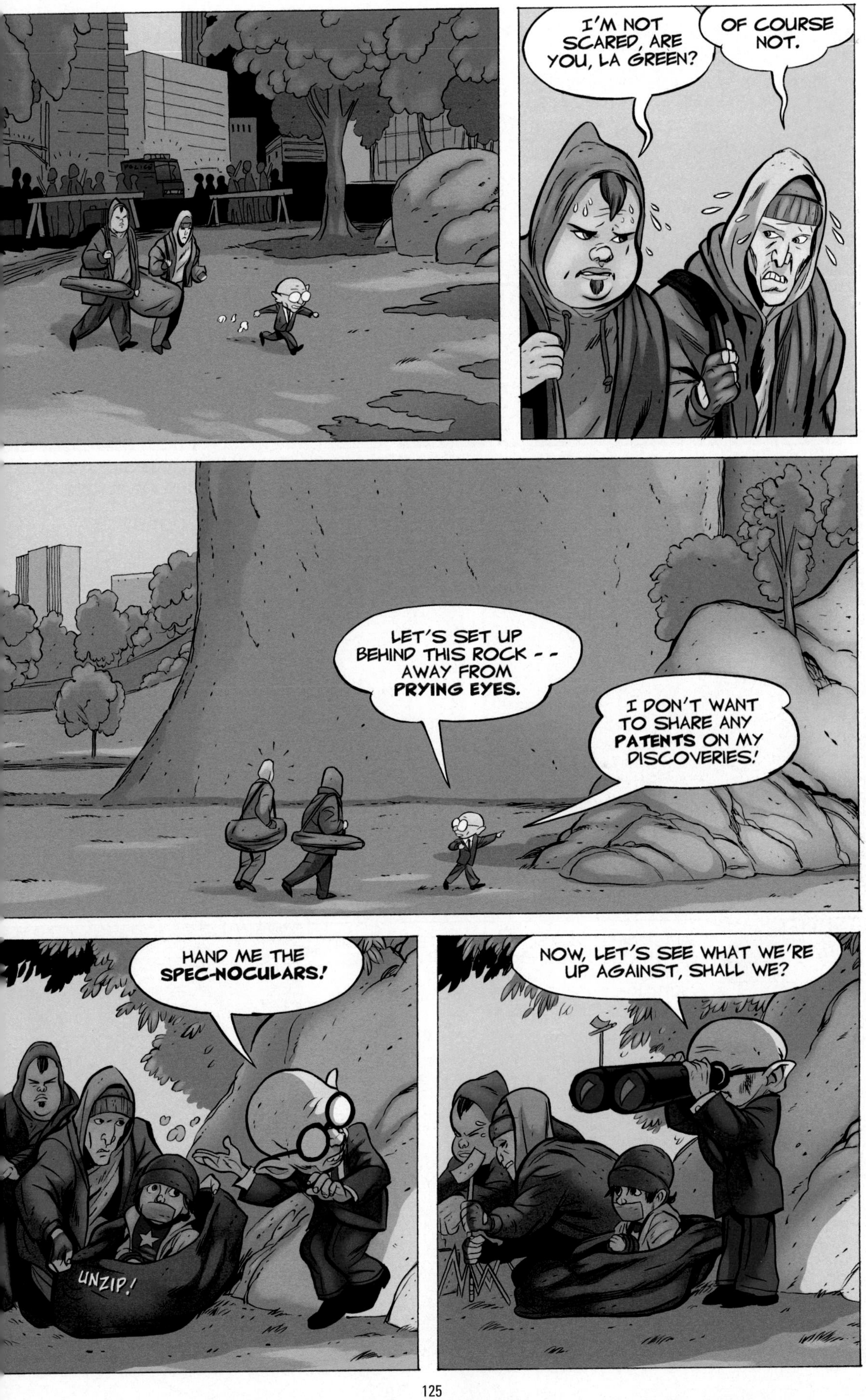
POLICE
I'M NOT SCARED, ARE YOU, LA GREEN?
OF COURSE NOT.
LET'S SET UP BEHIND THIS ROCK - - AWAY FROM **PRYING EYES.**
I DON'T WANT TO SHARE ANY **PATENTS** ON MY DISCOVERIES!
HAND ME THE **SPEC-NOCULARS!**
UNZIP!
NOW, LET'S SEE WHAT WE'RE UP AGAINST, SHALL WE?

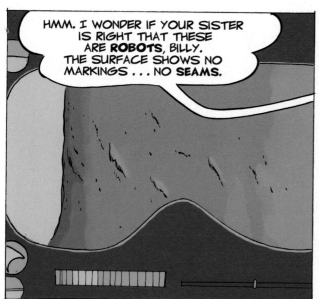

HMM. I WONDER IF YOUR SISTER IS RIGHT THAT THESE ARE **ROBOTS**, BILLY. THE SURFACE SHOWS NO MARKINGS . . . NO **SEAMS**.

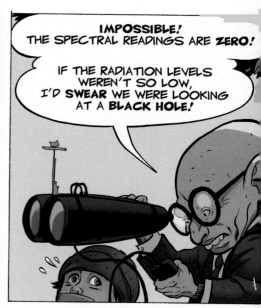

**IMPOSSIBLE!** THE SPECTRAL READINGS ARE **ZERO!**

IF THE RADIATION LEVELS WEREN'T SO LOW, I'D **SWEAR** WE WERE LOOKING AT A **BLACK HOLE!**

EH? WHAT'S THIS?

I'VE NEVER SEEN ONE OF **THOSE** BEFORE. I WONDER WHAT IT DOES?

ALL RIGHT, BOYS, THIS IS THE MOMENT OF **TRUTH**. YOUR GOVERNMENT NEEDS YOU TO RUN TOWARD THAT THING STICKING OUT OF THE MONSTER'S FEET. **READY?**

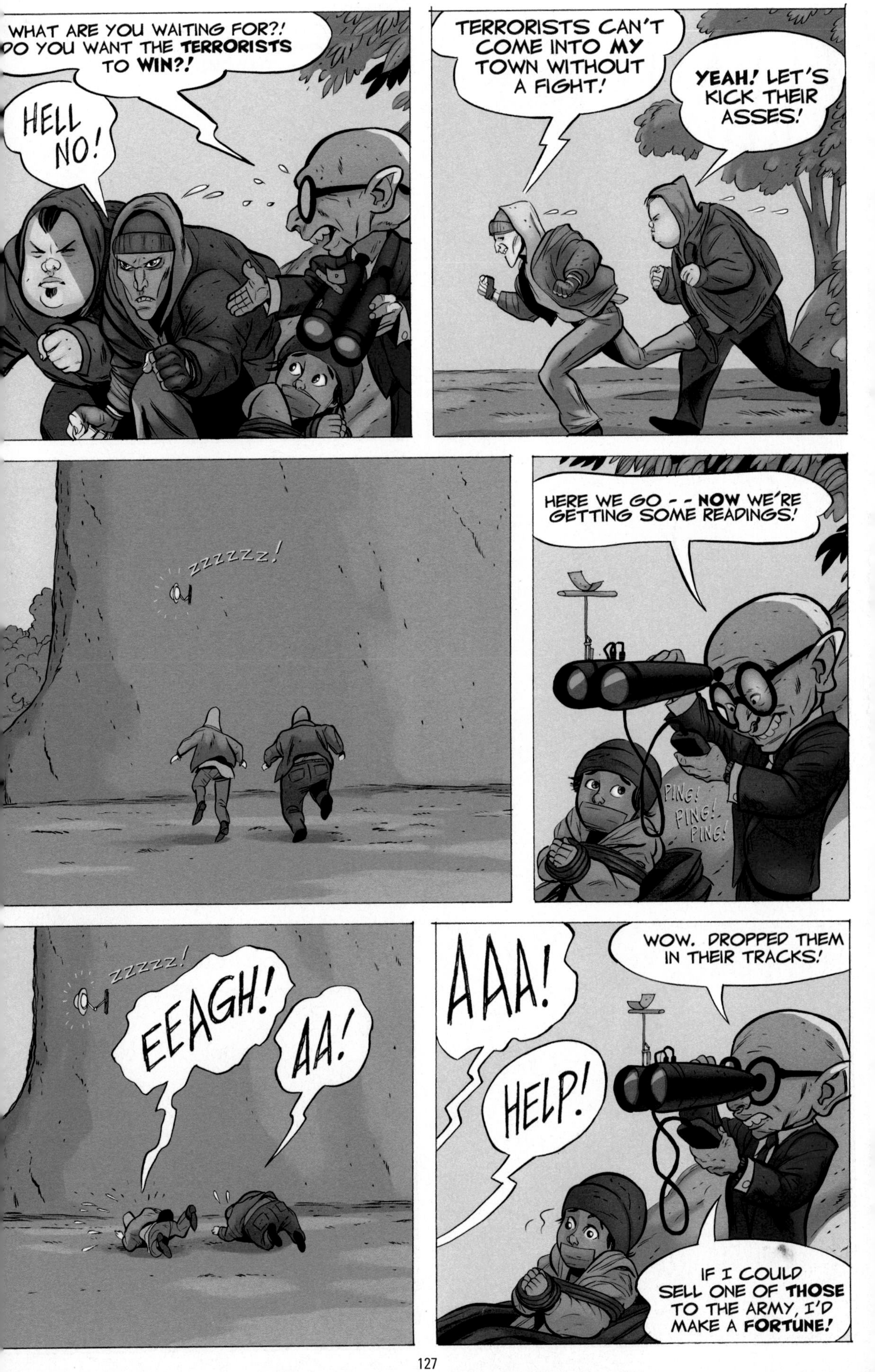
WHAT ARE YOU WAITING FOR?! DO YOU WANT THE **TERRORISTS** TO **WIN**?!
HELL NO!
TERRORISTS CAN'T COME INTO **MY** TOWN WITHOUT A FIGHT!
**YEAH!** LET'S KICK THEIR ASSES!
ZZZZZZ!
HERE WE GO - - **NOW** WE'RE GETTING SOME READINGS!
PING! PING! PING!
ZZZZZ!
EEAGH!
AA!
AAA!
HELP!
WOW. DROPPED THEM IN THEIR TRACKS!
IF I COULD SELL ONE OF **THOSE** TO THE ARMY, I'D MAKE A **FORTUNE!**

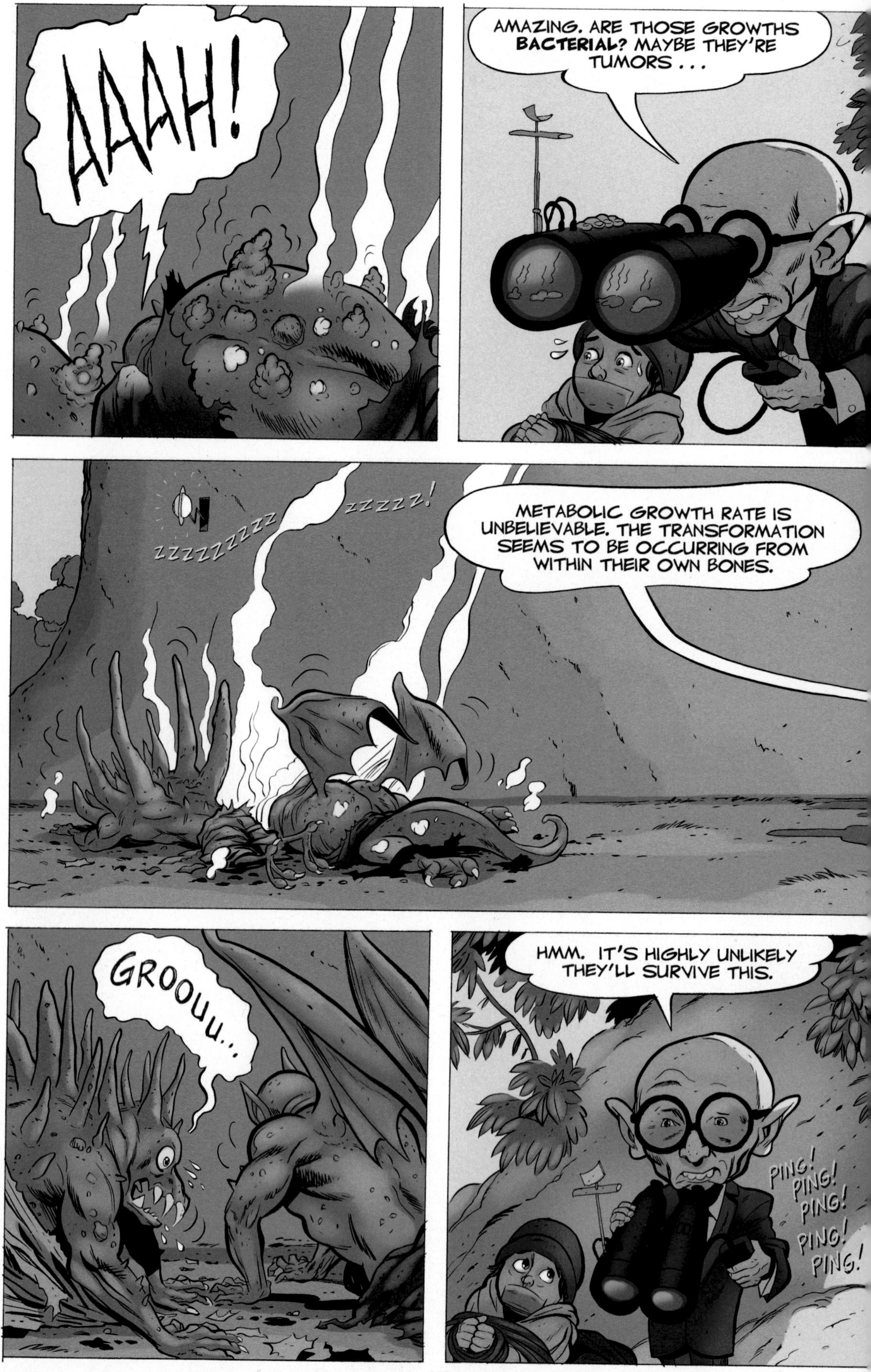
AAAH!
AMAZING. ARE THOSE GROWTHS BACTERIAL? MAYBE THEY'RE TUMORS . . .
ZZZZZZZZZZ
ZZZZZ!
METABOLIC GROWTH RATE IS UNBELIEVABLE. THE TRANSFORMATION SEEMS TO BE OCCURRING FROM WITHIN THEIR OWN BONES.
GROOUU...
HMM. IT'S HIGHLY UNLIKELY THEY'LL SURVIVE THIS.
PING! PING! PING! PING! PING!

RRRR!

NOW SEE HERE! DON'T YOU LOOK AT ME LIKE THAT! YOU WORK FOR ME!

MM. MM!

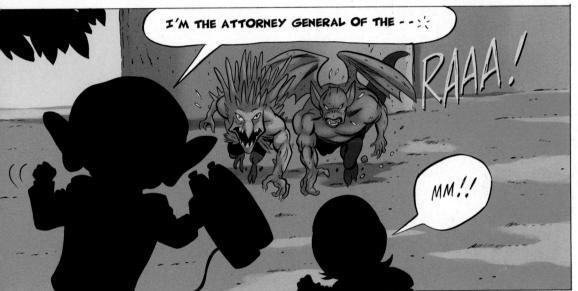

I'M THE ATTORNEY GENERAL OF THE - - ✳

RAAA!

MM!!

QUICK, BILLY! SAY YOUR MAGIC WORD - - WHY WON'T THIS BLASTED TAPE COME OFF?!

ACK! TOO LATE! EAT THE BOY!

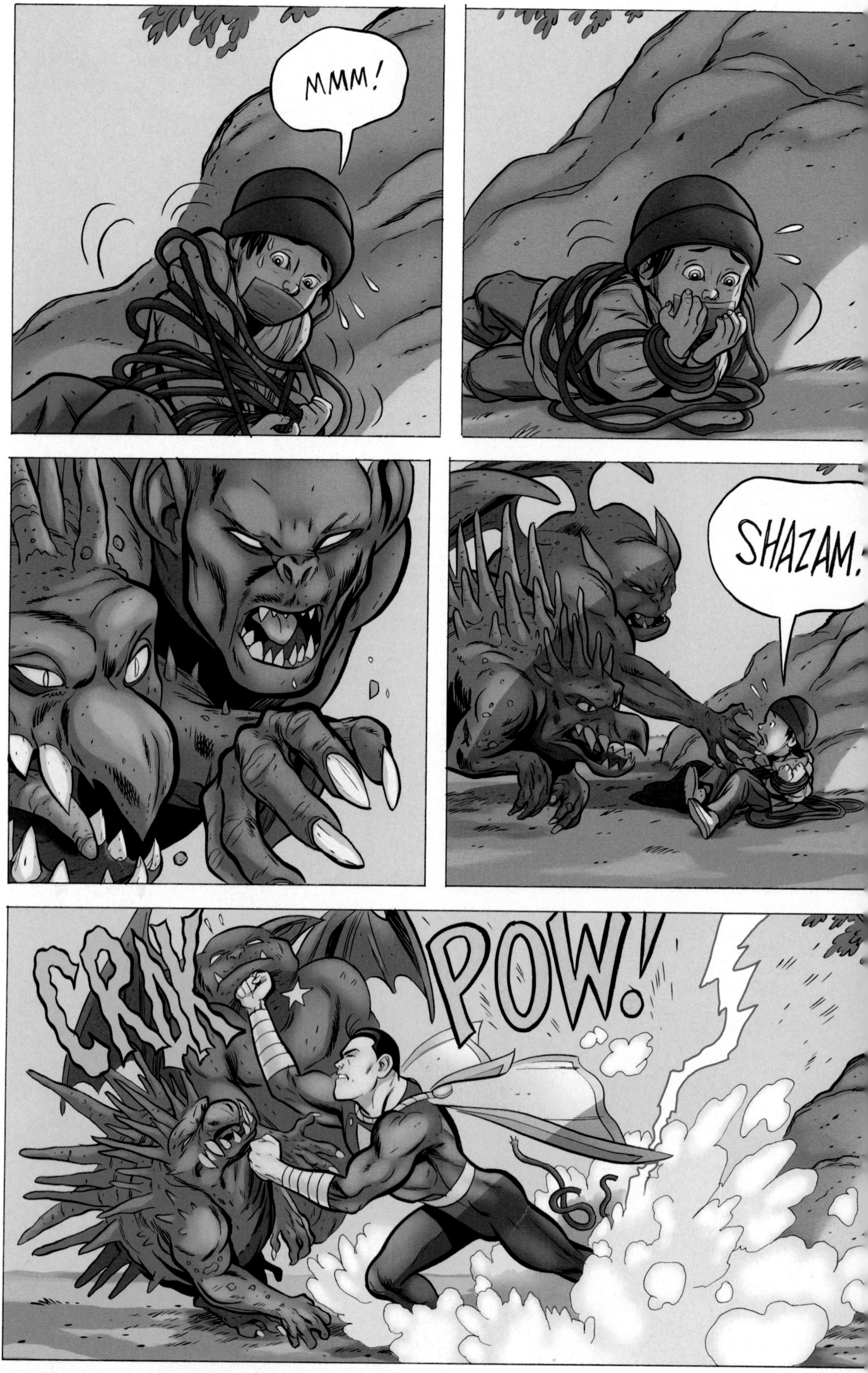
MMM!
SHAZAM.
CRAK
POW!

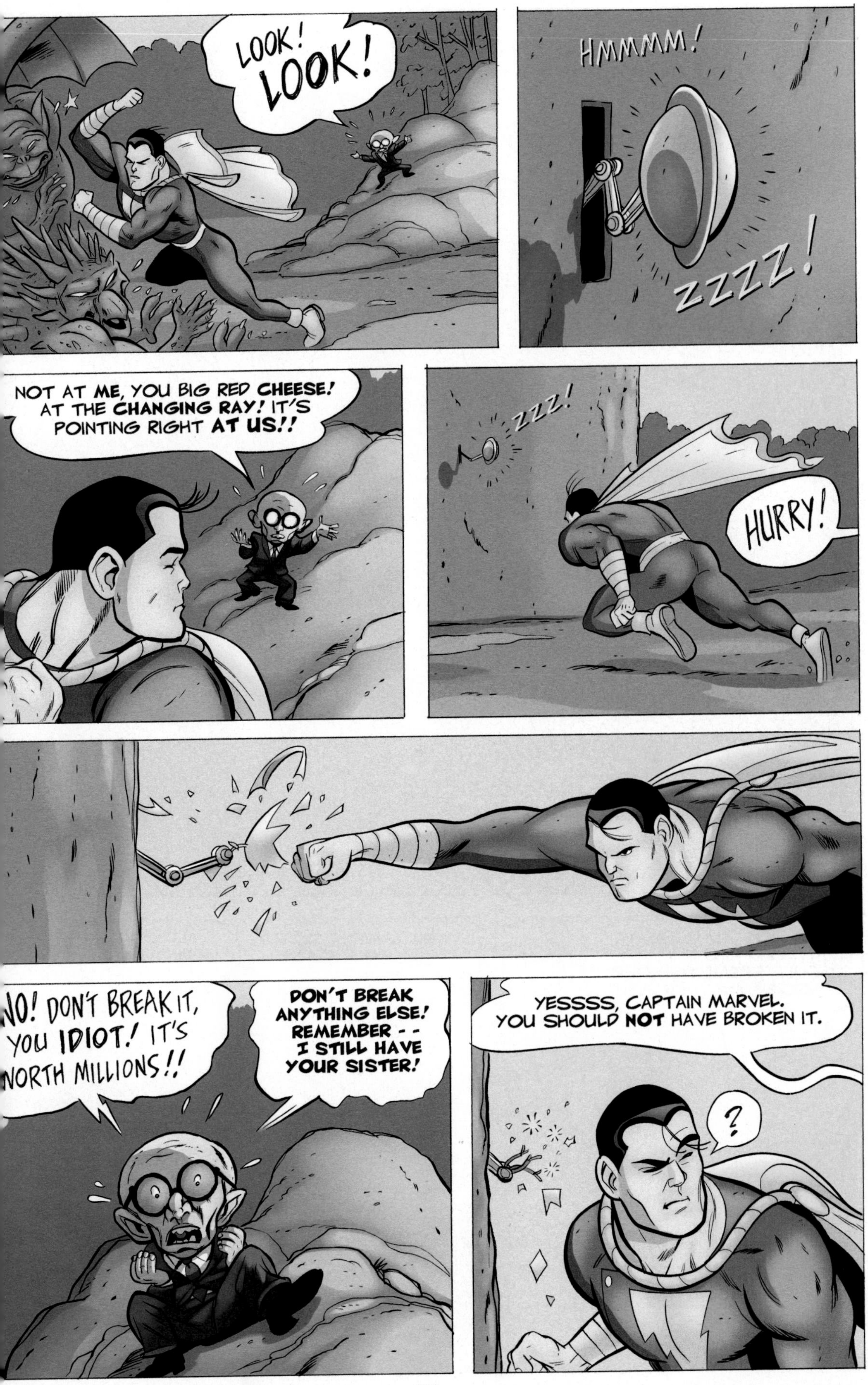
LOOK! LOOK!
HMMMM!
ZZZZ!
NOT AT ME, YOU BIG RED CHEESE! AT THE CHANGING RAY! IT'S POINTING RIGHT AT US!!
ZZZ!
HURRY!
NO! DON'T BREAK IT, YOU IDIOT! IT'S WORTH MILLIONS!!
DON'T BREAK ANYTHING ELSE! REMEMBER - - I STILL HAVE YOUR SISTER!
YESSSS, CAPTAIN MARVEL. YOU SHOULD NOT HAVE BROKEN IT.
?

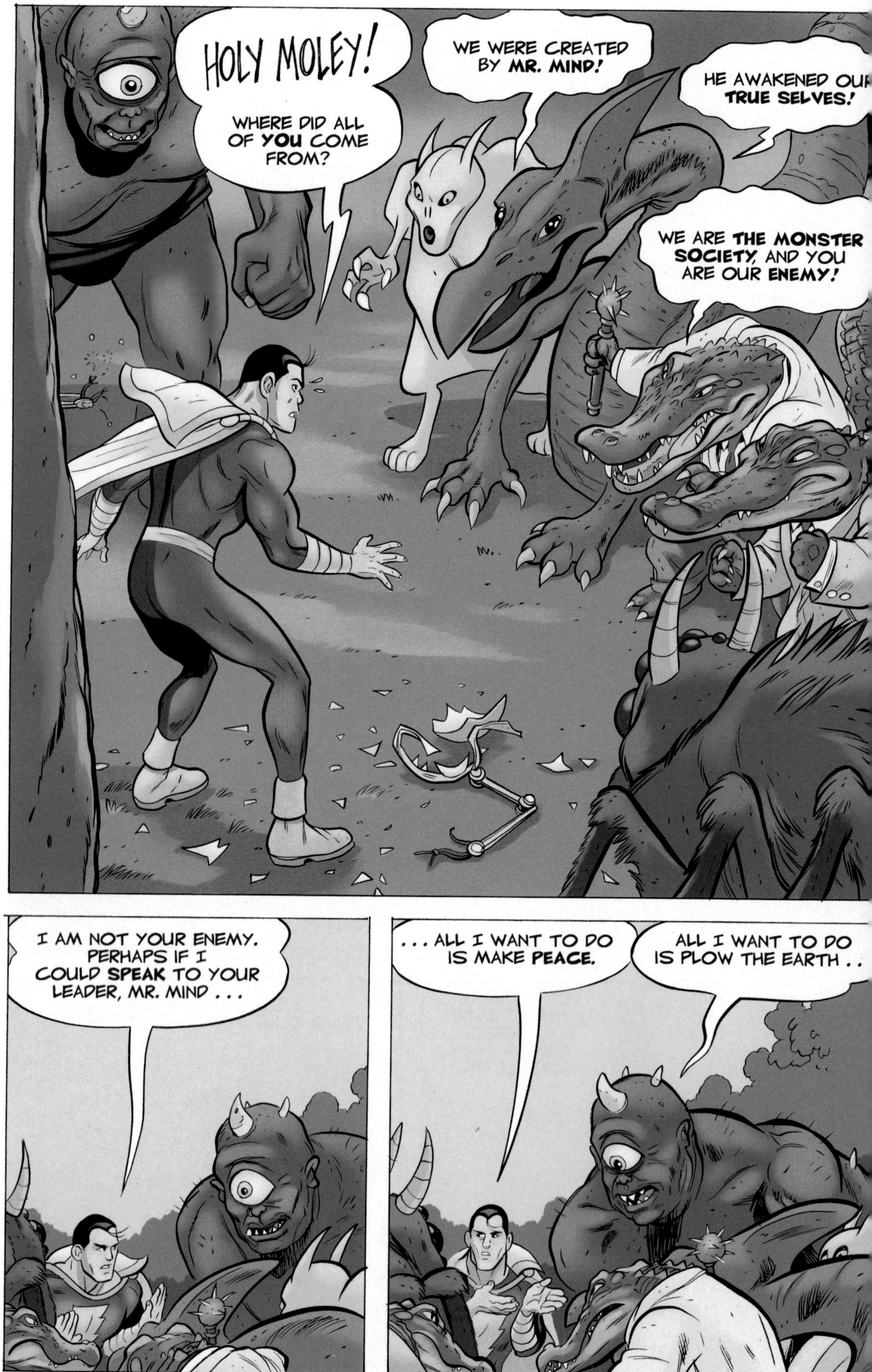

HOLY MOLEY!
WHERE DID ALL OF YOU COME FROM?
WE WERE CREATED BY MR. MIND!
HE AWAKENED OUR TRUE SELVES!
WE ARE THE MONSTER SOCIETY, AND YOU ARE OUR ENEMY!
I AM NOT YOUR ENEMY. PERHAPS IF I COULD SPEAK TO YOUR LEADER, MR. MIND . . .
. . . ALL I WANT TO DO IS MAKE PEACE.
ALL I WANT TO DO IS PLOW THE EARTH . .

133

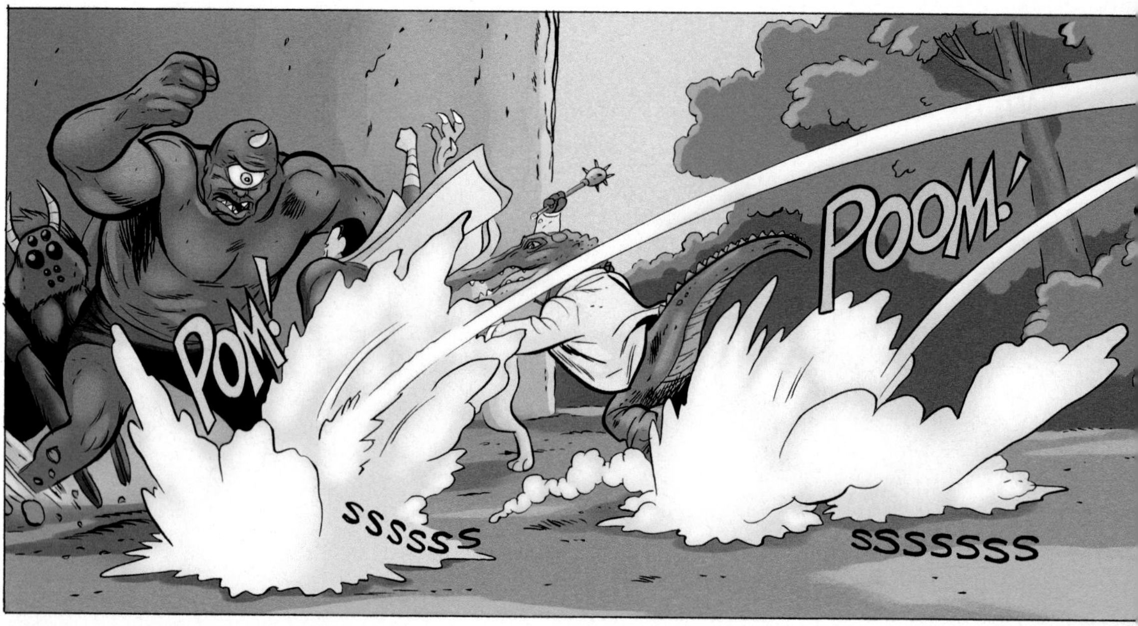
POM!
POOM!
SSSSSS
SSSSSSS

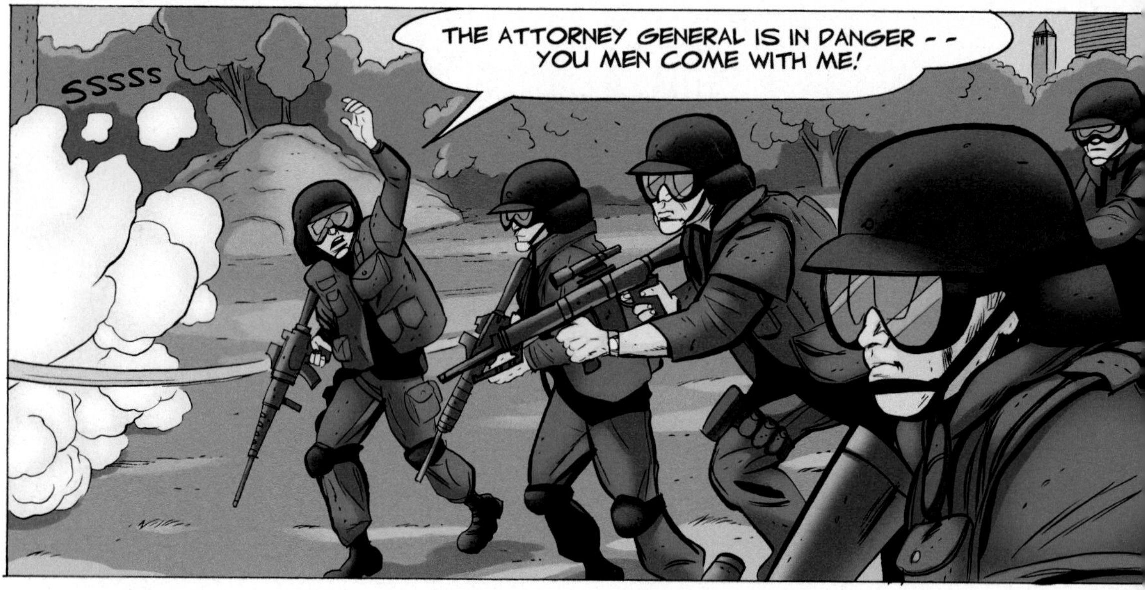
THE ATTORNEY GENERAL IS IN DANGER - - YOU MEN COME WITH ME!
SSSSS

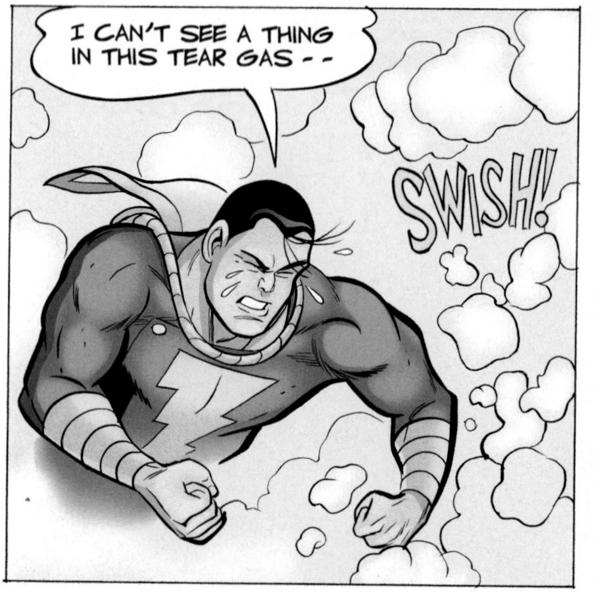
I CAN'T SEE A THING IN THIS TEAR GAS - -
SWISH!

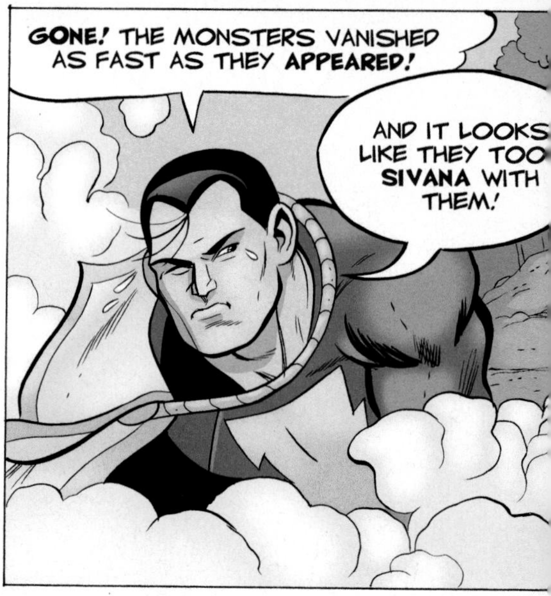
GONE! THE MONSTERS VANISHED AS FAST AS THEY APPEARED!
AND IT LOOKS LIKE THEY TOO SIVANA WITH THEM!

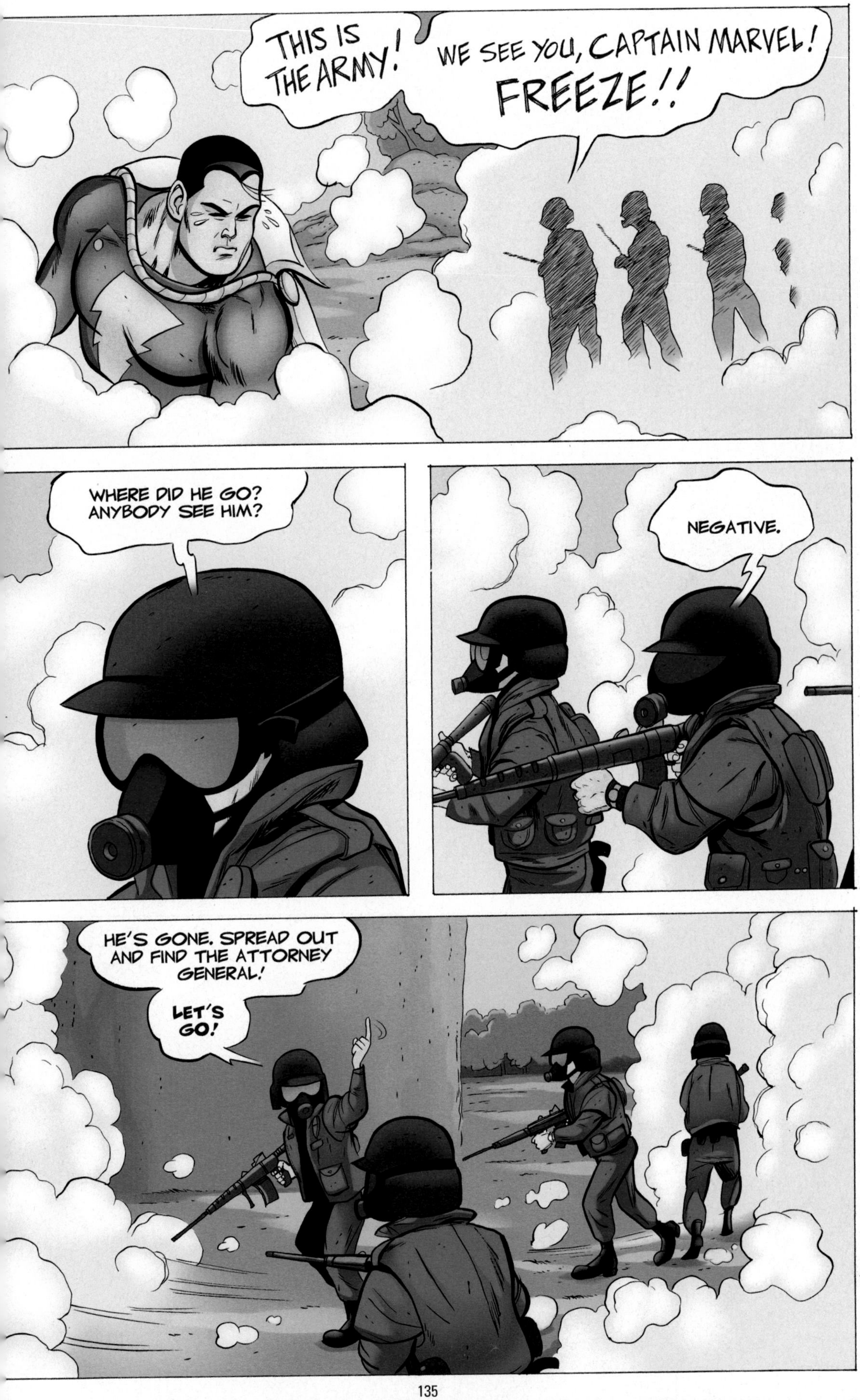
THIS IS THE ARMY!
WE SEE YOU, CAPTAIN MARVEL! FREEZE!!
WHERE DID HE GO? ANYBODY SEE HIM?
NEGATIVE.
HE'S GONE. SPREAD OUT AND FIND THE ATTORNEY GENERAL!
LET'S GO!

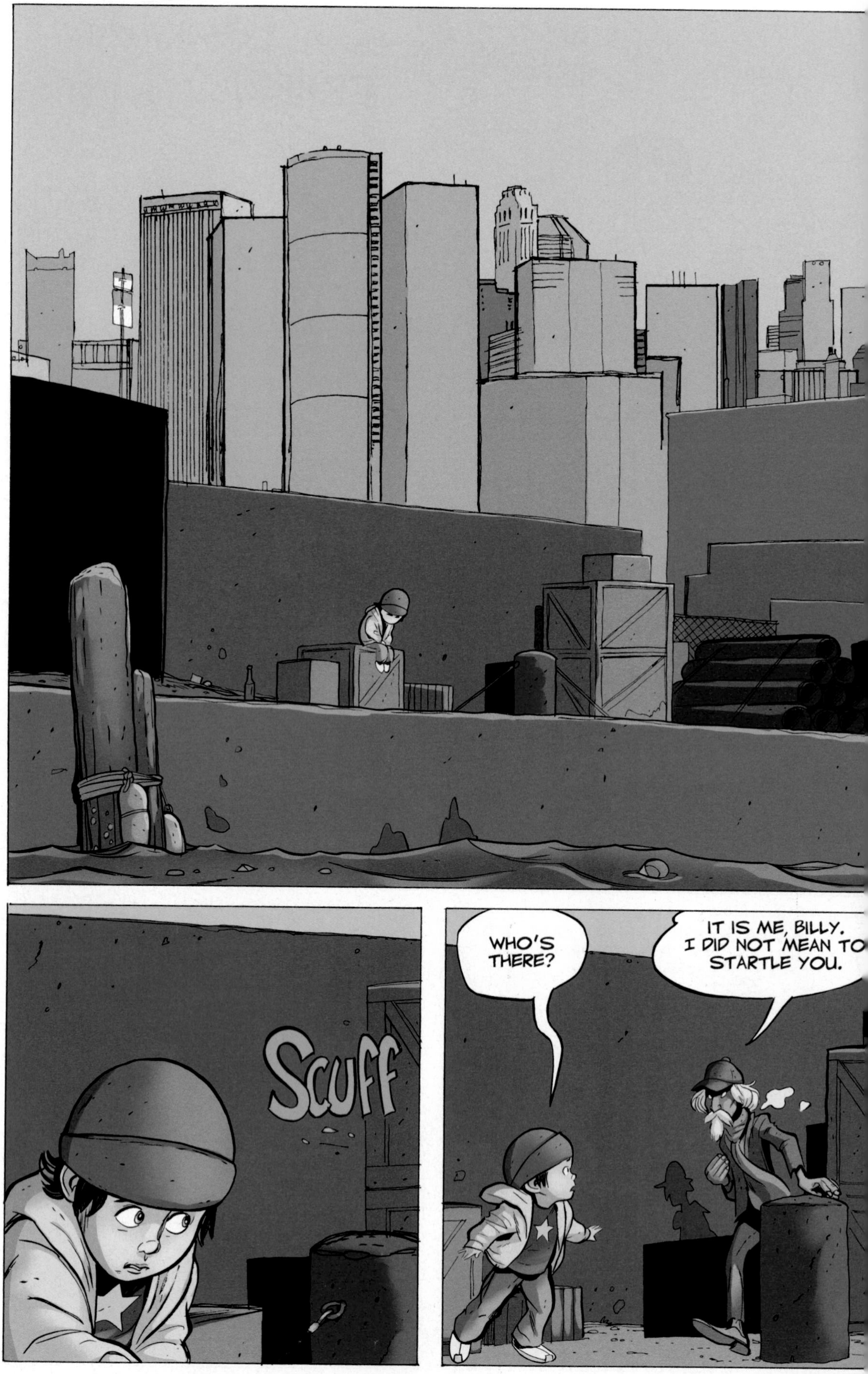
SCUFF
WHO'S THERE?
IT IS ME, BILLY. I DID NOT MEAN TO STARTLE YOU.

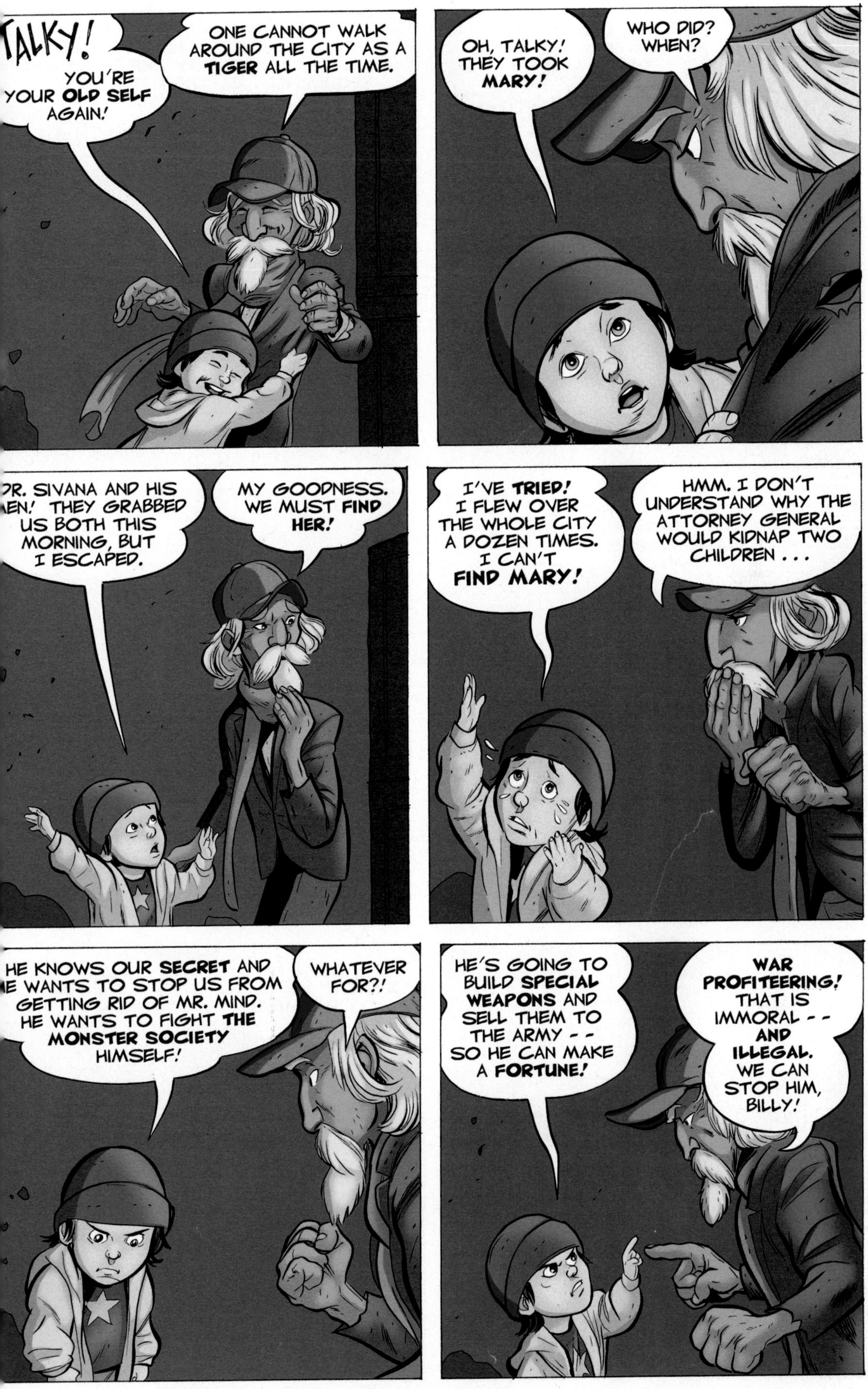
TALKY!
YOU'RE YOUR OLD SELF AGAIN!
ONE CANNOT WALK AROUND THE CITY AS A TIGER ALL THE TIME.
OH, TALKY! THEY TOOK MARY!
WHO DID? WHEN?
DR. SIVANA AND HIS MEN! THEY GRABBED US BOTH THIS MORNING, BUT I ESCAPED.
MY GOODNESS. WE MUST FIND HER!
I'VE TRIED! I FLEW OVER THE WHOLE CITY A DOZEN TIMES. I CAN'T FIND MARY!
HMM. I DON'T UNDERSTAND WHY THE ATTORNEY GENERAL WOULD KIDNAP TWO CHILDREN . . .
HE KNOWS OUR SECRET AND HE WANTS TO STOP US FROM GETTING RID OF MR. MIND. HE WANTS TO FIGHT THE MONSTER SOCIETY HIMSELF!
WHATEVER FOR?!
HE'S GOING TO BUILD SPECIAL WEAPONS AND SELL THEM TO THE ARMY - - SO HE CAN MAKE A FORTUNE!
WAR PROFITEERING! THAT IS IMMORAL - - AND ILLEGAL. WE CAN STOP HIM, BILLY!

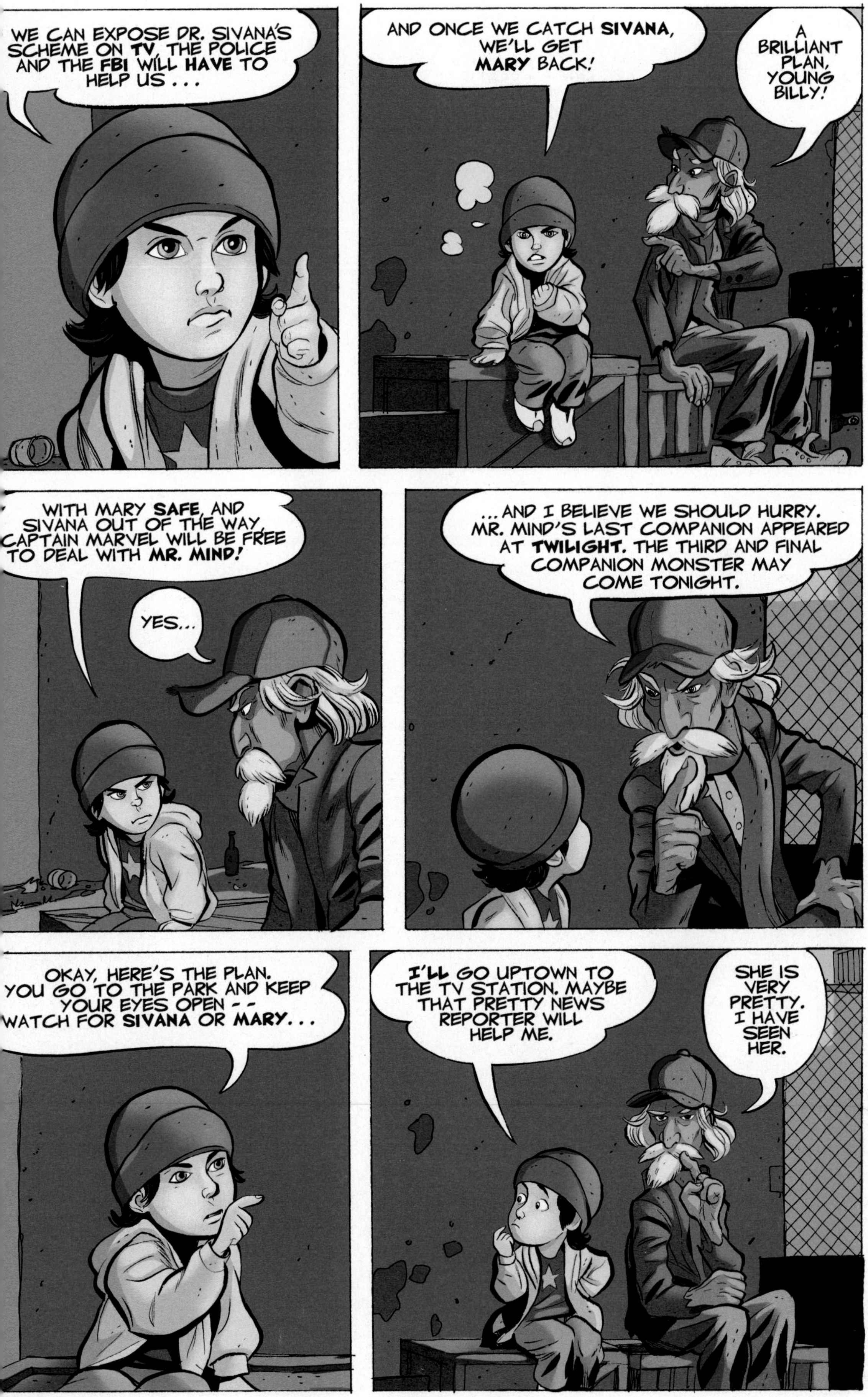
WE CAN EXPOSE DR. SIVANA'S SCHEME ON TV, THE POLICE AND THE FBI WILL HAVE TO HELP US...
AND ONCE WE CATCH SIVANA, WE'LL GET MARY BACK!
A BRILLIANT PLAN, YOUNG BILLY!
WITH MARY SAFE, AND SIVANA OUT OF THE WAY, CAPTAIN MARVEL WILL BE FREE TO DEAL WITH MR. MIND!
YES...
...AND I BELIEVE WE SHOULD HURRY. MR. MIND'S LAST COMPANION APPEARED AT TWILIGHT. THE THIRD AND FINAL COMPANION MONSTER MAY COME TONIGHT.
OKAY, HERE'S THE PLAN. YOU GO TO THE PARK AND KEEP YOUR EYES OPEN -- WATCH FOR SIVANA OR MARY...
I'LL GO UPTOWN TO THE TV STATION. MAYBE THAT PRETTY NEWS REPORTER WILL HELP ME.
SHE IS VERY PRETTY. I HAVE SEEN HER.

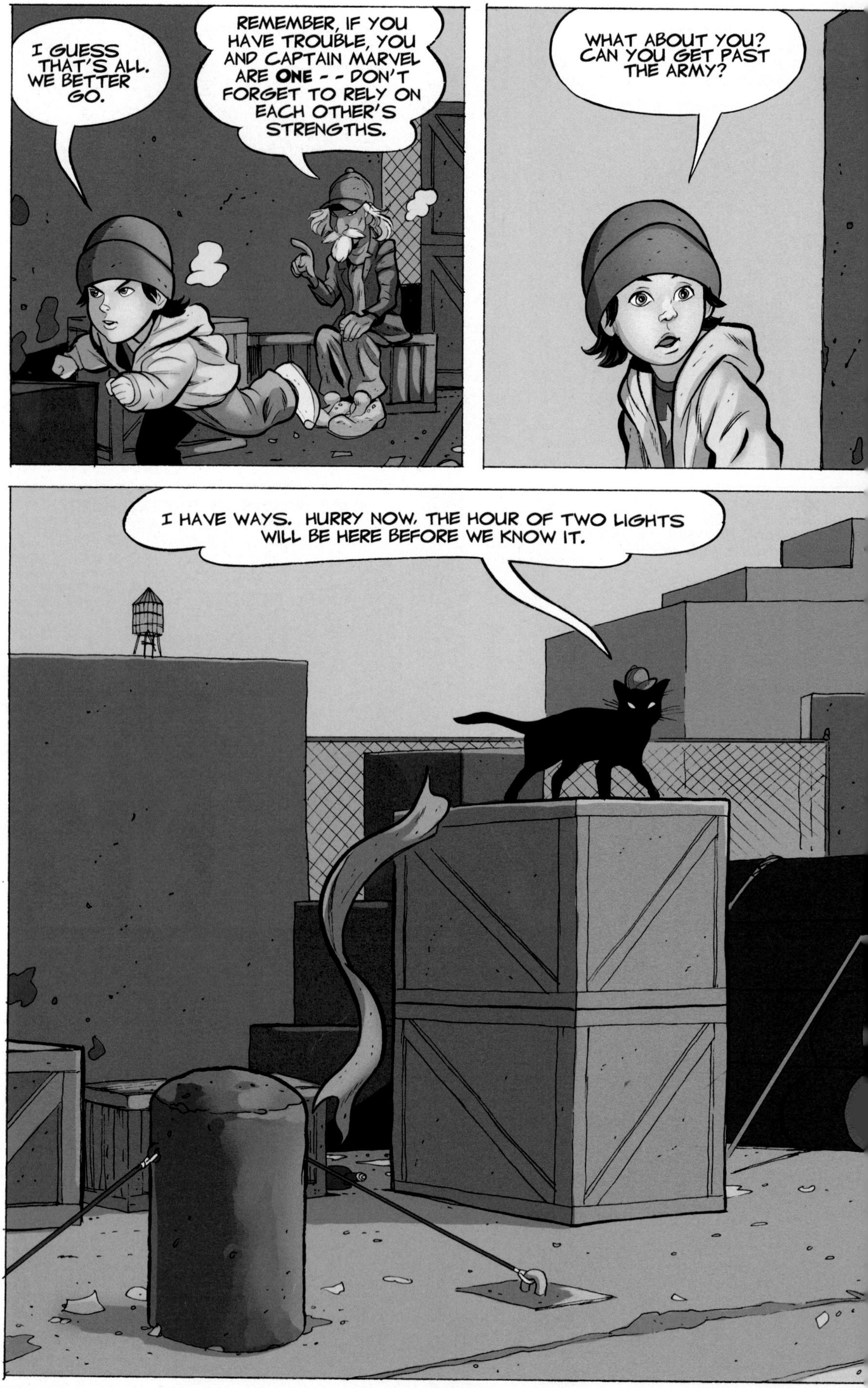
I GUESS THAT'S ALL. WE BETTER GO.
REMEMBER, IF YOU HAVE TROUBLE, YOU AND CAPTAIN MARVEL ARE ONE - - DON'T FORGET TO RELY ON EACH OTHER'S STRENGTHS.
WHAT ABOUT YOU? CAN YOU GET PAST THE ARMY?
I HAVE WAYS. HURRY NOW, THE HOUR OF TWO LIGHTS WILL BE HERE BEFORE WE KNOW IT.

143

145

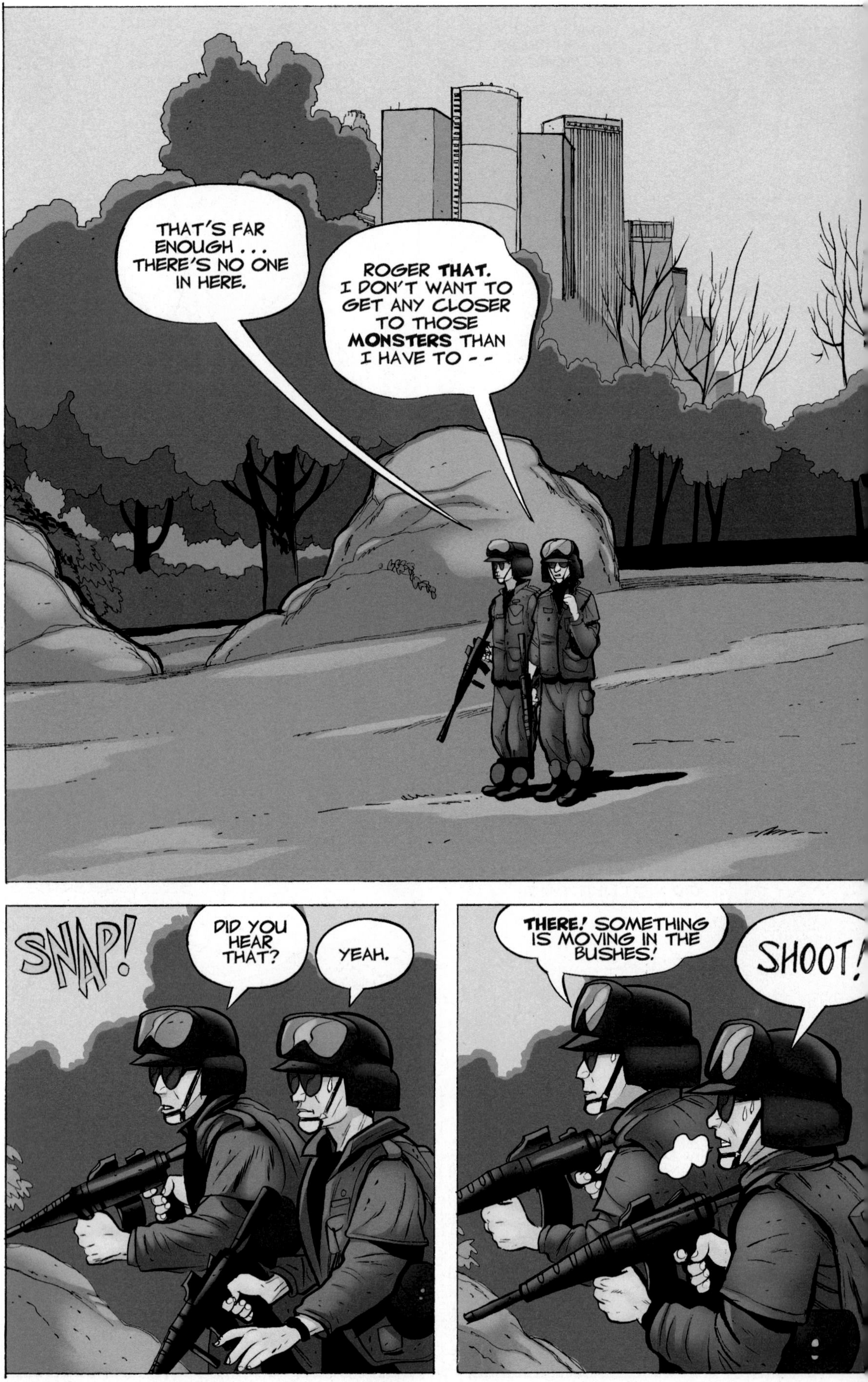

THAT'S FAR ENOUGH . . . THERE'S NO ONE IN HERE.
ROGER **THAT.** I DON'T WANT TO GET ANY CLOSER TO THOSE **MONSTERS** THAN I HAVE TO - -
SNAP!
DID YOU HEAR THAT?
YEAH.
**THERE!** SOMETHING IS MOVING IN THE BUSHES!
SHOOT!

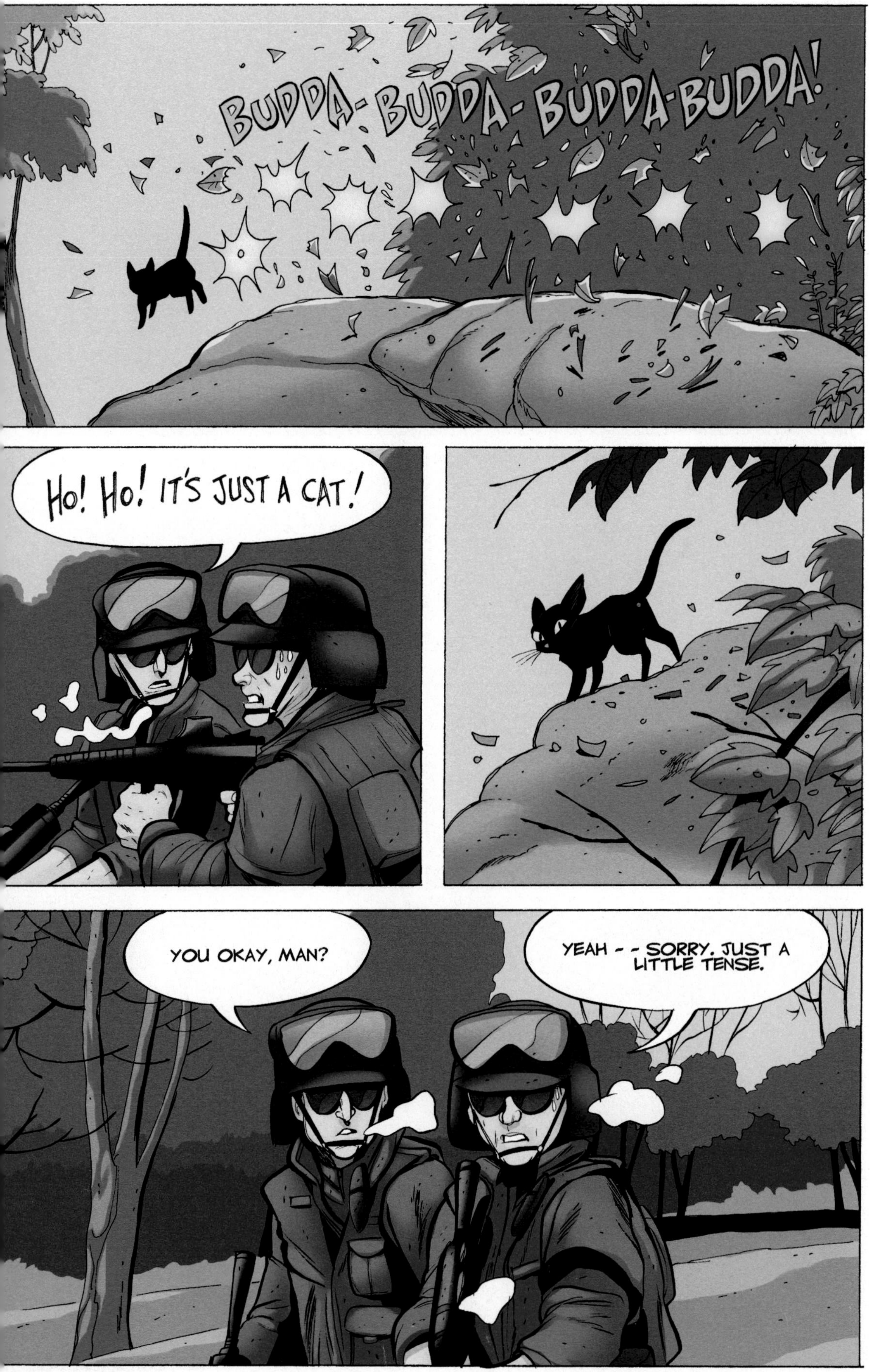
BUDDA-BUDDA-BUDDA-BUDDA!
HO! HO! IT'S JUST A CAT!
YOU OKAY, MAN?
YEAH -- SORRY. JUST A LITTLE TENSE.

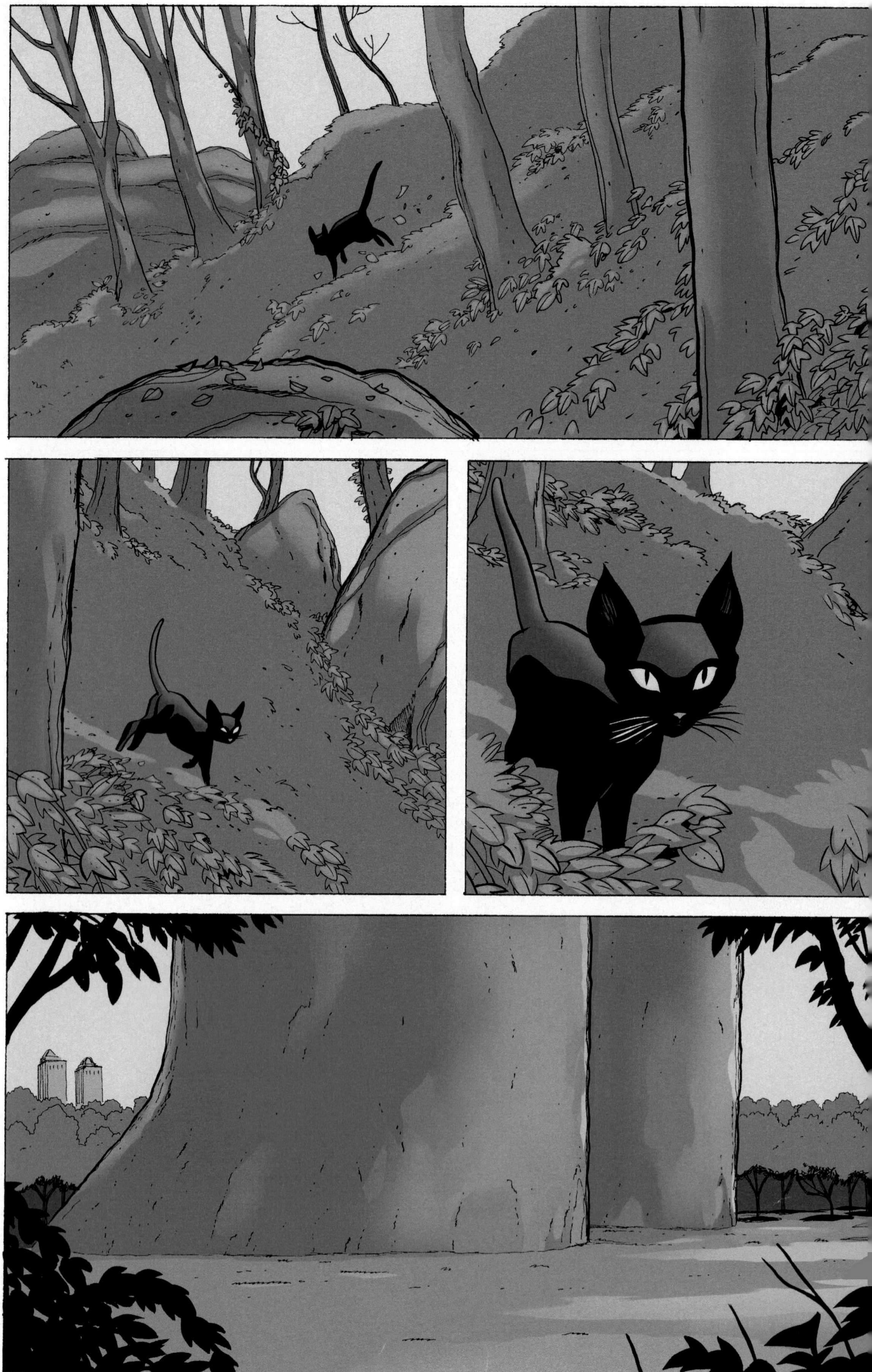

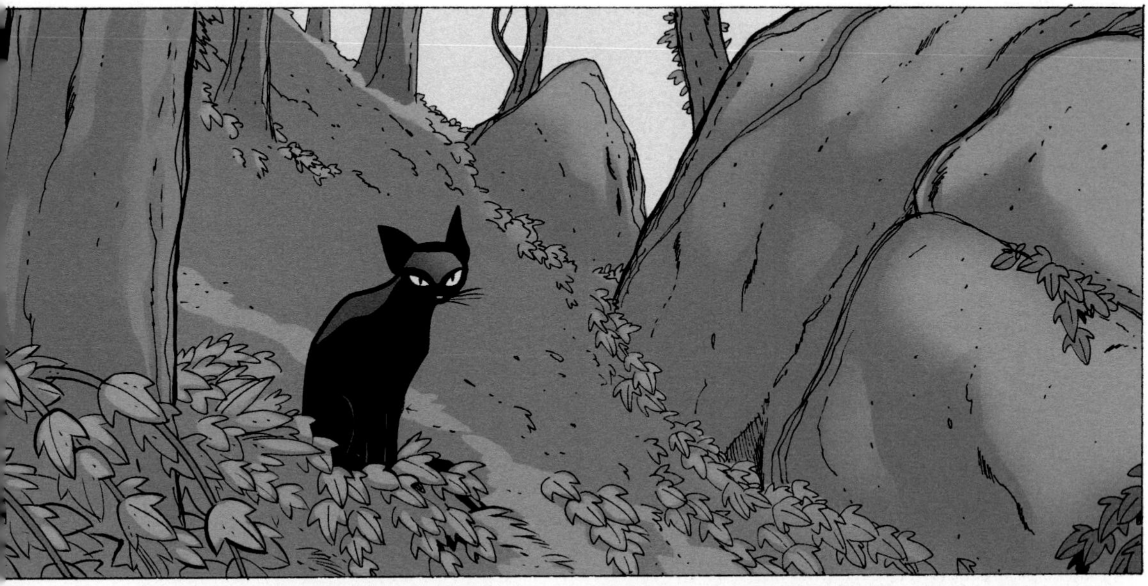

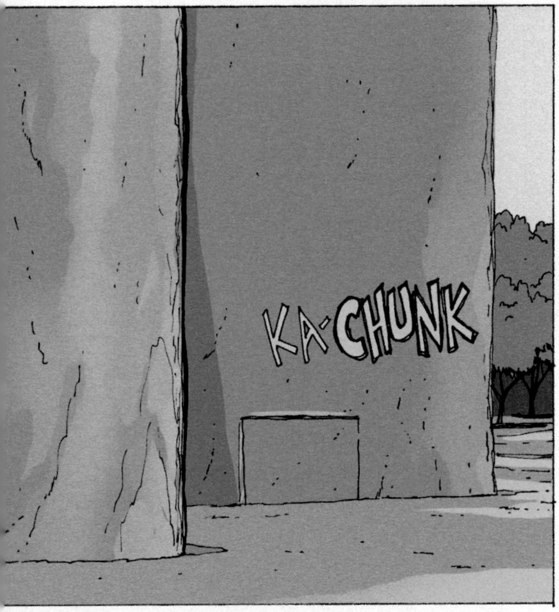
KA-CHUNK

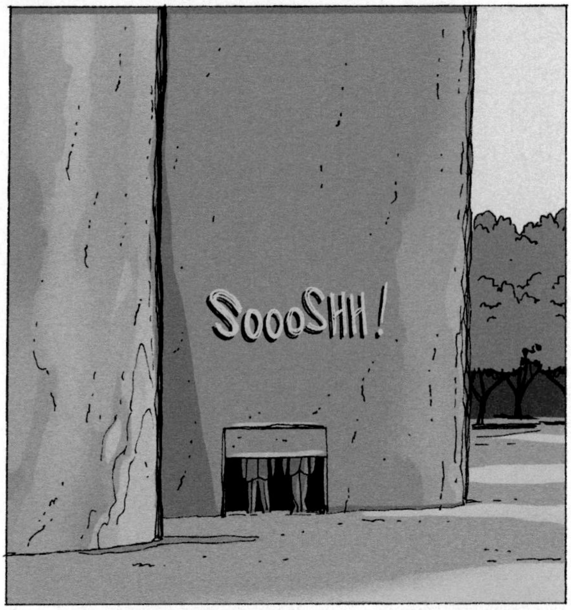
SooooSHH!

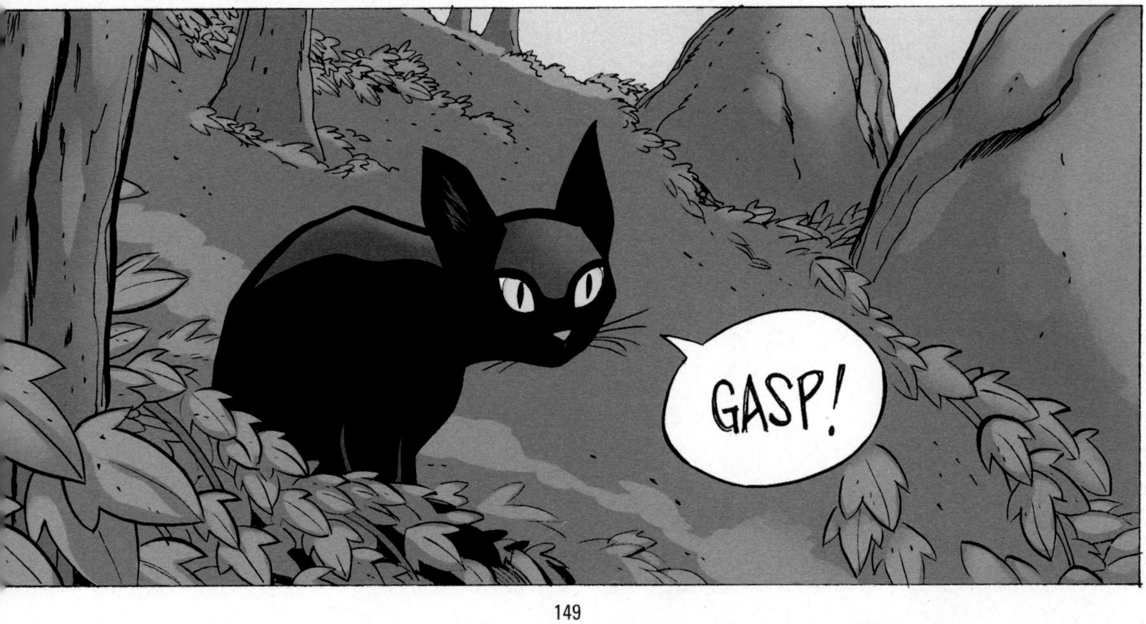
GASP!

THESE ARE INCREDIBLE CHARGES, CAPTAIN . . . MARVEL, IS IT?

NOT ONLY DO YOU ACCUSE ATTORNEY GENERAL SIVANA WITH WAR CRIMES, BUT WITH **KIDNAPPING** AS WELL. IS THAT RIGHT?

YES SIR, MR. MORRIS.

AMAZING. SO TELL ME WHAT YOU WANT FROM ME.

I'M HOPING SNN WILL HELP ME EXPOSE SIVANA'S **PLOT** . . .

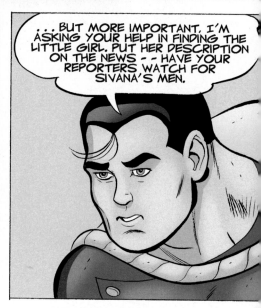

. . . BUT MORE IMPORTANT, I'M ASKING YOUR HELP IN FINDING THE LITTLE GIRL. PUT HER DESCRIPTION ON THE NEWS -- HAVE YOUR REPORTERS WATCH FOR SIVANA'S MEN.

OF COURSE WE WILL DO WHAT WE CAN TO FIND THE LITTLE GIRL . . .

BUT AS FAR AS **ACCUSING** ONE OF THE MOST POWERFUL MEN IN THE COUNTRY. . . I'M AFRAID WE'LL NEED A LITTLE MORE PROOF OF YOUR CLAIMS.

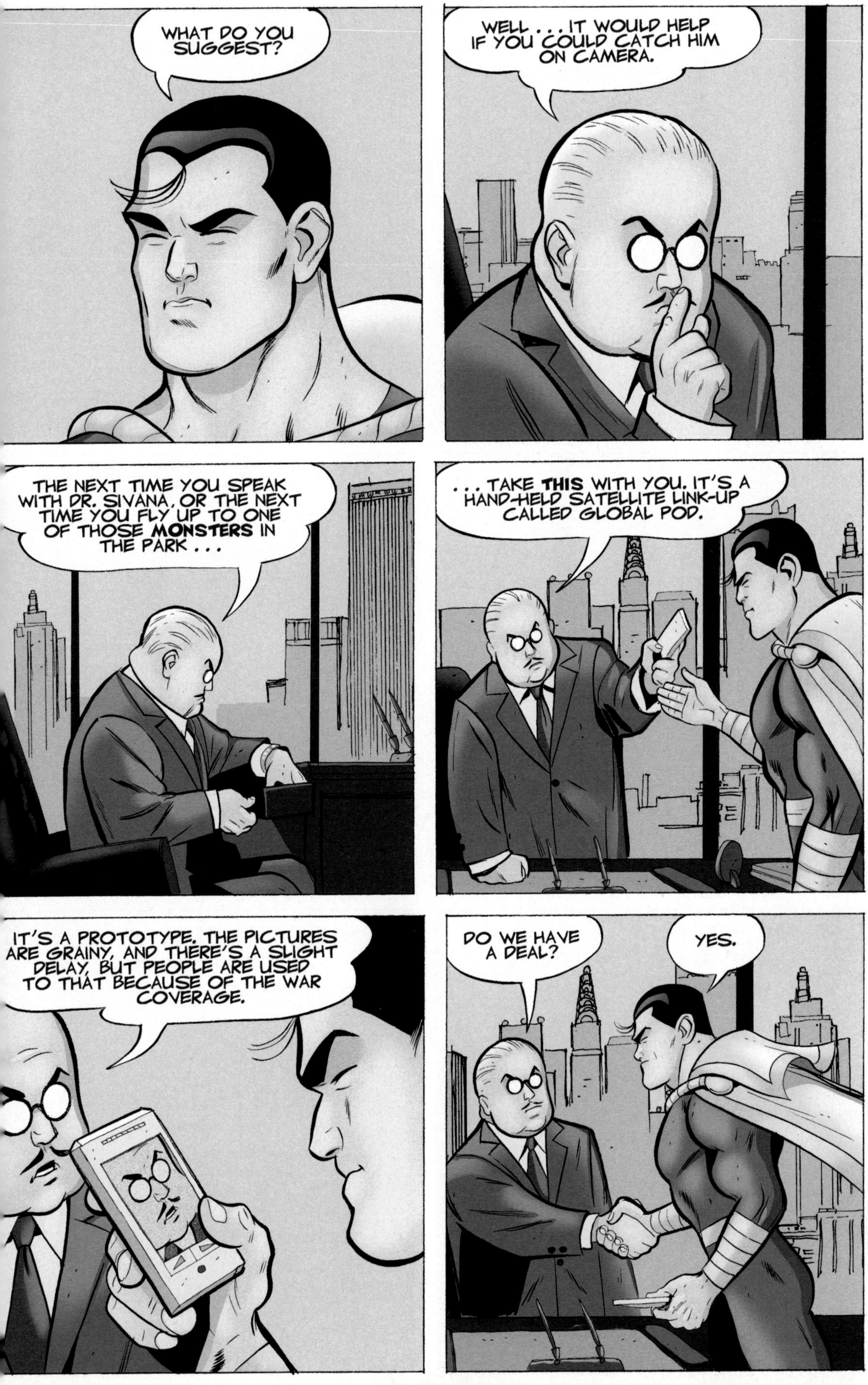
WHAT DO YOU SUGGEST?
WELL . . . IT WOULD HELP IF YOU COULD CATCH HIM ON CAMERA.
THE NEXT TIME YOU SPEAK WITH DR. SIVANA, OR THE NEXT TIME YOU FLY UP TO ONE OF THOSE MONSTERS IN THE PARK . . .
. . . TAKE THIS WITH YOU. IT'S A HAND-HELD SATELLITE LINK-UP CALLED GLOBAL POD.
IT'S A PROTOTYPE. THE PICTURES ARE GRAINY, AND THERE'S A SLIGHT DELAY, BUT PEOPLE ARE USED TO THAT BECAUSE OF THE WAR COVERAGE.
DO WE HAVE A DEAL?
YES.

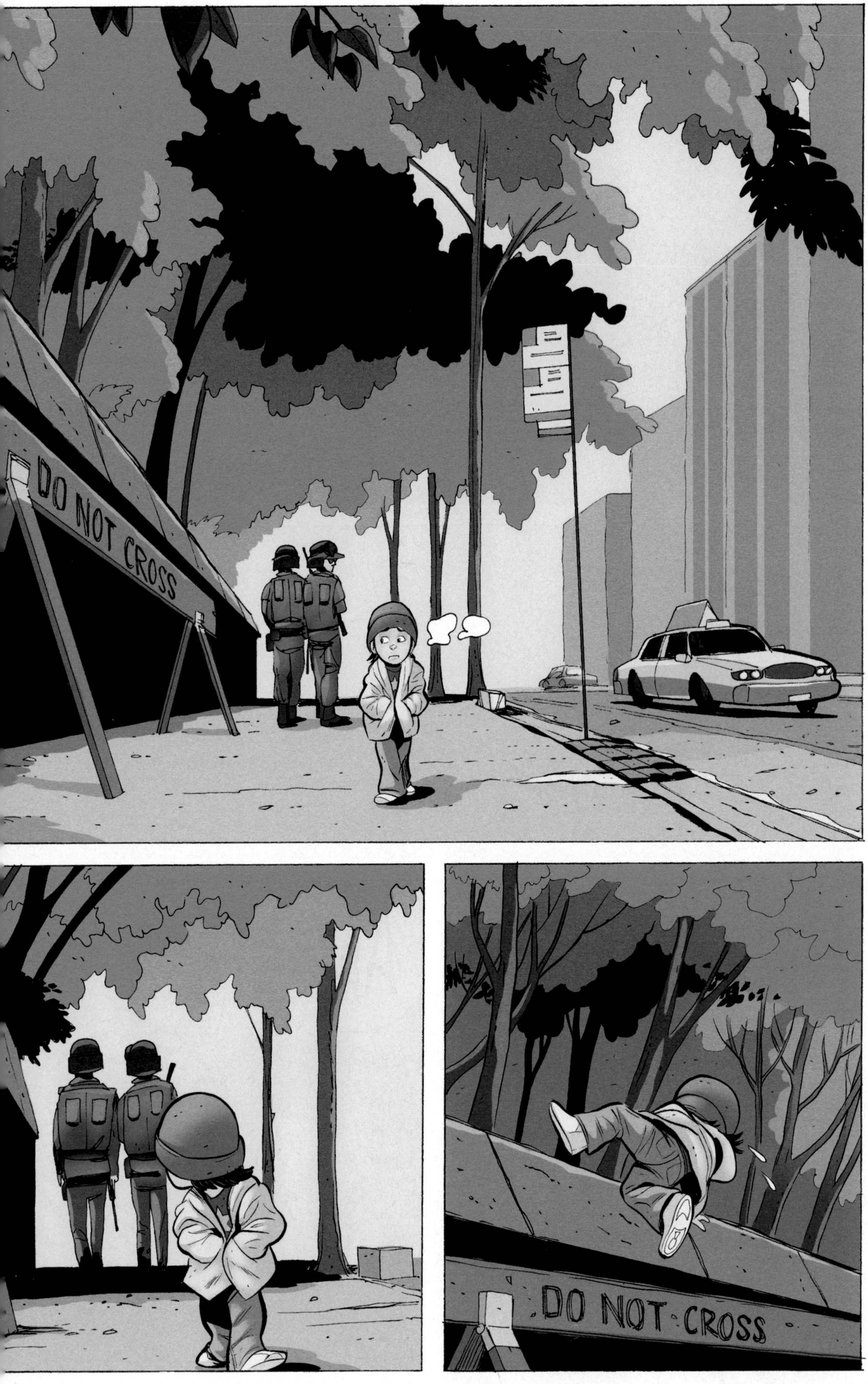
DO NOT CROSS
DO NOT CROSS

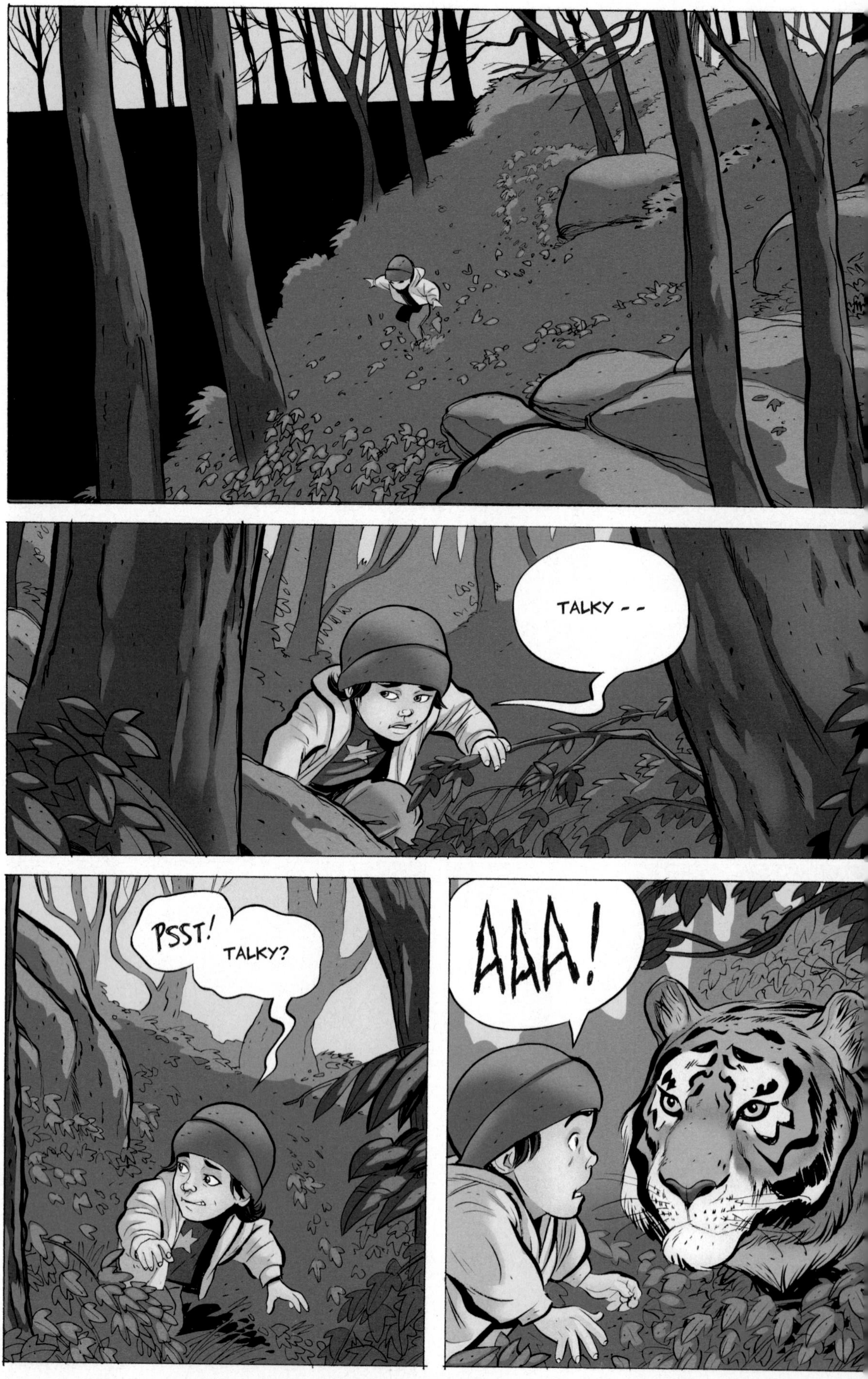
TALKY - -
PSST! TALKY?
AAA!

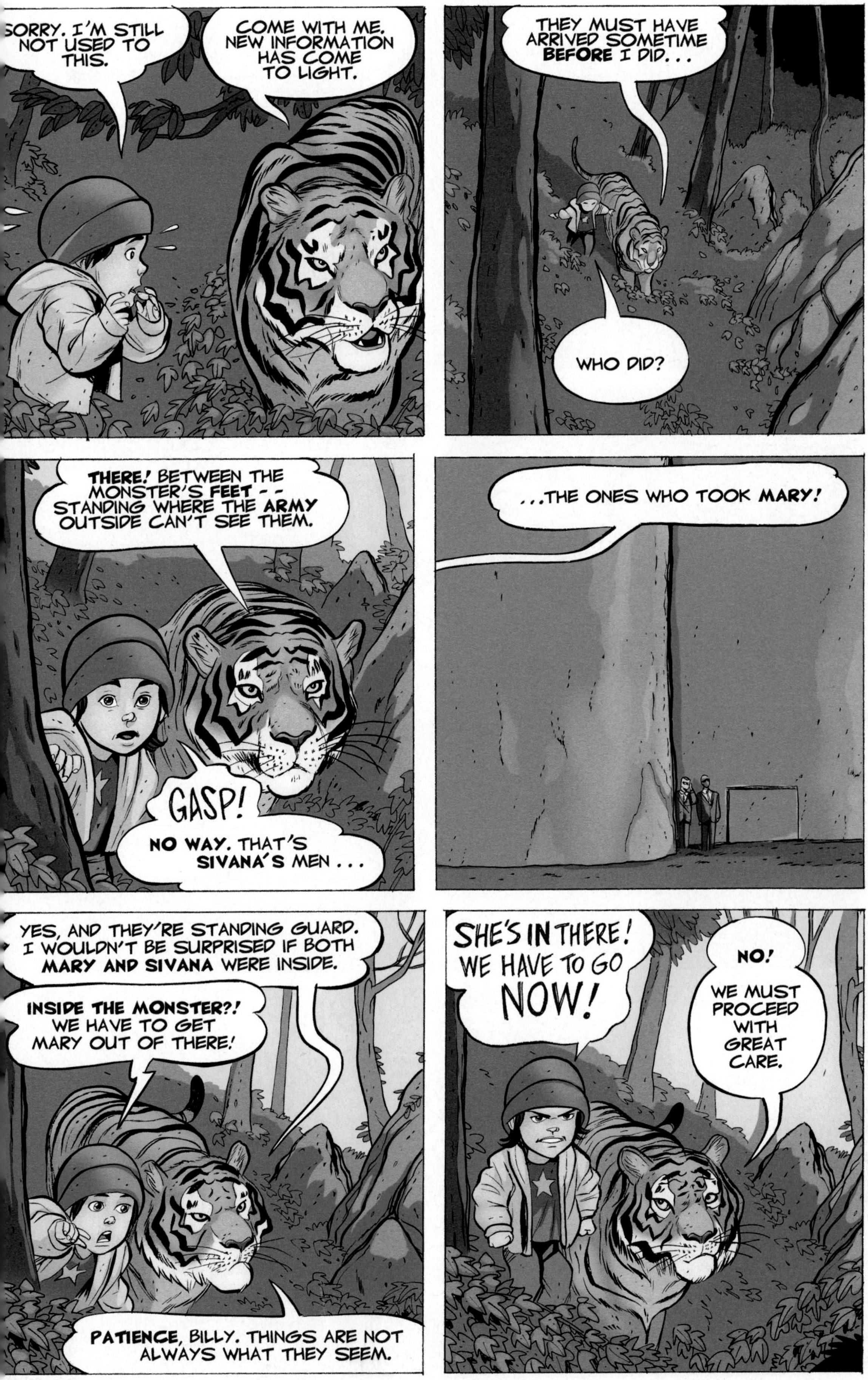

SORRY. I'M STILL NOT USED TO THIS.
COME WITH ME. NEW INFORMATION HAS COME TO LIGHT.
THEY MUST HAVE ARRIVED SOMETIME BEFORE I DID...
WHO DID?
THERE! BETWEEN THE MONSTER'S FEET-- STANDING WHERE THE ARMY OUTSIDE CAN'T SEE THEM.
GASP!
NO WAY. THAT'S SIVANA'S MEN...
...THE ONES WHO TOOK MARY!
YES, AND THEY'RE STANDING GUARD. I WOULDN'T BE SURPRISED IF BOTH MARY AND SIVANA WERE INSIDE.
INSIDE THE MONSTER?! WE HAVE TO GET MARY OUT OF THERE!
PATIENCE, BILLY. THINGS ARE NOT ALWAYS WHAT THEY SEEM.
SHE'S IN THERE! WE HAVE TO GO NOW!
NO!
WE MUST PROCEED WITH GREAT CARE.

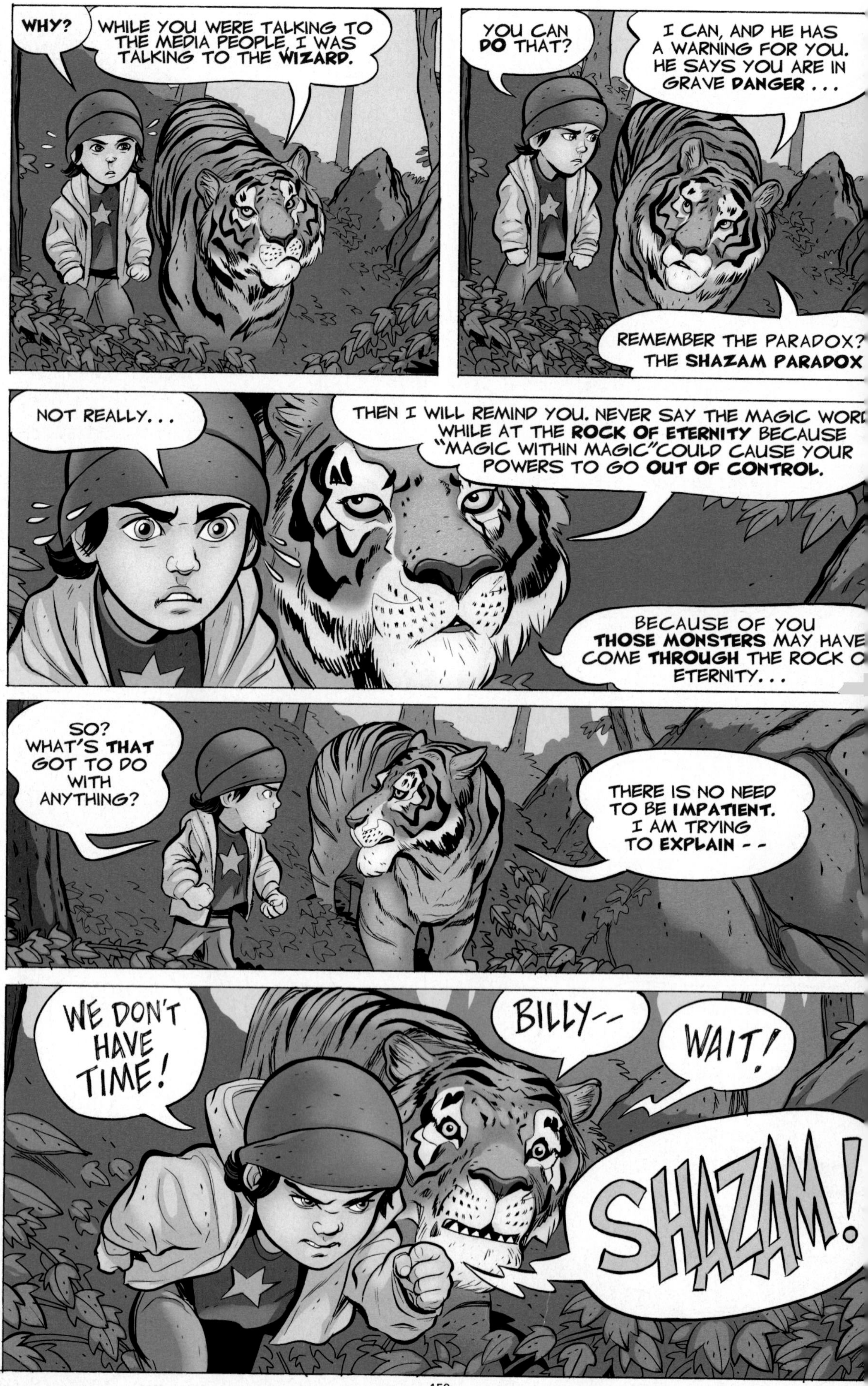
WHY?
WHILE YOU WERE TALKING TO THE MEDIA PEOPLE, I WAS TALKING TO THE WIZARD.
YOU CAN DO THAT?
I CAN, AND HE HAS A WARNING FOR YOU. HE SAYS YOU ARE IN GRAVE DANGER . . .
REMEMBER THE PARADOX? THE SHAZAM PARADOX
NOT REALLY. . .
THEN I WILL REMIND YOU. NEVER SAY THE MAGIC WORD WHILE AT THE ROCK OF ETERNITY BECAUSE "MAGIC WITHIN MAGIC" COULD CAUSE YOUR POWERS TO GO OUT OF CONTROL.
BECAUSE OF YOU THOSE MONSTERS MAY HAVE COME THROUGH THE ROCK OF ETERNITY. . .
SO? WHAT'S THAT GOT TO DO WITH ANYTHING?
THERE IS NO NEED TO BE IMPATIENT. I AM TRYING TO EXPLAIN - -
WE DON'T HAVE TIME!
BILLY- -
WAIT!
SHAZAM!

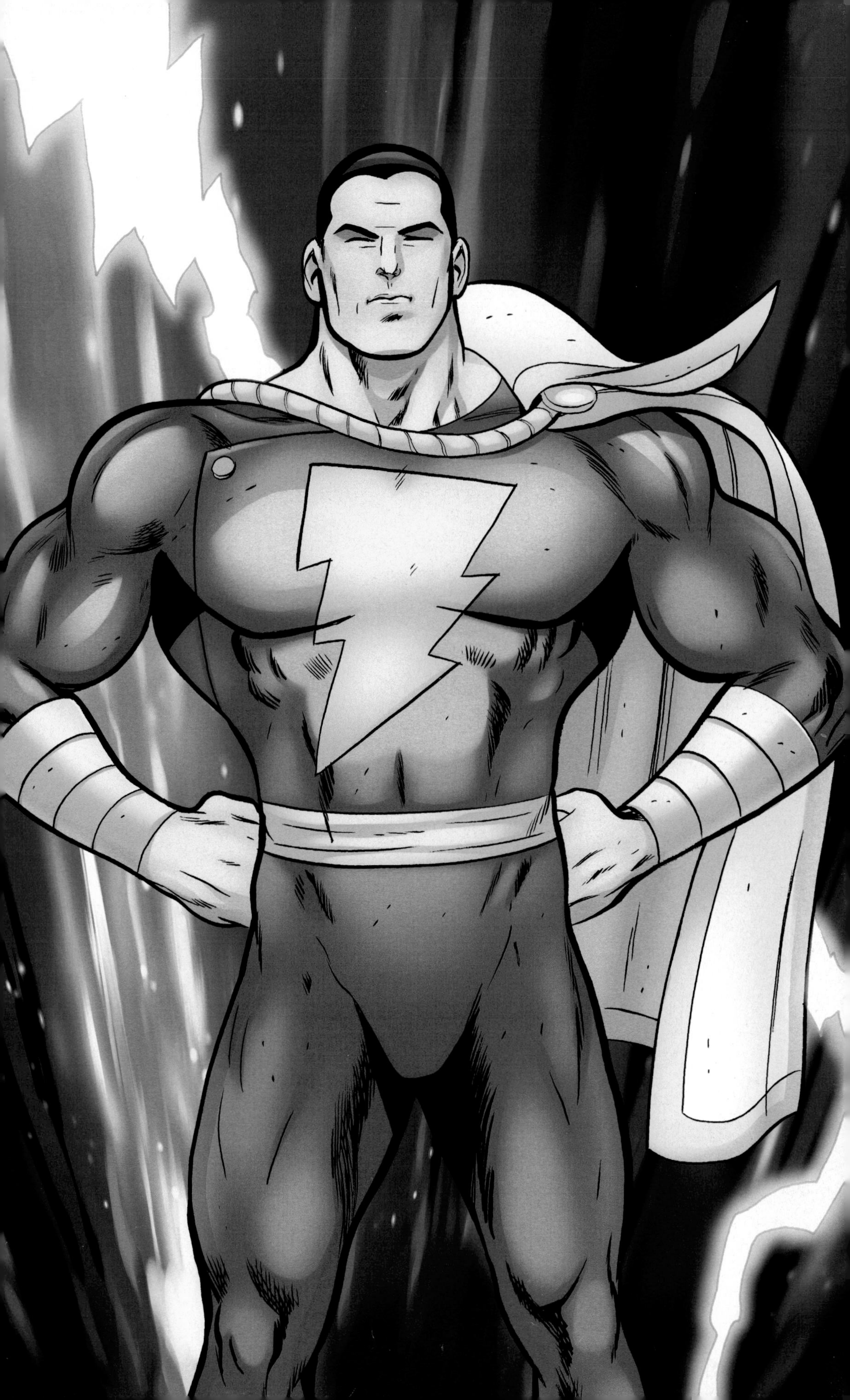

# THE MONSTER SOCIETY OF EVIL

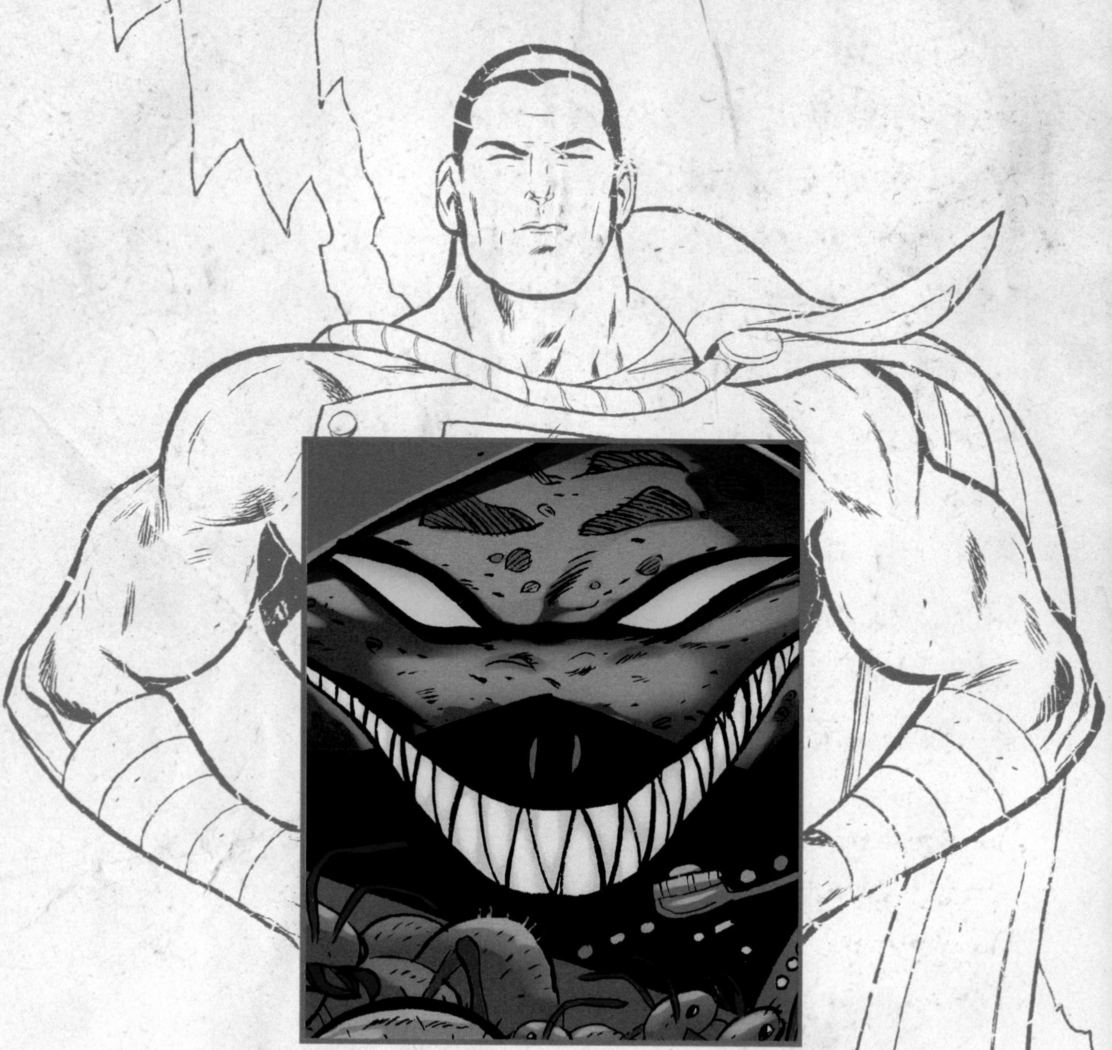

## CHAPTER 4:

# NI. NRMW NZPVH SRH NLEV!*

*THE MONSTER SOCIETY CODE

| A | B | C | D | E | F | G | H | I | J | K | L | M | N | O | P | Q | R | S | T | U | V | W | X | Y | Z |
|---|---|---|---|---|---|---|---|---|---|---|---|---|---|---|---|---|---|---|---|---|---|---|---|---|---|
| Z | Y | X | W | V | U | T | S | R | Q | P | O | N | M | L | K | J | I | H | G | F | E | D | C | B | A |

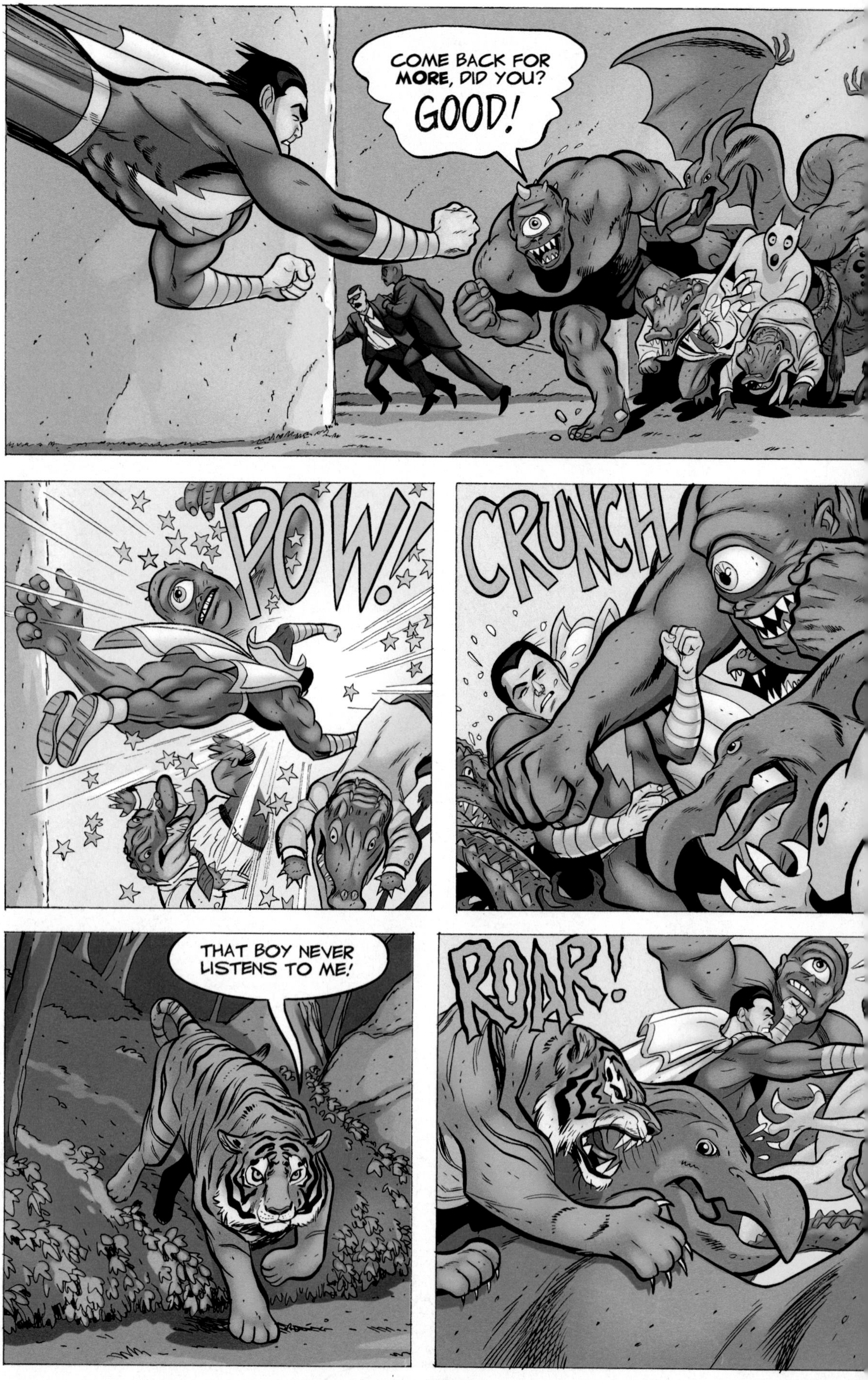
COME BACK FOR MORE, DID YOU? GOOD!
POW!
CRUNCH
THAT BOY NEVER LISTENS TO ME!
ROAR!

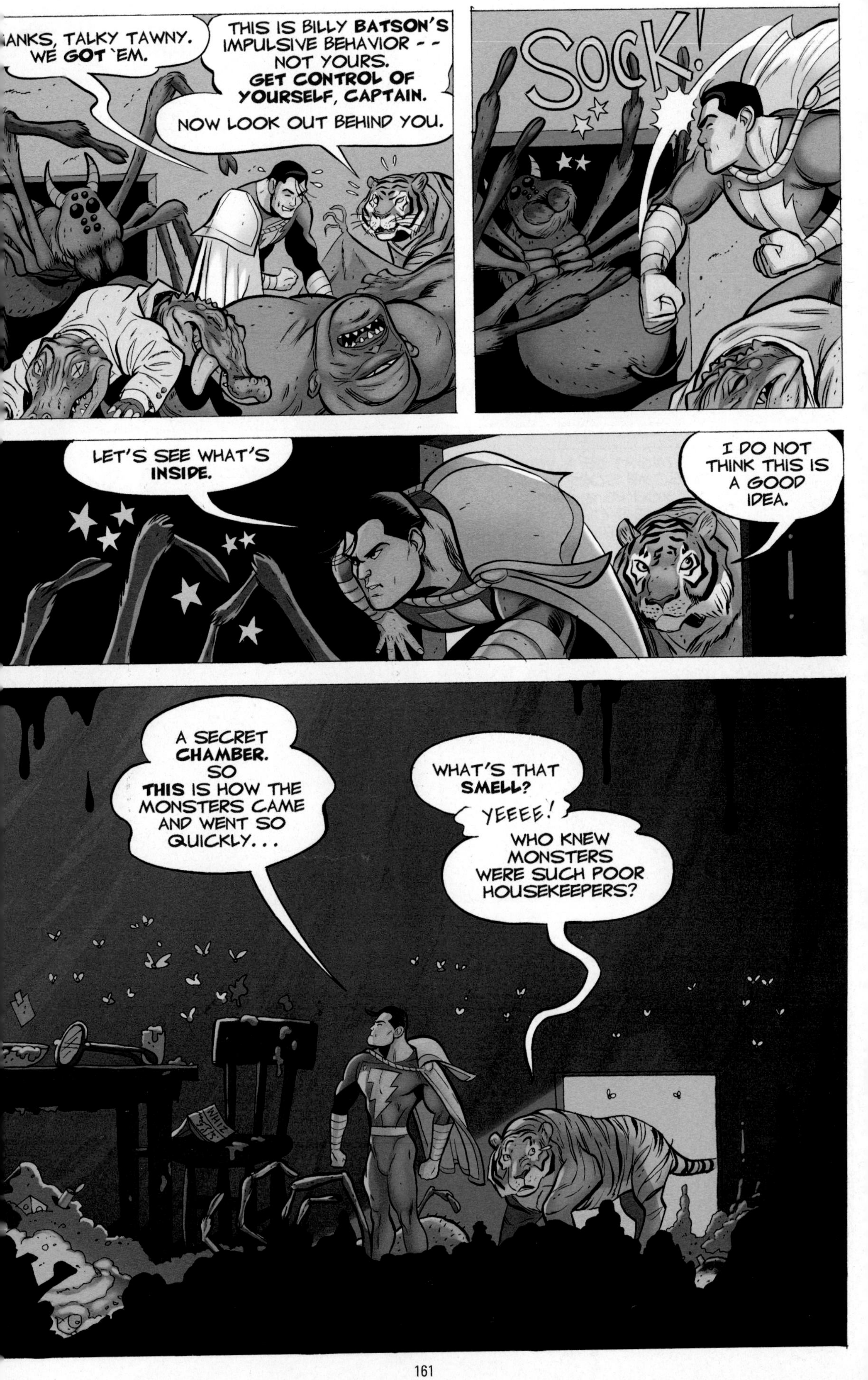

ANKS, TALKY TAWNY. WE GOT 'EM.
THIS IS BILLY BATSON'S IMPULSIVE BEHAVIOR - - NOT YOURS. GET CONTROL OF YOURSELF, CAPTAIN.
NOW LOOK OUT BEHIND YOU.
SOCK!
LET'S SEE WHAT'S INSIDE.
I DO NOT THINK THIS IS A GOOD IDEA.
A SECRET CHAMBER. SO THIS IS HOW THE MONSTERS CAME AND WENT SO QUICKLY...
WHAT'S THAT SMELL?
YEEEE!
WHO KNEW MONSTERS WERE SUCH POOR HOUSEKEEPERS?

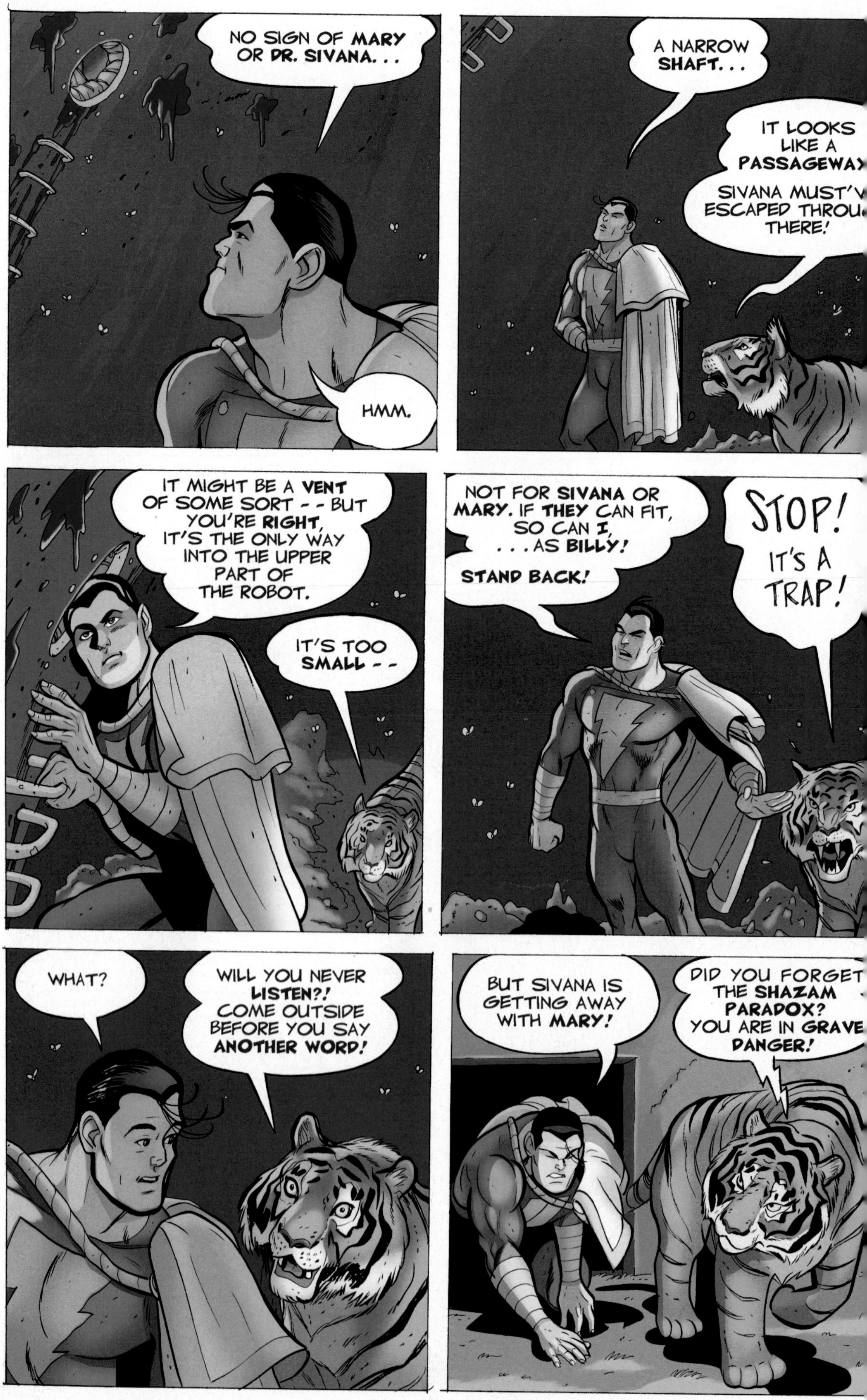
NO SIGN OF MARY OR DR. SIVANA. . .
HMM.
A NARROW SHAFT. . .
IT LOOKS LIKE A PASSAGEWA
SIVANA MUST'V ESCAPED THROU THERE!
IT MIGHT BE A VENT OF SOME SORT - - BUT YOU'RE RIGHT, IT'S THE ONLY WAY INTO THE UPPER PART OF THE ROBOT.
IT'S TOO SMALL - -
NOT FOR SIVANA OR MARY. IF THEY CAN FIT, SO CAN I, . . . AS BILLY!
STAND BACK!
STOP! IT'S A TRAP!
WHAT?
WILL YOU NEVER LISTEN?! COME OUTSIDE BEFORE YOU SAY ANOTHER WORD!
BUT SIVANA IS GETTING AWAY WITH MARY!
DID YOU FORGET THE SHAZAM PARADOX? YOU ARE IN GRAVE DANGER!

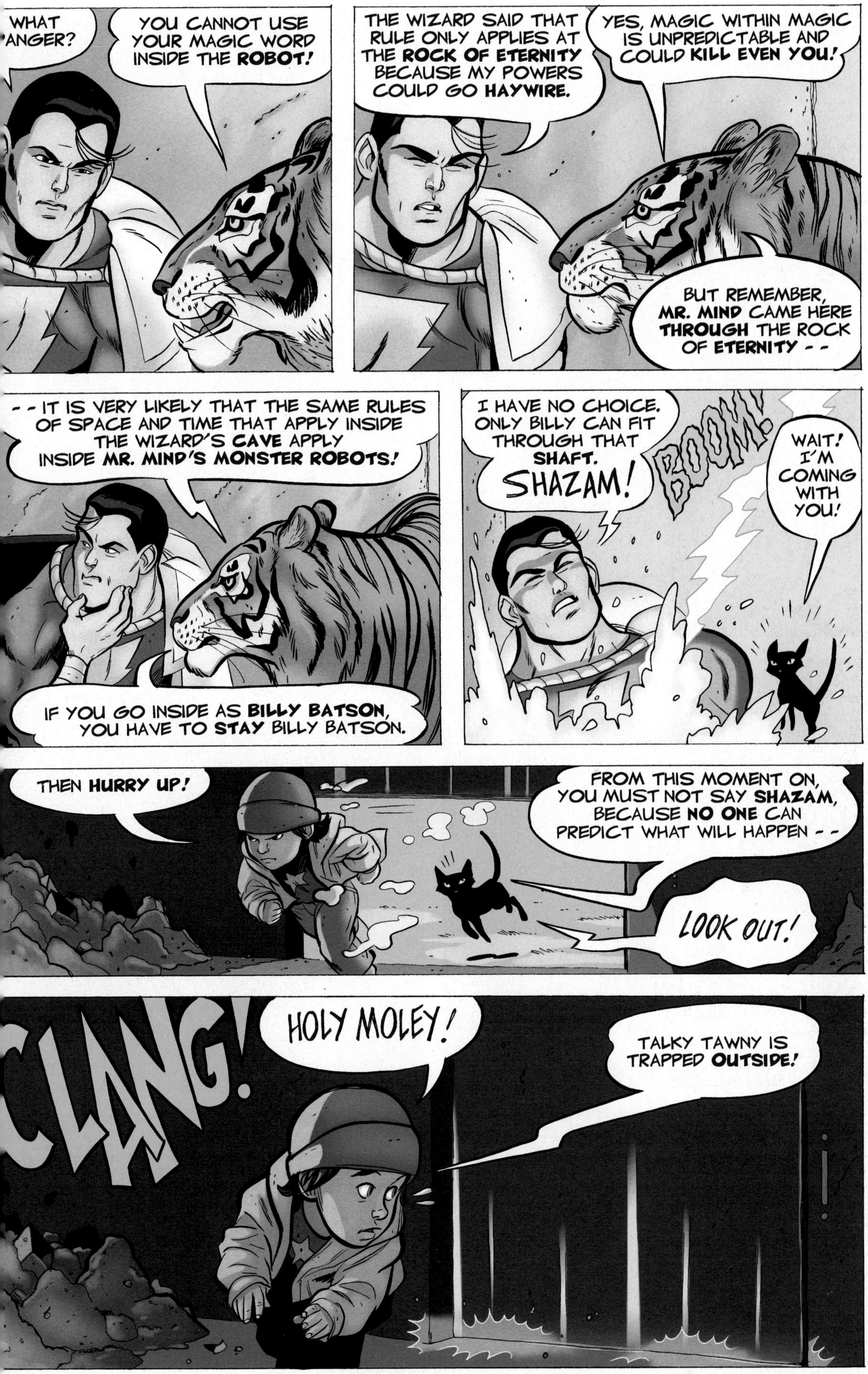
WHAT ANGER?
YOU CANNOT USE YOUR MAGIC WORD INSIDE THE ROBOT!
THE WIZARD SAID THAT RULE ONLY APPLIES AT THE ROCK OF ETERNITY BECAUSE MY POWERS COULD GO HAYWIRE.
YES, MAGIC WITHIN MAGIC IS UNPREDICTABLE AND COULD KILL EVEN YOU!
BUT REMEMBER, MR. MIND CAME HERE THROUGH THE ROCK OF ETERNITY - -
- - IT IS VERY LIKELY THAT THE SAME RULES OF SPACE AND TIME THAT APPLY INSIDE THE WIZARD'S CAVE APPLY INSIDE MR. MIND'S MONSTER ROBOTS!
IF YOU GO INSIDE AS BILLY BATSON, YOU HAVE TO STAY BILLY BATSON.
I HAVE NO CHOICE. ONLY BILLY CAN FIT THROUGH THAT SHAFT. SHAZAM!
BOOM!
WAIT! I'M COMING WITH YOU!
THEN HURRY UP!
FROM THIS MOMENT ON, YOU MUST NOT SAY SHAZAM, BECAUSE NO ONE CAN PREDICT WHAT WILL HAPPEN - -
LOOK OUT!
CLANG!
HOLY MOLEY!
TALKY TAWNY IS TRAPPED OUTSIDE!

164

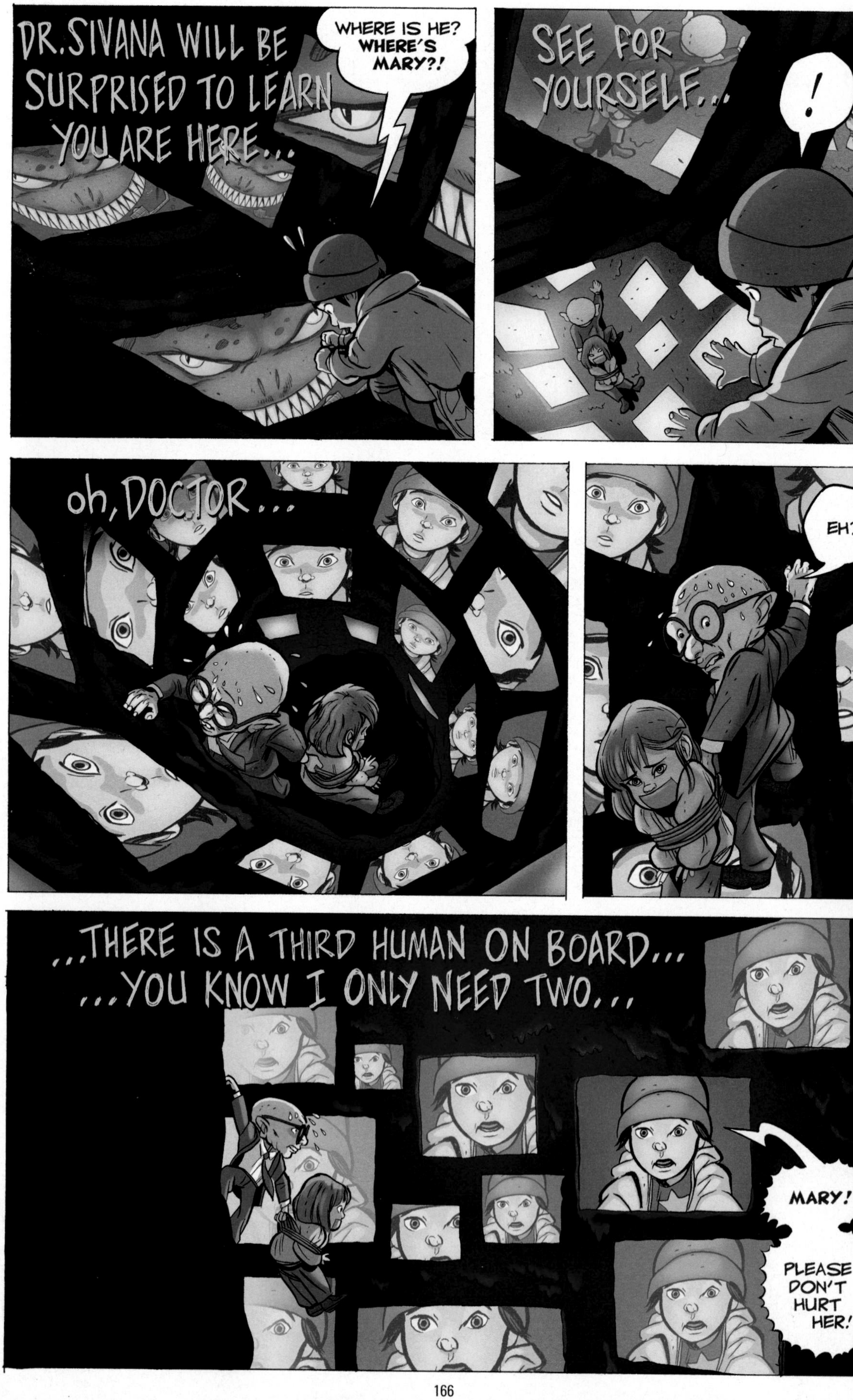
DR. SIVANA WILL BE SURPRISED TO LEARN YOU ARE HERE...
WHERE IS HE? WHERE'S MARY?!
SEE FOR YOURSELF...
!
oh, DOCTOR...
EH?
...THERE IS A THIRD HUMAN ON BOARD...
...YOU KNOW I ONLY NEED TWO...
MARY!
PLEASE DON'T HURT HER!

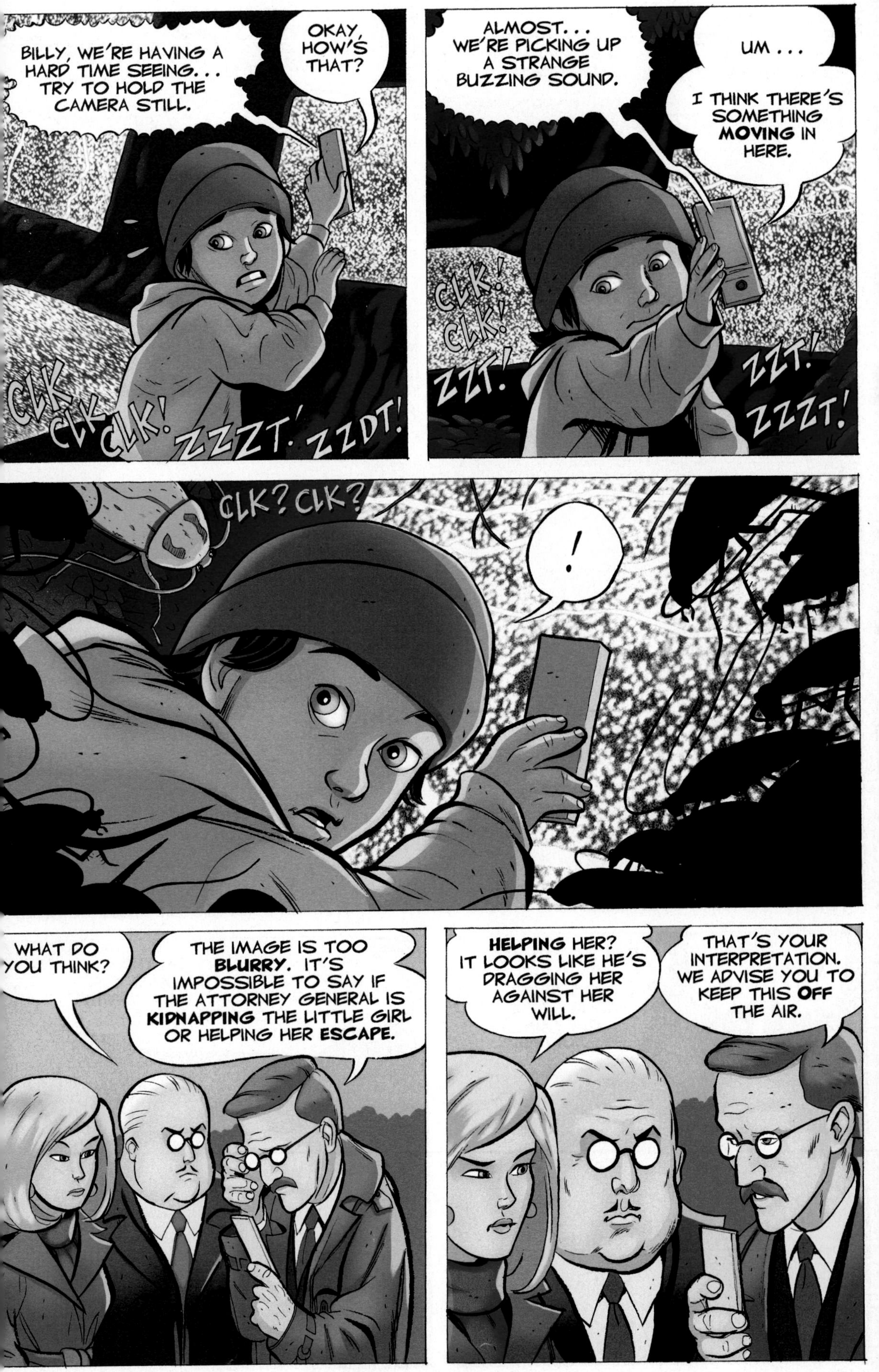
BILLY, WE'RE HAVING A HARD TIME SEEING... TRY TO HOLD THE CAMERA STILL.
OKAY, HOW'S THAT?
CLK CLK CLK! ZZZT! ZZDT!
ALMOST... WE'RE PICKING UP A STRANGE BUZZING SOUND.
UM ...
I THINK THERE'S SOMETHING MOVING IN HERE.
CLK! CLK! ZZT!
ZZT! ZZZT!
CLK? CLK?
!
WHAT DO YOU THINK?
THE IMAGE IS TOO BLURRY. IT'S IMPOSSIBLE TO SAY IF THE ATTORNEY GENERAL IS KIDNAPPING THE LITTLE GIRL OR HELPING HER ESCAPE.
HELPING HER? IT LOOKS LIKE HE'S DRAGGING HER AGAINST HER WILL.
THAT'S YOUR INTERPRETATION. WE ADVISE YOU TO KEEP THIS OFF THE AIR.

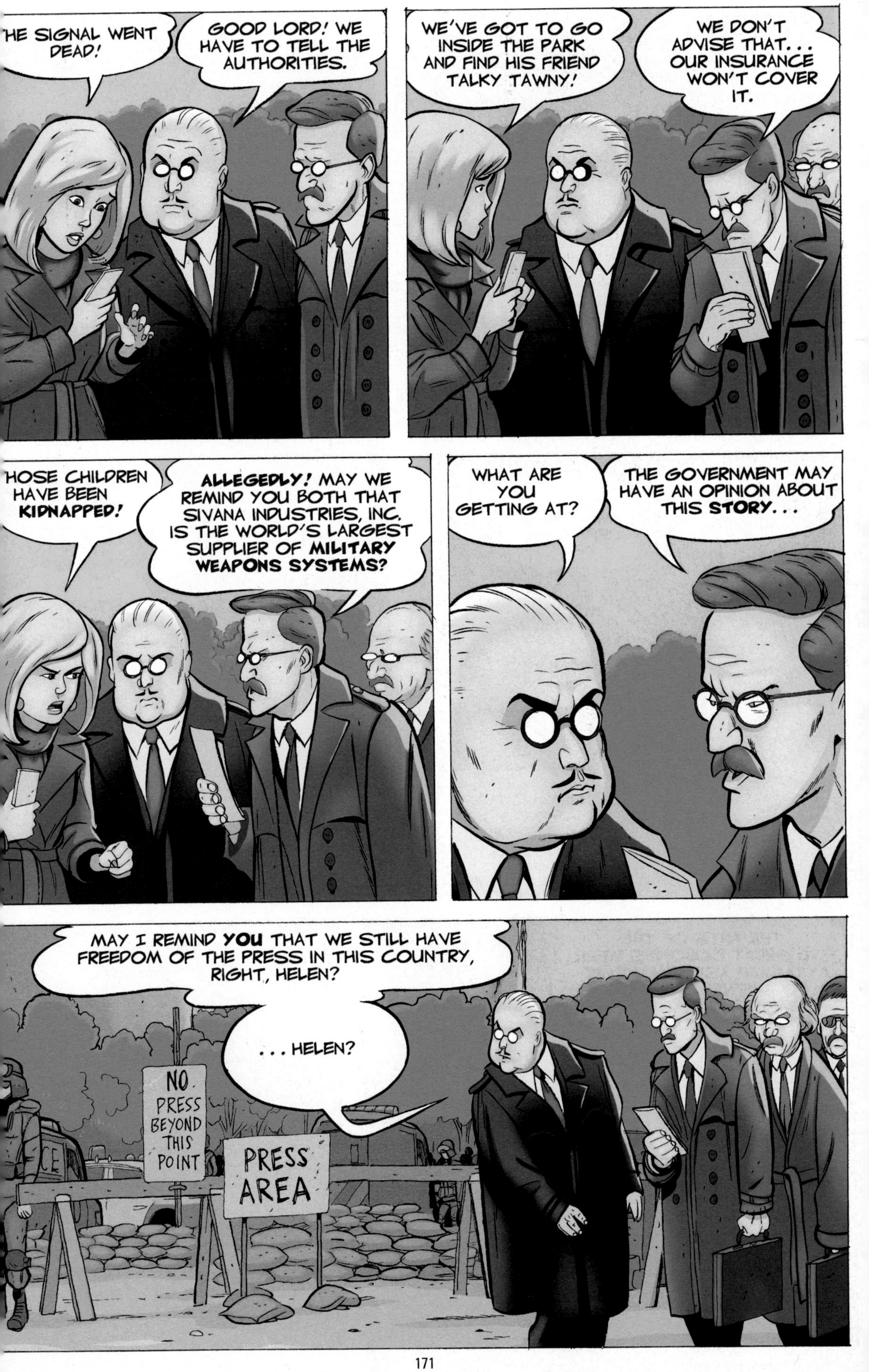

THE SIGNAL WENT DEAD!
GOOD LORD! WE HAVE TO TELL THE AUTHORITIES.
WE'VE GOT TO GO INSIDE THE PARK AND FIND HIS FRIEND TALKY TAWNY!
WE DON'T ADVISE THAT... OUR INSURANCE WON'T COVER IT.
THOSE CHILDREN HAVE BEEN **KIDNAPPED!**
**ALLEGEDLY!** MAY WE REMIND YOU BOTH THAT SIVANA INDUSTRIES, INC. IS THE WORLD'S LARGEST SUPPLIER OF **MILITARY WEAPONS SYSTEMS?**
WHAT ARE YOU GETTING AT?
THE GOVERNMENT MAY HAVE AN OPINION ABOUT THIS **STORY**...
MAY I REMIND **YOU** THAT WE STILL HAVE FREEDOM OF THE PRESS IN THIS COUNTRY, RIGHT, HELEN?
... HELEN?
NO PRESS BEYOND THIS POINT
PRESS AREA

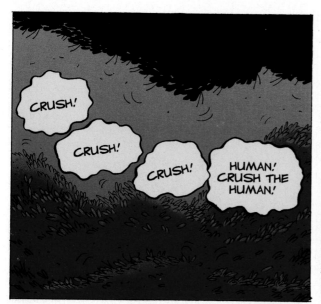

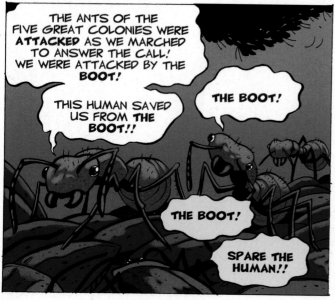

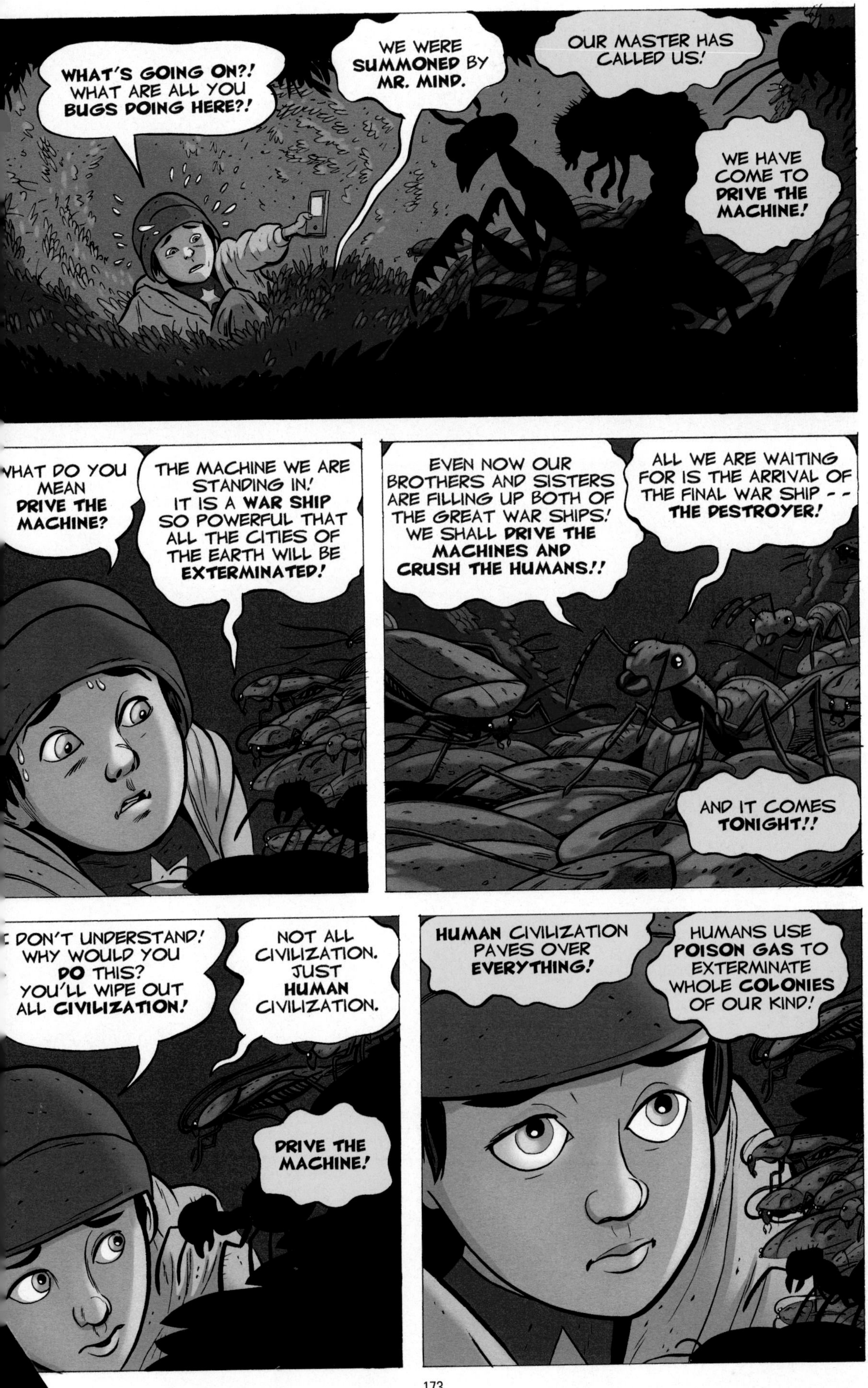
WHAT'S GOING ON?! WHAT ARE ALL YOU BUGS DOING HERE?!
WE WERE SUMMONED BY MR. MIND.
OUR MASTER HAS CALLED US!
WE HAVE COME TO DRIVE THE MACHINE!
WHAT DO YOU MEAN DRIVE THE MACHINE?
THE MACHINE WE ARE STANDING IN! IT IS A WAR SHIP SO POWERFUL THAT ALL THE CITIES OF THE EARTH WILL BE EXTERMINATED!
EVEN NOW OUR BROTHERS AND SISTERS ARE FILLING UP BOTH OF THE GREAT WAR SHIPS! WE SHALL DRIVE THE MACHINES AND CRUSH THE HUMANS!!
ALL WE ARE WAITING FOR IS THE ARRIVAL OF THE FINAL WAR SHIP - - THE DESTROYER!
AND IT COMES TONIGHT!!
DON'T UNDERSTAND! WHY WOULD YOU DO THIS? YOU'LL WIPE OUT ALL CIVILIZATION!
NOT ALL CIVILIZATION. JUST HUMAN CIVILIZATION.
DRIVE THE MACHINE!
HUMAN CIVILIZATION PAVES OVER EVERYTHING!
HUMANS USE POISON GAS TO EXTERMINATE WHOLE COLONIES OF OUR KIND!

OKAY, HELEN . . . GET READY TO GO **LIVE** - - IN THREE, TWO - -

THIS IS HELEN FIDELITY REPORTING LIVE FROM INSIDE THE PARK NOT FAR FROM THE FEET OF MR. MIND'S GIANT **MONSTERS!**

HELEN FIDELITY

NOT LONG AGO, **SNN** RECEIVED CALL FOR HELP FROM **INSIDE** ONE OF THE MONSTERS!

THE CALL CAME FROM A LITTLE BOY WHO CLAIMS HIS SISTER HAS BEEN **KIDNAPPED!**

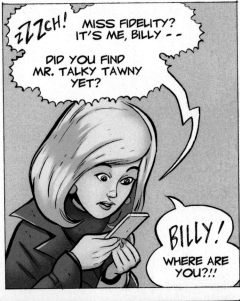

**zZZCH!** MISS FIDELITY? IT'S ME, BILLY - -

DID YOU FIND MR. TALKY TAWNY YET?

**BILLY!** WHERE ARE YOU?!!

I'M STILL INSIDE THE MONSTER ROBOT - - I MUST BE NEAR THE **TOP** BY NOW.

DR. SIVANA AND MARY CAN'T BE FAR AHEAD OF ME.

BILLY, WE ARE ON LIVE TV. CAN YOU DESCRIBE YOUR SURROUNDINGS?

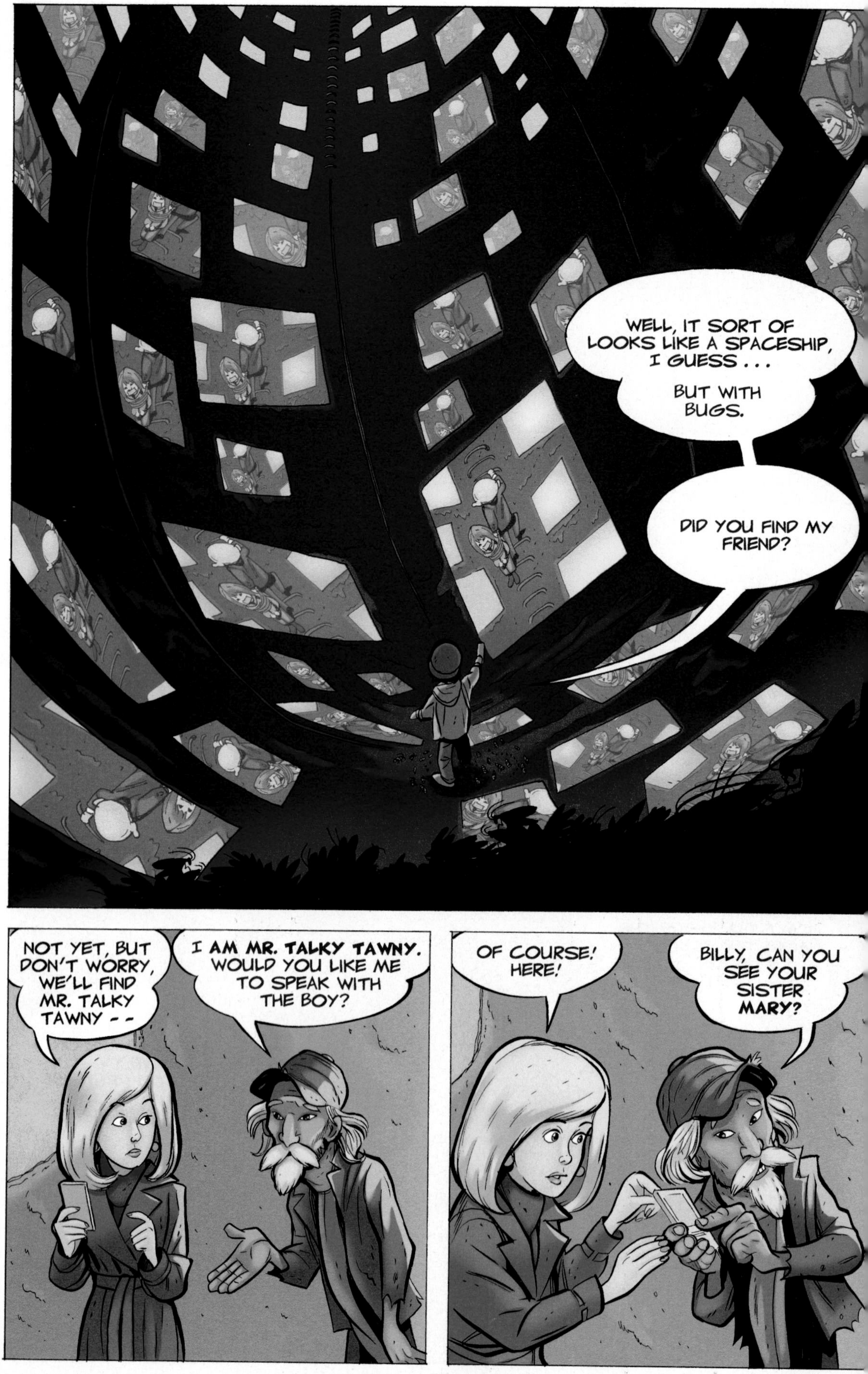
WELL, IT SORT OF LOOKS LIKE A SPACESHIP, I GUESS . . .
BUT WITH BUGS.
DID YOU FIND MY FRIEND?
NOT YET, BUT DON'T WORRY, WE'LL FIND MR. TALKY TAWNY - -
I **AM MR. TALKY TAWNY.** WOULD YOU LIKE ME TO SPEAK WITH THE BOY?
OF COURSE! HERE!
BILLY, CAN YOU SEE YOUR SISTER **MARY?**

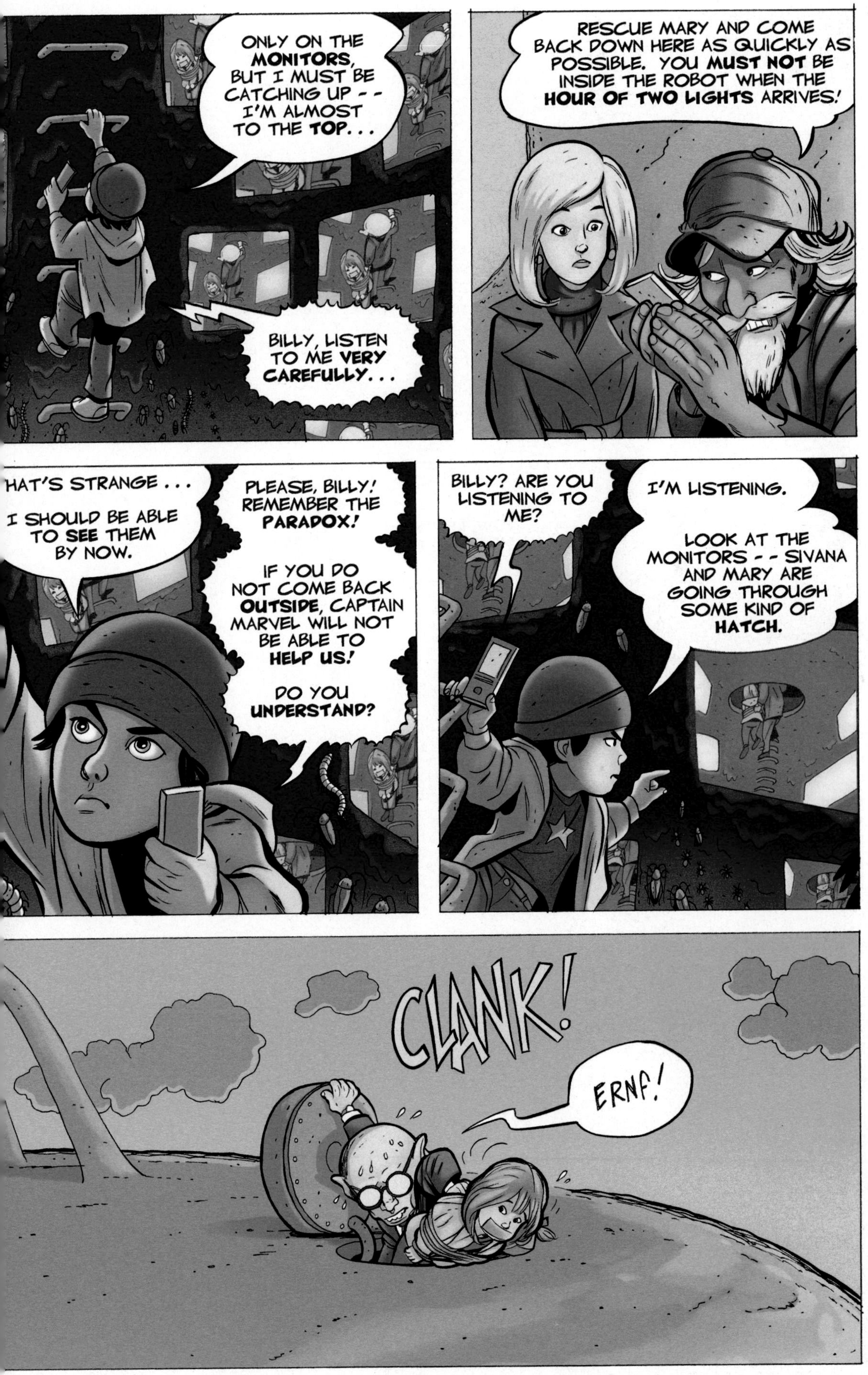
ONLY ON THE MONITORS, BUT I MUST BE CATCHING UP - - I'M ALMOST TO THE TOP...
RESCUE MARY AND COME BACK DOWN HERE AS QUICKLY AS POSSIBLE. YOU MUST NOT BE INSIDE THE ROBOT WHEN THE HOUR OF TWO LIGHTS ARRIVES!
BILLY, LISTEN TO ME VERY CAREFULLY...
HAT'S STRANGE...
I SHOULD BE ABLE TO SEE THEM BY NOW.
PLEASE, BILLY! REMEMBER THE PARADOX!
IF YOU DO NOT COME BACK OUTSIDE, CAPTAIN MARVEL WILL NOT BE ABLE TO HELP US!
DO YOU UNDERSTAND?
BILLY? ARE YOU LISTENING TO ME?
I'M LISTENING.
LOOK AT THE MONITORS - - SIVANA AND MARY ARE GOING THROUGH SOME KIND OF HATCH.
CLANK!
ERNF!

HEY! DO YOU GUYS SEE THIS? SIVANA AND MARY ARE ON TOP OF THE **MONSTER ROBOT!**

KLK! KLK!

GET SOME CAMERAS IN THE AIR! I WANT A CLEAR SHOT OF THIS!

ALL RIGHT, MR. MIND -- I BROUGHT THE GIRL TO THE TOP. **NOW** WHAT?

STRAP HER INTO THE COCKPIT!

OKAY, KID. LET'S GO!

FLASH!

WHAT TH--?

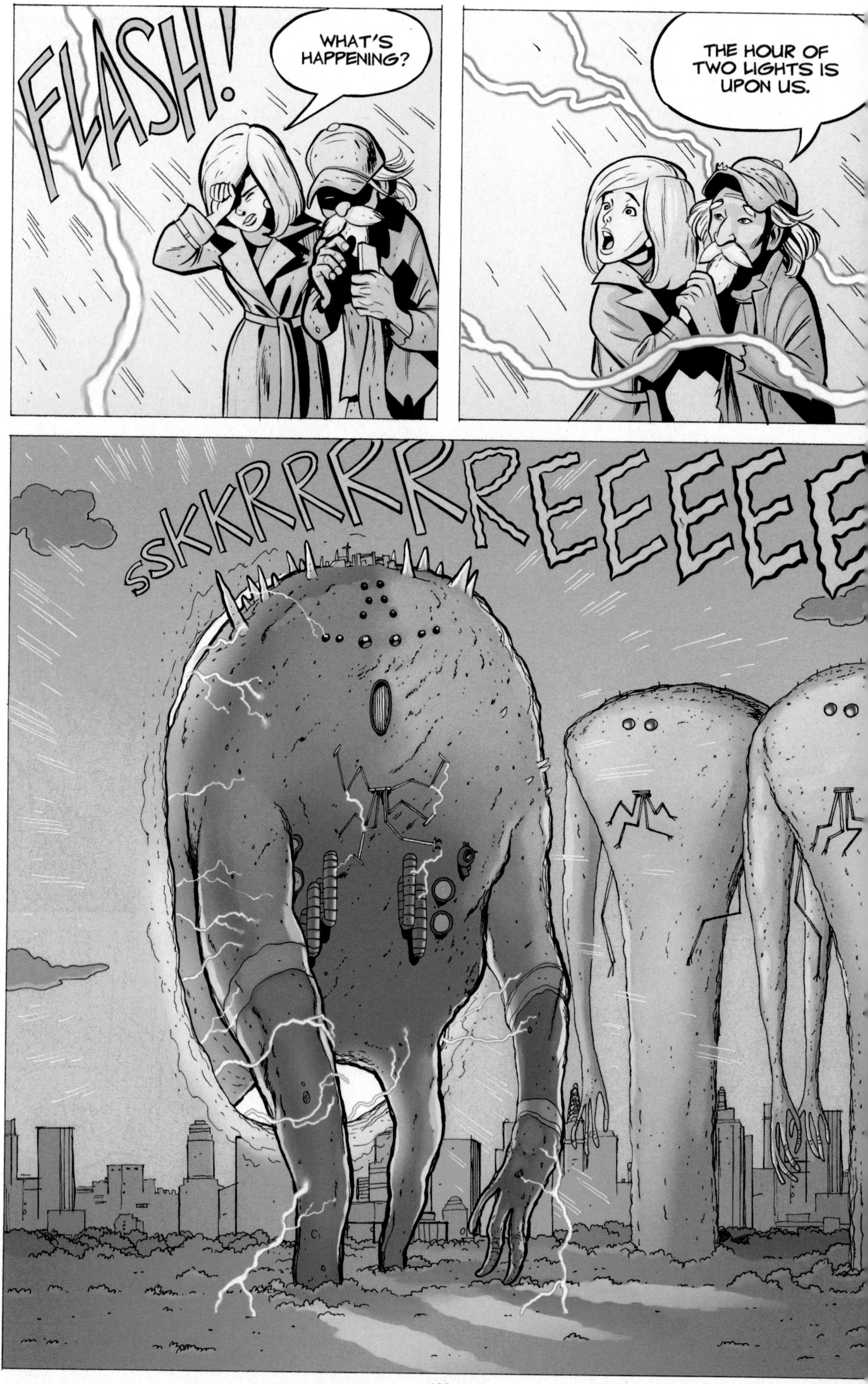
FLASH!
WHAT'S HAPPENING?
THE HOUR OF TWO LIGHTS IS UPON US.
sSKKRRRRRRREEEEEE

BILLY -- THE FINAL OMPANION IS HERE!!

ZZRKT! IT'S A WARSHIP CALLED **THE DESTROYER!** WE HAVE TO HURRY!

MR. MIND HAS TURNED THE INSECTS OF EARTH **AGAINST US** . . .

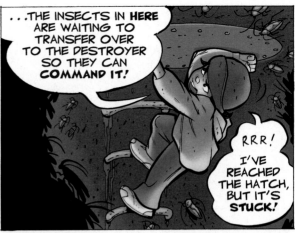

. . .THE INSECTS IN **HERE** ARE WAITING TO TRANSFER OVER TO THE DESTROYER SO THEY CAN **COMMAND IT!**

RRR! I'VE REACHED THE HATCH, BUT IT'S **STUCK!**

BILLY, PLEASE COME DOWN! WITHOUT APTAIN MARVEL WE ARE **DOOMED!**

LOOK BEHIND US!

INSECTS ARE FLOODING OUT OF THAT GRATE!

THEY ARE ALL GOING OVER TO **THE DESTROYER!**

THIS IS **HORRIBLE!** WHERE'S THE **ARMY?** WHY AREN'T THEY **BOMBING** THAT THING?

-- HOLD YOUR FIRE. DO YOU UNDERSTAND ME?

THE MILITARY IS TO **STAND DOWN** UNTIL YOU HEAR FROM ME.

ROGER THAT.

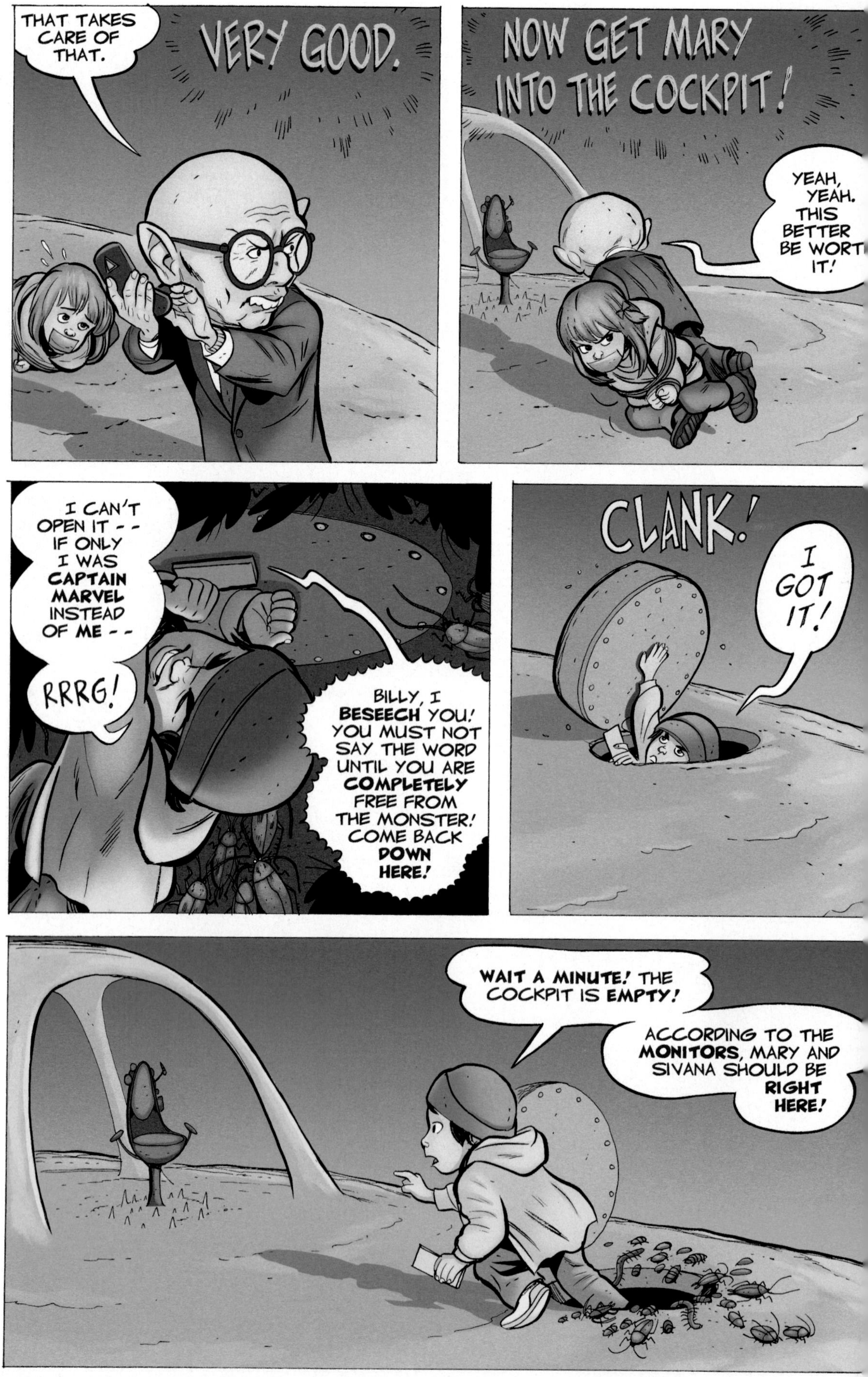

THAT TAKES CARE OF THAT.
VERY GOOD.
NOW GET MARY INTO THE COCKPIT!
YEAH, YEAH. THIS BETTER BE WORT IT!
I CAN'T OPEN IT - - IF ONLY I WAS CAPTAIN MARVEL INSTEAD OF ME - -
RRRG!
BILLY, I BESEECH YOU! YOU MUST NOT SAY THE WORD UNTIL YOU ARE COMPLETELY FREE FROM THE MONSTER! COME BACK DOWN HERE!
CLANK!
I GOT IT!
WAIT A MINUTE! THE COCKPIT IS EMPTY!
ACCORDING TO THE MONITORS, MARY AND SIVANA SHOULD BE RIGHT HERE!

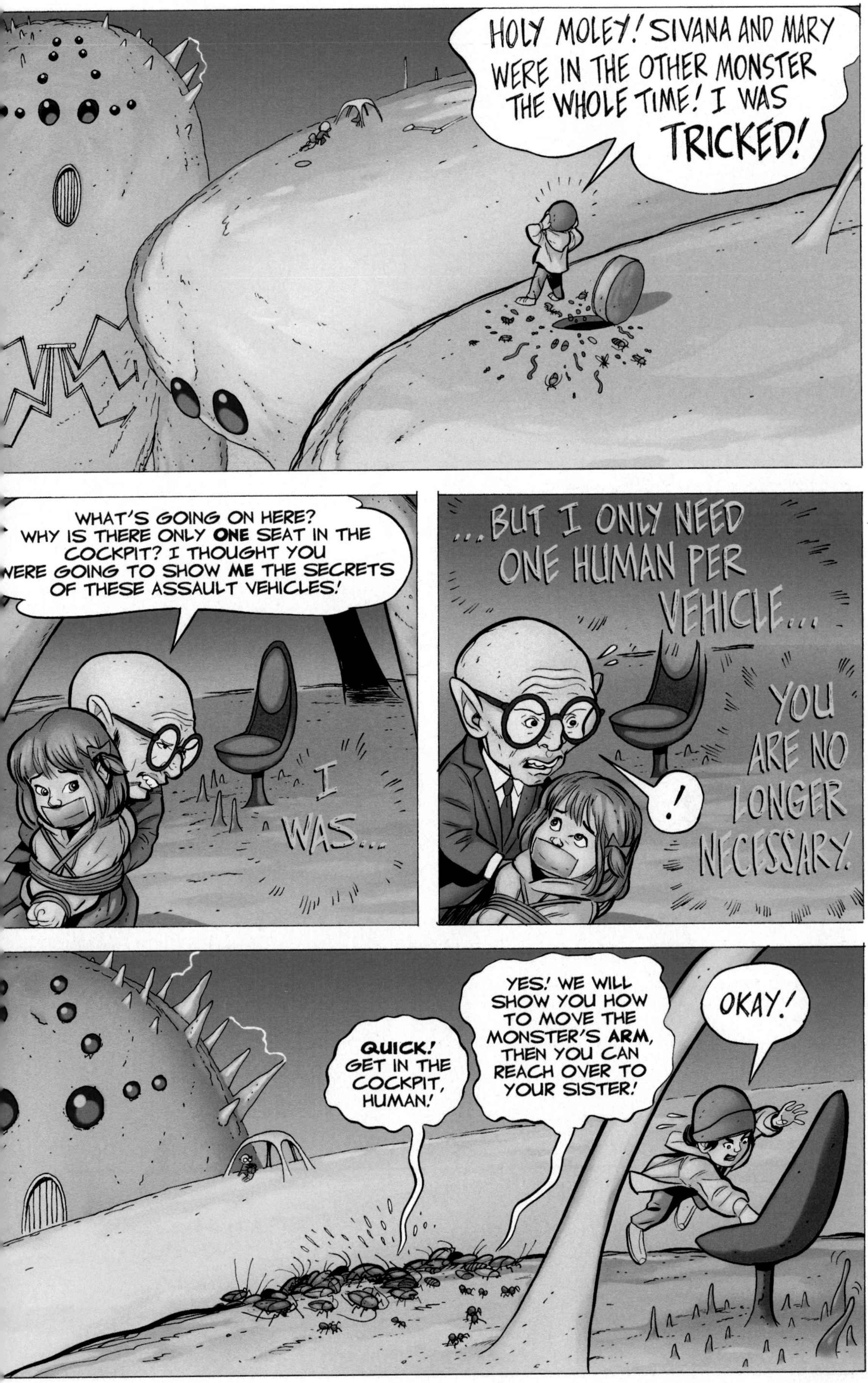
HOLY MOLEY! SIVANA AND MARY WERE IN THE OTHER MONSTER THE WHOLE TIME! I WAS TRICKED!
WHAT'S GOING ON HERE? WHY IS THERE ONLY ONE SEAT IN THE COCKPIT? I THOUGHT YOU WERE GOING TO SHOW ME THE SECRETS OF THESE ASSAULT VEHICLES!
I WAS...
...BUT I ONLY NEED ONE HUMAN PER VEHICLE...
!
YOU ARE NO LONGER NECESSARY.
QUICK! GET IN THE COCKPIT, HUMAN!
YES! WE WILL SHOW YOU HOW TO MOVE THE MONSTER'S ARM, THEN YOU CAN REACH OVER TO YOUR SISTER!
OKAY!

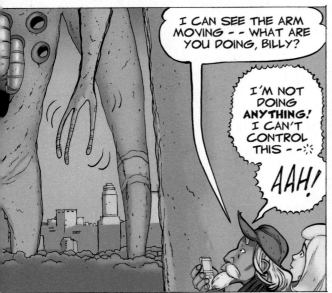

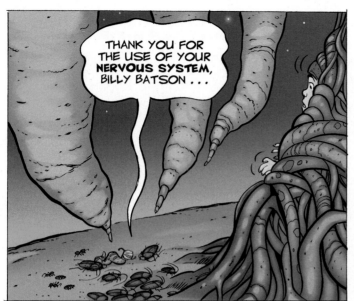

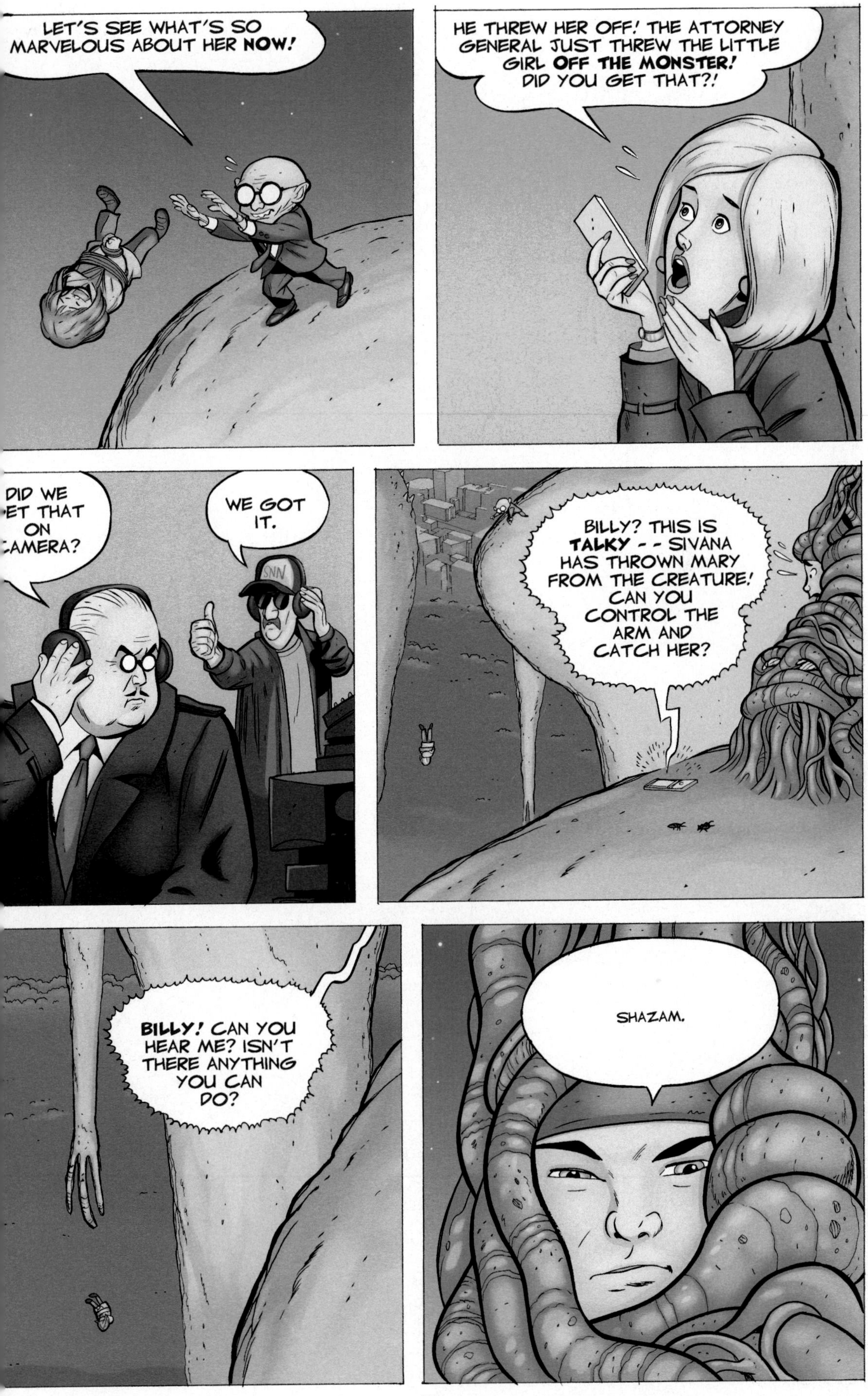
LET'S SEE WHAT'S SO MARVELOUS ABOUT HER NOW!
HE THREW HER OFF! THE ATTORNEY GENERAL JUST THREW THE LITTLE GIRL OFF THE MONSTER! DID YOU GET THAT?!
DID WE ET THAT ON CAMERA?
WE GOT IT.
SNN
BILLY? THIS IS TALKY - - SIVANA HAS THROWN MARY FROM THE CREATURE! CAN YOU CONTROL THE ARM AND CATCH HER?
BILLY! CAN YOU HEAR ME? ISN'T THERE ANYTHING YOU CAN DO?
SHAZAM.

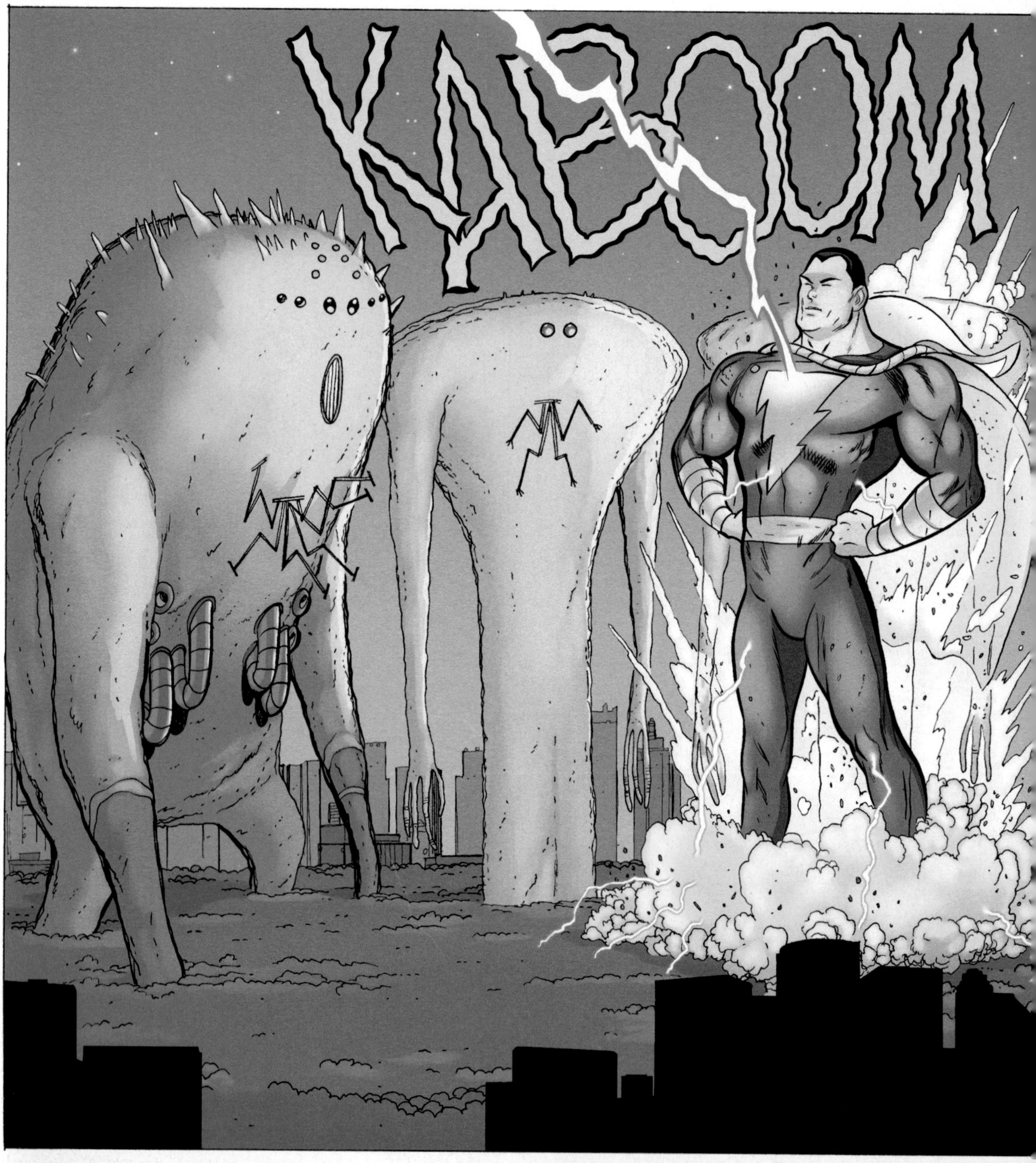
KABOOM

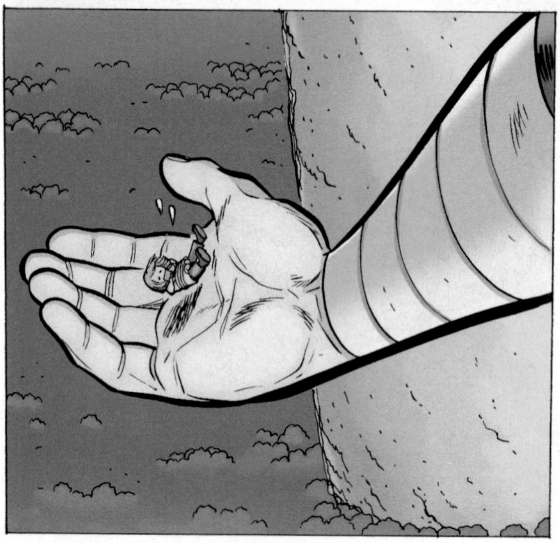

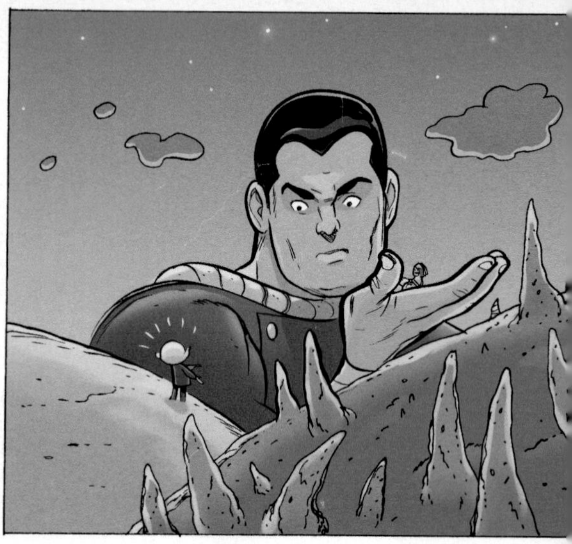

WHAT APPENED -- ?! oh--!

LOOK! THE INSECTS ARE ALL INSIDE THE DESTROYER!

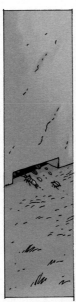

SHHK!

KILL CAPTAIN MARVEL!

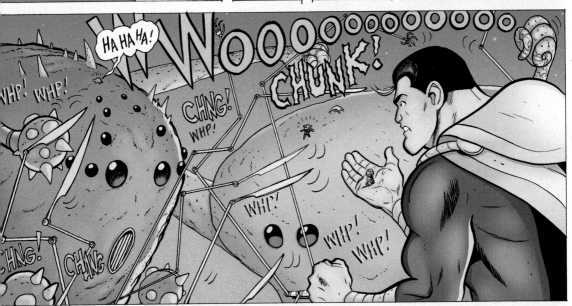

HA HA HA!

WOOOOOOOOOOOO

CHUNK!

WHP! WHP!

CHNG! WHP!

CHNG! CHNG!

WHP!

WHP! WHP!

POW

CRUNCH!

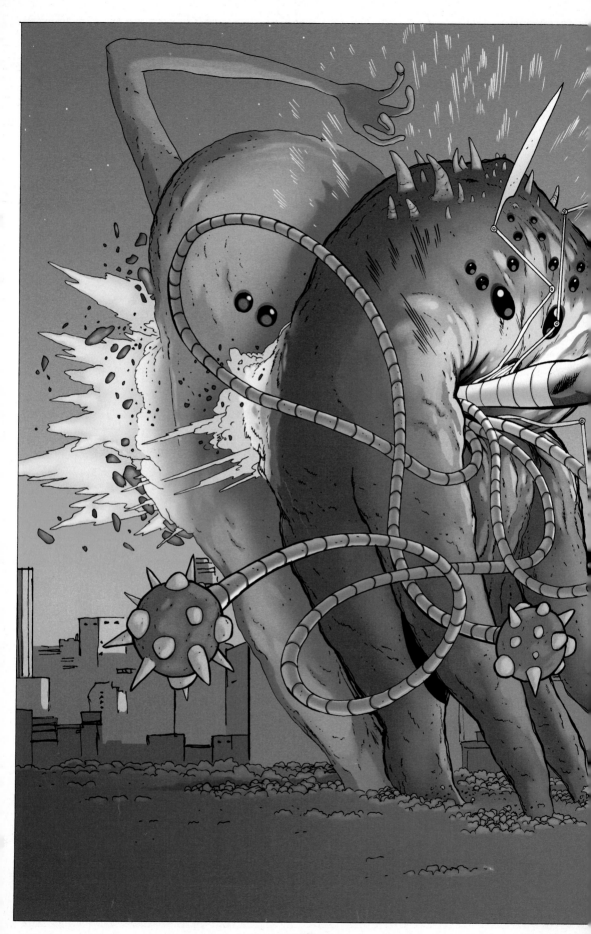

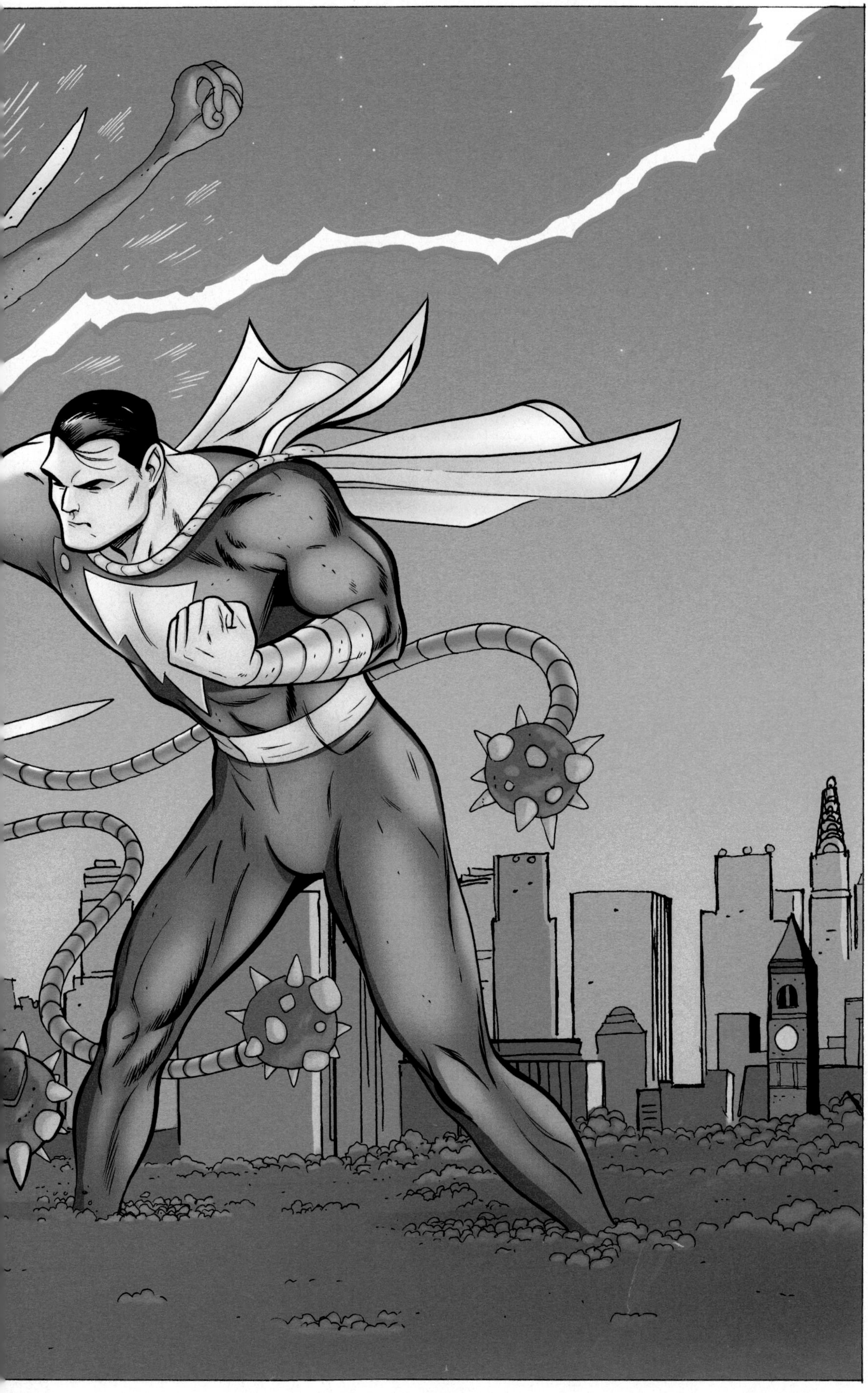

HOORAY!!!

GO, CAPTAIN MARVEL!!

OH, NO! THIS IS **VERY BAD!** CAPTAIN MARVEL PUNCHED HIM **TOO HARD!**

WHAT DID YOU SAY?

THE FABRIC OF LIGHT HAS BEEN COMPRESSED INTO A **SINGULARITY!** A SMALL **BLACK HOLE** HAS FORMED --

AND IT IS PULLING EVERYTHING BACK TO **ETERNITY** --

INCLUDING CAPTAIN MARVEL!

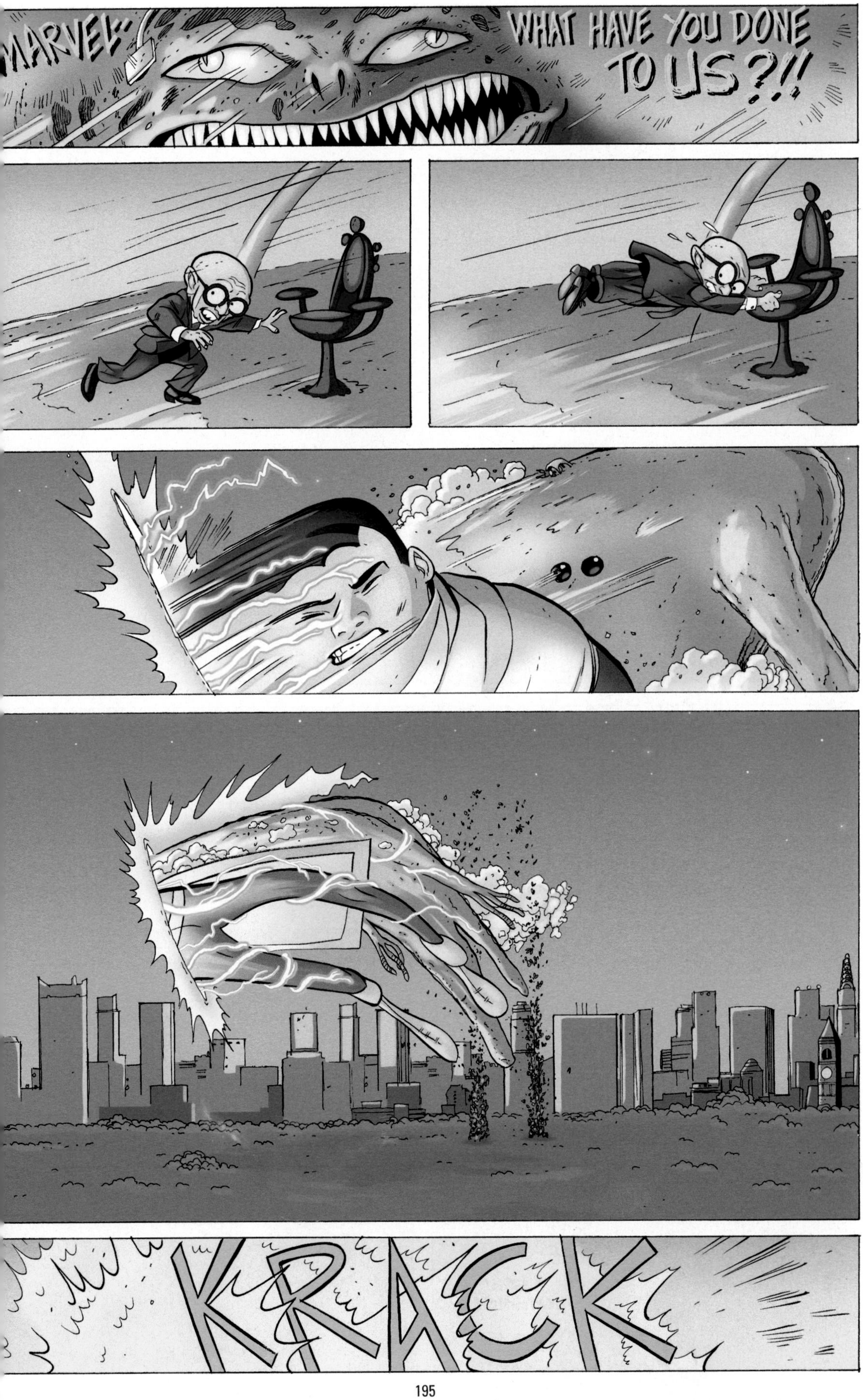
MARVEL--
WHAT HAVE YOU DONE TO US?!!
KRACK

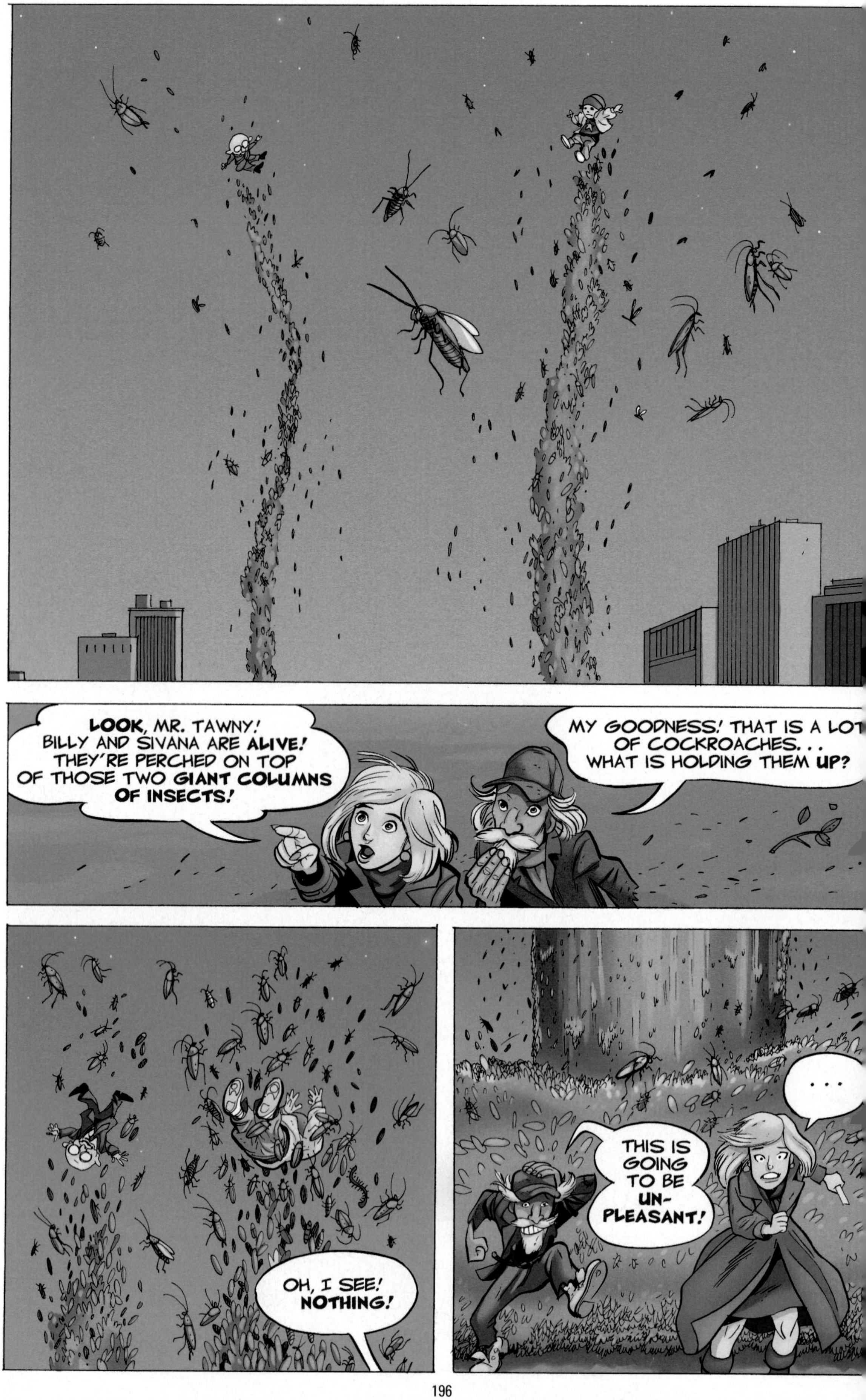
LOOK, MR. TAWNY! BILLY AND SIVANA ARE ALIVE! THEY'RE PERCHED ON TOP OF THOSE TWO GIANT COLUMNS OF INSECTS!
MY GOODNESS! THAT IS A LOT OF COCKROACHES. . . WHAT IS HOLDING THEM UP?
OH, I SEE! NOTHING!
THIS IS GOING TO BE UN-PLEASANT!
. . .

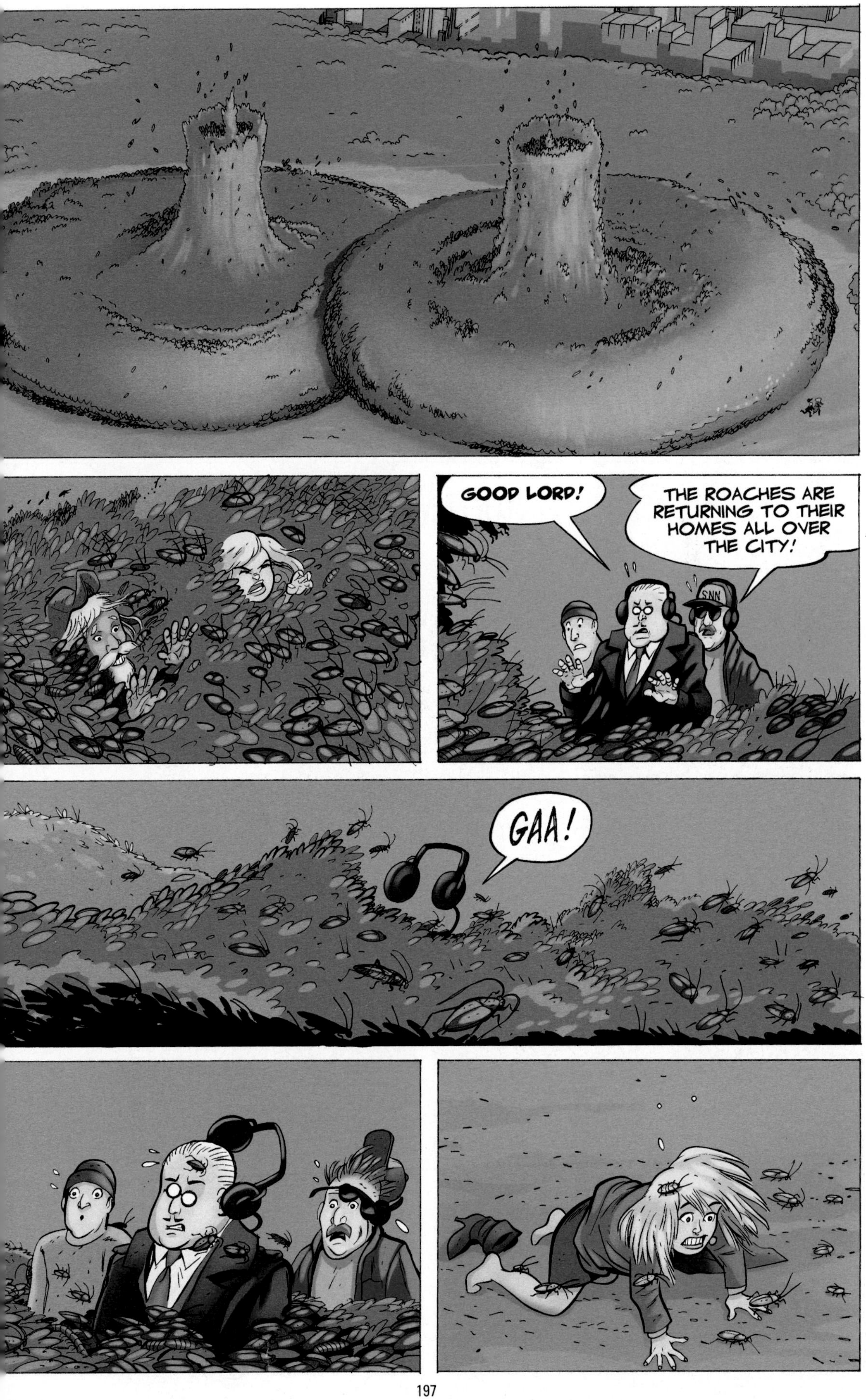
GOOD LORD!
THE ROACHES ARE RETURNING TO THEIR HOMES ALL OVER THE CITY!
SNN
GAA!

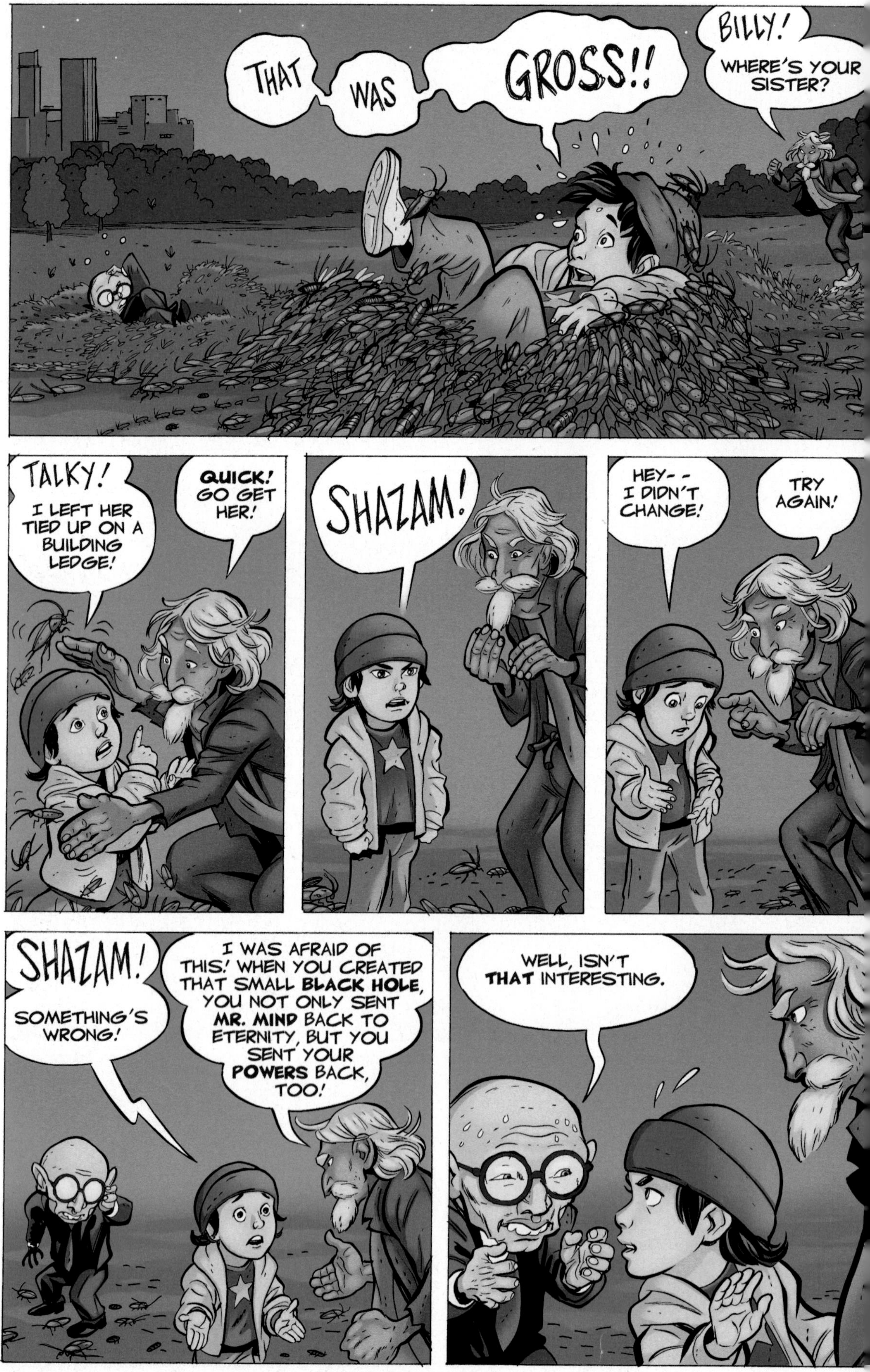
THAT WAS GROSS!!
BILLY! WHERE'S YOUR SISTER?
TALKY! I LEFT HER TIED UP ON A BUILDING LEDGE!
QUICK! GO GET HER!
SHAZAM!
HEY-- I DIDN'T CHANGE!
TRY AGAIN!
SHAZAM! SOMETHING'S WRONG!
I WAS AFRAID OF THIS! WHEN YOU CREATED THAT SMALL BLACK HOLE, YOU NOT ONLY SENT MR. MIND BACK TO ETERNITY, BUT YOU SENT YOUR POWERS BACK, TOO!
WELL, ISN'T THAT INTERESTING.

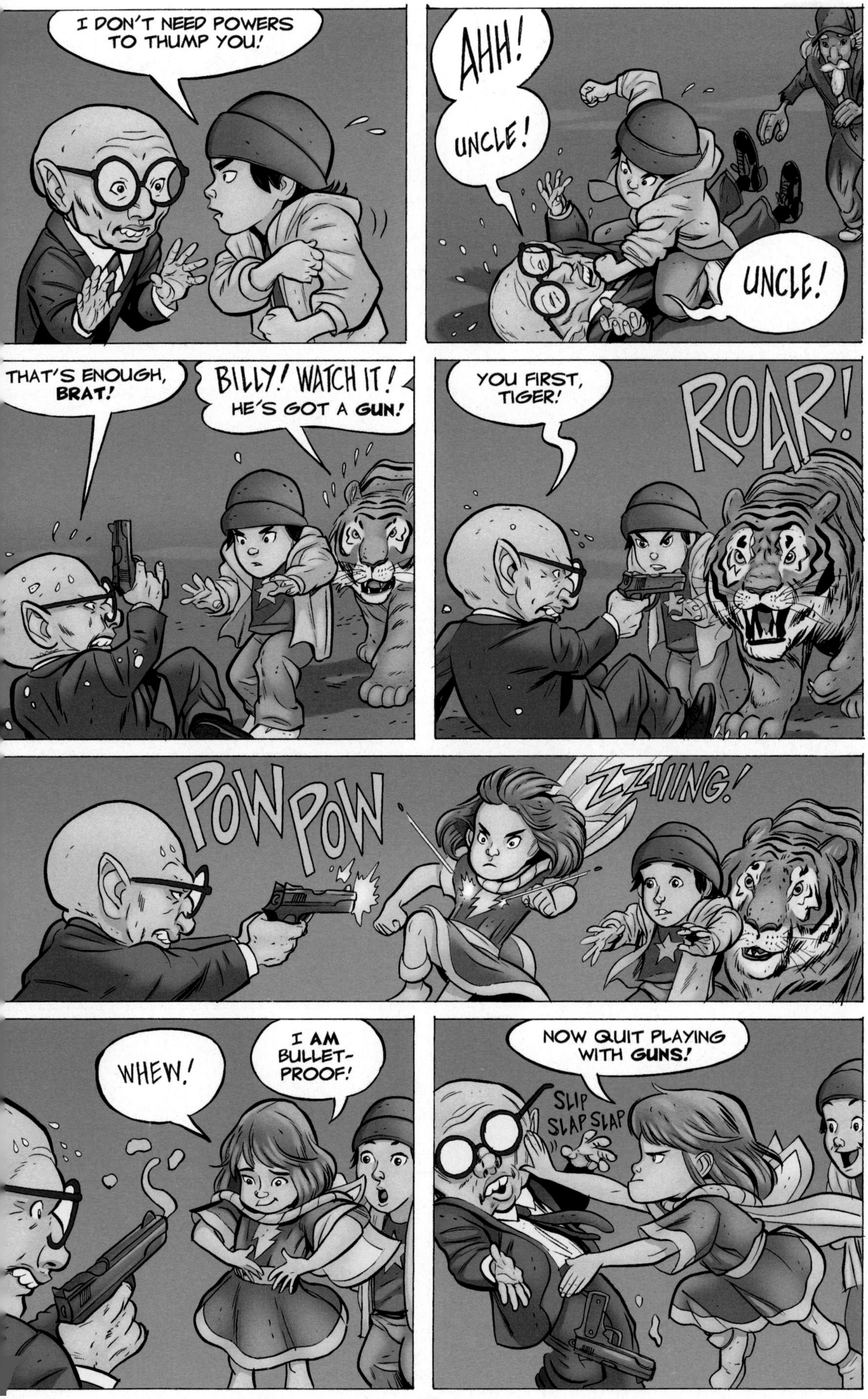
I DON'T NEED POWERS TO THUMP YOU!
AHH!
UNCLE!
UNCLE!
THAT'S ENOUGH, **BRAT!**
BILLY! WATCH IT! HE'S GOT A **GUN!**
YOU FIRST, TIGER!
ROAR!
POW POW
ZZIIING!
WHEW!
I **AM** BULLET-PROOF!
NOW QUIT PLAYING WITH **GUNS!**
SLIP SLAP SLAP

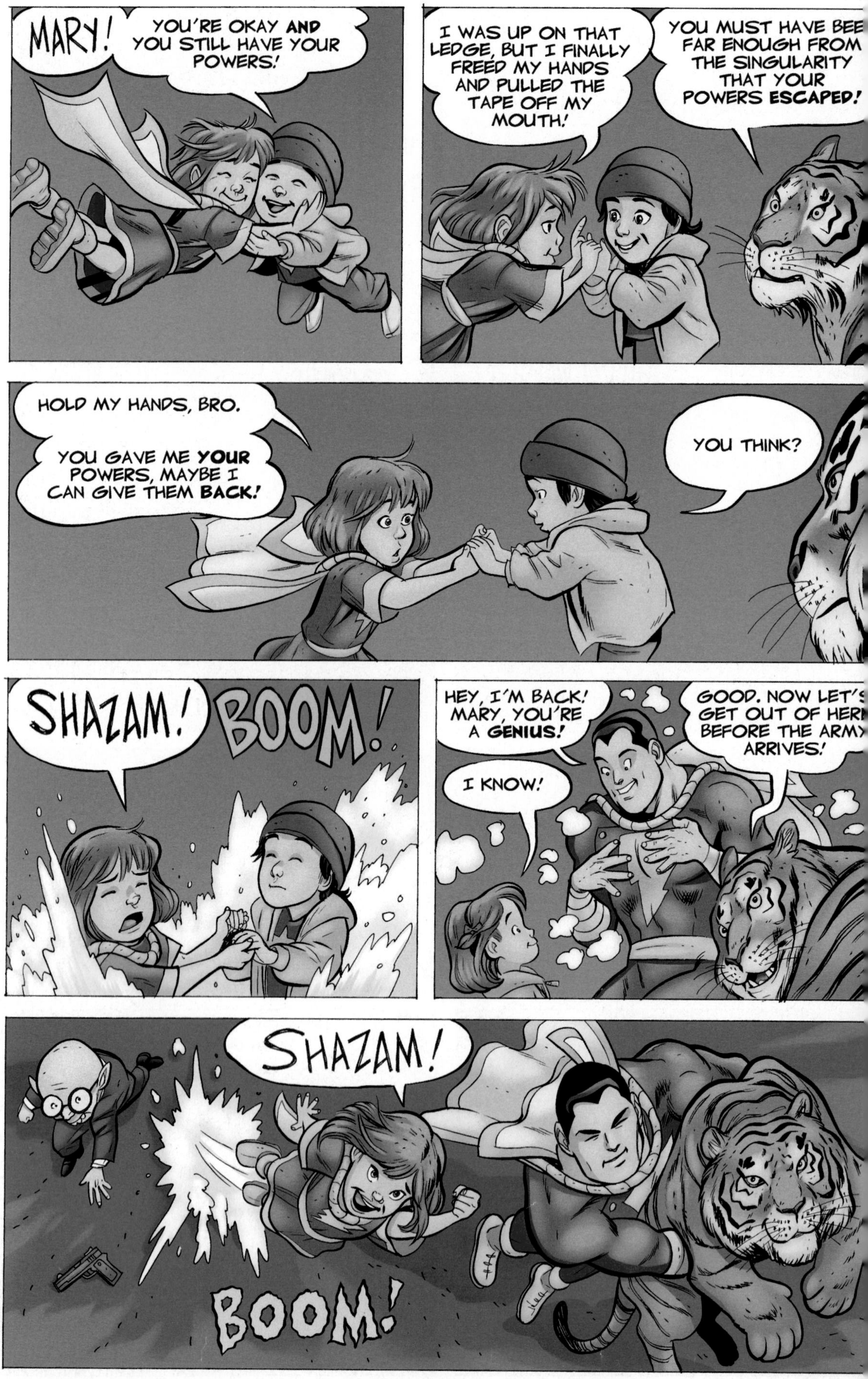
MARY!
YOU'RE OKAY AND YOU STILL HAVE YOUR POWERS!
I WAS UP ON THAT LEDGE, BUT I FINALLY FREED MY HANDS AND PULLED THE TAPE OFF MY MOUTH!
YOU MUST HAVE BEE FAR ENOUGH FROM THE SINGULARITY THAT YOUR POWERS ESCAPED!
HOLD MY HANDS, BRO.
YOU GAVE ME YOUR POWERS, MAYBE I CAN GIVE THEM BACK!
YOU THINK?
SHAZAM!
BOOM!
HEY, I'M BACK! MARY, YOU'RE A GENIUS!
I KNOW!
GOOD. NOW LET'S GET OUT OF HER BEFORE THE ARMY ARRIVES!
SHAZAM!
BOOM!

AS YOU CAN SEE, BILLY, ALL THE EYES ON THE IDOLS ARE NOW CLOSED.

THE INTERESTING THING IS --

MARY -- PLEASE STOP CLIMBING ON THE SEVEN DEADLY ENEMIES OF MAN. THANK YOU.

AS I WAS SAYING, THE INTERESTING THING IS THAT THE EYES CLOSED -- NOT WHEN CAPTAIN MARVEL VANQUISHED MR. MIND...

...BUT WHEN ATTORNEY GENERAL SIVANA WAS CAUGHT ON TAPE THROWING MARY OFF THE TOP OF THE MONSTER!

PRIDE

ENV

THAT MEANS DR. SIVANA WAS THE TRUE THREAT ALL ALONG!

WHAT ABOUT MR. MIND?

MR. MIND WAS DOOMED THE MOMENT IVANA PROVOKED YOU INTO USING YOUR MAGIC WORD.

PERHAPS **FATE** WAS CONTROLLING OUR WORM-LIKE FRIEND THE WHOLE TIME... WHO KNOWS? THE FORCES OF ETERNITY ARE NOT ALWAYS EASY TO UNDERSTAND.

IN ANY CASE, HE IS **CONNECTED** TO YOU, BILLY. AND NOW THAT HE HAS HAD A TASTE OF OUR UNIVERSE, I'M SURE MR. MIND WILL BE **BACK**. WE MUST BE **ALERT!**

HE'LL HAVE TO GO THROUGH **US**, RIGHT, BRO?

**RIGHT!**

OH, HEY--!

OH, MY **GOSH!** IT'S MR. MORRIS' **GLOBAL POD!** I FORGOT TO GIVE IT BACK!

BILLY BATSON, YOU HAD BETTER RETURN IT STRAIGHT AWAY!

I HAVE A FEELING MR. STERLING MORRIS WILL WANT TO HAVE A WORD WITH YOU, YOUNG MAN.

203

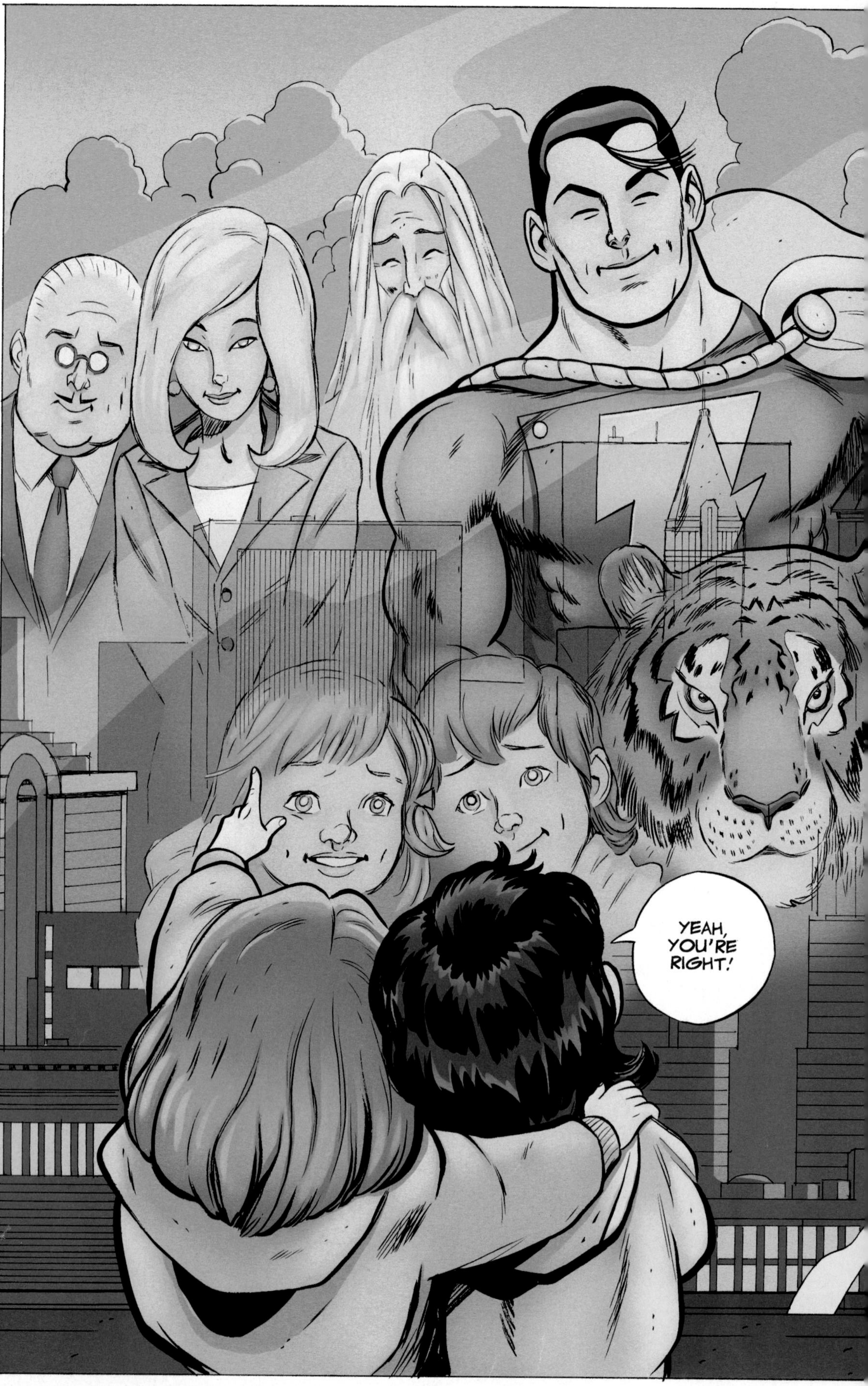
YEAH, YOU'RE RIGHT!

# THE MONSTER SOCIETY of EVIL

# GSV VMW?*

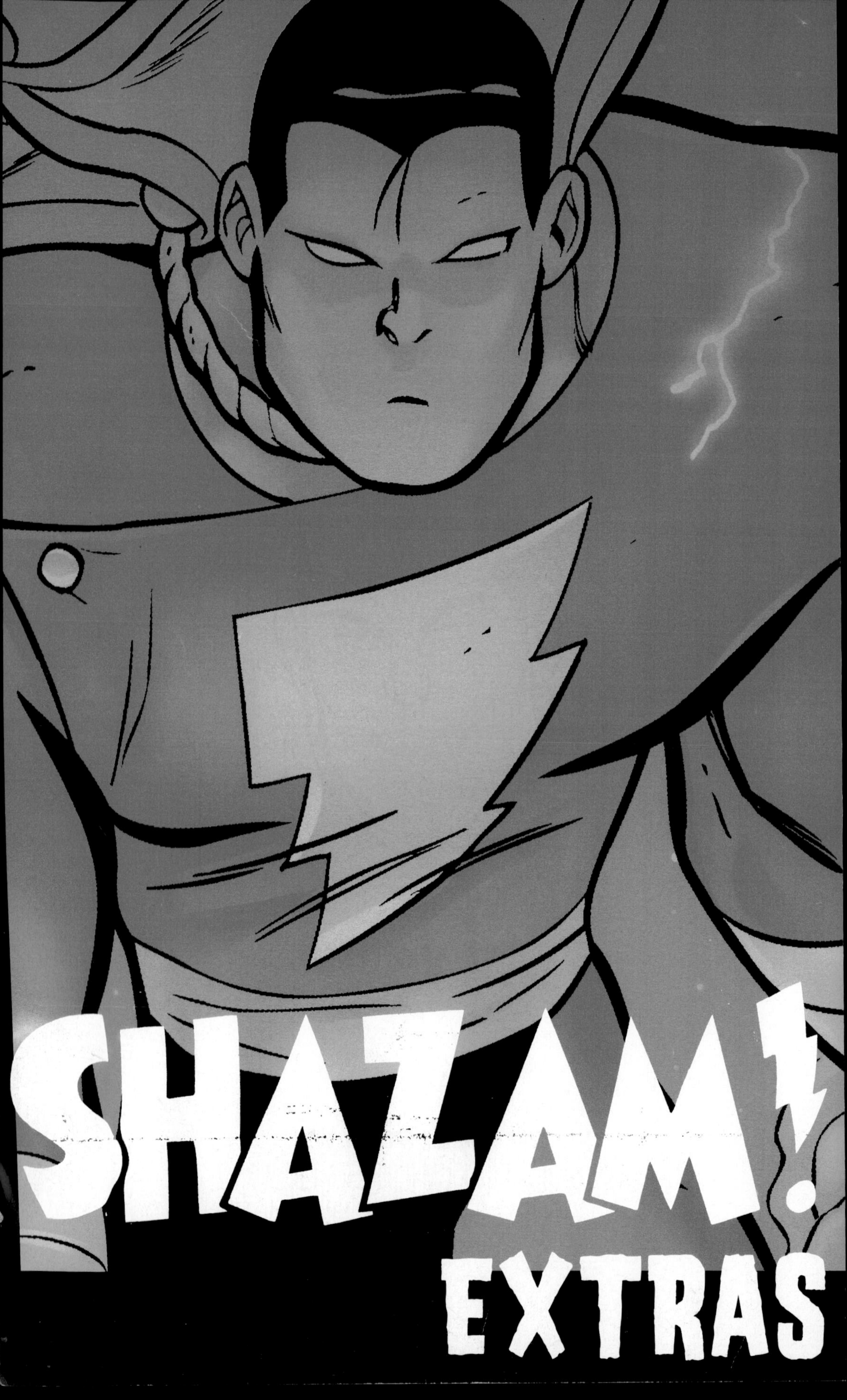
SHAZAM!
EXTRAS

# Afterword

One of the secret pleasures of making comics is doing the research; immersing yourself in history, science, mythology and of course, comic books.

Since Shazam is, at its core, a story built around a magic word, I followed the trail of Aladdin's Lamp, and Ali Baba's Forty Thieves to the 1,001 Arabian Nights, and other Near Eastern myths, where I found plenty of magic words, guardian genies, and the Wandering Ifrit, an amazing and ancient being that can change from human to animal form. Next, coming to terms with the Rock of Eternity required an exploration of space-time, so I happily dug out my books by Carl Sagan and Stephen Hawking. That's where I rediscovered singularities, an extreme phenomenon of physics where space and time are no longer separate. When time no longer exists, you have...eternity!

For a superhero story, especially one about Captain Marvel, the place to start is the Golden Age of comic books when *The Adventures of*

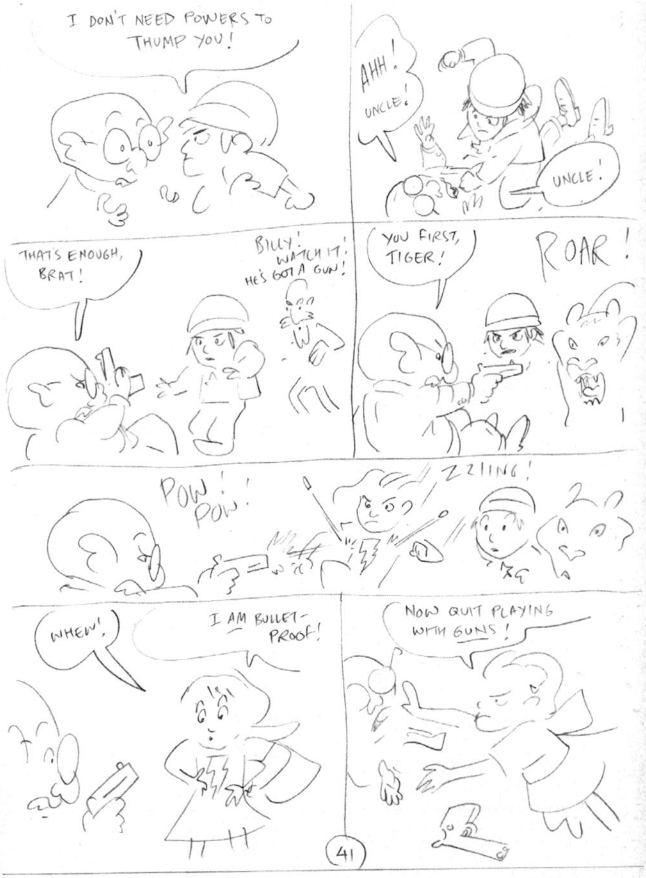

I DON'T NEED POWERS TO THUMP YOU!
AHH! UNCLE!
UNCLE!
THAT'S ENOUGH, BRAT!
BILLY! WATCH IT! HE'S GOT A GUN!
YOU FIRST, TIGER!
ROAR!
POW! POW!
ZZIING!
WHEW!
I AM BULLET-PROOF!
NOW QUIT PLAYING WITH GUNS!
41

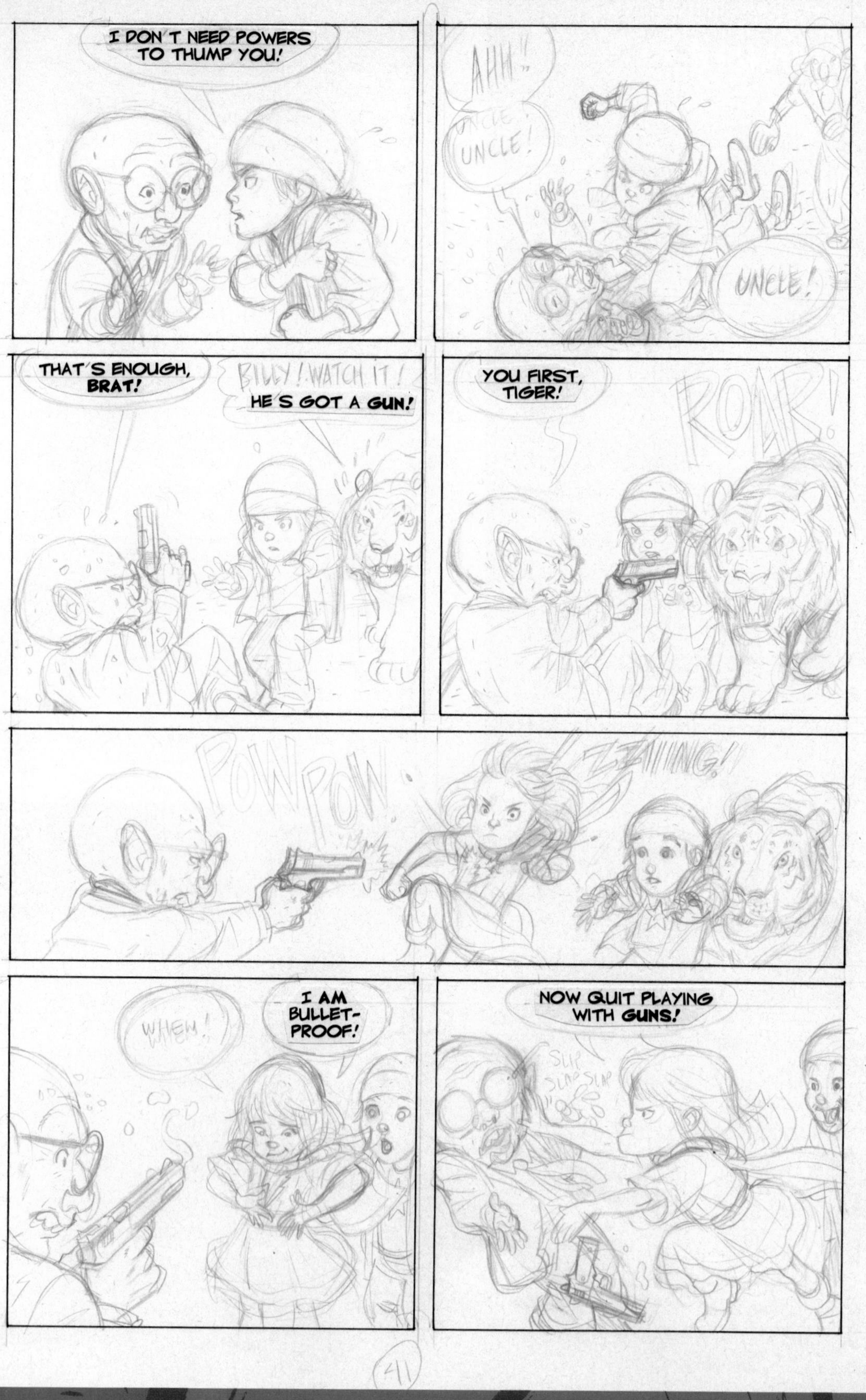
I DON'T NEED POWERS TO THUMP YOU!
AHH!!
UNCLE, UNCLE!
UNCLE!
THAT'S ENOUGH, BRAT!
BILLY! WATCH IT! HE'S GOT A GUN!
YOU FIRST, TIGER!
ROAR!
POW POW
ZZIIING!!
WHEW!
I AM BULLET-PROOF!
NOW QUIT PLAYING WITH GUNS!
SLAP SLAP SLAP
41

**Previous page:** Script for SHAZAM! №4, page 41.
**Above:** Blue pencils for SHAZAM! №4, page 41.
**Facing:** The same page with partial inks. I like to work on the faces first so the main acting is out of the way.

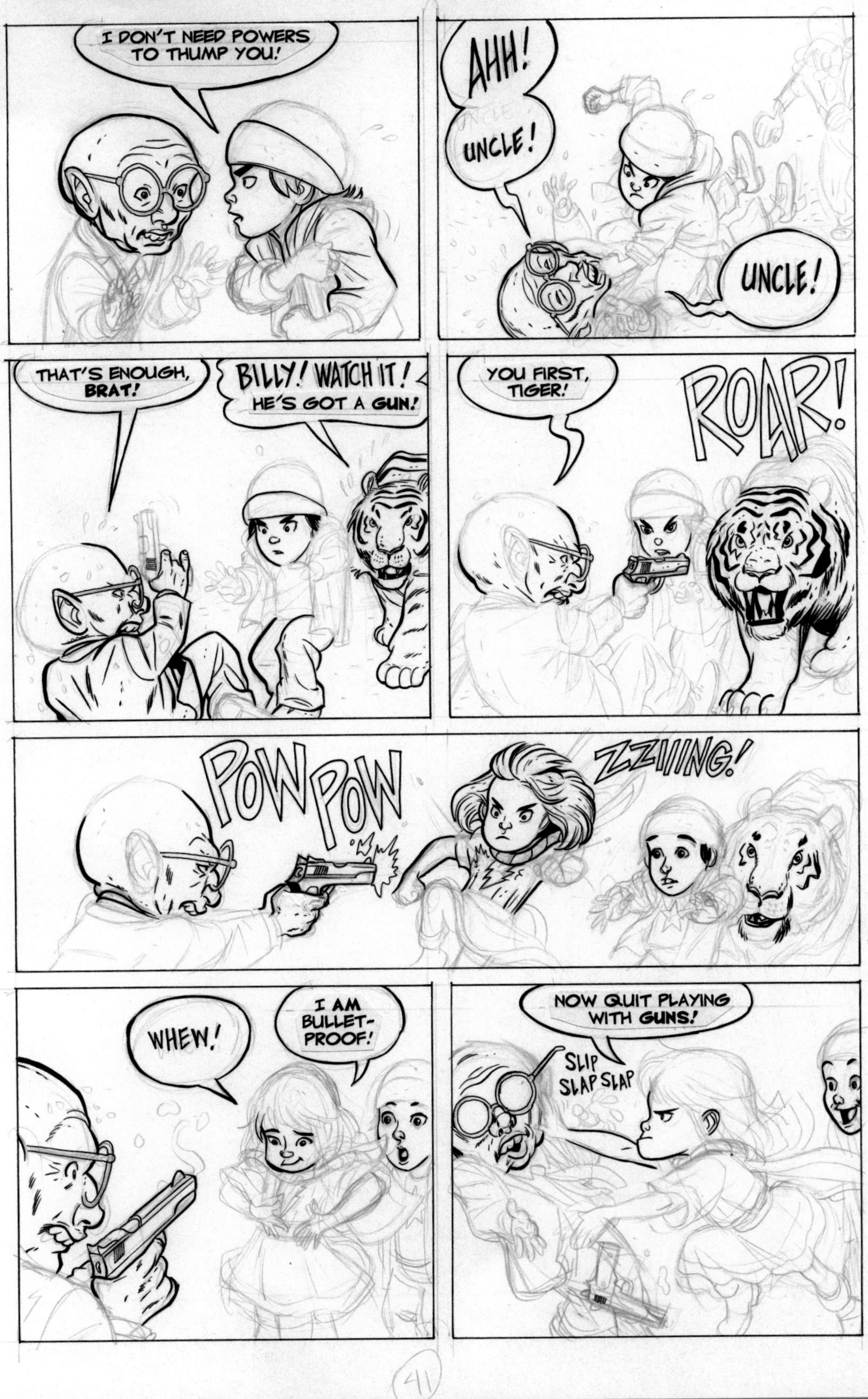

I DON'T NEED POWERS TO THUMP YOU!
AHH!
UNCLE!
UNCLE!
THAT'S ENOUGH, BRAT!
BILLY! WATCH IT! HE'S GOT A GUN!
YOU FIRST, TIGER!
ROAR!
POW POW
ZZIIING!
WHEW!
I AM BULLET-PROOF!
NOW QUIT PLAYING WITH GUNS!
SLIP SLAP SLAP
41

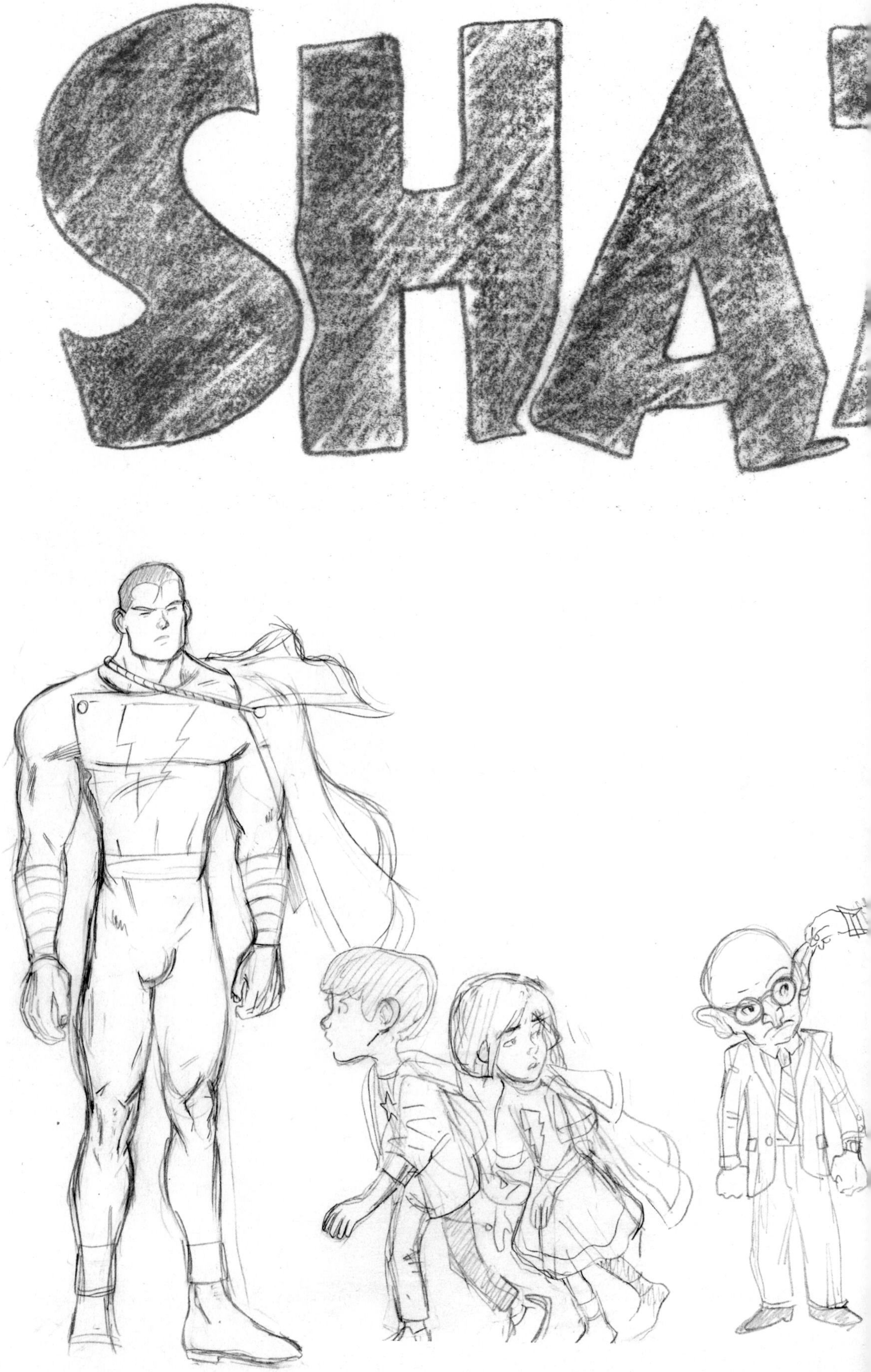
SHA

# LAM!
# SKETCHBOOK

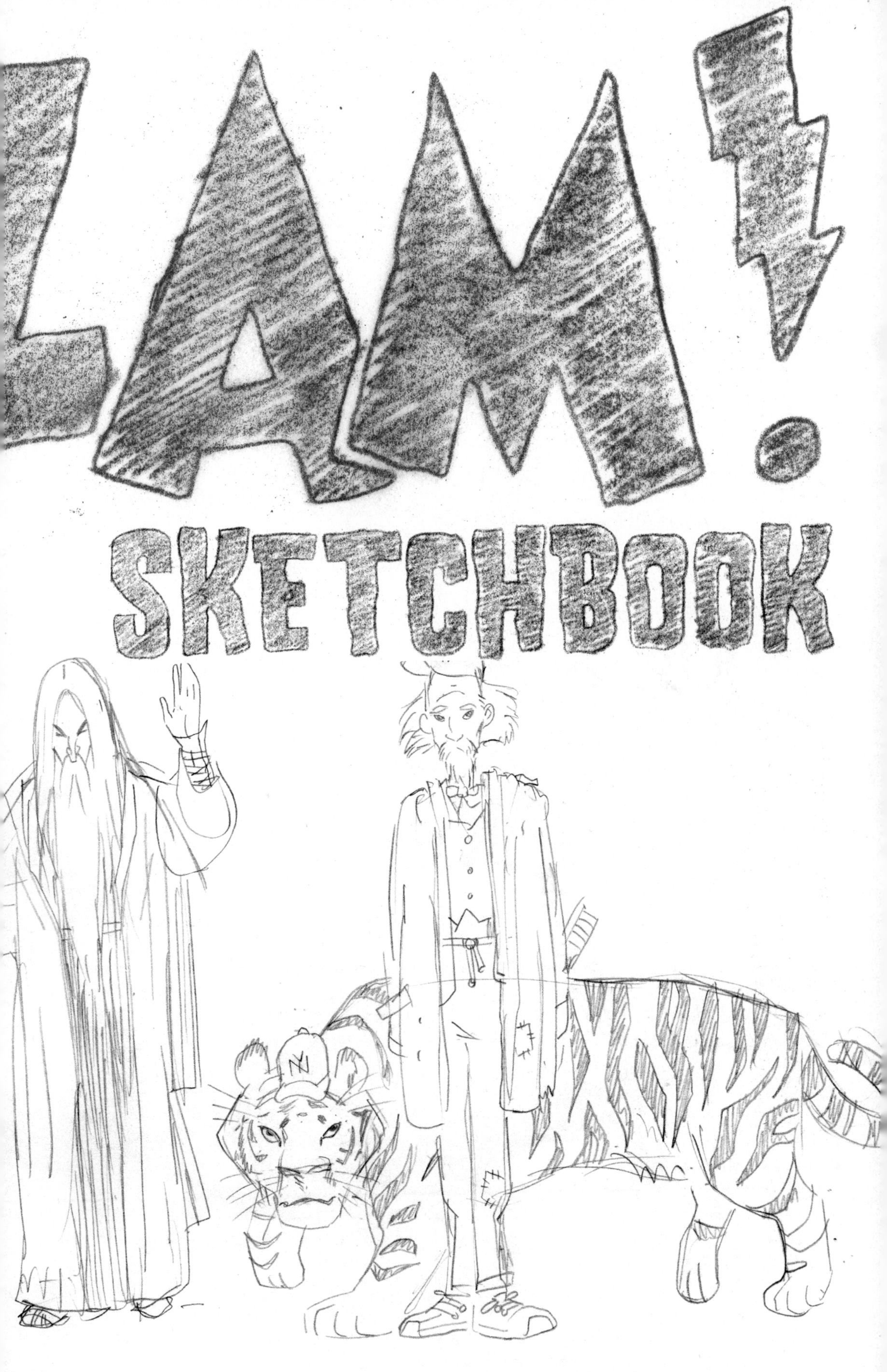

Nov. 16, 2001

CAPT. MARVEL NOTES

POSSIBLE
TITLES: WHIZ, BIG RED JUSTICE, CAPT. BILLY'S WHIZ BANG

CAPTAIN MARVEL IS A GENIE* (A SUPERNATURAL BEING THAT CAN TAKE
   HUMAN OR ANIMAL FORM AND INFLUENCE HUMAN AFFAIRS)
      * A JINNI IS A MOSLEM LEGEND -- I SHOULD RESEARCH MID-EASTERN MYTHOLOGY

C.M. IS BILLY'S PROTECTOR -- BUT IS ALSO PART OF BILLY.

C.M. IS OLDER AND WISER THAN BILLY, BUT ALSO FAIRLY NEW TO OUR WORLD.
   HE IS CURIOUS AND DISPLAYS A REAL ZEAL FOR LIFE AND EVERYTHING IT
HAS TO OFFER. (HE ESPECIALLY LOVES HOT DOGS, AND SOMETIMES BEFORE
CHANGING INTO MARVEL, BILLY LEAVES A COUPLE OF BUCKS OUT SO C.M.
CAN BUY A HOT DOG FROM THE GUY ON THE CORNER.)

BILLY LIVES IN NYC. HE IS HOMELESS AND AN ORPHAN. HE IS A STREET KID
HE KNOWS HE HAS A SISTER AND HE IS SEARCHING FOR HER.

STORY OPENS WITH BILLY SLEEPING IN ABANDONED BUILDING. A TROUBLEMAKER
   ENTERS AND STARTS TO BEAT HIM, BUT BILLY CHANGES TO C.M.
MARVEL CHASES OFF THUG, BUT THEN LOOKS AROUND AT BILLY'S QUARTERS.
   SOMETHING MUST BE DONE -- THIS IS NO PLACE FOR A KID.

BILLY LOVES STORIES ABOUT HERCULES AND OTHER GREEK MYTHS --- MAYBE THAT'S WHERE
ALL THE GREEK NAMES COME FROM THAT MAKE UP "SHAZAM."
   (THE OLD WIZARD SHAZAM IS SUPPOSED TO BE EGYPTIAN, BUT MAYBE IT ALL COMES
      FROM BILLY BATSON'S UNCONSCIOUS?)

MARVEL IS BILLY, AND BILLY IS MARVEL.

①

Nov. 16, 2001

QUICK PLOT IDEAS:

○ A DIMENSION RIFT OPENS UP AND A GIANT, ORGANIC ROBOT
APPEARS AND BEGINS CRUSHING CITY.

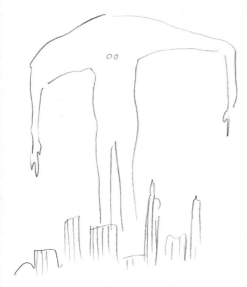

○ MORE ROBOTS APPEAR AND BEGIN A WAR
WITH EACH OTHER. THE HUMAN POPULATION
ARE INNOCENT VICTIMS.

○ SIVANA SUB-PLOT OF SENDING HUMAN SIZED
KILLER ROBOTS TO DEFEAT MARVEL.
MOSTLY COMEDY RELIEF. SIVANA IS A
WHINY, SELF-CENTERED PHONEY BONE-TYPE.

○ MAGIC IS A THEME HERE. BILLY GOES TO
A SIEGFID & ROY TYPE SHOW. HE MEETS
TALKY TAWNY -- WHO EITHER IS ANOTHER
JINN LIKE MARVEL, OR IS FROM THE
SAME DIMENSION AS THE GIANT ROBOTS

BILLY BATSON — A LONELY STREET URCHIN
THE WIZARD — AN ANCIENT HOLYMAN of UNKNOWN ORIGIN
MARY MARVEL — BILLY BATSON'S YOUNGER SISTER
SHAZAM — A POWERFUL PROTECTOR GUARDIAN FROM THE REALM of ETERNITY
TALKY TAWNY — A WANDERING IFRIT (A CREATURE ABLE TO TAKE THE FORM of MAJOR BEAST,
ALSO FROM THE REALM of ETERNITY
DR. SIVANA — A SELF MADE, POWER-HUNGRY GENIUS
MR. MIND — A MYSTERIOUS FORCE FOR EVIL

I started to jot down ideas as fast as they came. Some got used;
others, like Sivana's army of human-sized robots, didn't.

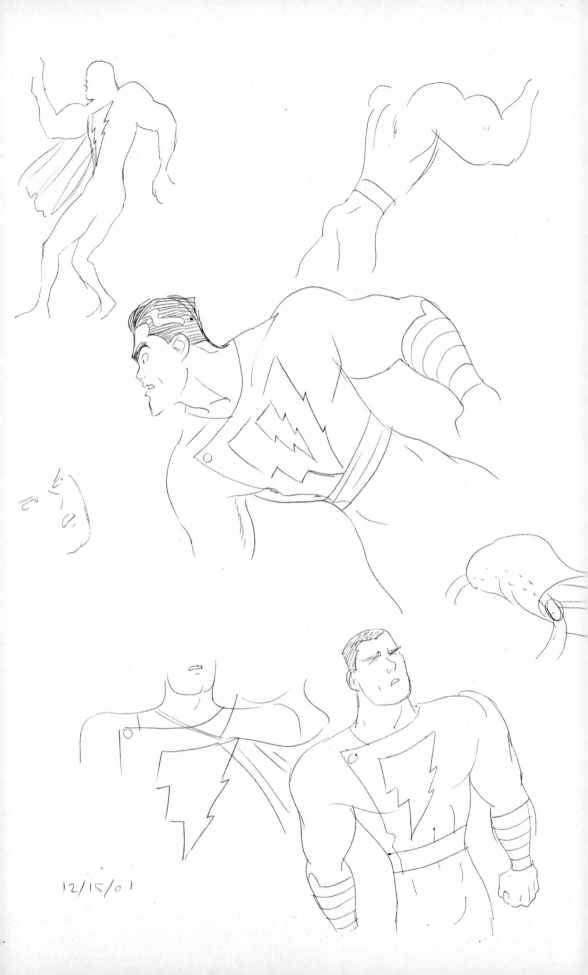

12/15/01

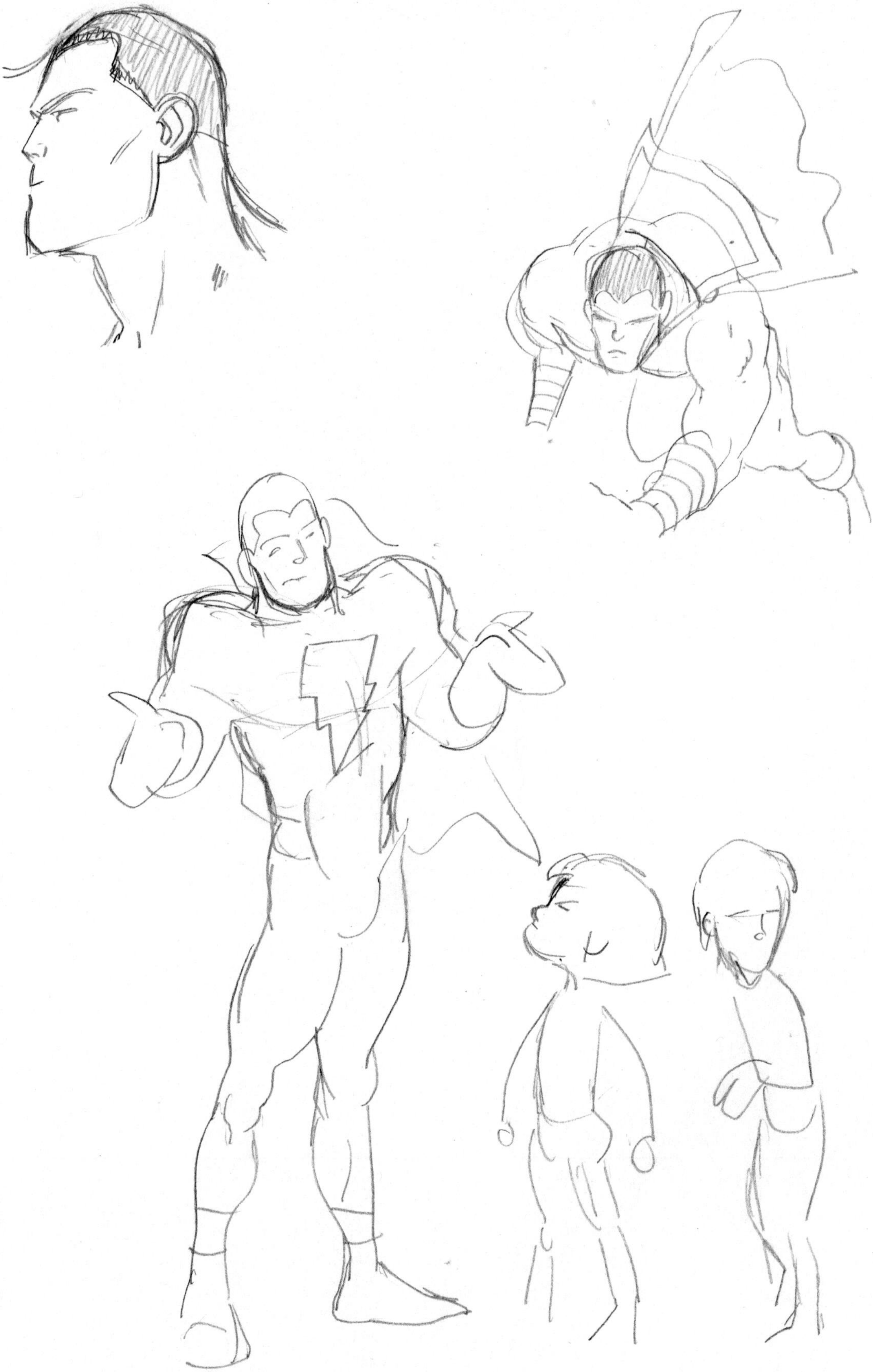

One big question was how realistic to draw Captain Marvel; dot eyes or whites; should his shirt have big shoulder seams or a buttoned flap? How large should his lightning emblem be? The original C.C. Beck artwork was very simple and clear, often verging on cartoony.

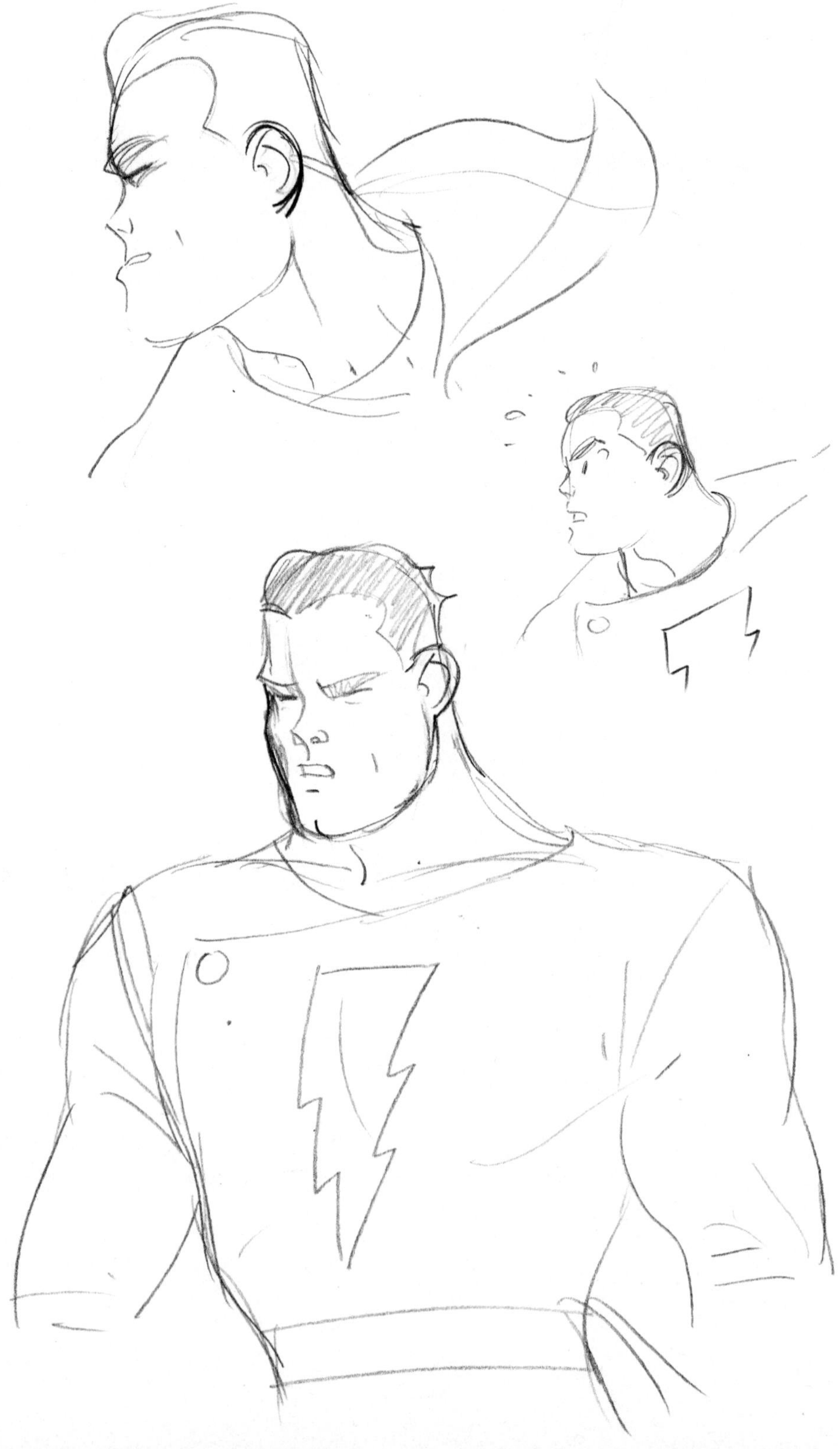

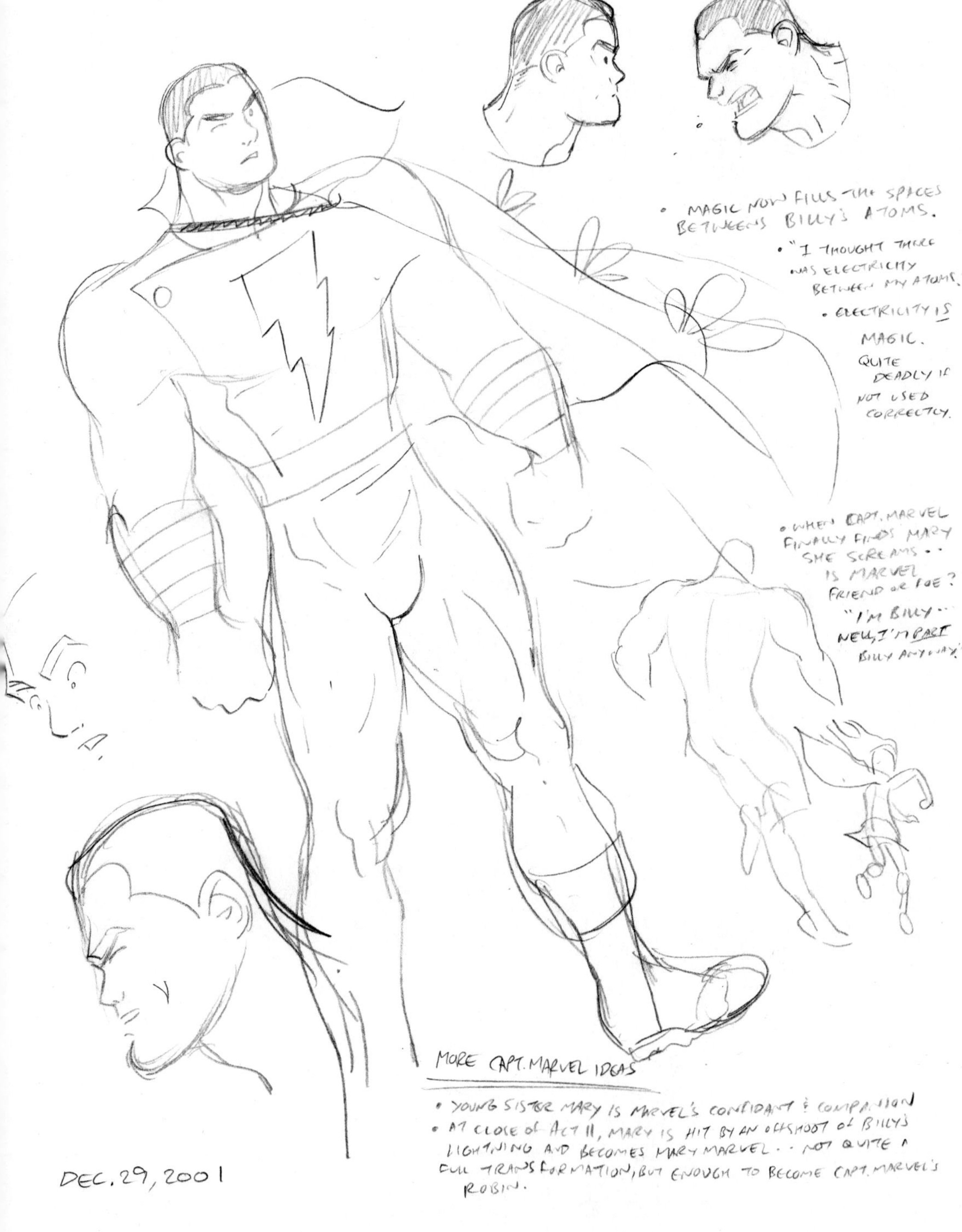
• MAGIC NOW FILLS THE SPACES BETWEENS BILLY'S ATOMS.
• "I THOUGHT THERE WAS ELECTRICITY BETWEEN MY ATOMS."
• ELECTRICITY IS MAGIC. QUITE DEADLY IF NOT USED CORRECTLY.
• WHEN CAPT. MARVEL FINALLY FINDS MARY SHE SCREAMS . . IS MARVEL FRIEND OR FOE?
"I'M BILLY . . . WELL, I'M PART BILLY ANYWAY."

MORE CAPT. MARVEL IDEAS

- YOUNG SISTER MARY IS MARVEL'S CONFIDANT & COMPANION
- AT CLOSE OF ACT II, MARY IS HIT BY AN OFFSHOOT OF BILLY'S LIGHTNING AND BECOMES MARY MARVEL . . NOT QUITE A FULL TRANSFORMATION, BUT ENOUGH TO BECOME CAPT. MARVEL'S ROBIN.

DEC. 29, 2001

This drawing of Mary ignited the whole story for me. Once I knew who Mary was, I suddenly knew who Billy and Captain Marvel were—her big brother! Note the C.C. Beck dot eyes.

DURING A CRISIS, MARY IS STRUCK BY A STRAY BOLT FROM BILLY'S MAGIC LIGHTNING.

TO BOTH THEIR SURPRISE SHE TURNS INTO MARY MARVEL

MARY DOES NOT HAVE THE FULL POWERS THAT HER BROTHER HAS. SHE IS INVICIBLE AND CAN FLY, BUT SHE IS NOT AS STRONG. NOR DOES SHE FULLY TRANSFORM INTO AN ADULT THE WAY BILLY DOES.

DEC. 29, 2001

AFTER THE FIRST TIME MARY IS ATTACHED, SHE IS UNHURT BUT STILL VERY SCARED, LIKE A CHILD, BUT THEN, GASPING WITH EXCITEMEN EYES WIDE, SHE SPRINGS TO ATTACK

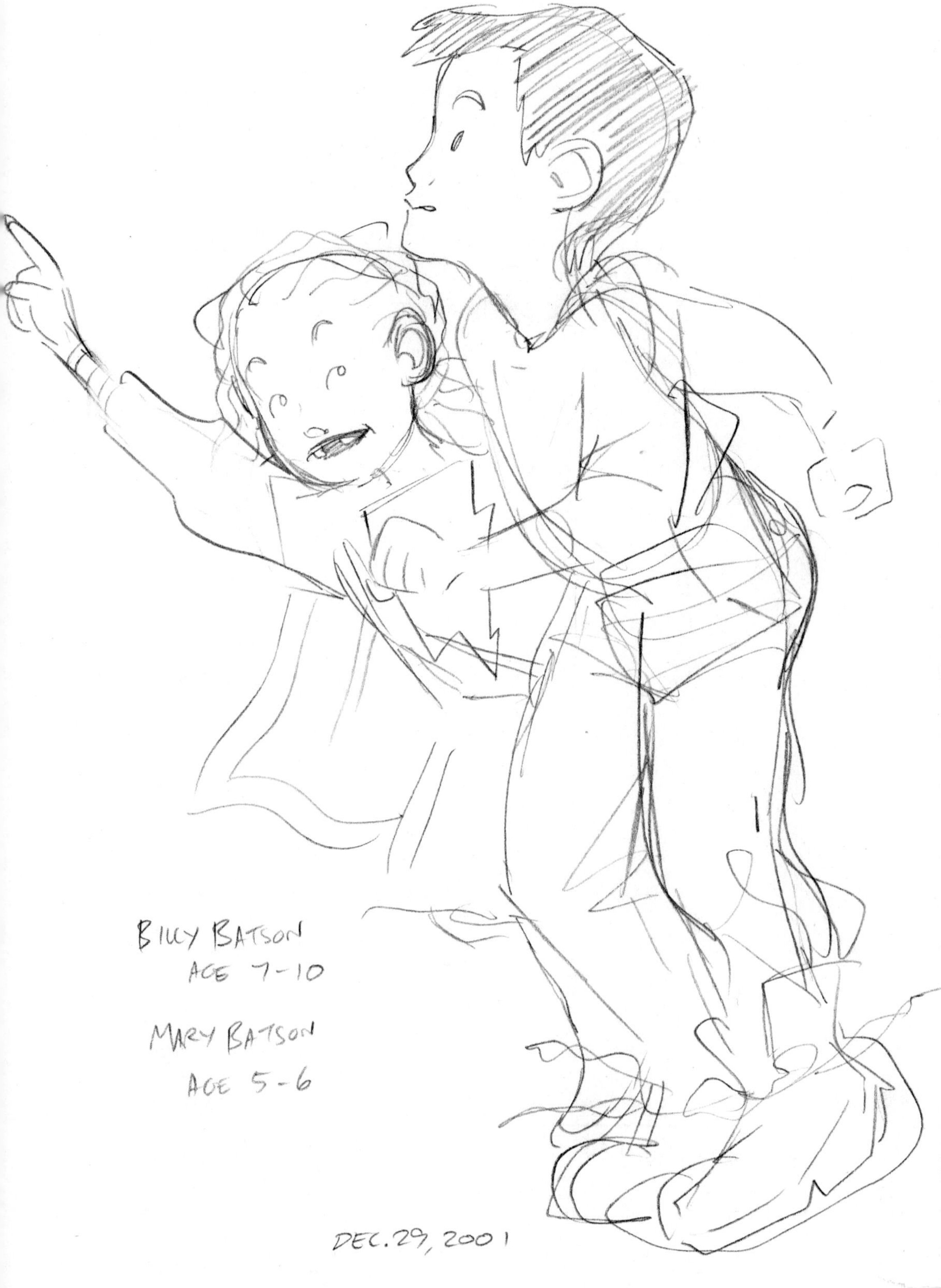

BILLY BATSON
AGE 7-10

MARY BATSON
AGE 5-6

DEC. 29, 2001

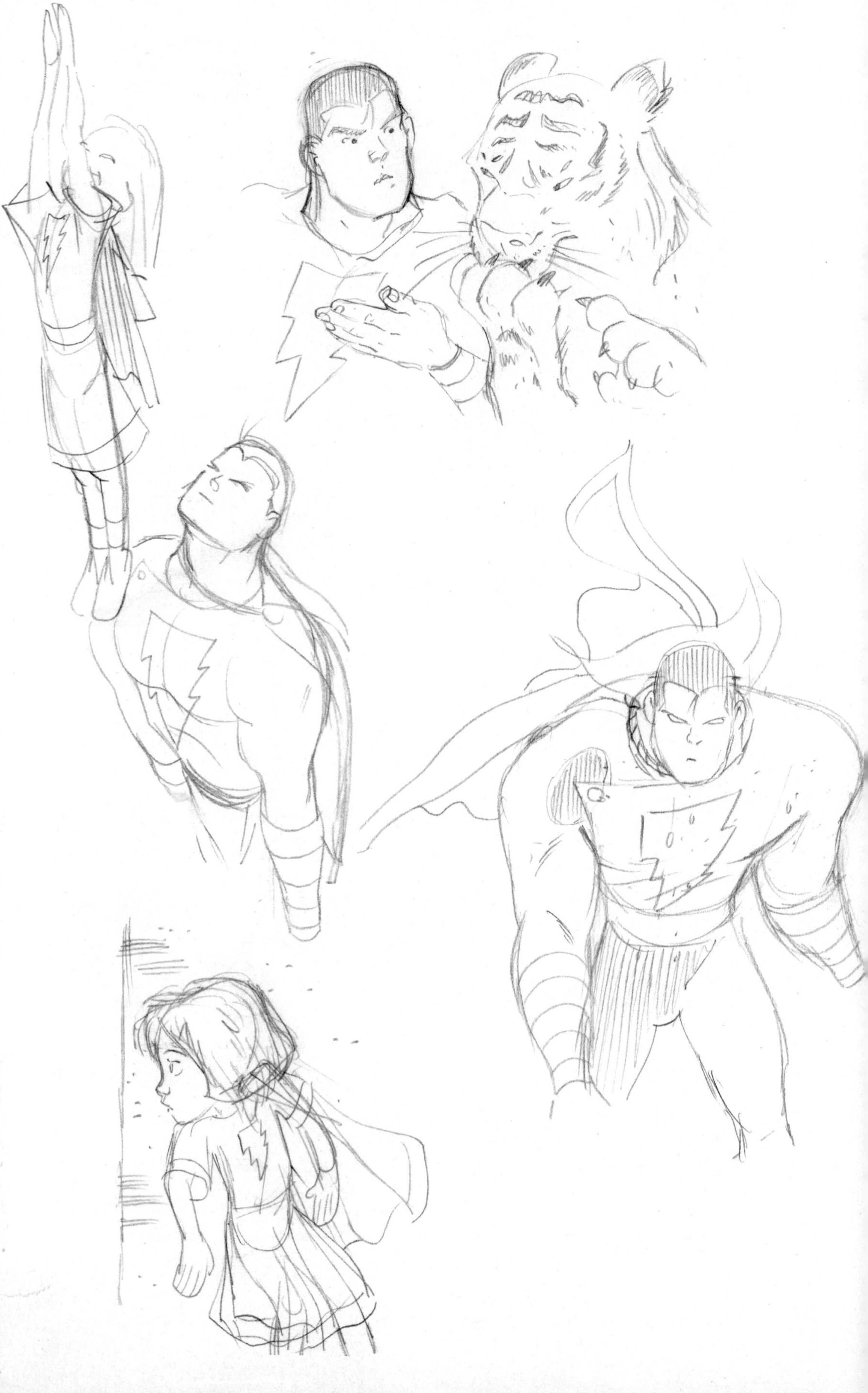

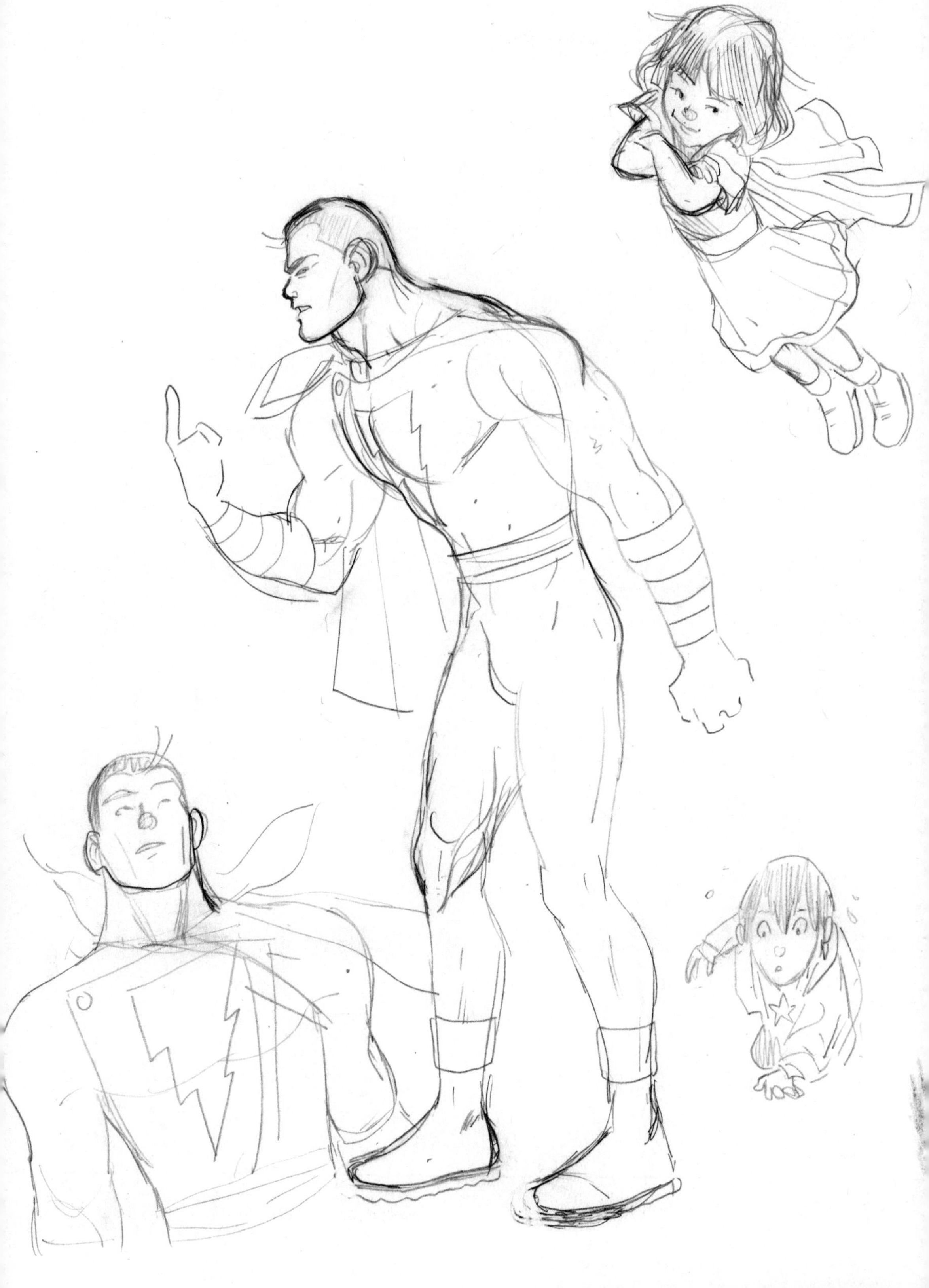

The main cast of characters began to fill out, gaining more natural weight, becoming solid. Two of these drawings actually made it into the finished book: one as a cover, the other as part of a full page.

These are some of my earliest sketches—
Billy is running like a human version of Fone Bone!

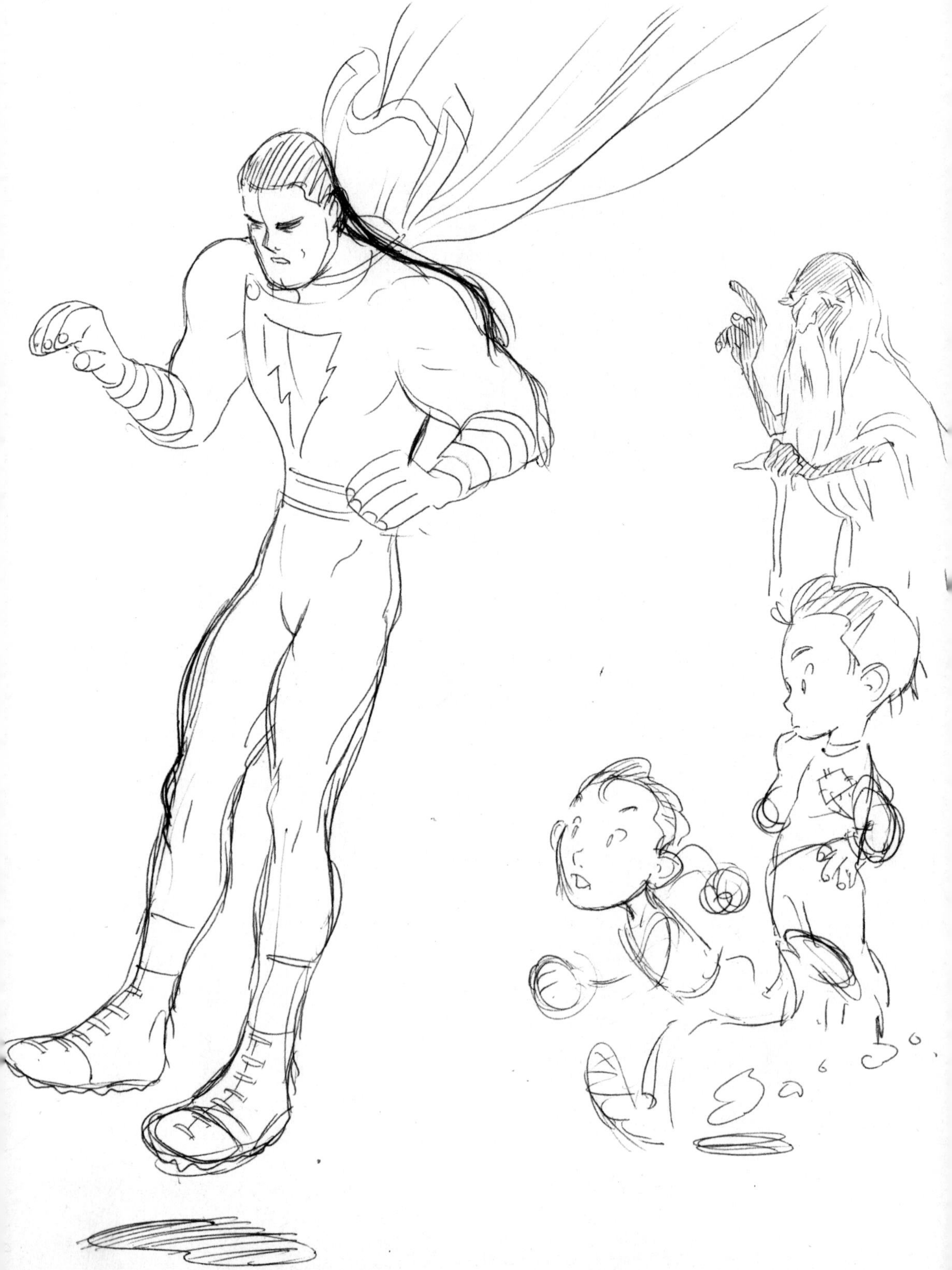

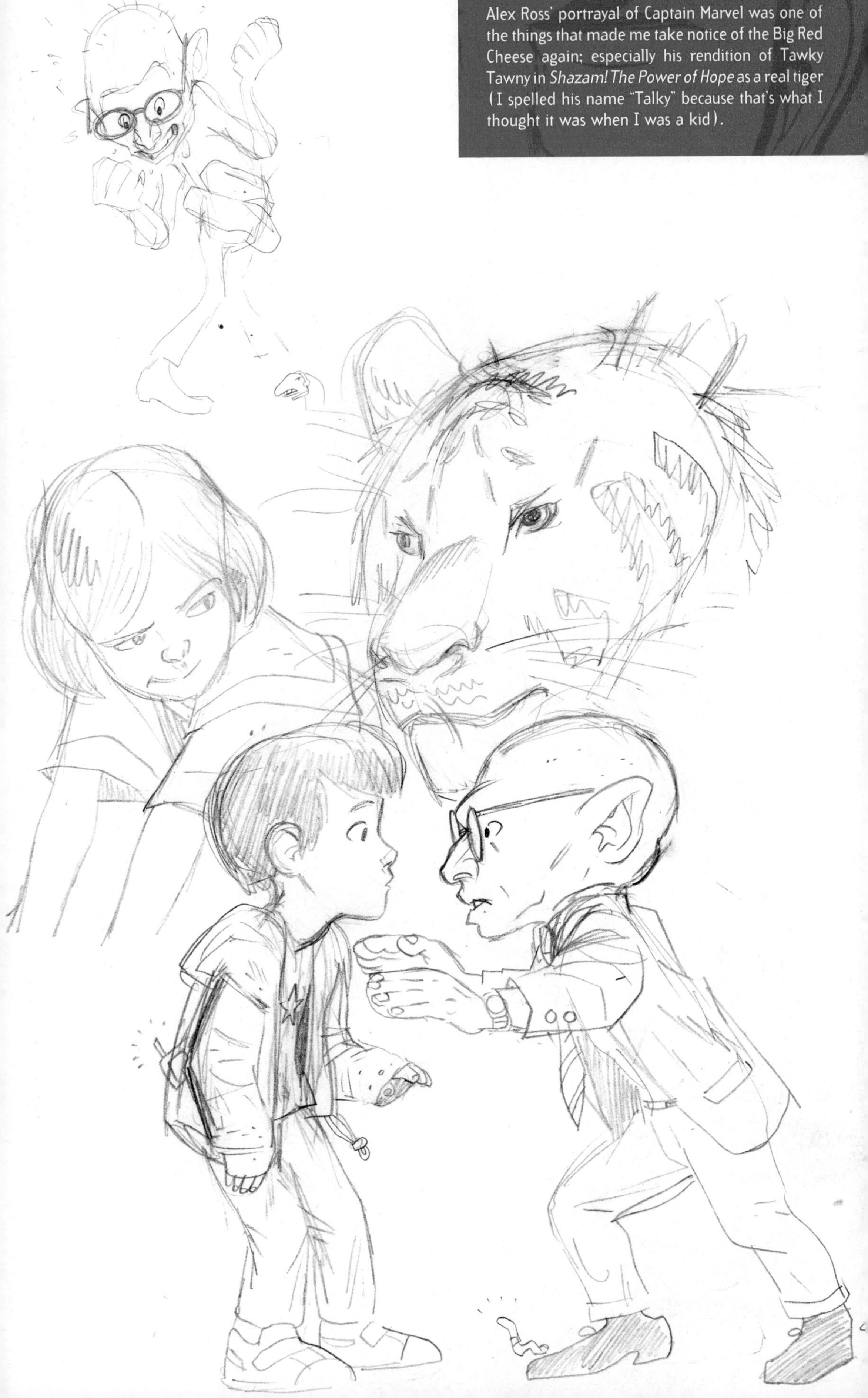

Alex Ross' portrayal of Captain Marvel was one of the things that made me take notice of the Big Red Cheese again; especially his rendition of Tawky Tawny in *Shazam! The Power of Hope* as a real tiger (I spelled his name "Talky" because that's what I thought it was when I was a kid).

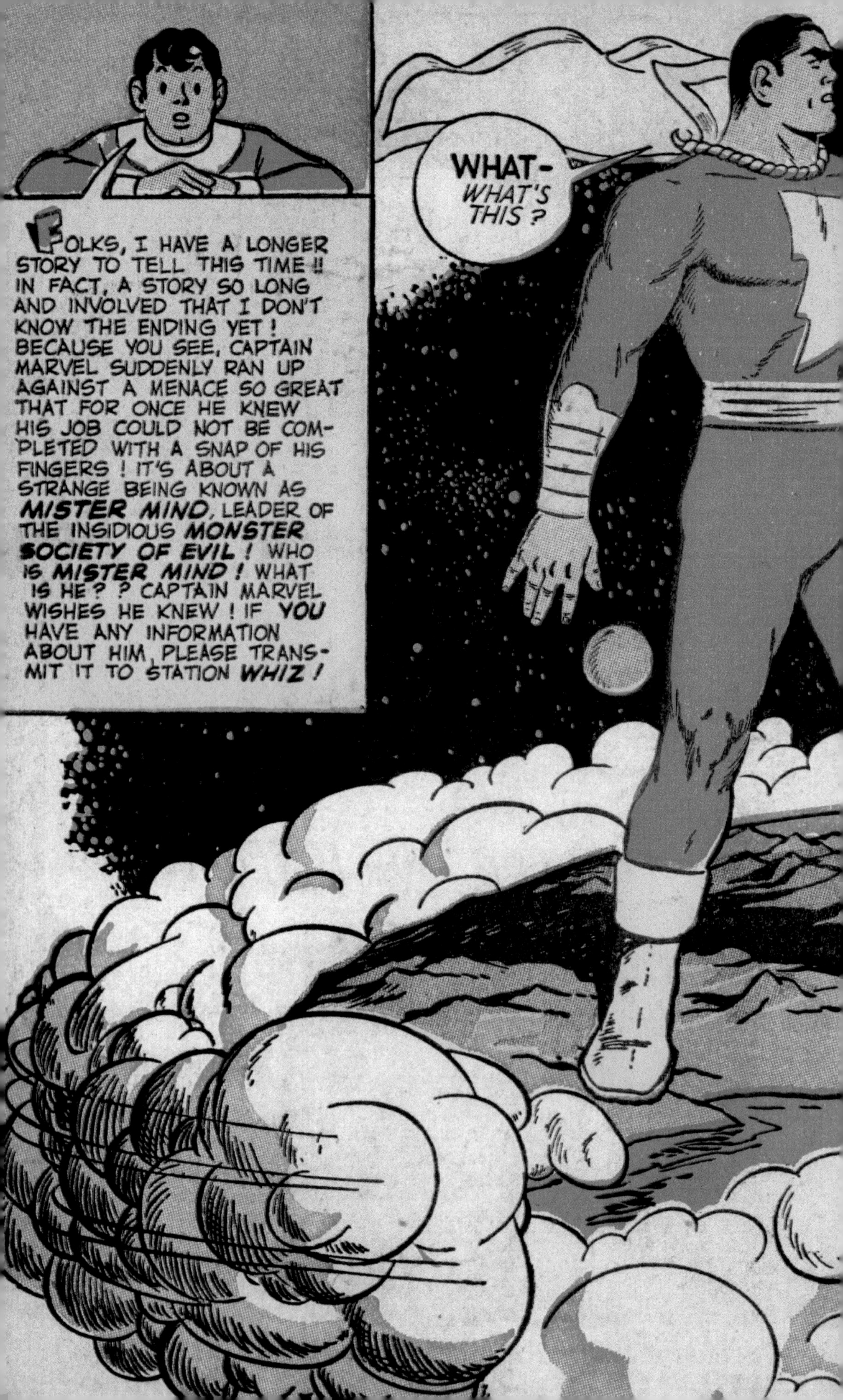
FOLKS, I HAVE A LONGER STORY TO TELL THIS TIME !! IN FACT, A STORY SO LONG AND INVOLVED THAT I DON'T KNOW THE ENDING YET ! BECAUSE YOU SEE, CAPTAIN MARVEL SUDDENLY RAN UP AGAINST A MENACE SO GREAT THAT FOR ONCE HE KNEW HIS JOB COULD NOT BE COMPLETED WITH A SNAP OF HIS FINGERS ! IT'S ABOUT A STRANGE BEING KNOWN AS MISTER MIND, LEADER OF THE INSIDIOUS MONSTER SOCIETY OF EVIL ! WHO IS MISTER MIND ! WHAT IS HE ? ? CAPTAIN MARVEL WISHES HE KNEW ! IF YOU HAVE ANY INFORMATION ABOUT HIM, PLEASE TRANSMIT IT TO STATION WHIZ !
WHAT- WHAT'S THIS ?

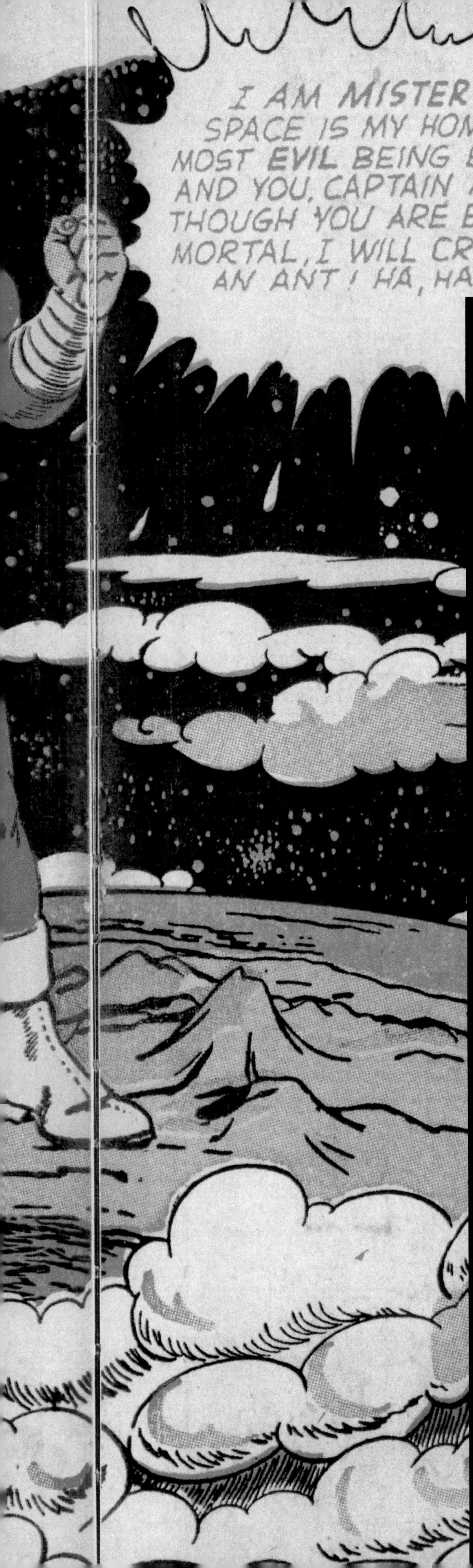
I AM MISTER MIND! SPACE IS MY HOME! I AM THE MOST EVIL BEING EVER TO LIVE! AND YOU, CAPTAIN MARVEL.. THOUGH YOU ARE EARTH'S MIGHTIEST MORTAL, I WILL CRUSH YOU LIKE AN ANT! HA, HA, HAAAA!!

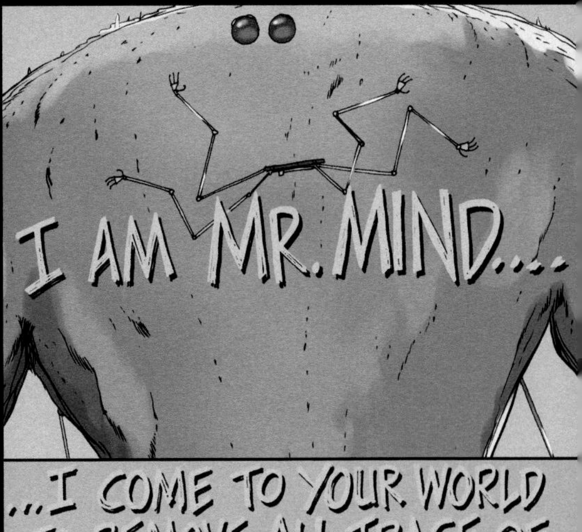
I AM MR. MIND....
...I COME TO YOUR WORLD TO REMOVE ALL TRACE OF HUMAN CIVILIZATION...

The original Monster Society of Evil was serialized in *Captain Marvel Adventures* nos. 22-46. It started with this two-page splash of a disembodied voice coming from the sky.

Inset above: Panels from the current MSoE.

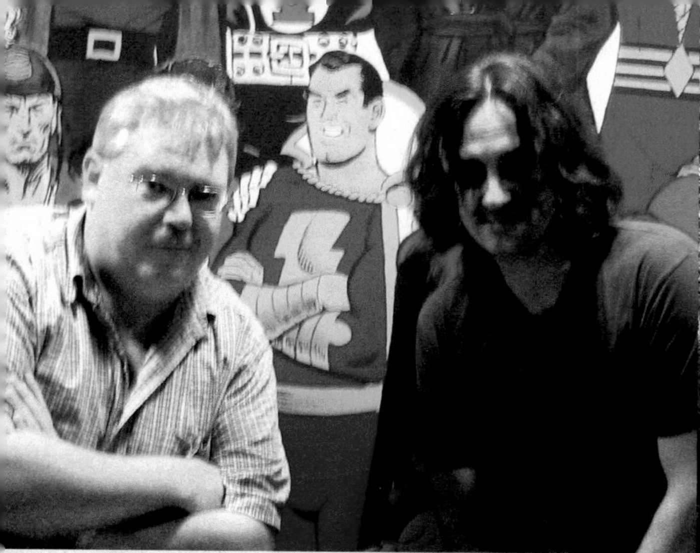

# 7/5/2006

## Shazam Production Journal: SHAZAM!

This will be the first of my SHAZAM! MONSTER SOCIETY OF EVIL production journals. I slipped into New York last week to meet with DC editor Mike Carlin about the four-issue miniseries I'm working on, SHAZAM! MONSTER SOCIETY OF EVIL. This is me and Mike, with the Big Cheese himself, in front of a mural at the DC offices.

Meanwhile, I needed to do some location scouting. The climactic battle in MSoE takes place in Central Park, so I spent Friday wandering around taking reference photos. Here are a few that will be used for locations around the giant monster's feet, like Sivana's Rock, and Talky & Billy's Rendezvous Point.

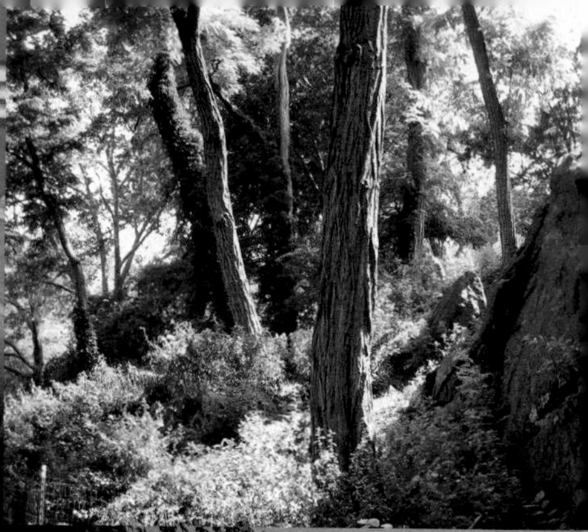

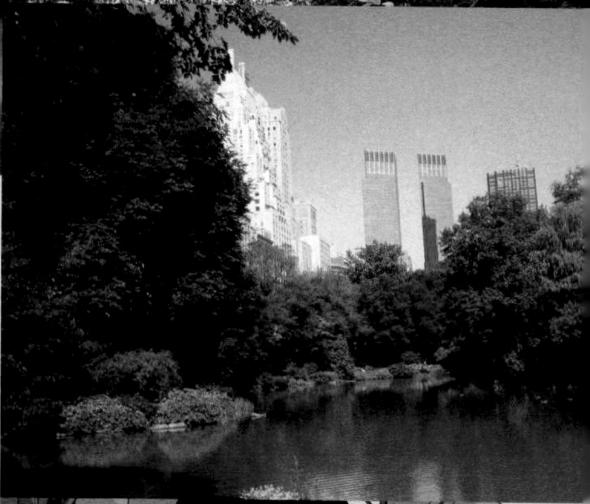

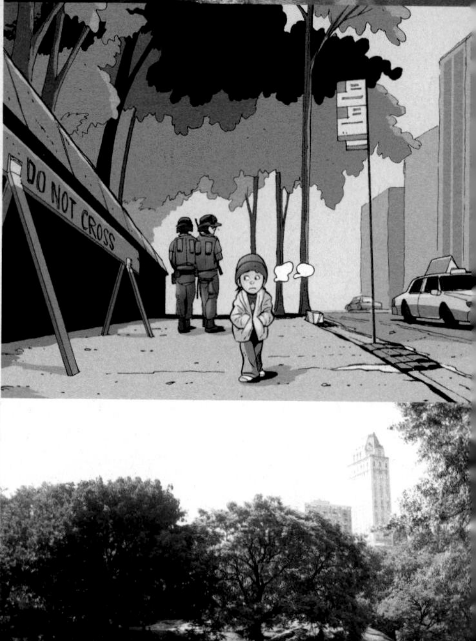
DO NOT CROSS

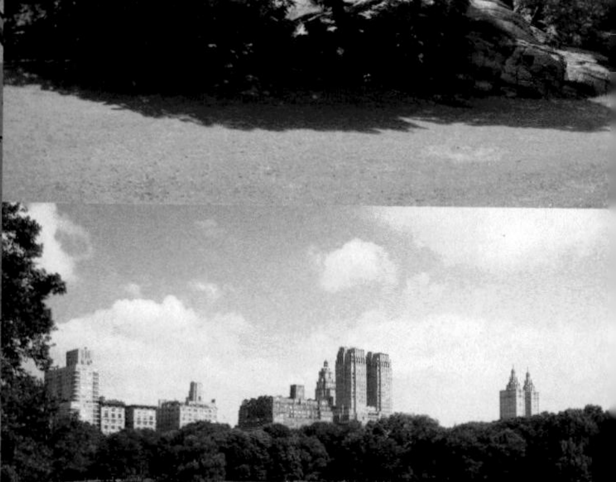

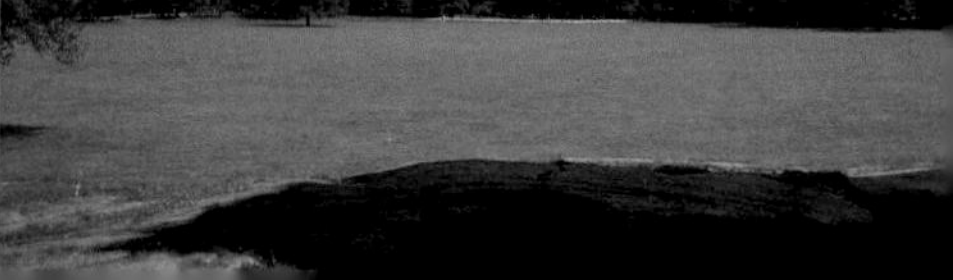

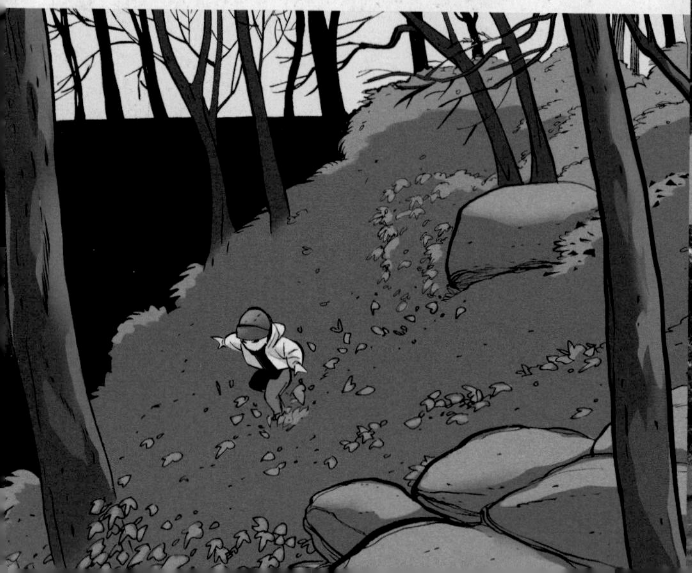

# 11/28/2006

## Shazam Production Journal: The Seven Deadly Enemies of Man

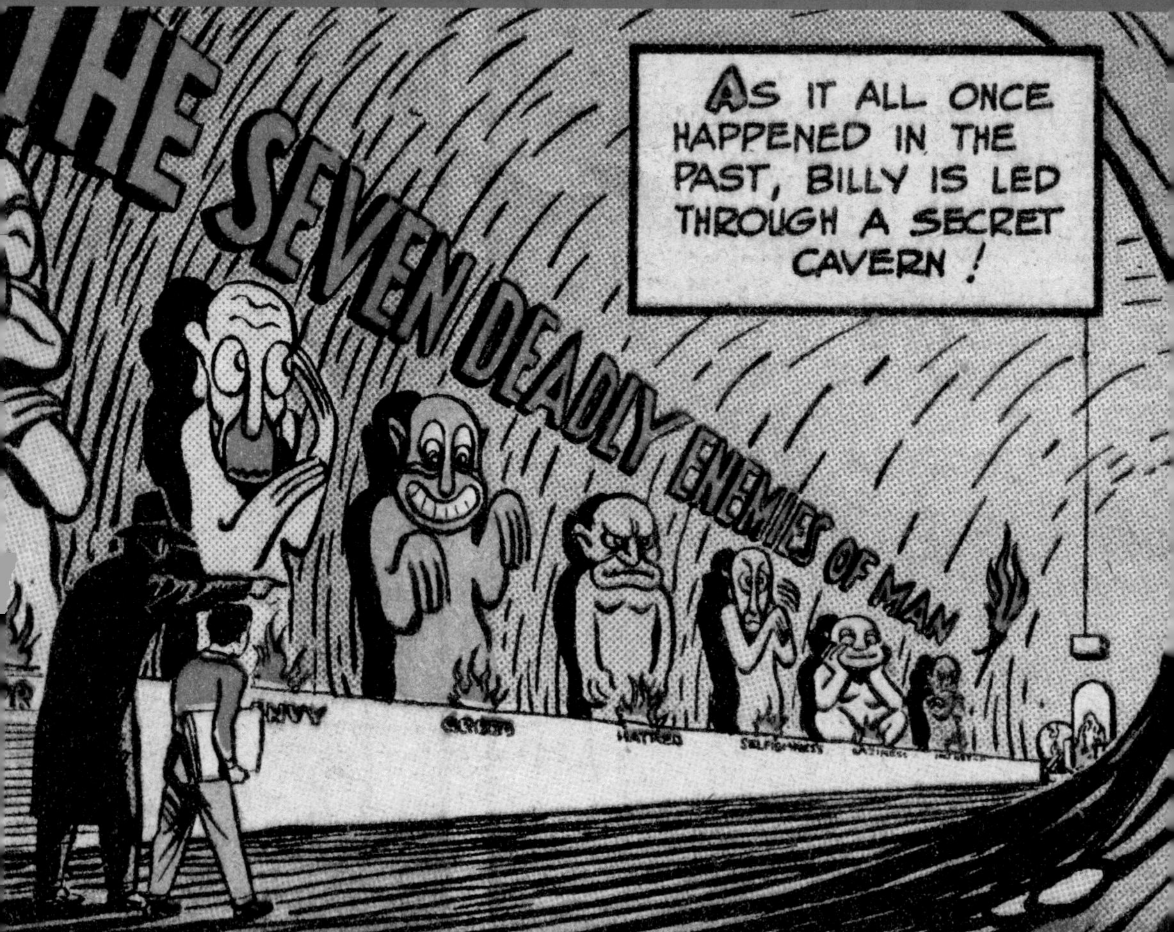
HE SEVEN DEADLY ENEMIES OF MAN
AS IT ALL ONCE HAPPENED IN THE PAST, BILLY IS LED THROUGH A SECRET CAVERN!
ENVY
HATRED

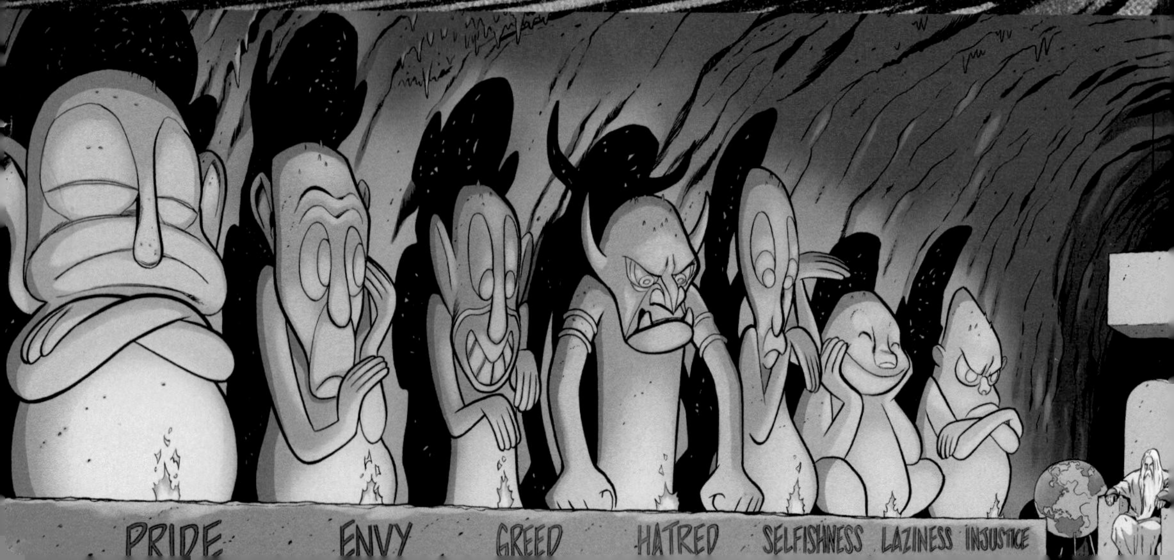
PRIDE
ENVY
GREED
HATRED
SELFISHNESS
LAZINESS
INJUSTICE

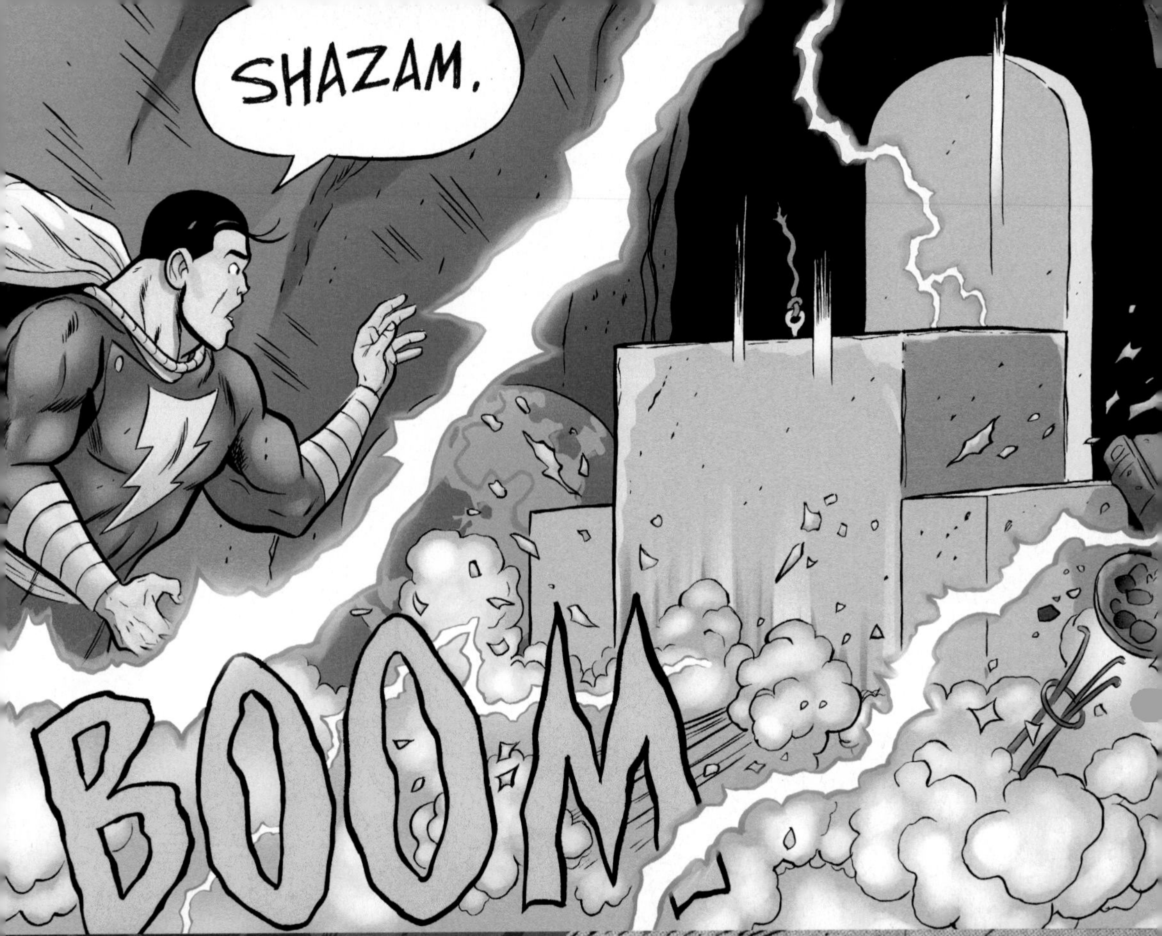
SHAZAM.
BOOM

Starting tomorrow, Nov. 29, the pages from SHAZAM! MONSTER SOCIETY OF EVIL that feature a portion of Captain Marvel's origin in the Hall of the Seven Deadly Enemies of Man will be up on the DC Comics website. Here are some of the panels from the Golden Age that influenced my version.

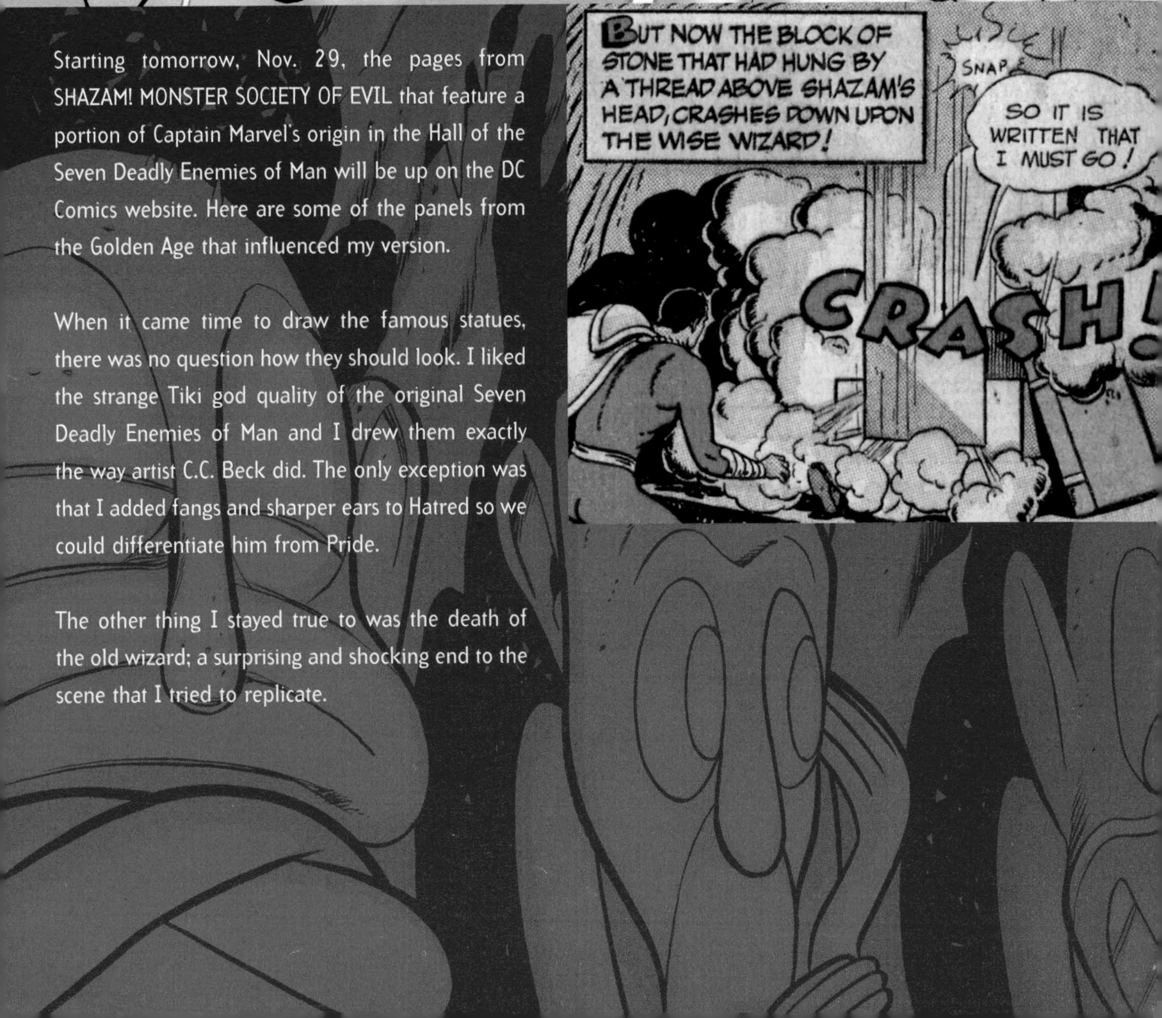
BUT NOW THE BLOCK OF STONE THAT HAD HUNG BY A THREAD ABOVE SHAZAM'S HEAD, CRASHES DOWN UPON THE WISE WIZARD!
SNAP
SO IT IS WRITTEN THAT I MUST GO!
CRASH!

When it came time to draw the famous statues, there was no question how they should look. I liked the strange Tiki god quality of the original Seven Deadly Enemies of Man and I drew them exactly the way artist C.C. Beck did. The only exception was that I added fangs and sharper ears to Hatred so we could differentiate him from Pride.

The other thing I stayed true to was the death of the old wizard; a surprising and shocking end to the scene that I tried to replicate.

# 12/8/2006

# Shazam Production Journal: Monster Societies and Secret Codes

Not long ago, I described the four-issue miniseries I'm working on as "Shazam: Year One" but, that's misleading. SHAZAM! MONSTER SOCIETY OF EVIL isn't really a "Year One" project as much as it's a remake of a nearly legendary comic book serial from the early 1940s. "Captain Marvel and the Monster Society of Evil" ran in monthly installments from 1943 to 1945 in *Captain Marvel Adventures* №22-№46.

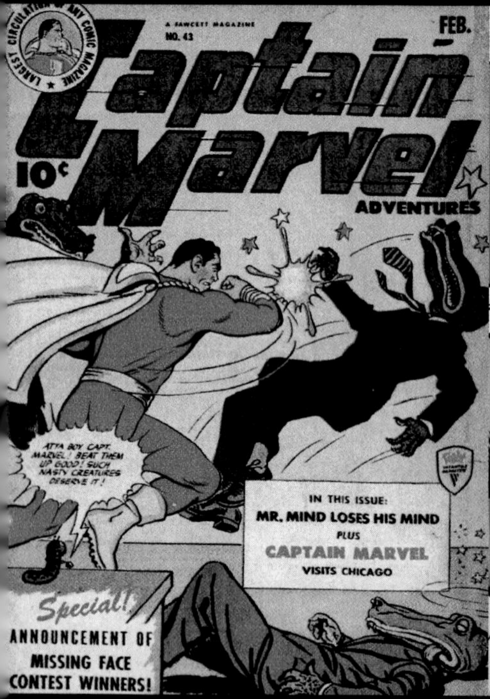
A FAWCETT MAGAZINE
NO. 43
FEB.
Captain Marvel
10¢
ADVENTURES
IN THIS ISSUE:
MR. MIND LOSES HIS MIND
PLUS
CAPTAIN MARVEL
VISITS CHICAGO
Special!
ANNOUNCEMENT OF
MISSING FACE
CONTEST WINNERS!

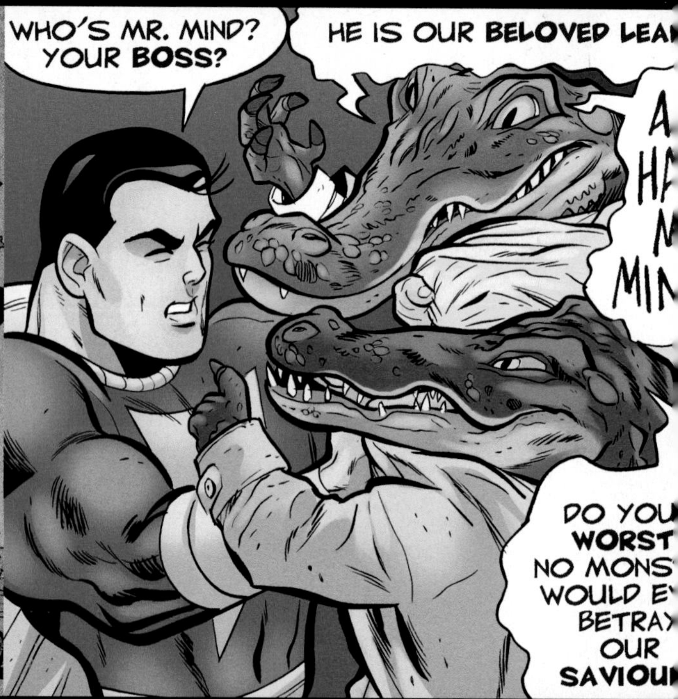
WHO'S MR. MIND? YOUR BOSS?
HE IS OUR BELOVED LEA
DO YOU
WORST
NO MONS
WOULD E
BETRAY
OUR
SAVIOU

It was the first really long story in comic books, and it was full of cliff-hangers and secret messages that could be read only if you had a Secret Decoder Ring. At the heart of the Monster Society are the monsters, of course, and my favorites from the original serial were the alligator people. In the original, they were crocodile men, but because I love Albert from *Pogo*, I made them alligator men.

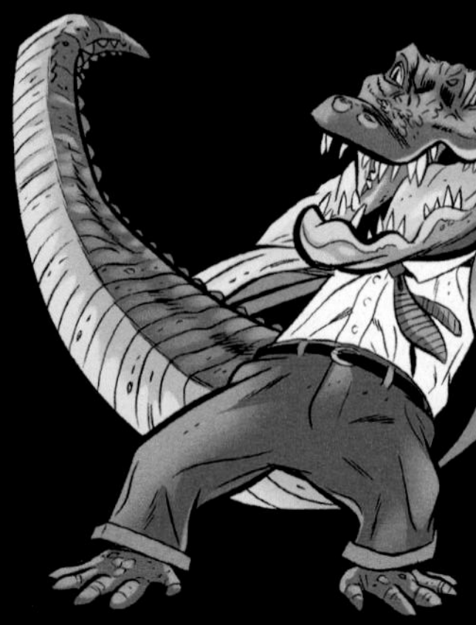

# 1/12/2007

## Shazam Production Journal: Mary Marvel!

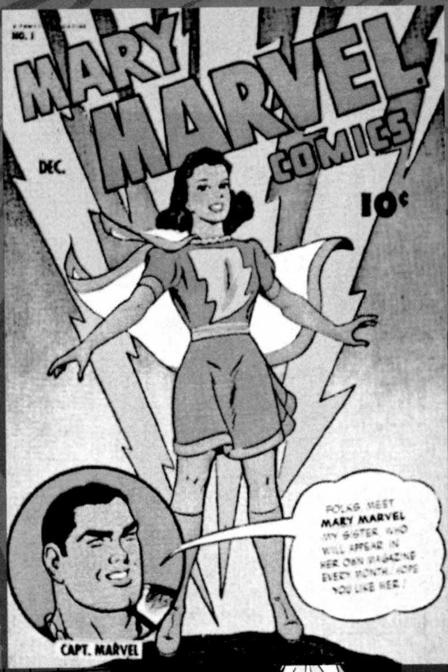

NO. 1
MARY MARVEL COMICS
DEC.
10¢
FOLKS MEET MARY MARVEL MY SISTER WHO WILL APPEAR IN HER OWN MAGAZINE EVERY MONTH. HOPE YOU LIKE HER!
CAPT. MARVEL


The plot of SHAZAM! THE MONSTER SOCIETY OF EVIL revolves around young, homeless Billy Batson's search for his long-lost sister Mary—who, it turns out, can share his powers.

One of the first things I did for this project was fill up sketch pages looking for the best way to draw her.

The image below left was originally going to be used for the cover of MSoE №2, and was widely seen in 2003, but it has since been pulled into the service of the story, flopped, re-colored, given word balloons and will be used inside the comic.

Up top is Mary on the cover of *Mary Marvel* №2 from the 1940s.

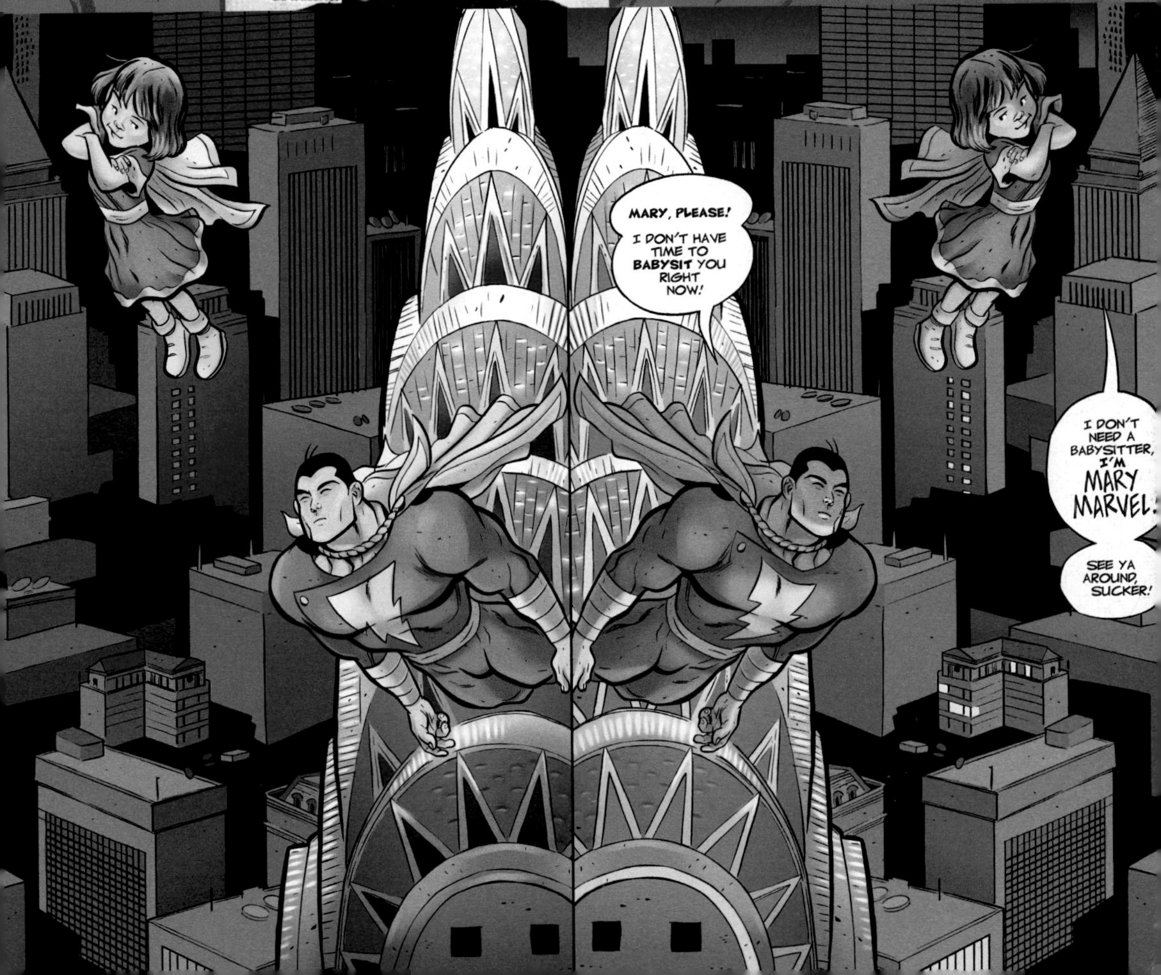

MARY, PLEASE!
I DON'T HAVE TIME TO BABYSIT YOU RIGHT NOW!
I DON'T NEED A BABYSITTER, I'M MARY MARVEL!
SEE YA AROUND, SUCKER!

# 1/18/2007

## Shazam Production Journal: Talky Tawny the Talking Tiger!

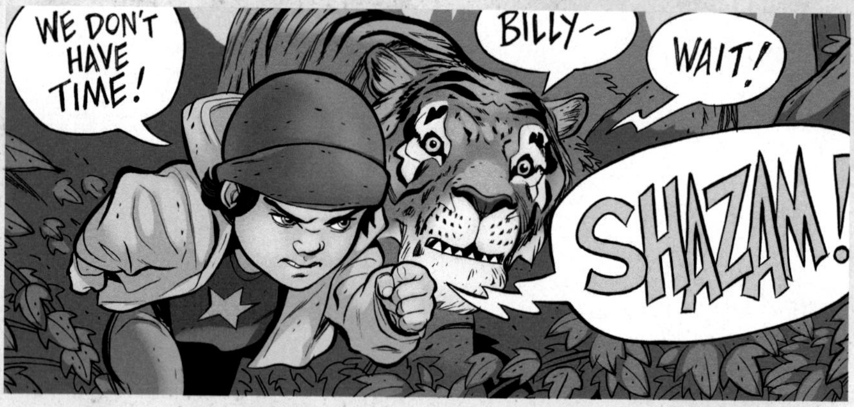
WE DON'T HAVE TIME!
BILLY--
WAIT!
SHAZAM!

Talky Tawny is one of those characters who causes people to roll their eyes. A talking tiger? And I admit he was handled pretty goofily in the '40s, but Captain Marvel's powers are more mythological than most—derived from ancient gods and sages—so wandering spirits and talking animals don't feel out of place to me. Gods and talking animals are part of our oldest storytelling traditions. The trick was to build a relationship between Talky and Marvel, connect them to each other, and then throw them into modern-day New York City. R zohl gslftsg rg dlfow svok ru R wivd srn orpv z ivzo grtvi, zm rwvz R krxpvw fk lm uiln Zovc Ilhh!

To the right are three stages of making a comic book panel from MSoE №3.

I use blue pencils because high contrast scanners can't see that color, and I won't have to erase the page later after it is inked, which can harm the drawings.

The next step is to ink the word balloons, so I know how much space they will take up. Then I usually go straight for the faces. The faces are where the acting goes on, so I want this done first while I still have the energy. Later on, as deadlines approach, and time runs short, I know this has been taken care of. You can see that I have changed Billy Batson's dialog, and added a balloon for Talky Tawny. Writing continues on into the final stages. Also note the smears—after all these years, I still put my hand in the ink...

After a little white paint to cover the smears, I finish the figures and start on the background. In this scene, Billy and Talky have rendezvoused in Central Park. I visited the park in June to see what kind of rocks and brush were there. Using my reference photos, I draw leaves and vines around their feet.

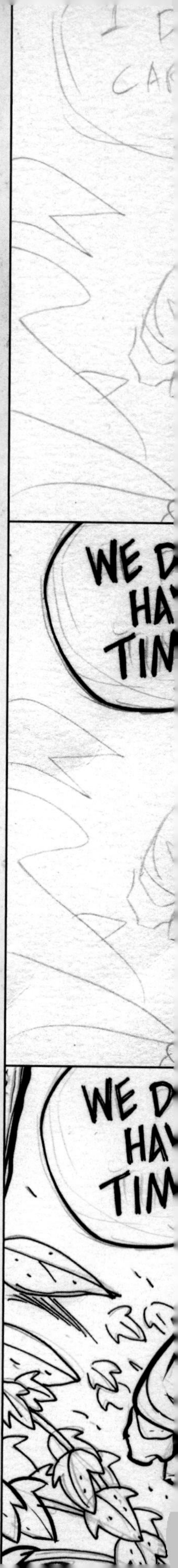

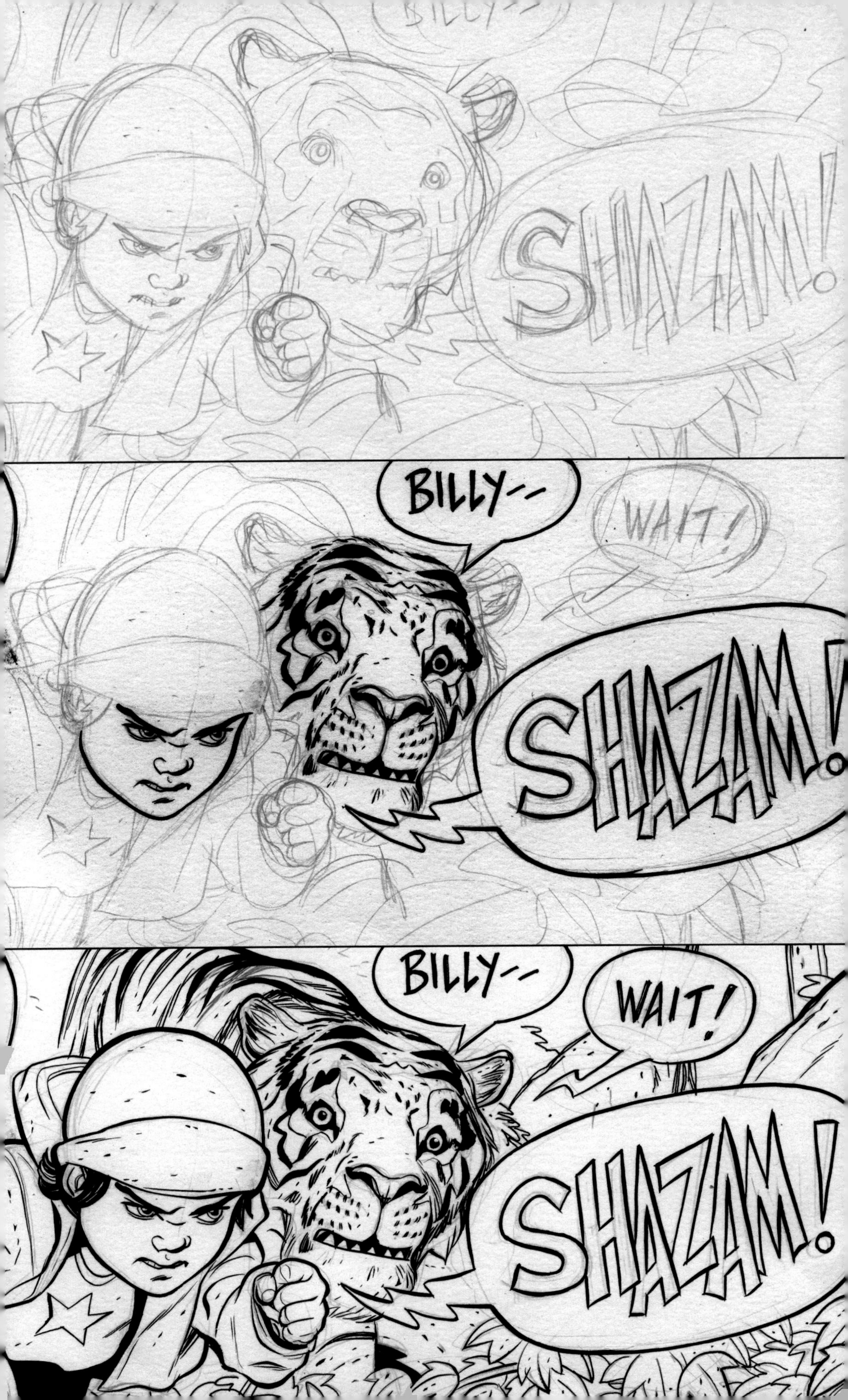
SHAZAM!
BILLY--
WAIT!
SHAZAM!
BILLY--
WAIT!
SHAZAM!

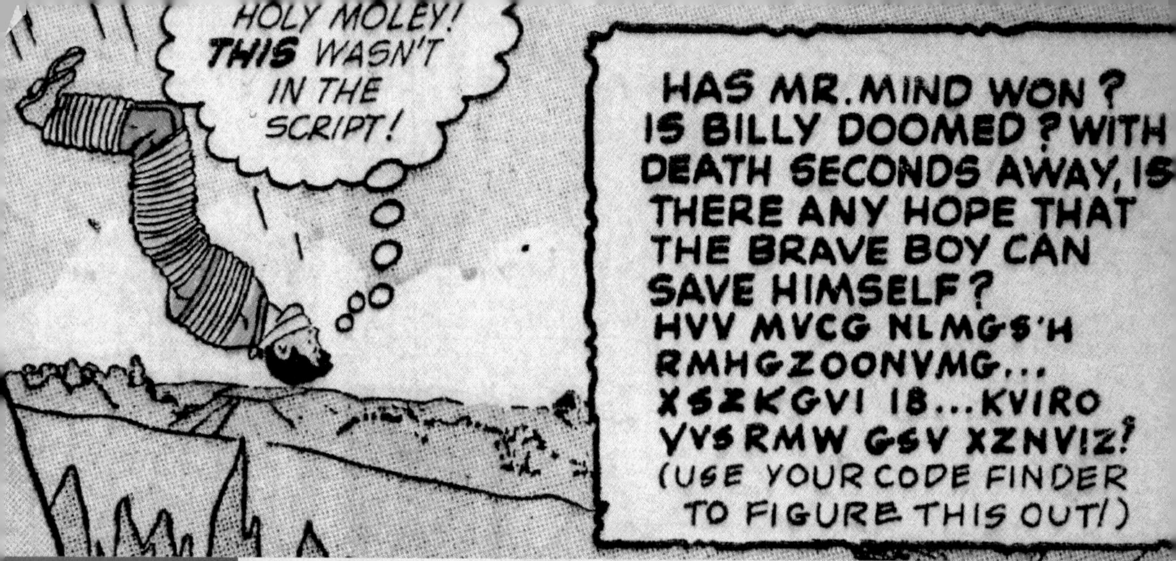
HOLY MOLEY! THIS WASN'T IN THE SCRIPT!
HAS MR. MIND WON? IS BILLY DOOMED? WITH DEATH SECONDS AWAY, IS THERE ANY HOPE THAT THE BRAVE BOY CAN SAVE HIMSELF?
HVV MVCG NLMGS'H RMHGZOONVMG... XSZKGVI 18...KVIRO YVSRMW GSV XZNVIZ!
(USE YOUR CODE FINDER TO FIGURE THIS OUT!)

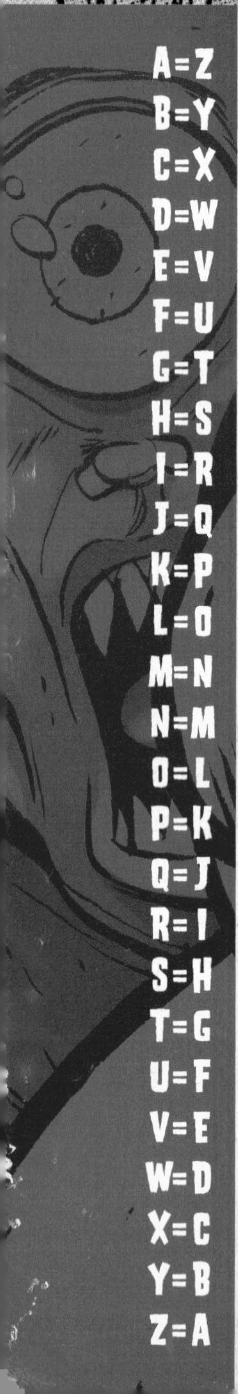
A=Z
B=Y
C=X
D=W
E=V
F=U
G=T
H=S
I=R
J=Q
K=P
L=O
M=N
N=M
O=L
P=K
Q=J
R=I
S=H
T=G
U=F
V=E
W=D
X=C
Y=B
Z=A

# 7/13/2007

## Final Shazam Production Journal; MSoE IS COMPLETE!

In the original serialization of the Monster Society of Evil in 1942, the secret code was used to tease the reader about the title of the next chapter. In our current version, the code is used in a similar way—to disguise the chapter titles that appear on the inside covers.

The covers were designed to look like old movie serial posters, which often had a frame for switching out a photo based on the newest chapter of the serial. I sent rough layouts to DC's art director Louis Prandi, who did a great job of putting the whole package together.

The New Monster Society of Evil was constructed in four chapters, each one spotlighting one of the major players. The code we used is based on the old Captain Marvel Fan Club Code and is the same one used in the original serial. I'll tell you what it is, but you can't tell anyone else, okay? The Monster Code is the alphabet backwards; A=Z, B=Y, etc. Here are the four decoded titles...

MSoE Chapter One: **Billy Has a Secret!**

MSoE Chapter Two: **Mary Takes the Cake!**

MSoE Chapter Three: **Sivana Comes On Strong!**

And our final installment,

MSoE Chapter Four: **Mr. Mind Makes His Move!**

INSIDE FRONT

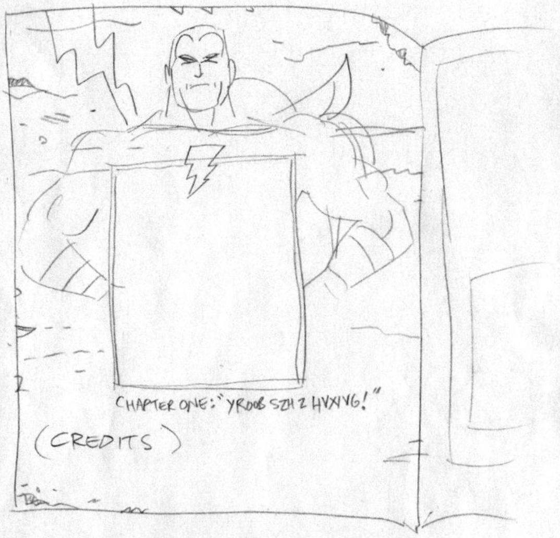
CHAPTER ONE: "YROOB SZH Z HVXIVG!"
(CREDITS)

INSIDE FRONT LOOKS LIKE OLD, VINTAGE MOVIE POSTER. INSIDE FRAME WILL BE IMAGE WE CHOOSE TO REPRESENT THAT CHAPTER. IN THIS CASE, A DETAIL FROM PAGE 20, PANEL 4. (A CLOSE-UP OF BILLY) THIS INSERT IMAGE SHOULD NOT BE WORN AND AGED.

INSIDE BACK

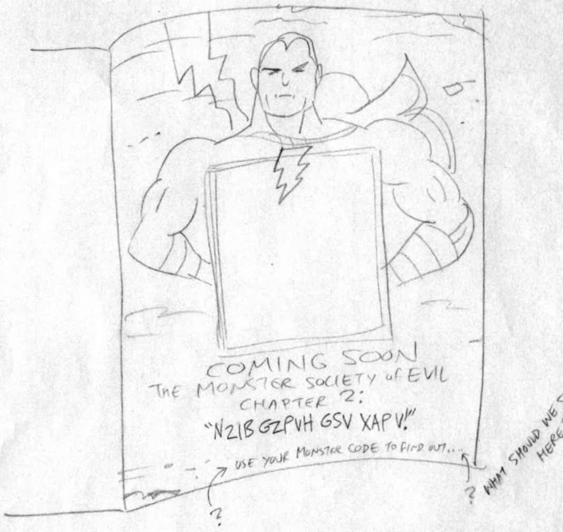
COMING SOON
THE MONSTER SOCIETY of EVIL
CHAPTER 2:
"NZIB GZPVH GSV XAPV!"
USE YOUR MONSTER CODE TO FIND OUT...
?
? WHAT SHOULD WE SAY HERE?

INSIDE BACK COVER - SAME IMAGE BUT WITH DIFFERENT COPY. INSERTED IMAGE WILL BE A PANEL FROM MSOE No. 2. IN THIS CASE, A CLOSE UP of MARY'S FACE FROM PAGE 47 of No. 2. AGAIN, THE INSERT IS NOT WEATHERED.

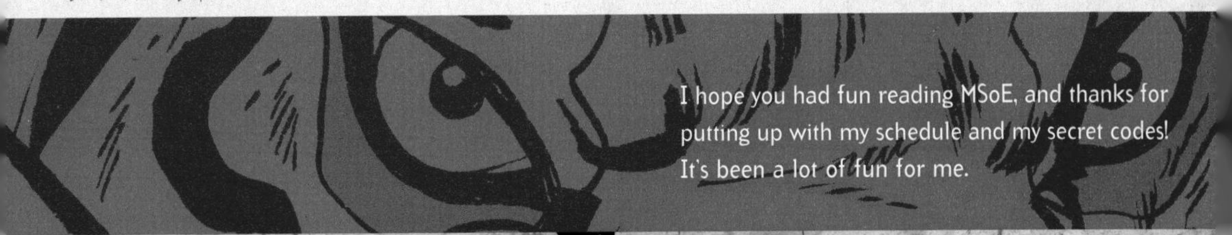

I hope you had fun reading MSoE, and thanks for putting up with my schedule and my secret codes! It's been a lot of fun for me.

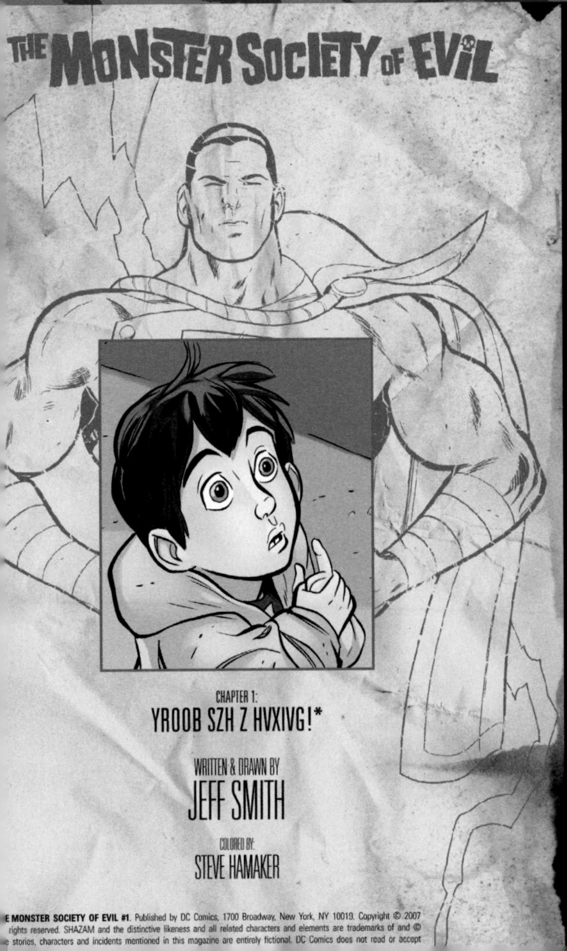
THE MONSTER SOCIETY OF EVIL
CHAPTER 1:
YROOB SZH Z HVXIVG!*
WRITTEN & DRAWN BY
JEFF SMITH
COLORED BY:
STEVE HAMAKER
E MONSTER SOCIETY OF EVIL #1. Published by DC Comics, 1700 Broadway, New York, NY 10019. Copyright © 2007
rights reserved. SHAZAM and the distinctive likeness and all related characters and elements are trademarks of and ©
e stories, characters and incidents mentioned in this magazine are entirely fictional. DC Comics does not read or accept

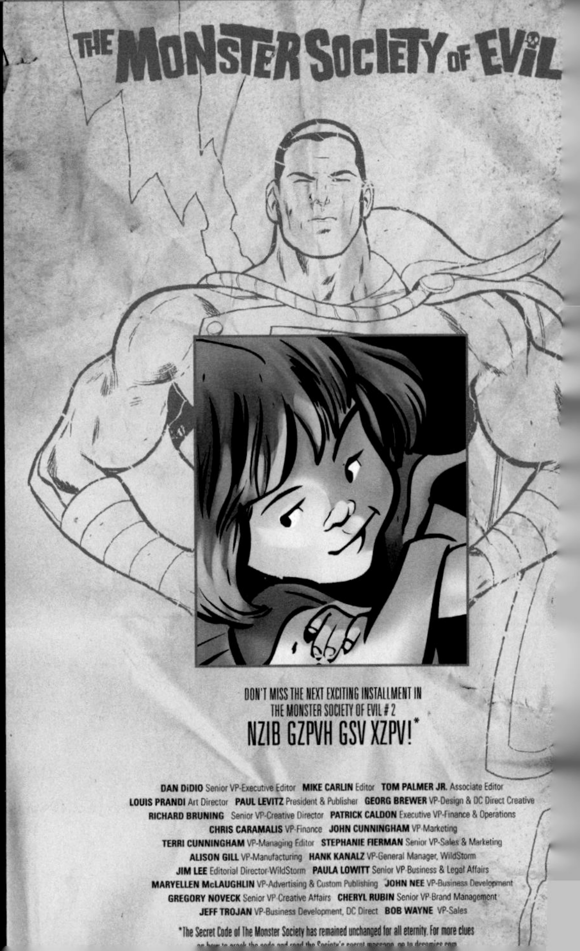
THE MONSTER SOCIETY OF EVIL
DON'T MISS THE NEXT EXCITING INSTALLMENT IN
THE MONSTER SOCIETY OF EVIL # 2
NZIB GZPVH GSV XZPV!*
DAN DiDIO Senior VP-Executive Editor MIKE CARLIN Editor TOM PALMER JR. Associate Editor
LOUIS PRANDI Art Director PAUL LEVITZ President & Publisher GEORG BREWER VP-Design & DC Direct Creative
RICHARD BRUNING Senior VP-Creative Director PATRICK CALDON Executive VP-Finance & Operations
CHRIS CARAMALIS VP-Finance JOHN CUNNINGHAM VP-Marketing
TERRI CUNNINGHAM VP-Managing Editor STEPHANIE FIERMAN Senior VP-Sales & Marketing
ALISON GILL VP-Manufacturing HANK KANALZ VP-General Manager, WildStorm
JIM LEE Editorial Director-WildStorm PAULA LOWITT Senior VP-Business & Legal Affairs
MARYELLEN McLAUGHLIN VP-Advertising & Custom Publishing JOHN NEE VP-Business Development
GREGORY NOVECK Senior VP-Creative Affairs CHERYL RUBIN Senior VP-Brand Management
JEFF TROJAN VP-Business Development, DC Direct BOB WAYNE VP-Sales
*The Secret Code of The Monster Society has remained unchanged for all eternity. For more clues

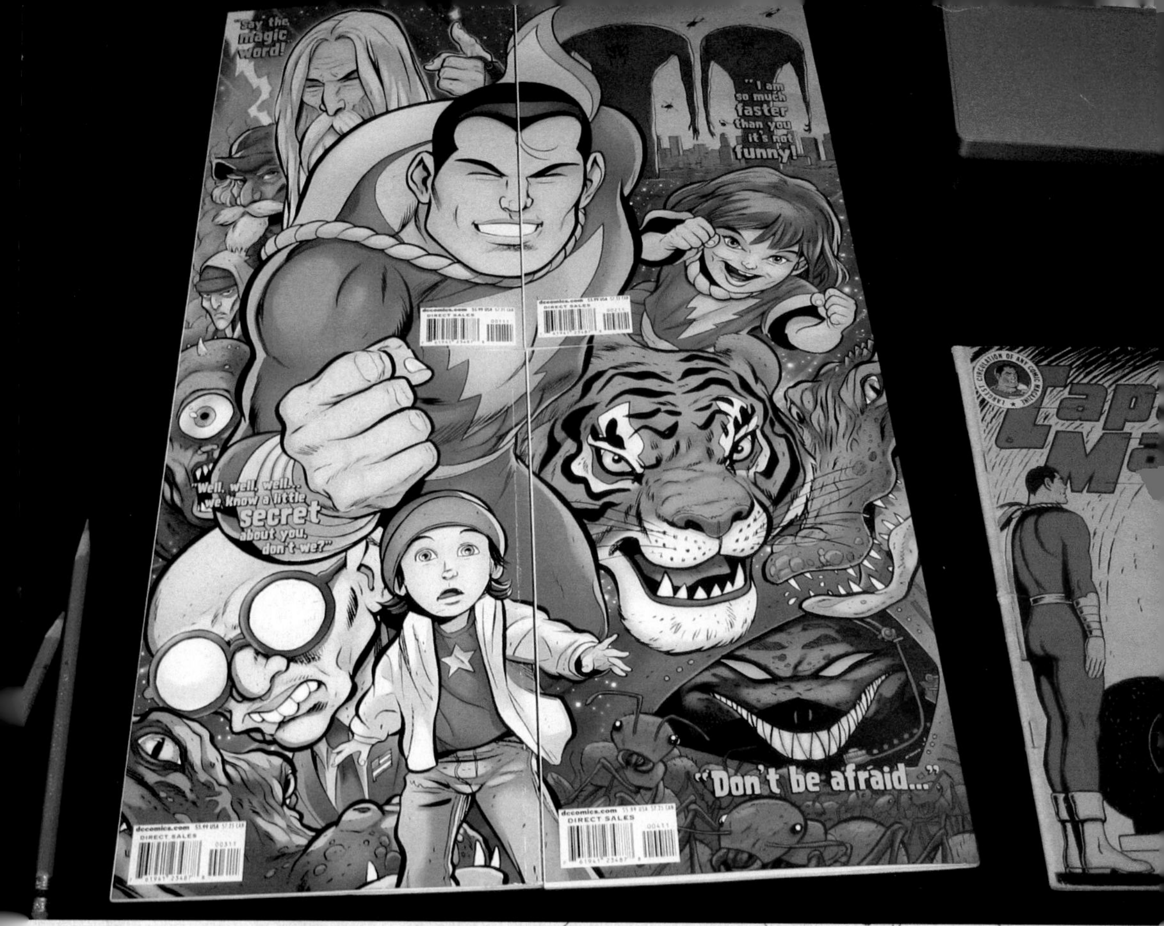
"Say the magic word!"
"I am so much faster than you it's not funny!"
"Well, well, well... we know a little secret about you, don't we?"
"Don't be afraid..."

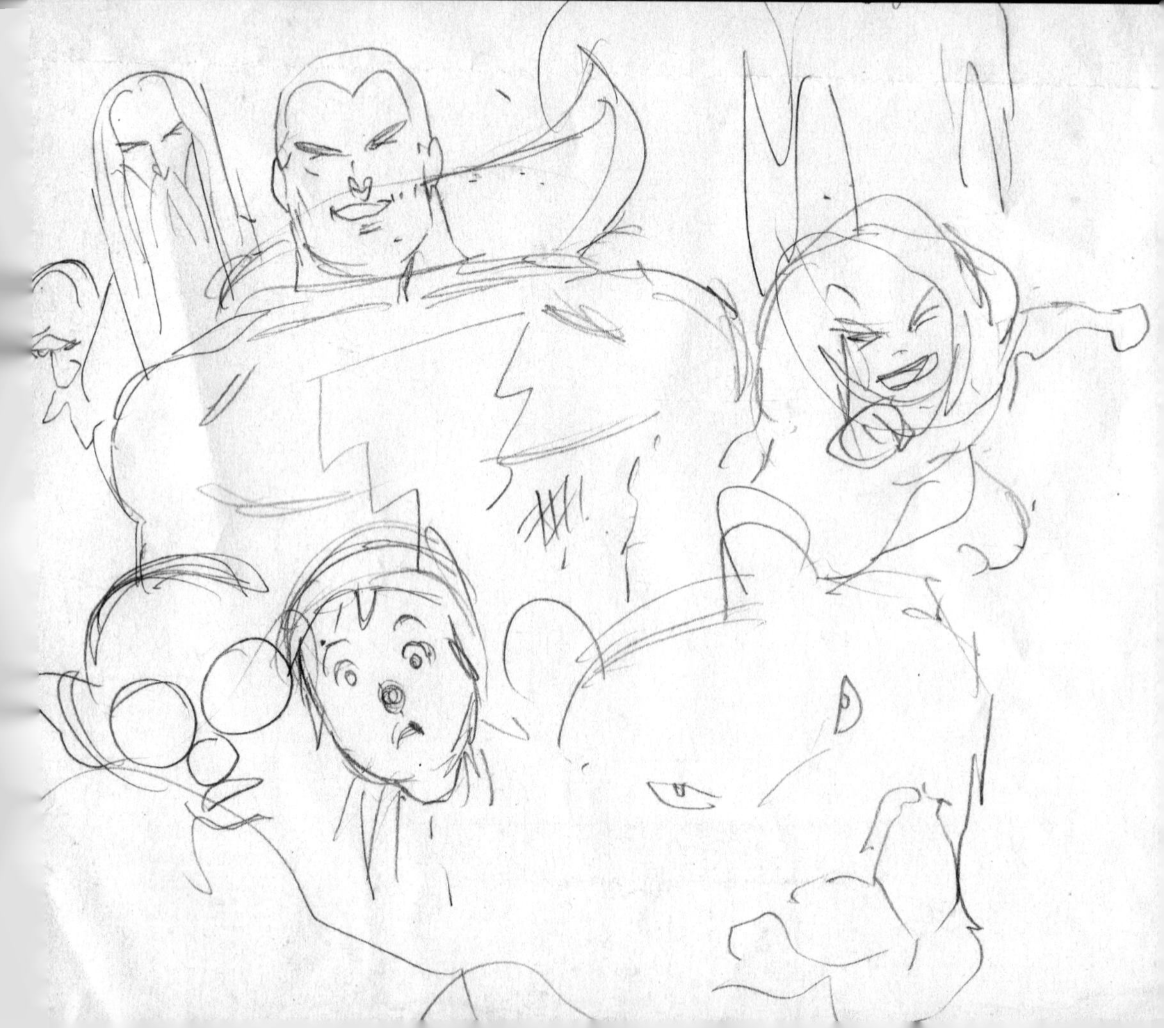

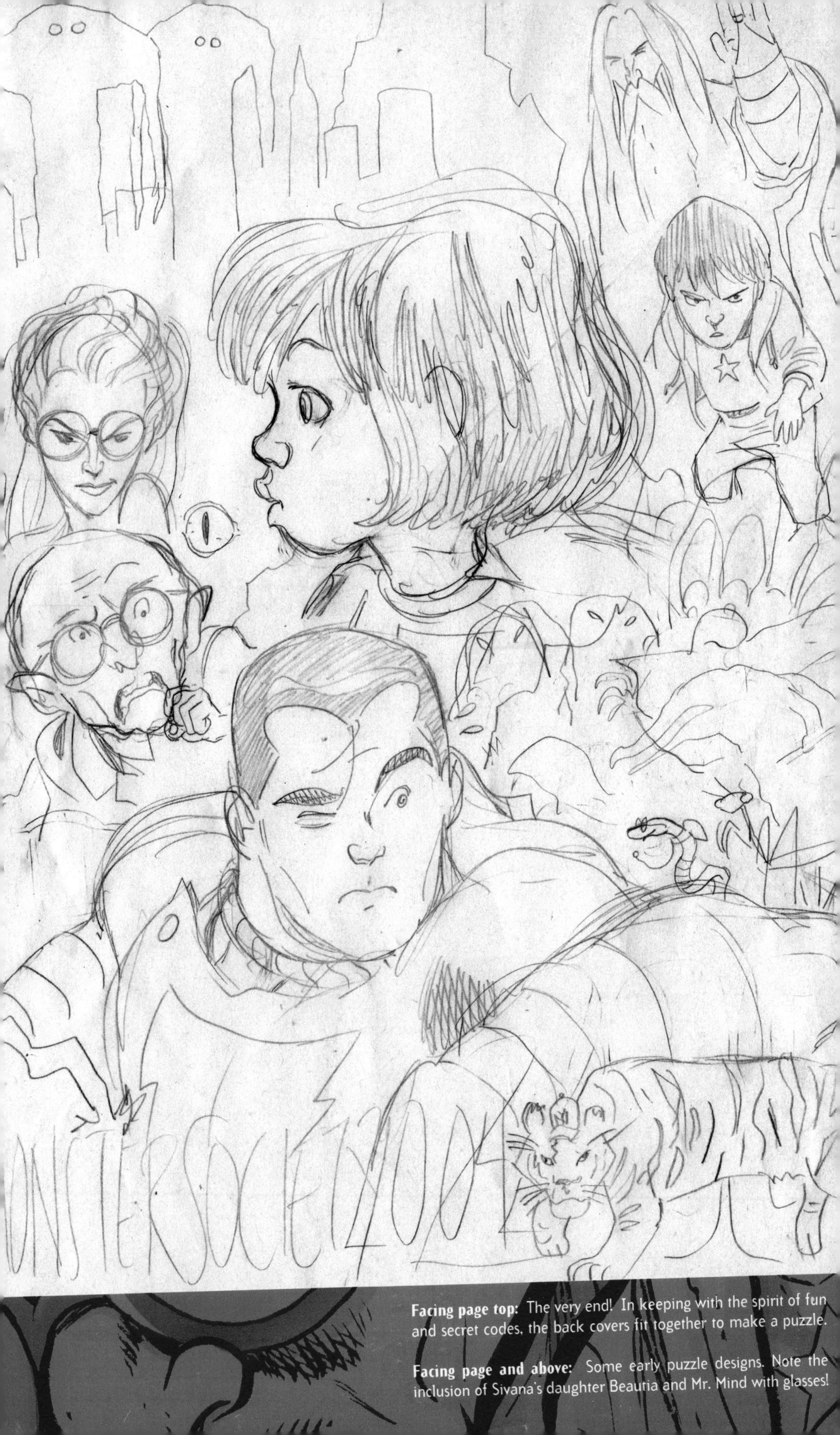

**Facing page top:** The very end! In keeping with the spirit of fun and secret codes, the back covers fit together to make a puzzle.

**Facing page and above:** Some early puzzle designs. Note the inclusion of Sivana's daughter Beautia and Mr. Mind with glasses!

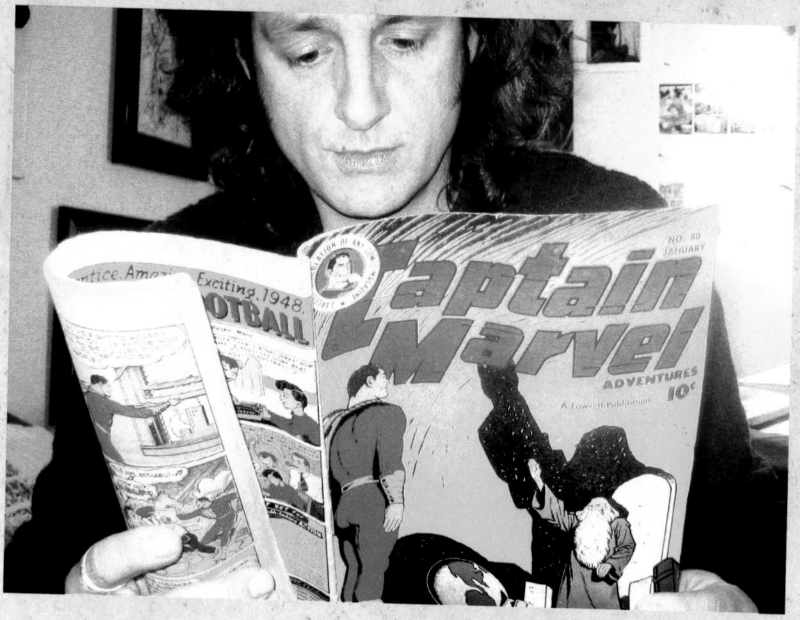
NO. 80
JANUARY
Captain Marvel
ADVENTURES
10¢
A Fawcett Publication

**Jeff Smith**

In 1991, Jeff Smith launched a company called Cartoon Books to publish his comic book *Bone*, a comedy/adventure about three lost cousins from Boneville. Against all odds, the small company flourished, building a reputation for quality stories and artwork. Word of mouth, critical acclaim, and a string of major awards helped propel Cartoon Books and *Bone* to the forefront of the comic book industry. In 1992, Jeff's wife Vijaya Iyer joined the company as partner to handle publishing and distribution, licensing, and foreign language publications.

In the spring of 2005, Graphix, an imprint of Scholastic Books, published a full-color version of *Bone: Out from Boneville*, bringing the underground comic to a new audience and a new generation. Between projects, Smith spends much of his time on the international guest circuit promoting comics and the art of graphic novels. The Boneville travel blog can be found at boneville.com.

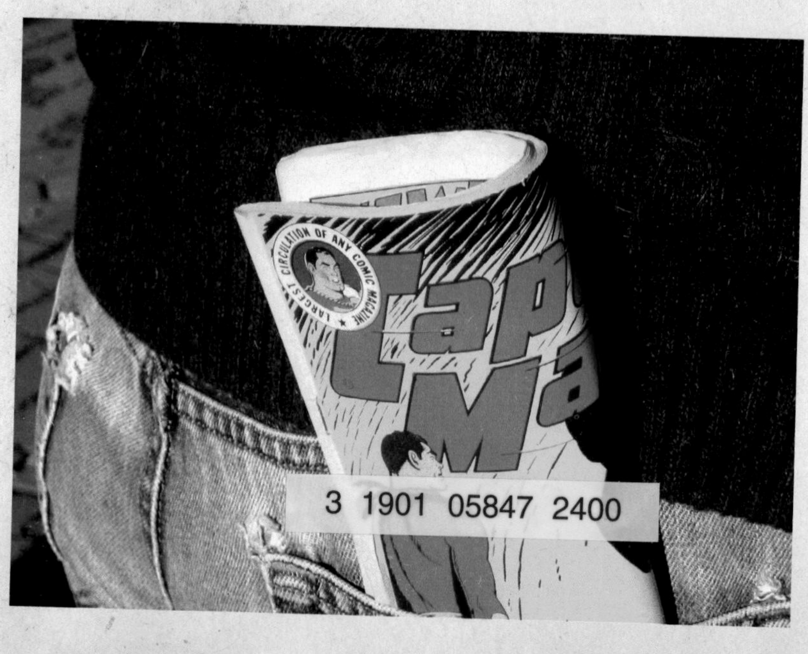
LARGEST CIRCULATION OF ANY COMIC MAGAZINE